THE
COMPLEAT
McCLANE

SELECTED BOOKS BY A. J. McCLANE

The American Angler

Spinning for Fresh and Salt Water Fish of North America

The Practical Fly Fisherman

McClane's New Standard Fishing Encyclopedia

Fishing with McClane

McClane's Field Guide to Freshwater Fishes of North America

McClane's Field Guide to Saltwater Fishes of North America

McClane's Secrets of Successful Fishing

McClane's Game Fish of North America
(with Keith Gardner)

McClane's Angling World

THE COMPLEAT

A Treasury of A. J. McClane's

Illustrations by Joseph Fornelli

McCLANE

Classic Angling Adventures

A. J. McCLANE

Edited and with an Introduction by
John Merwin

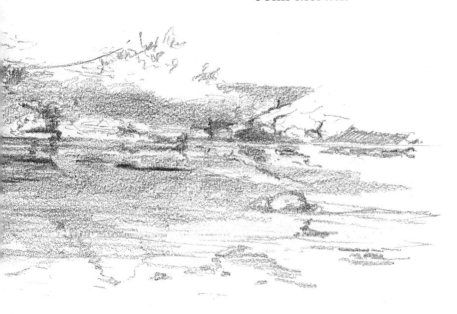

TT TRUMAN TALLEY BOOKS / E. P. DUTTON / NEW YORK

Published in the United States by Truman Talley Books•E. P. Dutton,
a division of NAL Penguin Inc.,
2 Park Avenue, New York, N.Y. 10016.

Published simultaneously in Canada by
Fitzhenry and Whiteside, Limited, Toronto.

Library of Congress Cataloging-in-Publication Data

McClane, A. J. (Albert Jules), 1922–
The compleat McClane.

"Truman Talley books."
Includes index.
1. Fishing.   2. Cookery (Fish)   I. Merwin, John.
II. Title.
SH441.M44   1988   799.1   87-36480
ISBN 0-525-24643-6

DESIGNED BY EARL TIDWELL

3 5 7 9 10 8 6 4 2

Grateful acknowledgment is made to the following magazines, where
portions of this book previously appeared:

Esquire: Chapters 30–33, 35. *Field & Stream:* Chapters 1–11, 13–20, 22,
23, 25, 29, 38, 40–45, 47, 48. *Fishing World:* Chapter 24. *Fly Fisherman:*
Chapter 39. *Food and Wine:* Chapter 34. *Gourmet:* Chapter 26. *Sports
Afield:* Chapters 12, 21, 27, 28, 36, 37. *Venture:* Chapter 46.

Contents

CONTENTS

Introduction

Before you're led too far astray, I have to explain that this—
The Compleat McClane—isn't a "complete works" by any
means. It is given as complete in the sense of Walton's *Compleat Angler,* meaning well-rounded, as in this book we happily share the extraordinary diversity of America's best-selling angling author: Albert Jules McClane.

As a practical matter, you have my absolute assurance
that this book will improve your fishing no matter what sort
of fishing you do. This, after all, is why most people buy
fishing books. When you consider that everything from panfish to piranhas—with a generous dose of bass and trout—is
covered within these pages and was written by one man over
a forty-year period, the word *compleat* becomes self-evident.

McClane's career as an angling writer in national media
so far spans four decades—almost three of those as Fishing
Editor of *Field & Stream*—and now in his sixties he's still
going strong. As a writer, he's one of a small handful in the
angling field who qualify as genuine stylists. As an angling
authority, he is simply without peer. The combination has
produced hundreds of thousands of loyal readers through the
years, most of whom will find material in this book that they
haven't seen before. And if you're meeting McClane for the
first time in these pages, I envy you the joy of your discovery.
It will change your fishing life.

He has fished in more countries for more species than I

can count, and he's been in the forefront of every major angling development since World War II—all imparted to the angling public in clear, concise McClane style. As if this weren't enough, the publication of his two books on fish cookery has established him as an international authority in this field as well. Small wonder his late friend and frequent angling companion Arnold Gingrich once referred to him as a "one-man conglomerate."

Through all of this he maintains a remarkable modesty. I cornered him in his Florida living room a few years ago and asked him how he felt about such an exceptional career. "I've just been a reporter," was his simple answer, which to me was a little like Henry Ford describing himself as a mechanic. But Al meant what he said.

At any rate, this book came about as a result of my coming to know Al as a genuinely diverse person. To reflect that diversity in some way, I divided the book into four sections, each of which reflects in print a part of the enthusiasm and skill he brings to the fishing life.

The first section—"Here's How"—offers McClane as the angling tactician. Spinning tackle, fly tackle, lines, leaders, and other aspects of the tackle game are covered in depth here, with an emphasis on showing you how to use your tackle more effectively.

Once you've mastered the method, you need to master the fish, which takes us into the second section: "Panfish to Piranhas." From bonefish to bass to brown trout, in fresh water and salt water, McClane's unsurpassed knowledge of gamefish behavior means you'll be catching more of your favorite fish more often.

Having caught them, you may have kept a few while releasing most, and you'll need to know how to handle the forthcoming confrontation in the kitchen. The third section—"The Gustatory Angler"—is designed to help you do just that with numerous tested recipes for all sorts of gamefish.

Finally, in "Ripples and Reflections," we look with McClane beyond the mechanics of fishing into such things as why people fish in the first place and the story behind his best-selling *Fishing Encyclopedia.*

Many of the forty-eight chapters in this book originally appeared in such magazines as *Gourmet* and *Esquire,* outside of what's normally considered angling media. None of these chapters has ever before appeared in book form. I've taken the liberty with each chapter of providing you with a brief introduction so there's some consistent perspective given the time span covered by this collection.

It's difficult to describe McClane without sounding adulatory and clichéd. But I think you'll find in these pages what Arnold Gingrich once said of our mutual friend: "This vintage McClane is the real McThing."

JOHN MERWIN

Dorset, Vermont
September 1987

Book One

HERE'S HOW

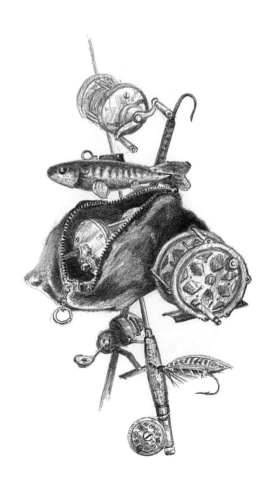

One of the reasons for McClane's success as an angling writer over the years has been his ability to explain fishing techniques and tackle in their simplest terms without insulting either the reader or the method. This section offers numerous examples of just that, which should be immediately helpful in your fishing.

As one example, thousands of spinning reels are sold in this country every year. They are superficially very easy to use and are commonly a beginner's first reel. Very few people can cast well with them, however, and casting well can make all the difference. McClane's explanation in this section will simply mean better fishing more often for you.

1

The Case for the Flea Rod

Graphite as a rod material has become so popular in recent years that many anglers are still surprised to find out that graphite wasn't used commercially in fishing rods before the early 1970s. This 1965 Field & Stream *article was written when bamboo was in wider use as a rod material, but as is true with so much of McClane's work most of the points made here apply just as well to the modern angler who confronts a bewildering array of graphite rods in almost every shop and mail-order catalog.*

Light fly tackle, if anything, has become lighter and stronger with the advent of graphite. Several manufacturers now offer two- and three-weight graphite rods (taking lines with nominal grain weights of 80 and 100 grains respectively) in a variety of rod lengths, and at least one maker has a bona fide one-weight rod scheduled for introduction within a year.

One thing to remember is that as rod length is reduced the weight differential between graphite and bamboo diminishes considerably. In shorter lengths—say less than 7½ feet—many contemporary bamboo rods compare favorably in performance with graphite as the slightly greater weight of the bamboo is relatively insignificant. And even though I have a closet full of graphite to choose from, my favorite and most often used small-stream rod is still bamboo.

From time to time I have written of the virtues of light fly tackle, not to dogmatize but to convert, and I have found many sympathetic minds. Some manufacturers became kindred spirits and in recent years began producing delicate wands ideally suited to modern angling. However, like a translated book, something was lost in the interpretation, and in a few cases the idea has been carried to ridiculous extremes. Merely chopping the bottom off a long rod does not result in a good short one. This, of course, is recognizable when the angler skewers his ear with a low forward cast, but aside from the dubious value of such tools, the original concept is in danger of being lost.

The real purpose of a light fly rod is to make it possible to cast a light line, long, fine leaders, and small flies. This basic premise is obscured, largely because we tend to believe that light tackle is more sporting—a suggestion that could be argued pro and con forever, as our idiom lends itself more readily to controversy than to the expression of pleasure. After all, how can you explain the thrill of holding a rod bent as tight as an archer's bow while a big brownie thumps against the current? Would one ounce less bamboo make that moment any more memorable? On the other hand, a rod that is too light, or one that lacks backbone to prod a shallow-water gamefish into motion, puts the premium on the reel, and in effect becomes a very unsporting tool. If you can't pressure a fish, there's little likelihood of getting him into the air. So the virtues of any kind of light gear must be measured against the job being attempted.

Most American trout fishing is done by wading, and a large part of it is accomplished in fast water with short, blind casts. This is as true on the Roaring Fork in Colorado as on the Beaver Kill in New York. Characteristically, we have to achieve a rapid casting tempo. An angler working upstream in hip-deep water doesn't float a fly more than a few yards before the fish is covered and a new cast is on the way. Thus, the lightest practical outfit has the advantage not only in being easier on the wrist but in hitting nearby targets. The case for the flea rod is really the value of short casts. Heavy tackle and distance casting have their roles in trout angling, but they have been overemphasized to the point that many neophytes appear on rivers with tackle designed for ranges well beyond the realistic 40-foot limit of everyday fishing.

The first question you have to answer is, Which line fits your fishing? Actually, you are better off buying a line to fit the stream and then finding a rod to fit the line, although traditionally our tools are purchased in the reverse order. As an arbitrary gauge, I'd say an efficient trout rod is something on the order of a 7½-foot stick weighing about 3 ounces and using lines in the IFI or the HEH class, which is a workable weight range for the short-cast artist. This may strike some ears as heresy, but except for steelheading and a certain few specialist forms of angling, such as swimming big streamer flies in the Andes or flailing spinners at Gods River square-tails, the problem we usually face is a 1-pound trout poised on nervous fins not 40 feet away. He is not bent on doing anything fatal, and the slightest splash will scare him.

Last summer provided the best fishing I can recall in many years. It was crowned by a 7½-pound brown trout taken from the upper Madison River on a dry fly, but mainly it was a four-month period in which, for a change, I seemed to be on the right rivers at the right time. My season's total ran well over several thousand releases with plenty of 2- to 3-pounders making their bids. Despite the fact that my car trunk was stuffed with fly rods, I kept using the same one over and over again. It didn't matter if the day's project was a pasture brook or a rugged canyon watercourse; I always uncased the same stick. Somehow it seemed suitable for every occasion, and I began to think that maybe I was getting in a rut. But though the Missouri may be seven hundred feet wide in spots, the fish on my bank lay behind boulders and frolicked in riffles where forty yards of wading and forty feet of casting did the trick.

The rod I used is made of heat-tempered bamboo; it is 7½ feet long and weighs exactly 2.74 ounces. It is slower than the sticks usually classed as having dry-fly action. The butt section works. It doesn't shrug off the load, but flexes down into the corks. Through trial and error I found two or three different lines for it. These are double-tapers, and because they weigh a little more than half as much as the average weight-forward line, it doesn't take much energy to hold them in the air and keep them going. Fortunately the rod's cycle is slow enough so it doesn't interfere with the line; it does what any good rod should—transmits energy to the cast and then ducks out of the way when a line loop is formed, without hindering its flight by excessive wiggling. The aluminum alloy reel is just 2⅞ inches in diameter and weighs 3 ounces, which allows for an HEH plus enough backing for the occasional large trout. So the whole outfit, line included, doesn't heft much over 6 ounces. I can swing it all day long without a blister. It has stopped big trout and Atlantic salmon without stress. In twelve years I have broken two tips in the usual way rods are demolished—with a car door.

Of course, you might not like this outfit. My astute angling companion, Arnold Gingrich, thinks it's pretty heavy gear. He uses a 6-foot, 3-inch rod that weighs 1¾ ounces, not only for trout but for salmon as well. This is a deadly little weapon and probably represents the ultimate in flea rods. But I can't get the work out of it that Arnold does; whatever smoothness I have in casting just collapses. I find myself thinking of the rod rather than the fishing. So basically what I'm talking about is a class of rods and their qualities rather than a specific model. There are several bamboo builders still in the business who glue delicate canes, and one of them, for example, offers at least four models ranging from a one-piece 6-foot, 1⅛-ounce stick to a two-piece 7½-foot, 3¼-ounce rod, which is about the gamut of the flea category.

These specifications scare a lot of old-timers away. However, modern 3-ounce rods, or 3X leader tippets for that matter, are not the featherweight calibers of yesteryear. They are

7

potent weapons. You'd have to go down to a 1-ounce rod and 8X points before you'd impress the local angler's club. In my case, I don't beat the air with a 2¾-ounce rod because I feel that it gives the fish a break. Quite the contrary. Trout already have built-in advantages. It just happens that this particular rod has proved its ability to handle a 120-grain line to 60 feet with strain, and it turns over 12-foot leaders as though they were sensitized. I'd feel naked without it.

Infighting with the flea rod is deadly. You have the advantage of quiet presentation with fine tippets and small flies, and because of the delicacy of the terminal tackle, drag is minimized. For every fish that might rise to a fly instantly, at least half a dozen more will leave their places and come downstream, inspecting the pattern as it floats. Sometimes this ends in a take if the fly is unencumbered by a tightening line. An E or F belly is, in my experience, just about the ideal. It doesn't require a bucketful of grease to keep it floating, and the fly and leader will hit the surface before the line. Automatically, you have an edge on the drag factor. If the line hits first, and nine times out of ten a heavy one will, it is swept back with the current, starting an unnatural pull against the fly even before it reaches the trout. This brings up a point that has caused some confusion: rod length is not necessarily a criterion of the line size needed.

I met a man on the Snake River in Wyoming who had paid a fancy price for a 5-foot fiberglass rod that has been touted as the ever-loving end of all miniatures because it flings a GBF. In fact, 200 grains is required to bend it. This is broomstick craftsmanship, and the rod is not in the flea category. It won't cast short distances, and, furthermore, a modern G point is far too coarse for critical trout in clear water. He was understandably disgusted with "light" tackle and wore the scars to prove it. Aside from the fact that his gear was downright dangerous, particularly in a crosswind where the short lever length of rod has to maintain maximum speed to keep so much line weight in the air, he was at a tactical disadvantage. Most G points start at about .036 inch, and many of them mike at .042 inch, which is a shade more than the belly portion of an HEH. The G point not only acts like a hawser on the water but requires a heavy leader butt (if we use the standard two-thirds of the diameter of the line as representing the appropriate diameter), which gets up to a fish-frightening .024 inch for a starter. Drawing that down to .006 within 9 or 12 feet makes a crazy leader.

Suitable line weights for flea rods usually run from 118 to 126 grains, which may be an IFI or an HEH. The fine I point or an honest H point will permit you to use leaders tapering from as little as .016 inch at the butt without sacrificing the necessary rigidity between line and leader, so you can get down to 6X or 7X within 9 or 10 feet. The new fly-line standard with its WFs and DTs and symbolic numerals still disguises the line-point diameter, which in some cases is so far out that it has no meaning here.

A line point of .022 to .026 inch is about right for transmitting the energy of the cast to a long, fine leader. There are several reasons why this is important; chief among these is the fact that the leader will turn over with a very few feet of line extended from the rod tip. In other words, you can make a 15-foot cast without flailing the rod, and have some control over the fly. However, the leader must be balanced. As I have indicated in this column many times before, a reliable formula is 60 percent heavy, 20 percent graduation, and 20 percent tippet. No matter what total length you want, the first 60 percent should consist of the butt, the next 20 percent of progressively smaller sections, until the last strand is within .002 of the tippet diameter, with the final 20 percent as the tippet itself. Do not use limp monofilament for this purpose; the ideal material is not soft, but rigid enough to transmit that last flea power of energy from the unrolling fly line.

A heavy line is easier to cast a long distance than a light one, and quite naturally the neophyte looks for an outfit that will heave out yardage with a minimum of effort. But at short ranges a heavy line is effective only in theory; the fact that more weight might be extended from the tip at any given length does not allow for the fact that the rod must be rigid, or nearly insensitive, to function smoothly at the range for which it was designed. Therefore, one component nullifies the other. As for being harmonious enough to make a properly balanced 9- or 12-foot leader (which you should be able to turn over by hand) lay out straight—it just doesn't happen. I remember Marvin Hedge remarking once that he could design a line for any distance a man wants to cast—100 feet, 150 feet, or 200 feet—but he doubted if it would be much good for fishing. The same thing applies to a fly rod.

I was so impressed with what I had read about Western trout streams that on my first trip to the Rocky Mountains years ago I bought an expensive 8½-foot rod. It was a real powerhouse and in fact earned a first place in regional competition with a 142-foot-long cast. But the practical limits of a heavy-caliber rod didn't occur to me while swishing a GAF over the front lawn. After I had about 35 feet of line on the grass I could make a smooth pickup and shoot to 80 feet with ease. What I didn't consider was that by adding a 9-foot leader my *minimum* effective cast was about 40 feet.

As things turned out, I found that the Madison or the Big Hole or any other sagebrush creek presented the same angling problems I had back East; targets appeared at short ranges, and most of the time I had not more than 20 feet of line in the air. Being able to cast across the river wasn't much help when trout were popping almost under my rod tip. I couldn't get accurate drag-free floats, and the fly came down like a ton of bricks. In a few days I was back to a standard 8-footer with an HDH and doing a lot better. This rod can push a line to 80 feet when necessary, but, more important, it turns over 25 feet with precision.

At short ranges a heavy fly line also makes hooking the trout difficult. It has more water resistance even when floating on the surface and requires more oomph in the strike. The difference is not particularly noticeable when fishing with big flies and 2X tippets, but when you start fiddling around with Jassids and 6X points, the slightest excited tug will pop the leader. Using flea tackle, however, a 6X point becomes part of an elastic unit capable of holding surprisingly large trout. The resilience of a well-made light rod will not only absorb the initial shock of a runaway fish but should be capable of putting the pressure on when necessary.

Undeniably, there are rivers, water conditions, and

methods of fly fishing that require something heavier than flea tackle to get results. However, these situations are less common than run-of-the-mill trouting where the accomplished short-caster will excel. The important thing in putting together an outfit is not to look for a line that will sail across the Missouri or a rod that will toss a lead sinker over the post office, but a modest set of tools designed to baffle a trout lying in plain sight.

[1965]

2

Exploring with Ultralight

Al McClane got me thoroughly hooked on ultralight spinning in the early 1960s through his Field & Stream *columns. While late-evening fly fishing in summer on our local brook still produced fish for me, the delicacy and distance of ultralight gear had me catching the same trout in broad daylight. Ultralight tackle also saved more than one day on Long Island Sound, when snapper, bluefish, or flounder came by the dozens to our little jigs while the bigger bass and bluefish were nowhere to be found.*

Not too much has changed with regard to ultralight since this article was written. Reels have gotten smaller and lighter, and often with better drag systems, thanks to the addition of Teflon drag washers. Lines in general are stronger for a given diameter. One important addition in the lure arena is the recent popularity of soft plastic baits. When attached to a miniature jig, these wiggle-tail "grubs" are especially devastating on smallmouth bass in both rivers and lakes, and on some saltwater species as well. One problem you may encounter is with the newer "ultra-

light" spinning rods made of graphite. Many of these are stiff to the point of being useless with ultralight gear. Not only will the rod not bend and load when casting a miniature lure, but it also won't bend and load of its own inertia in casting—as will light rods of either fiberglass or bamboo. After fussing with ultralight graphites for a while, I gave up and returned to fiberglass, either of a commercial make or converted from any number of good, light-action fly rods, where the softer action allows much greater accuracy in use.

There are days when you just can't win. Like the time last summer when I hiked into a swamp pond in central Wyoming that was reputed to hold big brook trout. Nobody could say for sure because nobody wanted to go there. It was only a mile from the road, but clusters of mosquitoes sounded their battle cry all the way, and at the pond I couldn't get within twenty feet of its edge. The water was sitting in a quaky, bottomless bowl of stewed spinach. It didn't even look like a trout pond. As I was about to leave, a heavy rise bulged the surface way out of fly range, so I mucked back to the car, rigged up my ultralight spinning rod, and returned to the pond. It was impossible to stand in one place very long because the bottom sank slowly beneath my feet. I tossed out a little wobbling spoon and in a few minutes skidded a handsome squaretail over the moss. Then it occurred to me that I couldn't release my fish without throwing them back twenty feet, so I quit. But circumstances of a less peculiar nature are the very essence of hairline fishing.

Ultralight spinning tackle is not a universally effective method of angling, but on hard-fished rivers like the Tippecanoe in Indiana, the Saint Joe in lower Michigan, the Flint in Georgia, or the lower Connecticut in New Hampshire it will get results when other methods fail. In salt water, ultralight has proved to be equally remarkable—so much so that it is opening new possibilities in marine angling. What makes the method fascinating to so many people is not merely the pleasure of using featherweight tackle but the fact that it's designed for a lure-weight class of $\frac{1}{20}$ to $\frac{1}{8}$ ounce. These tiny baits attract gamefish and panfish that are otherwise difficult to catch with artificials. Ultralight gear is meant specifically to deliver a lure at fishable ranges with minimum disturbance combined with maximim efficiency.

The redear sunfish, or shellcracker, is a good illustration of the value of ultralight. This is an important panfish in the South and many parts of the Midwest. Redears are big, weighing a pound or more, and extremely good eating. Unfortunately, as the name "shellcracker" suggests, they forage principally on crustaceans and mollusks, such as scuds, crayfish, and freshwater mussels. They seldom hit flies or panfish bugs, but can often be induced to strike a *very* small jig.

A nylon peewee jig of $\frac{1}{16}$ or $\frac{1}{10}$ ounce hopped along the bottom sometimes scores as heavily as live bait. The jig achieves an action that appeals to all species with similar appetites; this includes smallmouth bass and brown trout when they are gorging on crayfish and scuds, and pompano and lookdown that have a passion for sand bugs. There is a long list of both fresh- and saltwater fish that feed selectively either part-time or all the time on aquatic life that no other artificial imitates.

The reason for the jig's attraction probably is that most crustaceans and mollusks are bottom-dwellers that hop when disturbed. Even a scallop can jump off the sand by jetting water through its valves, and its motion is not unlike the backward sculling of an alarmed crayfish, scud, or shrimp. So the erratic behavior of a correctly fished skirted lure (not the vertical thrust and drop from the side of a boat but the horizontal, low-rod-tip method with long casts and artful bottom bouncing) may resemble food forms that our plugs, spinners, and flies cannot emulate. However, it takes a cobweb line to cast and operate a microscopic lure. Conventional gear is out. But this is only one reason why ultralight is unique as an angling method.

As the name of the game implies, the art of hairlining is done with refined tackle; rods of 3 ounces or less and lines of 3-pound test or less are used. The majority of ultralight rods are from $4\frac{1}{2}$ to 6 feet in length and weigh about $1\frac{1}{2}$ to

2 ounces. For smooth casting and absolute precision, the rod should have a soft action without excessive vibration. The tiny lures have no real weight and they cannot make the rod flex properly. You can flip a ⅜-ounce plug backward with an ordinary spinning rod and it will "load" the tip, but a 1/20-ounce lure merely goes along for the ride, even on a fragile shaft. Put the ultralight lure on a stiff tip-action rod and it will sail in all directions because the rod does little bending without load, and the movement is so greatly accelerated that the angler cannot "feel" his cast.

So rod action is of prime importance. Second, the guides must be properly spaced and correctly designed. A high-set, straight-legged gathering guide standing well away from the rod is vastly superior to the common low-set guides. High-set guides might not look as neat or fit in small rod cases, but they add yards to a cast by minimizing line slap. When closed-face spin-casting reels are used, the size and position of rod guides aren't too important. Although the line might "spin" just as rapidly when leaving the spool of a closed-face reel, it is immediately choked down under the nose cone, and the hole through which it escapes has the same dampening effect in reducing the spin as a whole set of guides on a regular spinning rod.

A matching reel for the ultralight rod is smaller than standard freshwater models and usually weighs from 6 to 8 ounces. Its most important feature is the drag. Although no friction brake is 100 percent efficient, try to find the best one obtainable. A sticky drag isn't a critical factor in ordinary fishing, as you can back off if necessary and let the line and rod absorb the pull of a running fish momentarily. But with 2-pound test it's a different matter. Remember that the force required to start the drag working is at right angles to the spool—over the roller mechanism—and all the stress is confined to a few inches of line.

So it must start smoothly and run without a hitch. Naturally, if you use the reel in salt water, it's necessary to wash and clean the drag mechanism each fishing day, because the slightest coat of residual salt on the pressure spring or between the washer and spool interface will cause it to stick.

15

Don't fret about the capacity of ultralight reels because they all hold more than enough line (over 200 yards); the most popular size is approximately 2-pound test with a diameter of .006, which is comparable to a 5X leader tippet in fly fishing.

Another virtue of ultralight gear is that it can be cast in very shallow water where an orthodox lure would bang bottom instantly. I am thinking now of a river like the Buffalo in Arkansas that all but evaporates in the summer months, yet holds fine smallmouths just the same, or any typical mountain stream that hides fish under sun-bleached rocks. Your quarry might be weighed in pounds, even though the water level is measured in inches. Here a miniature spinner can sink and snag, but with the right technique it's possible to control the swim.

Let's go back to basic spinning technique for a moment. In all open-faced reel casting, your forefinger controls the line. It holds the line free of the spool preparatory to the cast; it retards the flight of the lure by touching, or "feathering," the line as the loops spin off; and it stops the cast on target by pressing lightly against the spool. With standard gear under ordinary conditions, the angler then turns the handle and closes the bail to commence his retrieve.

When using ultralight in shallow water, however, one more step is necessary. Keep your forefinger against the spool and raise the rod slightly, giving the lure some forward momentum, then close the bail. In practice this becomes a blended movement with the lure swimming back—not sinking—while the bail is flipping to the closed position. If you retrieve in the normal manner without bringing the rod up, and release your forefinger before turning the crank handle, you lose a critical fraction of a second during which the bail gathers slack and the lure sinks. The manual control makes it possible to churn a spinner through ankle-deep water.

Once you have mastered the correct finger technique, you can work upstream. Any gamefish is easily spooked at considerable distances in low, bright water; and in view of the fact that your casting range is often limited to fifty or sixty feet with ultralight baits, it's wise to exploit their head-to-current position. In fishing a typical stretch of river, aim your casts beyond the places where you think the fish are holding. If there's a deep pocket under a midstream boulder, for example, shoot the lure ten or fifteen feet above it and swim the spinner back near the pocket so that it draws the fish out.

Although the size of an ultralight lure is deceptively natural and creates very little impact on the surface, anything that hits the water directly over a fish is going to arouse suspicion. To work an undercut or bring the bait around a submerged log, aim at a spot that looks safely empty to prevent a chain reaction of one fish frightening another; then, with the whirling blade creating tension on the line, lead the lure into the hold at the right depth and speed. Always try to find a natural entrance to the lair of a brown trout or a smallmouth. Like most predators, these gamefish are keenly aware of food lanes—in fact, they take up residence with that in mind.

Ultralight can be a big migraine for the man who hasn't done any spinning before, because the almost invisible line has a way of escaping an extended forefinger. It even gets caught in calluses or little skin abrasions. But where the beginner really gets into trouble is with line twist.

Not using a proper snap swivel with a rotating lure is one source of trouble, but it's minor in comparison to the yardage twisted by cranking against a stationary object, like a husky fish. The line, which is stretched against its weight and at right angles to the path of resistance, turns back on the spool in twists as it passes over the roller mechanism. When a heavy fish is played incorrectly even with standard spinning tackle, the line will become a tightly snarled mass of loops the moment all tension is released.

The correct way to regain line is by pumping. This is a stroking motion—a gentle upward sweep of the rod that prods the fish in your direction. When the fish shows signs of weakening, press your forefinger right against the spool and raise the rod slowly backward, then lower it quickly and reel in the slack. The slack will not twist. Never, under any circumstances, crank the reel when your quarry is stationary and unyielding. The fish must continually be prodded with gentle nudges of the rod.

By holding the rod high, keeping as much line as possible

out of the water, and taking advantage of the full bend of the rod, you can finger the spool and make the stretch of the monofilament wear the fish to exhaustion. The elasticity of the line acts as a shock absorber. In fact, the more yardage the fish peels off, the easier you can control the situation. Line breaks often occur because the angler snubs a green fish just a rod's length away, where sudden lunges or jumps can't be counteracted with the flexibility of the tackle. The antireverse should be in the on position until the fish has been brought to net. But don't attempt to land a lively gamefish with hairline until he's absolutely whipped.

There is a wide variety of ultralight lures on the market, including spinners, spoons, plugs, and jigs. As with any method of fishing, it's a good idea to stock at least a few of each type. I have never really been able to figure out why a brass spinner will work better than a silver or perhaps a black one on a particular day, or why fish will refuse the spinner and grab a tiny wobbler. I do believe that immunity to strikes of a particular lure probably has a lot to do with its popularity—the more the fish see it, the less frequently they accept it.

Fish can become conditioned to specific baits, so consistent success requires not only variation in presentation but in form and color as well. I have many times witnessed the cycle whereby a popular lure in a certain stream or pond suddenly loses its attraction, then some tourist comes along with a novel bait and slays them. With ultralight, however, we have to work within fairly well defined limits, using the lightest spinners in the shallowest water and heavier spinners or wobblers in slightly deeper places. The depth differential might only be a foot, but even miniature $\frac{1}{16}$-ounce spoons have a faster sinking coefficient and must be hurried along.

Of course, these are things the hairline angler learns for himself. Every lure, however, must have needle-sharp hooks. I file the barbs off trebles just to make it easier to release fish, and if the lure is a type that can be fitted with a pair of ice tong–style single hooks, I remove the treble altogether. The survival rate of returned fish is very high if they are handled carefully.

Ultralight is also a boon to the man who lives near the seashore. A reader in Brooklyn, New York, wrote to say that because he wasn't able to get a vacation very often he discovered a world of angling at his own back door in Sheepshead Bay. Among other things, he has learned a technique for catching herring on artificials—a sport that can be enjoyed to the hilt with ultralight gear.

But whether you travel by subway or sea skiff, the results in salt water are often exceptional. Few hairline fans seek large fish. The real fun is bottom-bouncing inshore waters for the variety of species that can be caught. As a general rule, a natural white nylon or polar-bear-hair jig of 1/10-ounce with a short, hollow skirt (so that it flexes) will produce results. If the water is crystal-clear, a yellow or pink jig might work better. As with redear sunfish, a tiny jig will hook such species as flounders, croakers, cutlassfish, and the shy mangrove snapper—all fish that seldom take artificials. Add the pompano, lookdown, sennet, spotted seatrout, ladyfish, Spanish mackerel, red drum, and whiting, and you have a sample of a typical morning's catch. In colder waters you can expect flounders, weakfish, snapper blues, whiting (sometimes called minkfish or northern kingfish), the common mackerel, school stripers, scup, and even puffers, or blowfish. Hopping the little jig along channel edges and over shell beds is apt to produce a dozen or more different kinds of fish. The contents of a day's bag merely reflects which part of the coast you explored.

Of course, ultralight tackle does have its limitations. Not long ago I was fishing a small pond with a Tennessee boy who is hotter than a stove lid with ultralight. We went around the lily pasture like a pair of otters, barbing one bass after another. They fell all over each other trying to grab a 1/8-ounce surface plug. But the fish were about the same size—1 to 2 pounds. We were convinced it was a runt population.

Before quitting we lingered in a cattailed cove for maybe half an hour, casting from one side to the other, but the fish weren't any larger here. Chet had just motioned toward the car when another bass nailed his plug. In the next instant the surface erupted and a mossback of well over 10 pounds engulfed the hooked fish. Crafty Chet tried to feed the little bass

19

to the monster like a live bait, hoping it would swallow the plug too, but Grandpa got wise to the game and spit Junior loose. Naturally we stayed until dark trying to make our miniature plugs look like frantic bass, but that was the last we saw of the cannibal. No doubt a tourist type will come along one day with something the size of a striper plug and get the surprise of his life. But think of all the fun he'll miss.

[1965]

3

Untangling the Tangled Leader

A fly-casting proficiency that allows line, leader, and fly to land on the water in a manner acceptable to the fish is a real bugaboo for beginners. Part of the problem is technique. Part of the problem is usually poorly balanced tackle. McClane here addresses both in a manner that should be helpful to any fly fisherman, regardless of his experience level. I say this because even the so-called professionals have days when they hope nobody's looking at their snarled leaders. I have fished with many of them and know this to be true. I also have sometimes wished I'd been carrying a copy of this article in my fishing vest.

It's worth noting that the material here on leader design has been reiterated by McClane in various ways over the years. The development of nylon monofilament during and after World War II led McClane and Charles Ritz into lengthy experiments with leader design. The basic leader designs McClane describes here have been international standards for almost thirty years, largely because of their work.

One sunny morning on Paradise Creek in Pennsylvania, I rounded a bend in the river and saw a large trout lying in shallow water just a few yards from shore. I say "large" in a comparative sense, as I was in short pants almost four decades back and any fish over ten inches long looked immense. His black-spotted skin was like the hide of a leopard and the longer I stood there, the bigger he became.

The fish obviously didn't see me, as he continued to push his snout against the surface, slurping in a parade of floating insects. While the trout was innocently feeding, I whipped out my line and let 'er rip. Although Paradise Creek lived up to its name in those days, I doubt if that fish could have found the fly even if he'd sorted out the tangle of line and leader that suddenly confused him.

This kind of casting was so common during my first season of fishing that I believed getting a freely drifting fly on the water was pure luck. My source of instruction at the time was a movie-gram booklet that one of the tackle companies used to publish. By flipping through the pages you could see the rod go back and forth. That was about all I had learned—how to flip the pages.

Then, and probably in self-defense because I was scaring the wits out of every trout around Henryville, a gentleman by the name of Lee Allen took pity on me. When astream he wore a tweed jacket and a necktie—which impressed the blazes out of everybody. Lee was one of the all-time greats in Pennsylvania waters, but finding me underfoot twenty hours a day must have been a traumatic experience for a contemporary of George LaBranche. For lack of talent I spent my day running from fish to fish, hoping to find one that would be stupid enough to cooperate.

Mr. Allen and I collided in the dark one night on the path below the dam, and my downhill momentum bowled him over. I think he said "God! Do you ever go to bed?" Or maybe it was *will* you ever. Anyhow that blew it. The next day I was flailing the greeny run in the gorge when he came wading out and pried the rod loose from my cramped fist.

"Get the line off your ears and listen to me." That's the way our brief relationship began.

Looking back on these happy summer days now, I realize that Mr. Allen's simplified instruction encompassed a few points that a beginner may overlook. I was equipped with the world's worst gear, including a five-dollar seamed tubular rod and a level enameled line that terminated in a Japanese gut leader. The very first thing I learned was that a skilled fly caster can perform with almost anything resembling tackle. My eyes bugged out when Lee Allen took my rod and swished the fly over the bubbly and promptly hooked a chub. Species didn't matter—it was a glorious fish.

"Now I want you to do the same thing," he demanded. He could have asked mc to climb Mount Everest with more promise of success. I showed him two or three fancy tangles, including the one where I wrapped both line and leader around the rod. My adopted instructor had the patience of a saint. Before the afternoon was over he taught me how to make a high back cast. Remarkably, the tangles disappeared.

A high back cast is the cornerstone of effortless fly casting. It is rarely mentioned except at casting clubs, where nuances of technique are what people think about, and work at. If a back cast is aimed high (rather than just flipped overhead to the rear), you *have* to make a perfect cast forward.

The line should not travel on a plane parallel to the water. Make the back stroke skyward so it rises about 30 degrees above your head, then check the forward stroke at eye level. The clock analogy of stopping the rod between twelve o'clock and one o'clock, or just beyond vertical, on the back cast is correct for ordinary casting; however, it's almost impossible for a beginner to hit that stroke perfectly with his line under control and the rod bent.

To make a high, smooth back cast, the line must be *slid* off the surface. The tendency always is to lift or literally jerk a fly line upward. Because of water resistance, slack is thrown into the cast and immediately any real control is lost. The line will fall downward in the rear, and if you've created even a few little curves in the line, you'll never get a clean shoot forward. A fly line is slid off the water to a supporting cushion of air (instantaneous though it may be), and it stays there while unrolling because of the velocity that you gave it with the rod.

Overcoming water resistance against the line, thereby

achieving a perfect high back cast with no loss of speed, requires only one simple movement. While the line is extended on the surface, reach forward with your left hand (assuming that you are a right-handed caster), grasp the line between thumb and forefinger, just below the first guide, and pull it briskly toward your body. When the line is moving across the water perfectly straight, then and *only* then, begin to raise the rod for your back cast. Don't let go of the line with your left hand. It will slide off the surface with barely a ripple, providing sufficient speed to put a bend in the rod. Without that bend you might just as well be holding a cow by the tail.

It didn't take me long to get the feel of a proper back cast, as I recall. Mr. Allen was pleased with his efforts by the end of our first informal lesson.

I didn't tangle too many leaders after that, but instinctively I was aiming directly at the water or a rising fish and putting the line down so hard that even little troutlings fled in panic. He explained how the final forward cast should be aimed at a spot about three feet over the target and the rod checked slightly when the line straightens to cause the fly to drop softly on the water.

My presentation, such as it was, improved enough to earn strikes, but I probably had a hundred chubs and trout hit the fly before hooking one very small brownie. Either I struck too late or hit the poor fish so hard that the leader snapped. Striking with the rod should be more of a quick tightening, practically simultaneous with the flash of the fish. A trout recognizes the deception in an artificial almost instantly, and if the hook is not set in this brief moment, the fly is ejected. Large fish generally take a fly more slowly and deliberately than the small ones, and this is particularly true in slow water. A big trout is likely to take the fly with almost no surface disturbance; just a tiny bubble might mark his rise to a floating fly. If you were to strike this fish as fast as a small one, you would probably pull the fly away before it was actually accepted.

The speed of your strike is gauged to some extent, then, on the size of the fish, but the power of the strike also depends on the length of line out and whether it is submerged or on the surface. It takes very little force to set a hook, with most of the force being used to overcome the inertia of a long sunken line when fishing a wet fly, and the force needed is greatly lessened with a floating line and a dry fly.

Despite my working at the high back cast that first season, I still tangled my leader once in a while, but there wasn't much I could do about it. Back in the 1930s we had only two choices of materials for a leader: Japanese gut, which had little rigidity and even less after it soaked up water—although it sold for ten cents a coil; and silkworm gut, which was astronomically expensive in the post-Depression years. Silkworm gut still commands a devout audience and a considerable price. Japanese gut worked for maybe the first hour of fishing, then it became so pliable that it had no more rigidity than thread. When the leader started to flop back on the fly line, it was time to put on a new one.

Today, of course, the neophyte angler has an advantage in the various synthetics that provide greater strength in all diameters without significant loss in pound-test rating. Synthetics are also manufactured in hard and soft finishes, which makes it possible to put rigidity in the taper where it is needed (roughly the butt section and first two-thirds of the leader) while using the soft finish in the tippet section for greater flexibility.

Next to a high back cast, the most important thing to learn is what makes a balanced leader. If you toss a line high and straight (without dips and curves) in the rear and the leader still tangles on the forward cast, then it isn't tapered correctly. At the risk of being dogmatic, this is an absolute, or as reliable a law as anybody can inscribe in the tenets of fly casting.

The problem is that instead of throwing a weight, as the bait caster does, you are unrolling a weight endwise to the direction of motion. Mechanically, it's cockeyed. When a fly line is unrolling forward, the section that has unrolled is the only section that is pulling forward. Unless it has some weight, it can't pull fast or hard, and it will not pull the line you want to shoot for any distance unless it is pulled upon by a heavier portion turning ahead.

As the loop unfolds and straightens, the front taper quits

pulling entirely, the shooting line stops, and if the applied energy on your part was properly calculated, the front taper has enough momentum left to straighten its own length and deliver the final impulse that will straighten the leader. Throughout the flight of the line, various components united in a continuous propulsion of the whole—only the leader played no part. It added nothing to the cast but waited for the last instant when it was pushed forward by the momentum of the line.

A leader is not selected simply on the basis of length and diameter suitable to fish of various sizes and intellects. Equally important is its taper. When your leader is properly balanced, you should be able to take the butt end between your fingers and cast it out straight. No line, no rod, just leader. This can't be done with a kinky leader. Pull it through a piece of soft rubber until it's perfectly straight before testing. If it lays out neatly by hand, then you know the taper is okay. However, if it tangles in actual casting, the chances are that the butt diameter is too small for your line. The great majority of leader problems resolve themselves in this one point. The butt section must have enough rigidity (a combination of diameter and stiffness) to transmit to the tippet the energy imparted by the line, which is about one flea-power at that final impulse.

The tippet section of your leader is important also. If the fly is too large or has too much air resistance for the tippet diameter, you will throw knots in it, or the fly will fall back on the leader. There is a rule of the thumb in this connection, which usually solves the problem. As a general rule for matching tippets to hook sizes, paste this on the inside of your hat:

Tippet	Fly
0X	#2 to 1/0
1X	#4 to #8
2X	#6 to #10
3X	#10 to #14
4X	#12 to #16
5X	#14 to #18

| 6X | #16 to #22 |
| 7X | #22 to #24 |

Whether a leader sinks or floats doesn't have anything to do with its tangling, but it can be a worrisome question to the beginner. Although it is extremely important that the leader be rubbed perfectly straight, I doubt if it matters whether it sinks unless you are fishing a wet fly or nymph that requires that it go under.

Experts will raise a bloodshot eye at the idea that a floating leader is just as effective as one running below the surface, but I am convinced that trout see it one way or the other, and any attempt to hide it underwater is wasted effort. Trout will even hit the knots in a leader when they're busy gorging on midges.

To convince myself, I spent many a chilling day in a wet suit with scuba gear studying the subject from the trout's point of view and could only come to the conclusion that a sunken leader is *more* visible, with its double image reflecting against the surface when it's an inch or so under the water, than a floating leader, which frankly I always had more difficulty finding.

Leader shadow on the bottom is of no consequence because from the trout's position facing the current, his view of the river is horizontal and upward. To a fisherman standing in the water and looking down on the full length of it, the shadow may be alarming, but a trout has no such advantage. The important thing is that the leader makes it possible for an artificial fly to arrive on the stream like a natural insect. And achieving that depends on how smoothly you present your casts.

The last time I saw Lee Allen was toward the end of summer. On this particular day, a gusting crosswind that promised stormy weather made my casting look like it did at the beginning of summer. There are two kinds of wind that foul everything up: a strong head wind and a crosswind from the rod-wielding side of the caster. Short of a real hat-lifter, a head wind is the lesser of evils if you keep your back cast up.

Casting directly into a strong wind slows down the forward motion of the line with ordinary casts, but this can be minimized by a slight change in speed and direction. The lift, back cast, and pause are made in the usual way, but the difference is in the forward cast, which is harder, with more wrist emphasis, and continues until the rod has almost reached horizontal. In this cast, the line travels forward in a lower plane, and the advancing line rolls out in a narrow loop. Thus, the wind resistance is considerably reduced because of the lower plane of flight and because of the smaller "front" presented by the curve of the advancing line.

A crosswind is more difficult to cope with. If you are a right-hand caster and the wind blows from the left, there's no problem. But if it comes from the right, the line tends to drift toward the rod and can catch the tip or the back of your neck.

As winds often do, this late-summer blow emptied the surrounding forest of insects and the trout were going crazy. Even though I was pitching my back casts high, a crossing gust would catch the line, and if I didn't duck fast, the fly would put a new part in my hair. Mr. Allen appeared on the gravel back, carrying a really large brown trout by the gill. He had a broad grin on his face.

"Well, you've learned to duck. Come over here and let's see your leader." I waded ashore and we examined it. It was full of wind knots. He gave the tippet a gentle pull and it snapped. Then, much to my astonishment, he removed his leader—a genuine 90-cent silkworm gut from William Mills in New York—and tied it to my line.

"Now, I'm going to show you a special cast. You'll have to practice it, but it's worth learning." We stood side by side in ankle-deep water like always, except this time he motioned me to his rod side. "This is a backhand cast, so you're safe on my right." Lee worked out a few yards of line in fast strokes, then eased into his smooth rhythm, throwing the line high over his left shoulder. It drifted slightly in the wind, but with a sharp forward motion, it turned over neatly, laying the leader out straight.

When he handed me the rod, I didn't do a very good imitation. The motions were awkward, and I couldn't get much distance. As I recall, it took a couple of seasons before my backhand developed any speed, but at least he showed me how to untangle one more tangle.

The backhand cast is made by a right-hander with his arm held across the front of his body and the rod pointing to the left. A southpaw makes the cast in the opposite plane, with arm held across the front of his body and the rod pointing to the right.

The cast is very simple to execute: With palm facing down and thumb on the top of the grip, your rod should be at a 45-degree angle, quartering away from and a few inches in front of your body. Pick up the line for a back cast, using the full forearm, pivoting at the elbow, and moving your shoulders slightly in the direction of the cast. The rod should stop at a 45-degree angle, quartering away from and to the rear of your body. Start the forward cast by coming closer to the vertical plane on the left side of your body, but do not cast just with your wrist. Lower your forearm slightly, and use the elbow pivot with wrist emphasis. In both the back and forward strokes, a slight left-hand pull will add speed to the line and help the turnover. Practice your backhand every chance you get. It's also a good one to use when fishing with a tree-bordered bank on your rod side.

I still can't get through a day of fishing without hanging the fly around the leader at least once. However, there's some satisfaction in knowing what I did wrong, which is the only way to learn any game.

[1970]

4

Performing Arts

*Learning to vary your retrieve is one of the most sub-
tle—and important—arts in all of angling, whether
you're skittering a big dry fly over a Madison riffle or
twitching a plastic worm past a lock-jawed largemouth. Very little has changed since McClane did this
piece for* Field & Stream *in 1971, although, if anything, the lessons here have become even more important as many waters have become harder fished.*

*As a practical matter, and after you've digested
the following information, the best teachers of retrieving methods will be the fish themselves, so exper-
iment. A seemingly oddball method that you uncover
by simply fooling around may be the only one that
works in a particular spot on a particular day—all of
which, of course, being no guarantee that the same
thing will work tomorrow or next week.*

In 1910, the lure-making business, far from being the considerable industry it is today, was almost a novelty trade in
America. James Heddon had made the first floating-and-div-
ing plug called the Dowagiac Minnow; then William Jamison

issued a challenge in *Field & Stream:* "I offer to meet any angler on earth, manufacturers of artificial baits preferred, in a three-day fishing contest, on any lake within 500 miles of Chicago to prove that the sportsmanlike Coaxer, with its humane armament, will actually catch more fish than any other bait on the market, or the live frog or minnow."

This war whoop didn't disturb Mr. Heddon, but one Ans Decker, who was promoting a top-water plug with a revolving head called the Decker Hopatcong, took up the gauntlet—much to his regret.

The Jamison versus Decker affair was reported with clinical detachment by *Field & Stream,* but then, as now, the magazine had an army of bass experts among its readers whose enthusiasm was reflected in such precontest letters as "If I had a million dollars, I would bet on Ans Decker in the coming fishing contest . . ." "If the Coaxer wins I will be the most surprised fisherman in this country . . ." "The Coaxer never fails so it's no contest." Even though Jamison or his bait clearly outpointed Decker by a score of 28 to 16, this Armageddon of the weed beds resolved nothing. The postcontest letters to the editor kept the pot boiling: some said that Congress Lake, Ohio, scene of the duel, was too deep for a Decker plug, or that it was too early in the season and the water was too cold, ad infinitum. Votes poured in for the Cooper's Porker and the Hildebrandt Spinner, which "anybody knows would beat them both."

In the years since, countless thousands of lures have been cast into limbo, but the baits that survived the paralyzing skepticism of both fish and fishermen have become household words. It's obvious that every lure must fit its purpose—a deep diver when the fish are down and a surface bait when the fish are hugging shore. However, what makes a favorite lure may not be the extras that the manufacturer added but more likely what the fisherman has learned to do with it.

There is a torpedo-shaped surface plug that is virtually the standard lure for snook in Florida waters. The most popular way of fishing it is with the so-called whip retrieve, using fast, sharp strokes of the rod tip to keep the bait running swiftly on top. It performs like a frantic mullet. But like any lure, it doesn't always produce strikes, and when the snook are ignoring it, most of us continue to retrieve in the same fashion. When reeled slowly through the water the plug has all the animation of a wooden cigar.

However, Ray Bradley, a professional guide who operates in the Everglades region, has proved to me on various occasions that when snook are not responding to a fast playback, the plug will trigger violent strikes if barely moved at all, Ray simply flips it near the mangroves, then cranks a few turns to get his line tight, and proceeds to jiggle the bait on the surface with gentle wrist twitches. After creating a slight rocking motion in the plug he gives the reel several fast cranks and stops the lure abruptly to repeat rocking it again. Although this would be a painfully slow retrieve over any distance, the strike usually comes within the first five or ten feet of the plug's swim. There is a definite rhythm to Ray's retrieve, which takes practice to duplicate. But the important lesson, which the daring William Jamison evidently discovered early in the game, is that the angler is more important than his lures, and learning how to get the most out of each one is infinitely more rewarding than shuffling through the tackle box.

The art form common to all methods of angling is to find the patterns of behavior or, conversely, the patterns of success in any given body of water with a particular lure. This has become most apparent to the plastic-worm craftsmen who ply their trade on Southern impoundments. A particular depth, a bottom contour, a type of weed bed or gravel bar becomes the key to earning strikes. Knowing where to expect bass and how to work the lure is only learned through experience, and both factors vary according to the season. A depthfinder and a thermometer are standard equipment to the serious reservoir fisherman. Likewise, the skilled trout angler will spend part of his career on a small stream. The nimble rapids and quiet pools of miniature watercourses are the very essence of fly fishing. Here the game is resolved in stalking, casting, and—equally important—observing. Occasionally we find a visible riser, but more often success lies in reading the water carefully and inducing a hidden trout to take. Squatting, crawling, hiding, and casting in situations that would give a squirrel claustrophobia are not without compensations. Mainly, you can *see* how the fish react to various lures and retrieves. Little rivers are a fountain of information that is applicable to nobler waters where any reaction short of the positive usually goes unseen.

Some generalizations can be made about the ideal retrieving speed for various gamefish. For example, a moderately fast retrieve will attract chain pickerel, northern pike, and muskellunge, whereas largemouth and smallmouth bass are more frequently caught by reeling slowly. However, certain lures, and especially spoons, will sometimes catch bass when retrieved very rapidly. The slowest retrieves are most productive of panfish such as yellow perch, bluegills, and crappies. In general, trout are taken at a much slower pace than, say, landlocked salmon or coho salmon, but the chinook salmon prefers lures that are barely moving. Landlocked salmon are often caught on trolled flies and spoons at speeds of eight to ten miles per hour; coho at four to eight miles per hour; and chinook at one to two miles per hour. In salt water you can hardly retrieve a lure fast enough to catch dolphin, barracuda, jack crevalle, roosterfish, and any of the mackerels. These species are often caught at speeds in excess of twelve miles per hour and often up to twenty miles per hour on trolled baits. Yet other saltwater gamefish such as the red drum, bonefish, and tarpon favor a lure that just dawdles along. Naturally, there are exceptions to every rule, but the experienced angler has at least some idea of what speed range he can operate in and still expect strikes.

Obviously, some plugs require more manual dexterity than others; those with metal arms or lips or deeply curved bodies that are designed to wiggle or dive through increased water resistance cannot in some cases be operated at varying speeds. A good example is the popping plug. The general procedure with a popper is to let the lure sit for a moment after making a cast, then give it a sharp jerk with an upward snap of the rod tip, pause, and repeat the action. This movement is solely in the wrist of the hand holding the rod when

33

casting with spinning gear. The other hand should hold the reel crank stationary, so that you can be ready to strike instantly. Most fish are difficult to hook on a surface popper because they usually knock the lure upward when rushing from below. The rod strikes shouldn't be too violent or the disturbance will make the illusion unnatural. The pauses in between each "pop" should be long enough to permit the plug to remain motionless. When the speed is right, you should get at least two pops out of the plug before there's enough slack in your line to require reeling. After taking up the slack, the action should be repeated, the time between pauses and pops should be varied. If fishing is slow, we're all inclined to rush things along, but a popping plug doesn't work when it's literally churned over the surface. Poppers are not designed for fast retrieves. The slanting, concave face pulls the plug body under, and it will flip end over end or tangle in the line. Second, the total effect is complete chaos, creating a noise and a wake but very little action. Of course, the village idiot might splinter it, but you can get better results by switching to a cigar-shaped plug with propellers fore and aft. The tiny blades churn just enough to attract a hiding largemouth or pickerel, yet the bait can be retrieved at top speed.

But aside from the mechanical aspects of fishing a lure, both the spin caster and the bait caster have to think in terms of tackle performance before ultimate retrieving speeds can be reached. One reason, for instance, why small reels are a handicap in many phases of saltwater casting is not that they lack the capacity or inherent strength to handle the fish but rather in having a minimal rate of line recovery. Your outfit might be perfect on a bass pond, but the gear ratio, the cranking radius, and the spool diameter of the reel just can't move a lure fast enough to trigger a solid strike from a barracuda or a ladyfish, for example. There are many species of fish that habitually follow, swat at, and swirl behind an artificial lure because the bait isn't moving fast enough.

The story is by now apocryphal—only because it has happened so often to so many anglers—where two men fishing from the same boat using identical lures defy the law of averages in that one scores fish after fish while his partner strikes out. Often as not, the unsuccessful angler is using a reel that just won't bring the lure to its effective swimming speed. These days with high gear-ratio spinning reels, even the terms *slow retrieve* and *fast retrieve* have to be measured with a practiced eye, as what looks slow to one man can be a brisk pace to another.

Shortly after William Jamison made his claim to fame, three nationally known casting experts put on a demonstration in a Michigan lake, which started as a gag but proved its point better than the participants expected. Fred Peet, William Dilg, and Clark Venable fished for bass using a carrot, an ear of corn, and a frankfurter as their lures. These were rigged with treble hooks, and though the hot dog merely disintegrated, the carrot and corn "plugs" took fish. The trio of champions worked their baits like surface lures with all the artsy-craftsy maneuvers we have come to recognize as skillful retrieving.

Equally ludicrous, and a tale that bears repeating, were the promotional efforts of one Buck Perry. I never could duplicate his system and I doubt if many of the outdoor writers who were invited to witness his demonstrations ever figured it out. Mr. Perry would perform on a totally unfamiliar bass lake employing a heavy trolling outfit to tow a lure that resembles a bent shoehorn. His technique was to roar around the pond with his outboard wide open. It's hard to believe that a bass would even see the bait, much less intercept it, but Buck caught strings of fish everywhere he appeared. This doesn't mean that any other lure can be trolled at full throttle and catch bass, but it suggests that the only limit to a potentially effective retrieve is how rapidly you can manipulate the bait. Slow is easy; but without the right tackle, fast can be impossible.

As a general rule, in spinning for most gamefish the retrieve should not be held at a steady pace. An erratic playback is usually more effective than a constant wobble or spin of the lure. A blade should be maneuvered in such a fashion that it rises and falls, turning and flashing with the slack, then suddenly darting forward again. Yet there are situations where all those practiced deceptions that make a fish believe a piece of metal is edible can be defeated by a strong current. It requires a sensitive hand to maintain a lifelike retrieve.

On fast rivers, and especially deep ones, the spin-stick artist must constantly relate the speed of the current to the speed of his lure. The usual approach in working a broad run is to cast quartering upstream. As the spoon enters the water, the line is slack, but it quickly begins to belly with the current pulling the lure along. Inevitably, there is some variation in how fast different lure weights and designs sink or swim, but a certain amount of slack is desirable until the bait swings around downstream; it should be just enough to maintain the right depth. When the lure begins to arc against a tightening line, you may want to slack off once again. This tightening causes the wobbler to rise from the bottom to the top (an attraction in itself), but the angler who has enough manual skill to anticipate the peak of that movement and pay out more line can prolong his retrieve at fish-holding depths. Steady reeling in this cast, or any attempt to "pump" more action into the retrieve, will only result in raising the spoon to the surface, leaving it flapping like an angry pancake on top. At times, of course, even a churning spoon is effective, but as a rule we get our best results near the gravel on big streams at slow to moderate speeds.

The key to your retrieve depends on how you hold the rod. There is no such thing as one position for all lures or all fish. In tarpon fly fishing, for example, you have to hold the rod so that the tip will be pointed directly at the fish. This would be difficult if the tarpon required a fast-moving lure, but fortunately the silver-king is caught on an almost motionless or slow-draw retrieve. By holding the rod down, the angler can make the essentially powerful overhead strike. This is neither desirable nor necessary in trout fishing, where the fly rod is most often at a 45-degree angle, and the strike a mere tightening of the line.

In all other forms of casting, the correct rod position for any type of retrieve depends on the lure itself and the length of line extended on the water. If you are using a surface plug designed to run over the surface, it will be necessary to hold the rod tip high at first when the lure is forty to fifty yards out.

Then it can be gradually lowered as the reel fills and your rate of line recovery becomes greater. The skilled caster automatically compensates for the increasing speed of the lure as he cranks it back, possibly starting with the rod at a 60-degree angle and lowering it to the horizontal or even pointing it at the water to one side to keep a popper working right up to the boat. The important thing is maintaining enough manual control so you can still set the hook.

In the sixty-odd years since Jamison versus Decker, virtually nothing has changed as far as the performing arts are concerned. To make a plastic plug or a metal spoon look like food to a gamefish still requires not only the correct tackle but a dexterous hand.

[1971]

5

The Spider
Dry Fly

For several reasons, spider-style dry flies have gone out of fashion with fisherman in recent years, but not with trout. Until the recent trend toward the widespread breeding of roosters especially for fly tying, the longer-fibered hackles required for spiders were hard to obtain. Also, since the early 1970s most development of American dry-fly patterns has centered on increasingly exact imitation, and the so-called attractor patterns—within which category spiders fall—have undeservedly languished.

All of this means a big opportunity for the modern dry-fly angler. Fussy trout on hard-fished waters will still climb all over a spider—all the more so because they almost never see them these days. You won't find spider patterns in most fly shops or catalogs these days, but given a copy of this chapter any good commercial fly dresser can whip you up some in a hurry.

There was a brook trout who lived in a flat pool at the head of our night pasture, just where the stream broke out of a hemlock stand. This fish had a casual innocence in the way he would rest at the very tail of the run, inspecting those flies that I threw at him day after day. I would come from below him and, by hiding in a screen of tall grass, make a thirty- or thirty-five-foot cast that put the fly directly in his line of vision. In all fairness to my trout, he did strike on two different occasions and I missed both. But as the summer passed, he became more and more indifferent. Apparently this brookie spent his whole day in exactly the same place, because I would find him there nearly every time I went out. My trouble was in avoiding the drag. The fly would float a few feet and at the instant my trout started for it, the fly would kick up a little wake, sending him scurrying across the pool and under a boulder. As any angler knows, a situation like this can become an obsession.

Late one afternoon I found my problem fish in his regular position, so I tied on a Cream Spider and wished it well. The fly settled easily and came dancing downstream while the line, caught in the faster currents nearby, started to race out of control. I gave some slack, but in the fraction of a second drag was inevitable—the belly of the line pulled at the fly. Spiders, however, are not ordinary flies. Instead of skimming through the surface, the fly spun and bounced off the water in a startling broad jump, and my trout was fastened to the hook. I should like to pause and reflect on what followed, but the brookie did little more than thrash about, arriving at my net with the passive dignity of a spent champion.

If you were to fish every day during that period of the year when trout rise to floating flies—using a spider or variant—you could catch your daily share of trout and probably hook some of the largest ones that will ever come to any dry fly. I won't even make exceptions about where you do this fishing. Provided it is water with a normal fly-eating trout population, you are going to get a chance at every fish who wants to be caught and even a few who usually know better. The only qualification is that you have a reasonable aptitude for casting. Your observer bows to all rebukes he is going to get for this bigotry, but I'll allow no shoddy substitutions on the end of my leader. The Case of the Spider is in point, and I record it even though we are spying on the weakness of trout.

Of all trout flies, the one you can least afford to be without is the spider. It can be a Brown Spider, a Badger Spider, a Blue Dun Spider, or whatever kind you like, but at least one of these high-yielding floaters should be in the kit of every serious fly fisherman. The spider is thought to imitate long-legged insects like the crane fly, spider, or water strider. True or not, they seem to suggest insect life in general, because they are usually effective when caddisflies, midges, and mayflies are on the water. In appearance, the spider-type dry fly consists of a relatively small hook tied with extra-large hackle. Although they are sometimes made without bodies or tails, in my experience a fly so tied is much less effective. When the spider is tied with a tiny pair of wings, it is properly called a *variant,* but in recent years the term has become arbitrary, and many variant patterns are now wingless. The great attraction of this fly is its ethereal, almost lifelike ability to dance across the surface. It will even turn around on the water, and the slightest change in current or puff of wind will send it skating for a few inches before floating again. The secret of course is in the hackle, which may be two inches or more in diameter, depending on the hook size. Hook and hackle are out of proportion to each other, the hackle being roughly three or more times greater than the hook would regularly require in an ordinary dry fly.

The reactions of trout to a spider-type fly are different from their responses to ordinary flies. Logical behavior among trout is nothing more than a pleasant myth at best, yet the spider commonly causes the fish to rise above the surface and take the fly going down. Now whether this is because the fly actually excites them or because the sensitive movement of a spider simulates an active insect about to take off, I am not sure. I have caught many trout this way, and over a long period of time the only impression left me is that the fish were anxious that the fly should not escape.

I found a brown trout on the Willowemoc below Harry Darbee's place last summer. The fish was rising in a length of bouncy water between two pools, and after trying several casts with a Cahill he stopped his feeding. For a moment he drifted backward with the current, sinking very slowly, but when the fly didn't come down again as he expected, we both felt relieved. A minute passed and he was back at the surface. Quite obviously, I had him on guard and the next cast would be my last chance. I took off the Cahill and knotted on a small Blue Dun Spider; the safest way to try any trout is to suggest an insect form, showing him little to find fault with. Don't mistake this scrap of learning for scholarship—it is an axiom on which fly fishing rests and you can do with it as you please. I cast the spider so that it fell several yards above his station, and even as the fly floated I knew the trout would take. My Blue Dun rode jauntily over the water, standing on the tips of its hackles. The trout dashed directly at the fly and then jumped clear of the surface—snatching the spider as he came down. Here was an otherwise reluctant fish suddenly inspired to be an acrobat. Unusual? Not in the least.

The spider-type dry fly is strictly an American innovation. On foreign waters the term *spider* means a long-hackled wet fly, and I point this out because many tackle shops stock the imported kind, which are not the same thing. I've often wondered how the chalkstream fly fisher overlooked the possibility of a long-hackled floater in his still-water casting. The spider really excels on glassy streams. In very fast and broken water a rough, hair-bodied fly or a bivisible would be more effective, as it requires a sizable mouthful to tempt a trout to the top. But in slower places the sparse, free-floating spider leaves nothing to be desired. I use three patterns almost exclusively: a Cream Spider with a gold tinsel body, a coch-y-bonddu spider with gold body, and a Blue Dun Spider with a condor quill body. These represent the three major insect colorations—cream, brown, and blue-gray. I also have quite a number tied with mixed hackles—grizzly and brown, grizzly and ginger, furnace and ginger—and these work equally well. The important thing to remember is that the hackle must be stiff, long, and sparse so that the overall effect is no more than a suggestion of insect life. You can't achieve this impression with webby neck hackle. A proper spider is made from spade hackle—the wide hackle found on a rooster's throat. Sometimes on a gamecock skin you'll find saddle hackles that are perfect for making spiders. As a rule, however, they are a bit too short.

The hooks I like best are #14 and #16 short shanks of very light wire, but don't hesitate to try #18 or even smaller; I have used them down to #20 even on heavy fish. Tom Moore showed me some fantastic fishing one day in the channel between Yellowstone and Shoshone lakes—using nothing but #18s and #20s.

It is interesting to note that the spider dry fly is almost foolproof in presentation. No matter how clumsily you shoot your cast, the fly will come delicately to the water—provided you do not use too heavy a leader. As a rule of thumb, a 9-foot leader tapered to 3X at the point is nearly correct for all light trout lines, and if the tippet section of the leader is 30 inches or longer you just can't bungle a cast. Spiders will not spin or twist a light leader, and although they have a little more air resistance than orthodox dry flies, once the cast is checked they have a slow, deliberate flight to the surface. Furthermore, the spider is less apt to drag on the water, because a pull on the line will send the fly hopping out of trouble. Remember, this fly cocks on the tips of its long hackles and tail with the hook well above the surface. It can even be cast directly downstream and purposely dragged against the current; if your line is floating high the spider will simply walk upstream. Spiders will not get mashed after a few fish are taken and most patterns are wingless—a feature that many skilled anglers appreciate. In my opinion, wings are only important when greater visibility is needed or when a spentwing hatch is on the surface. Spentwing flies are in a more limited fashion just as unique as the spider. Speaking of being unique, that reminds me of a day on one of our northern New York trout streams.

A storm started to move over West Canada Creek one afternoon, and as high winds blew upriver, the trout began rising in a strong ripple near the far bank. Pale-colored duns were hatching in numbers, but as the wind grew they skidded and skated on the surface, at times even being blown directly upstream. The fish were not taking them evenly; they slashed and jumped at the unpredictable insects. The whole performance smacked of spider fishing, and by the time great thunderclaps were overhead, I netted my sixth trout and ran for the car. West Canada is a heavily fished stream, and ordinarily a bag of six trout would have been an extremely complex procedure. The point is that spiders are especially effective on windy days. If you use a long, fine leader, the spider will skate and leap like a frustrated mayfly. Sometimes you'll get the same effect in heavy rivers where the currents conflict but the surface is flat.

The Thompson River is not a trout stream in the usual sense of the word, for the river is deep and in some places more than a quarter-mile wide. One is bewildered at first by the currents that merge and run in every direction—marked by streaks of froth that gather in patches of foam that revolve slowly, then dissolve. Floating logs go down in funnel-shaped whirls and reappear later amid hissing air bubbles. I have fished the Thompson for steelhead in its quieter parts around Kamloops and further south in British Columbia, but in the northerly primitive country near Clearwater drainage, there are some remarkable dry-fly waters. On one morning, fishing with Don and Sally Carter, we caught and released well over one hundred rainbow trout. They came so easily that we lost interest in catching them.

But the day I have in mind was the time when a school of big rainbows were "making the tour" around a froth-covered pool. The fish were on a spree, but no splash marked their feeding. A broad tail appeared and disappeared where a trout picked flies out of the foam; then another and another. Sometimes they would swim and rise in a straight line, finally getting on the tops of the long glassy rollers that surged against the rock shore, and then they'd move back out into the main current to make their circuit again. I was fishing with Bill MacDonald this trip; Bill is the angling editor of *Forest and Outdoors,* and his fly-rod skill is exceptional. In two hours of casting, we each managed to hook just one small trout. It was difficult fishing; the constant change in direction and length of the cast, frequent fly changing, and steadily rising trout made the perfect background for something miraculous to happen, and it did. Bill tied on a spider and after a few casts he was fast to a leaping rainbow. Those big rainbows suddenly hit our casts again and again, coming up and over to take the spider on a downward turn. There would be a terribly long pause before the trout took off, and many of them snapped our leaders on the first wild run. As in most of that country, the fish were of a size—while more abundant Clearwater fish had been 2-pounders, our Thompson trout were 3-pounders.

Spiders are especially productive in lake fishing. There is one troubled situation in particular, that of high-altitude Western lakes, where midges are the predominant food form; here the spider will frequently take fish that are obviously feeding on insects that seem no larger than the head of a pin. Why this should be, I am not sure, but the spider is a very satisfactory attracter when trout become narrowly wise in the isolation. I was discussing high-lake trouting with Frank Dufresne recently, and we discovered that we had identical experiences in widely separated areas. Most people are under the impression that remote trout populations are easy marks—this is not even a fair generalization. Frank pointed out that in the hundreds of mountain lakes in which he has fished, the majority demanded tiny flies and delicate tackle, and short of actual midge fishing the spider was the most reliable.

Mile High is a lake formed on a great bed of stones in northern British Columbia. The place Don Carter and I fished that afternoon was a narrow bay where the trout rose merrily, leaping as regular as clockwork. At first glance we thought this was going to be another Clearwater episode, but as the afternoon passed neither one of us had struck a trout, even though we covered one after another. There were many different sedges, midges, and even a few mayflies on the water, and we tried imitating every one of them. Don took the paddle once more, and we made our third and fourth circuit of the bay. Purely through the process of elimination I finally arrived at the fly box that held my spiders, and within a very short time we were catching trout. They weren't the biggest fish we saw feeding, but a dozen husky Kamloops rainbows came to net. Until this Mile High junket, I had never attached any real significance to spider fishing on mountain lakes. In the light of more recent events, I'm fairly well convinced that this is the dry-fly man's answer to flat-water trout at any altitude.

Large trout are not by nature free risers to the dry fly. Big brown trout especially stay out of sight and do their feeding at hours when most anglers are sound asleep. Yet let the green drake or salmon fly hatch by the thousands and these clouds of temptation clog his brain, halting all the rational traffic that a cannibal trout must direct down avenues of safety. Insect food gets out of proportion to his ability to resist it, and for a brief period you and I are in a position to meet the legendary monster. Although a spider could resolve this conflict, there are many kinds and patterns of flies that simulate green drakes and salmon flies—and dozens of them catch trout. But what fly will sometimes bring a hook-jawed brown to the top when there are not great fly hatches or when there is nothing on the water to imitate? I have asked that question of many skilled dry-fly men and the spider was elected by unanimous vote.

[1953]

6

Creep 'n' Crawl

Until recent decades, most American trout fishermen learned their early lessons along a small brook where the short-pants angler quickly found that not staying out of sight simply meant no fish. In these times especially, when the novice fly fisherman may be in his or her thirties and older, starting often with a fly-fishing school on a larger river, the mysteries of small-stream trouting can be almost insurmountable. Happily, this particular story (first published in 1956) is a good example of McClane's timeless counsel and can help any novice to better catches on smaller and still uncrowded waters.

I'll add something here that A. J. himself has mentioned in other works, which is how to get a better drift of the fly in such cramped quarters. Check your final forward cast abruptly as it straightens in the air, the shock of which will cause your leader tippet to recoil slightly. This creates just a little slack in the leader tippet near your fly; enough to add a few inches of extra, drag-free drift in a miniature pocket.

There is a portly gentleman in New York City who dines at the best clubs, and when the headwaiter bows, you know the old boy isn't on his stiff list. He wears a vest and pays his tab from a Mark Cross wallet. He is an angling-type citizen, however, and when he kisses off the éclat of Gotham you will find him by miscellaneous brooks, crawling around in places that would give a squirrel claustrophobia. I have stumbled over him from year to year on the small-stream circuit. He wears a bile-green jacket covered with trout flies and the expression of a man about to find the Holy Grail. The last time I saw him he was reconnoitering a pool on the upper Willowemoc with a crew-cut character in an Abercrombie outfit. The survey came to an abrupt and untimely end when the landowner came out and told them to get the hell off his property.

All brook fishermen are a little wacky, and any moppet showing the slightest inclination to crawl for the headwaters should be promptly inoculated against angling's most communicable disease. Lacking such protection, he may at some point in his adult life be bitten by this most potent bug when he is completely vulnerable. He will become an addict and nothing in this wide world will ever make him change his ways. I know. This is how it happened to me.

Bob Ward stopped by the house one day and interrupted a book I thought I was writing. His hip boots are rubbed thin at the knees, for in the Ward concept all upright casters are no-forehead types doomed to live on bark and berries. Bob told me about a brook full of improbable trout, and an hour later I was a candidate for the creep 'n' crawl society. It's a funny thing about small streams; they are often smaller at the mouth than they are at the source. This one coming down from Bear Wallow, for instance, looks like a spring seepage where it enters the river. Actually, most of the flow runs under gravel for at least twenty yards before hitting the main stream. This is quite common in mountain country, and on several occasions in the past a cursory investigation has paid off in handsome fish.

We started casting several hundred yards from the mouth where the stream bubbled and tumbled through moss and rhododendron. To keep from falling over each other we alternated pools going up the mountain. There weren't any flies on the water, but any drab, buggy-looking floater will usually take trout. I tied on a Ginger Spider and almost every cast brought a strike. The trout were small at first, so I often pulled the fly away from them at the last instant, but when we reached the section below the wallow some pools were five and six feet deep, with brookies running close to a pound. Bob creeled a 14-inch native below a little waterfall, and just before we quit for lunch I came upon a long run of still water between granite ledges. I didn't even try to see a trout this time, but kneed my way up to the tail of the pool.

Small-stream technique is nearly all horizontal casting. Wave your rod overhead a few times and you'll spook every trout within ten yards. I have one advantage in that I use a very short fly rod, which allows me to work close to vertical. This is a further advantage from a squatting position. Teasing line out foot by foot, I got a good bend in the rod and shot my fly up to the head of the pool. It was a calculated risk. The falling line would inevitably frighten any fish holding near the lower end of the run, but I counted on arousing a few big trout in the deeper water before the little buggers tore for cover. The fly never had a chance. The line unrolled and *bang,* there was a beautiful crimson-bellied native turning end over end in the narrow arena. The trout ripped line through the pool, and for about ten minutes he put on a Barnum & Bailey performance—from clown to acrobat with a flip of his tail. I have caught bigger brook trout, but none prettier or more perfectly stalked. It was a day—and a fish —to remember.

The toughest trout I can recall stalking was a big brown that lived under the suspension footbridge below our summer home. I have to cross the bridge every day to get groceries or mail, and for several weeks I saw this fish leaning close to the foundation. There were three other sizable browns that stayed out in the main current, all wearing gill tags I gave them last year, but the instant I saw their shadows they spooked. They still do. The big one held directly under the bridge, however, and if I walked quietly and peeked over the planks I could get a quick glimpse of him wiggling into a crevice under the foundation.

I fished for that trout nearly every morning and evening. I tried flies of all kinds, long casts, casts from the bank brush and casts from the opposite bank. No soap. Then I crawled out on the bridge one evening, poked a few inches of my rod over the side and let out just enough line so that the fly dimpled the water. I depended on the noise of his splash or the movement of my rod to signal a strike; I got both. We had a wild time for a few minutes, with me trying to get off the bridge and him going in the opposite direction. The leader finally broke and I haven't seen the old hookbill since. For years, though, I have caught countless trout around bridges, dams, and cut banks, using these tactics. Getting off a rock-and-roll suspension bridge was the detail I neglected in this instance.

Casual observers are apt to think that people who scrinch along brooks swatting mosquitoes and getting their seats wet are just trying to escape these tension-producing atomic days; nothing could be further from the truth. The creep 'n' crawl society is dedicated to the proposition that small streams operate on the short-term payment plan. A gent can always get action. This motto has been adopted by thousands of American anglers from East Coast to West. When the big-river man becomes a doorbell pusher in late August and September—making blind stabs at the water, hoping that somebody is home—our brook caster is right in the living room. The cold tributary waters usually hold an eager population of trout that will gobble nymphs, floating insects, minnows, crayfish, frogs, just about anything that falls in the water. They're hungry, but they're not easy marks. The premium is still on stalking and skillful casting. The point is that a real student of miniature waters is prepared, nay eager, to match wits with every trout he meets.

The great fascination of small-stream fly fishing is that you can frequently see your trout. Maybe he will be rolling head and tail under a hemlock bough or feinting left and right in the rippling places around a boulder, but his stance shows that he's more interested in looking at a new fly than contemplating the old one. Of course, you aren't admitted to this heady intimacy while standing upright. Nothing spooks a trout quicker than the sight of man. A deer, a cow, even an otter can amble along the brook with impunity; you cannot. Peek through the alders or stub your toe and you create havoc. But crawl along the bank as if you're looking for a lost collar button and the trout won't give you a tumble.

The angle at which a trout can spot you varies considerably, but it's hard to miss if you approach the fish from a position just as close to the ground or water as you can possibly manage (this becomes tricky as you get older). If there is any natural cover, take advantage of it. If the only approach silhouettes you against the sky, then creep, crawl, and throw a low line. I have crawled along streams in Maine, Vermont, New York, Michigan, Virginia, California, Oregon, Montana, Idaho, Wyoming, and various parts of Canada, and while at first I was long on fervor and short on organization, now I carry a minimum of gear.

The tackle for small-stream fly fishing is anything nonregulars happen to have or the specialized tools this department reviewed some time back. I personally prefer midget fly rods and light weight-forward lines. The most important component is the leader. If you use a long one, casting will be difficult. Most casts on small streams are in the 25-foot class, and often you will be in a position where 15 feet is maximum. With a regular 9-foot leader, 6 feet of line would have to flex your rod and turn the flimsy nylon over. There are two ways of meeting the problem. One is to use a very short leader, about 5 feet, and the other is to use a slightly longer double-tapered leader. You can turn a balanced double taper over with your hand. I designed one that is a comfortable 7½ feet long and it's ideal for short casts. Here are the specifications: 18 inches of .014, 6 inches of .015, 6 inches of .017, 15 inches of .019, 9 inches of .015, 9 inches of .013, 12 inches of .011, and 15 inches of .009. This will roll with very little line extended. The trouble with regular tapers in short lengths is that you often get in places where the trout are shy, and on abbreviated pools the ideal is to cover them with leader only.

For small-stream work I prefer spider-type dry flies. I feel the spider is best because it has a very light impact on the surface, it rides high on the current and it acts alive. A Blue Dun spider can make big trout roll twice, bark, and fetch. When the light is bad I sometimes use a Ginger spider, and if the stream is frothy I go to bivisibles. Bivisibles aren't quite as potent, but they float like a cork in rough water and the two types can be used interchangeably.

I never bother imitating any hatching insects. Trout in miniature streams are not truly selective; they grub out a meager existence by river standards and a well-presented dry fly is bound to get their approval. The size of the fly is important. If you get short strikes from good fish it means the one you are using is too large. I don't know why size makes a difference, but I would guess that trout in small streams, especially at high altitude, are conditioned to hatches of tiny insects and are suspicious of outsize imitations.

My turnaround selection is the nymph. On the way upstream you probably spotted a good trout that lit for cover because your big feet grated on the gravel at the wrong moment. Presumably you made a note of the place and are going to try him again. I use nymphs for a second chance because this kind of fly appeals to all trout and they're not likely to question its origin after spooking from a floater. Patterns such as the Sens Caddis dressed on #14 hooks are especially good; they are excellent imitations of caddis larvae, which are the main dietary staple of the small-stream trout.

It isn't often good tactics to work a brook in a downstream direction. The fish can see you much more easily, and unless there's a head of water flowing, the distance your line can drift is limited. If the brook is running bank full and you have a camouflaged approach to the pool, you might swim the nymph down, but I think it's worth walking to get below a cautious fish.

Fishing the nymph is scarcely different from working a dry fly. After estimating the position of your trout, make your cast so that the nymph drifts back to his hold. Let the current move the line and leader as the fly swings toward him. If the water is quiet and your nymph sinks to the bottom, try a slight twitch to make it drift free again. That faint movement may bring a rod-pounding strike. Wet flies are effective, and so are the midget streamers and bucktails at times, but in general I have better luck with sparsely dressed nymphs. The only wet-fly pattern I carry is the McGinty, with its wings cut down to stubs. A bee imitation is productive on Western streams during the summer months.

Creep 'n' crawl, anyone?

[1956]

7

Spinning-Reel Accuracy

The finest compliment I ever had in fishing came from a charter-boat skipper with whom I shared a day full of bluefish on the many tide rips off Nantucket Island. After I'd fooled around with various kinds of tackle during the morning, he allowed as how I was okay with a fly rod, pretty good with a conventional rod, but was one of the worst spin casters he'd ever seen. It was a compliment, of course, because I'd worked hard on the former methods but had never given spin casting a second thought. It just seemed so simple.

More people fish with spinning tackle than with any other kind, but few do it really well. Most neophytes these days get handed a spinning reel for starters because it's easy to operate. Unfortunately, this is seldom accompanied by a good casting lesson. As with other kinds of tackle, accurate casting is the key to success, and spinning has its own brand of subtlety in this regard. Here's a very important casting lesson that will prove invaluable for beginner and veteran alike.

Last summer I worked as a guide at the Circle S Ranch in Wyoming. Let me hasten to explain that my amateur standing is intact since I made the twenty-six floats on a no-pay basis. In fact there were probably moments when the dudes felt they deserved a better fate.

In any case I rowed 416 miles for no other reason except that the camp was short of help—and I wanted the experience. There is plenty of white water on the Green and New Fork rivers, which certainly took some of the sag and spread out of my waders. We fished by floating into the remote pools and riffles, then getting out of the boat and working the water carefully with dry flies.

One morning I went down the best part of the New Fork with a gentleman who had just taken up spinning. I am not violating a confidence in saying that to "Mr. Smith" the fixed-spool reel was a disembodied unit he viewed as the Orinoco Indian must regard an electric dishwasher.

After I'd maneuvered the boat among piano-size boulders and swung the stern into a long, greeny pocket that screamed big fish, he would toss his spoon into a willow or over a barbed-wire fence or anything else that happened to be on the bank. We all miss our target now and then, but I discovered what every professional guide must already know: some anglers can't hit the water. Perhaps you'll find this hard to believe, but in one hectic session I watched Mr. Smith make eight consecutive casts, not one of which landed in the river. We'd no sooner get him unstuck from one place (while rowing like mad to keep the double-ender from bolting into the rapids) than he'd snag another piece of landscape. It was then I realized that patience is a useless quality unless one knows exactly what to do with it, and in backbreaking self-defense I had to teach him how to cast.

Casting with the spinning rod does become automatic. And there's no reason why it shouldn't be accurate. The best casters, on the river or on a platform, are completely relaxed and totally unconcerned with the mechanical motions involved. When a fish shows or a pocket comes into view, the expert eyes it and bends the rod, and the lure finds the target. The chances are—if he deliberately stopped to estimate range and wind, then take aim—he'd miss a barn door. Exactly the same elements are involved as in shotgun handling; the bird shooter must learn to shoulder his weapon correctly and swing until the movement becomes reflexive. There is no second-best style. He doesn't shoot from the hip, the armpit, or the bridge of his nose, and if he took a calculated bead on a pheasant, he'd be lucky to collect a tail feather. By the same token, an accurate caster has mastered the basic stroke and doesn't deviate from it. Although he may split the target with his eyes and rod, it is automatic response that "feels" the lure to the bull's-eye. In every cast he holds the rod the same way, brings it up in the same path, and releases the line at the same point in his downstroke. Developing a consistent style and sticking to it is nine-tenths of the battle.

Accuracy is an obvious asset to the angler, and at times it can be absolutely essential to success. One of the best examples I've ever witnessed occurred the first time I fished a Florida canal for bass. These slab-sided waterways are tricky. They produce huge largemouths to the expert caster, but he's got to know where and when to fish them. Emory Lindsey was showing me L-7, one of the older canals, built in the days when they simply gouged a trench through the glades with a dragline (the technique now is to allow some slope along the banks to provide adequate spawning areas for the fish). I worked from the bow, and he sculled the skiff from the stern, holding a canoe paddle in one hand and his rod in the other. I cast like a robot, laying the plug within a foot of the bank, then twitching it back in short jerks. I was pleased as hell with my performance, but only a few small bass found it entertaining. Emory, who rarely made a cast except when he seemed bored, hooked a fat bass seemingly whenever he felt like it. He clamped four on the stringer that ran from 5 to 6 pounds. Being a polite companion, he didn't offer any advice until I asked for it, and when he wrestled another monster over the floorboards, I was bewildered.

"You're not casting where the fish are," he announced. "If you look real close, you'll see little bitty cuts in the shore that go back two, mebbe three, feet. You wouldn't believe an old daddy bass could git up in there, would ya? Well, that's where they hide. Man, you could cast all day at that bank, but unless your plug goes right plumb center in that pocket, you ain't gonna catch nothin' but little bass."

I didn't really understand why two or three feet would make that much difference in results. A bass should hear and attack a plug within that radius if he's hungry at all. But not in canal fishing, it seems. I began concentrating on Emory's cuts, which required a shade more accuracy than just pounding the bank, and the very first cast that hit the bull's-eye produced a fine 5-pounder. After that I hooked one hefty bass after another. We probably released sixty or seventy fish. When the spring-season water conditions are right in south Florida canals, the fishing can be phenomenal, but the pros who rack up the lunkers are teacup accurate. I believe that these shallow "tables" back in brushy banks are used as spawning areas, as well as convenient sources of forage, which probably accounts for the size of their inhabitants.

The casting style to develop with the spinning rod is a smooth chopping motion of the forearm. True, you can toss the lure out with a mere wrist snap, but using the forearm has several advantages that also apply to bait casting and fly casting. For one thing you can get more elevation with the forearm; by starting with the hand low and using a short arc you can make very short, accurate casts. As the arc is lengthened and the hand raised higher you can apply more power and achieve greater distance. A pure wrist motion, on the other hand, has a definite limit; it is not a consistent movement among inexperienced casters, and it is tiring particularly when lures larger than ¼ ounce are used. With the forearm (as well as some wrist action) you can achieve absolute precision and the maximum distance. This is the style used by the best tournament casters.

As in shotgunning, accurate casting begins with gripping the weapon properly. You should grasp the corks of a spinning rod with your fingers split around the reel leg—with two fingers in front and two in back. Some men with exceptionally large hands might find this uncomfortable and prefer one finger in front and three in back of the reel leg, but this is rarely necessary. Your thumb should be on top of the handle. It is important to keep your hand as relaxed as possible. Starting with a relaxed hold, you shouldn't squeeze down on the rod grip until the rod is stopped, an instant before power is applied to the back cast. To begin the cast, crank the handle so that the bail, pickup finger, or roller (depending on the type of reel) is on top and the lure is hanging about six inches from the rod tip, and then pick up the line so that it rests over the first joint of your forefinger. Your finger should bend just enough to lift the line free from the roller. Next, reverse the crank handle approximately one-quarter turn. At this point the pickup mechanism should be at the bottom of the reel, the line held in check by your forefinger. Do not squeeze the line against the rod grip, but hold it on the ball of your forefinger; the weight of the lure will create enough tension to keep the line tight. Now with your left hand snap the pickup open.

Aiming a cast requires no more thought than swinging the barrel ahead of a crossing bird or blotting one out as it rises going away. The motions are fluid. You have to keep your eye on the target. The extended rod is just a blur—it is pointed in the right direction, and you are aware of it, but your eyes are focused on the spot you want to hit. Mr. Smith belted the eight out of eight casts into the trees so regularly that it was easy to make a fairly accurate caster out of him. I simply kept asking him what he was looking at when he made a cast, and it finally dawned on him that whatever he looked at was what he was going to hit. You can't aim a rod accurately at one place and look at another; your eye and hand must be coordinated. So before you cast forget about the hazards, because they exist—and staring at them is not going to help.

In your first practice session hold the rod so the very tip is slightly above eye level, with the shaft splitting the center of the target. Your arm should be relaxed. Try to estimate how much speed the rod will need to shoot the lure the proper distance. Bending at the elbow with an upward and backward forearm motion, start the rod toward vertical, accelerating its speed until the rod is twelve o'clock high, and then stop the movement by squeezing the rod grip. The momentum of the lure will pull the rod tip back into a casting bend. As the lure pulls hard against the rod, start the forward chop with some wrist emphasis—and release the line from your forefinger as you pass the eleven-o'clock position (viewing the clockface with the angler facing left). When the line has been released, move your finger away and to the right of the spool. If you are trying for a very long shot over open water, don't allow the line to come in contact with your finger at all. In accuracy work, however, you will want to slow the cast down, since the common tendency is to overshoot a target. To "feather" a cast, simply tip your forefinger in toward the spool, and the escaping coils of line will hit your fingertip, thus retarding the flight of the lure.

Establishing the correct release point is important. If you let go of the line too soon, the lure will go too high and drift off target. If you release too late (after the rod tip has started to turn under), the lure will bang at your feet or, at best, splash down a few yards away. The lure must hit the right trajectory every time before you can be accurate. There are little nuances that the expert might add in releasing a shade earlier to get a high-arc cast in a tail wind for distance or a trifle late in getting a flat trajectory when bucking a head wind, but in the beginning—forget it.

You will find in using lures of various sizes that the proper distance between the tip of the rod and the bait itself must vary in proportion to its weight. For example, with an ultralight spinner weighing about $1/10$ ounce, you'll get the smoothest casts when the lure is suspended about 12 inches below the tiptop. A $1/4$-ounce lure will probably handle best at a point about 6 inches below the tiptop, and a $3/8$-ounce lure should be within 2 inches of the tiptop. There is no hard-and-fast rule because much depends on the stiffness of the rod. A "fast" rod, for example, never resists bend sufficiently to toss a light lure very far or very accurately. A little experimenting with different weights on your favorite rod can make a big difference in results.

Of course, there are lures that are impossible to cast accurately. Not because of the lack of weight but because of the shape. Some real fish catchers, such as air-resistant banana-shaped plugs and pie-plate spoons or spinners, are constitutionally incapable of going in a straight line. For most purposes when one is blind fishing it won't matter, but where accuracy is essential, old-timers will stay with a lure that comes as close to the thick-bottomed, narrow-necked tournament plug as is practical. Cigar-shaped plugs, pear-shaped spoons, and narrow-blade spinners with weighted shafts can be dropped on a dime. Some leadhead jigs cast well, depending on their weight and skirt length, but many of the lighter ones with stiff bucktail bodies whirl like a dervish in the air, thereby defeating accuracy and weakening the line as well. This has been a constant migraine to flats casters who hunt grubbing fish.

Accurate casting is extremely important in saltwater fishing. There is nothing haphazard about pegging a lure at a tarpon or bonefish. Let the lure land behind either one, and nine times out of ten they'll go busting off the flat. You have to lead both of these gamesters, whereas others such as the redfish or any of the sharks won't even touch a lure unless it's planted right under their noses. Even a large shark presents a small target when it's moving and the skiff is drifting in a wind. Other species, such as the mutton snapper and giant barracuda, often require a different kind of accuracy in placing the plug or spoon twenty or thirty feet ahead of and beyond the cruising fish so the lure can be retrieved to intercept their path. The saltwater caster has to be accurate not only on visible targets when they're cruising the shallows or feeding on the surface, but also when searching for cover-seekers such as the dolphin, cobia, and tripletail. Floating driftwood, old crates, and mats of seaweed offer the same cover to some saltwater species that a brushpile or bed of lily pads allows freshwater fish. Buoys and channel markers are so attractive to the tripletail that in many places he's known as a "buoy bass." His passion for shade is a well-known failing; Southern anglers put treetoppings on the water and fish under them with dead shrimp. Without this camouflage, however, Gulf Coast anglers work from one channel marker to the next, searching every piece of debris between. This is the routine approach, and on a calm day the fish can be seen quite easily at distances of seventy and eighty feet.

Accuracy with the spinning rod doesn't always mean casting at a fish. For one thing the splash of the lure may spook him. Furthermore, most of our freshwater fishing consists of blind casting at unseen targets. Let's take a river situation. Before the angler can pull life into his lure, he has two points to consider: The cast should be made from a position that permits the widest coverage of the water so that wading around to make subsequent casts is minimized; and it should be aimed at a spot where it will drift or swing in front of a fish without snagging in the stream bottom. It goes without elaboration that you can cast a long line and still be a very poor fisherman.

In a typical pool with a fast current at its head the direction of the flow pitches off toward one bank or the other, then eddies back, forming slack pockets along the deeper side. There might be a ledge, a stand of willows, or a string of boulders along the bank. The picture is not always the same. But the important factor is the current itself. Most anglers simply aim for the deepest spot and then reel the lure back through the middle of the pool. Sometimes this will catch fish; however, the largest stream dwellers are more likely to be holding in the slack pockets and undercut banks on the far side. This is especially true of trout; the fish are usually under something, and in the case of big brownies, at least, they are not apt to follow a lure out in the middle of a pool in broad daylight. If you can place your spinning lure accurately against the far bank with a cross-stream cast, so that it falls at the head of the flow and swings ten or twenty feet down into the slack pockets, the chance of drawing a large trout from his den is much better.

I made three floats with Mr. Smith last summer, and between trips he worked out on the lawn using a rubber practice plug. He was getting pretty good by the time we did the canyon float on the upper Green. This is a wild piece of water. Here the stream has a steep gradient and wicked stretches of jagged boulders that grin over the surface like dragon's teeth. I had never floated it before, nor had anyone at the ranch.

The fishing was spotty. We went through long rapids that didn't seem to hold any trout, then we'd hit a mile or two that was literally alive with rainbows. Smith could do no wrong. The trout hit everything in his box, and the banks were so far apart that even an expert couldn't hit the trees. But the cast that I remember was made when we passed a small island. The double-ender was moving at breakneck speed, and I windmilled the oars to keep us from the rocks. At the foot of the island the current swept in from both sides creating a small eddy—a logical spot for any trout with sense enough to get out of the midstream. Without hesitating, Smith copped out a 25-yard cast that dropped the spoon dead center. A rainbow churned out of the water and did a whip stall, hanging over the Green just long enough to thrill both of us. He looked a yard long. There wasn't much Smith could do about it; the trout hit the deck with his engine wide open as we vaulted over the whitecaps in the opposite direction. The reel screamed for a minute, then the line snapped.

Mr. Smith was disappointed, but better days are ahead. As we hiked to the truck he swished his rod at imaginary targets and made a popping sound with his tongue.

[1966]

8

Micro Power!

Sooner or later, most fly fishermen will face the choice of using size 20 patterns and smaller or not taking fish. As McClane points out in the following story, hatches of miniature aquatics together with miniature streamside terrestrials are found along all of America's trout rivers. On a season-long basis, they are almost always more important to both trout and fishermen than the larger and better-known mayfly hatches, which may only last for a week or a month at most.

Historically, the fine art of small flies is a recent one. Even into the 1950s, a full range of hooks down to size 28 wasn't widely available. And only in very recent years has nylon-monofilament technology progressed to a point at which 8X leader material (.003 inches in diameter) is both viable and commercially available. With the evolution of appropriate tackle has come an increasing interest in microfishing, an interest that now allows more anglers to extend their seasons into the summer and fall on many waters, long after the major hatches of larger flies have disappeared.

There are frustrating days in every fishing season when trout rise with abandon, though not recklessly, at what looks like dandruff or soot floating on the surface. These dimpling fish can drive the average angler bonkers as they *sip* and *slurp* at almost invisible food forms, and indeed they will often hit the knots in a leader rather than the perfectly presented Royal Coachman drifting gaily over their festive board. It's hard to believe that even a small trout would spend its energy gathering microscopic insects that are so small hundreds would be needed to fill a tablespoon, yet some of the biggest fish rise freely on these occasions. In a less technically oriented age the condition was known as "the angler's curse" and was reason enough to pack up and go home. Now that light-wire hooks are made to #28 and monofilament extruded to 8X, it can be a blessing in disguise. Any phenomenon that causes trout to feed voraciously is a promising situation. Skilled casters of the minutiae take fish when all else fails, but the game requires steel nerves, a controlled hand, and perfectly matched tackle. It also helps to have a blimp-size ego to suffer frequent deflation at the outset—regardless of how many felt soles you have worn to the nub.

Fishing with micros is the total refinement of our fly rod arts. Its mystique evolved on Pennsylvania limestone streams and the spring creeks of Montana. There are more days when the "ultimate" fly is essential on these silky waters, but the game has no geographic limitations. From Maine to Oregon and points south we have numerous rivers, usually highly alkaline, that produce microaquatic insects by the ton and are periodically invaded by equally small terrestrials. This demands leader tippets of less than 2-pound test with flies dressed on #20 to #28 hooks. For the most part you will be fishing at 6X and 7X and about a 1-pound pull is the measure of your success. Although it may seem impossible to take trout consistently on such frail terminal gear, once you get the feel of it, breakoffs are much less common than one would expect. As far as hooking fish is concerned, when these tiny points get a proper bite in skin or cartilage, the barb is difficult to remove even with strong tweezers. However, this cannot be accomplished with the wrong fly rod.

One of my first experiences with micros was back in the

days when I didn't need Granny glasses to find the hook eye. I was fishing New York's West Branch of the Ausable with Jim Deren in its quiet flowing upper reaches. Fish were popping everywhere, but except for a couple of little brook trout, bent on a suicide mission, an incredible number of selective browns countered every move on the board. Deren must have brooded on a midstream boulder for an hour, staring at his fly boxes like he was planning some chess strategy. Every once in a while he'd say *"Ah"*—but fastening an *"Ah"* on our leaders proved nothing.

Ed Hewitt wrote a booklet about midge fishing during the late 1940s, but nobody wanted to fiddle with 6X Spanish gut, nor did many anglers seriously believe that a #20 hook would hold a trout. Being an astute Manhattan tackle dealer, Deren had ordered a dozen of the Black Midge pattern dressed by the artful Scots lass Liz Greig. So with a final *"Ah"* we again distinguished ourselves. I was using an 8½-foot powerhouse of a rod made by Lew Stoner that could toss a flatiron over the post office, and whatever Deren darkly threatened the fish with wasn't any gentler in its response to .005 drawn gut. Unlike modern monofilaments gut has little elasticity.

The fact that we caught even a few cooperative trout was simply the law of averages at work. The maddening thing was that within an hour the Ausable's celebrated 16- to 18-inch browns consumed Deren's dozen like so much popcorn and we couldn't do a thing about it. The slightest underpull as the fish took skidded the fly off their teeth or on the next rise provoked a firmer hand response and a broken leader.

In a micro situation it is possible to switch to a finer tippet and tiny flies with some chance of success, but the *average* trout rod of 8 or 8½ feet is invariably too stiff in the tip section. The tip must be delicate with sufficient power for casting but resilient enough to act as a "cushion" when you strike the fish. No rod material can beat bamboo for this purpose; fiberglass and the higher-impact graphite, which performs so well in ordinary fly fishing, have too much rigidity to provide the buffer that *pulls* rather than drives the barb into skin. The stiffer a rod tip, the greater the ratio of breakoffs. Essentially, a 7½-foot length of about 2½ ounces is ideal, but if the rod is over 3 ounces in weight and promises to make long casts, be wary. To increase its range, the tip has to be beefed up, which is splendid for most trouting. In fishing the micros, however, distance is seldom important, since you are casting to visible targets rather than searching the water blind. Most casts are short, as microfeeders are usually intent at their eating pleasures, a foible that bodes good tidings for the already compromised angler.

The other tackle components, line and leader, must of course be integrated. A #3- or #4-weight line has minimal surface tension to overcome at the strike. A heavy fly line contributes to broken tippets simply because it has to be pulled with more force when setting the hook. Here again it's possible to use a #5- or #6-weight line, but with each increase (not only in weight but diameter) the margin for error is infinitely greater. The very act of striking a fish becomes a reflex, and the speed of your normal reaction measured by years of working with 3- and 4-pound-test leaders is in itself difficult to control. You can hit a trout a proper wallop with 2X or 3X, but micro tippets are unforgiving. You are allowed no more than a tightening of the line. It helps to think of your strike as merely taking the stretch out of the leader. The fly is so small that the fish will not reject it instantly as it would a larger artificial, so the speed of your response is not critical.

For good presentation and a drag-free swim with micros, a long leader is necessary, certainly no fewer than 10 feet and preferably 12 to 14 feet in length. My usual leader formula is 60 percent heavy to 40 percent light with respect to diameters, but in addition, and this is very important when using the minutiae, it also reads 60 percent *stiff* monofilament to 40 percent *soft*. A stiff nylon or any other rigid material prohibits a lifelike drift of the tiny fly, which has virtually no buoyancy to resist the pull of the tippet.

Furthermore, it's easier to cast a "slack" leader with soft monofilament, which delays drag and permits the micro to cover those first few critical feet over a rise without a hint of artifice. I like a long tippet of no fewer than 24 inches, and while 6X and 7X are the rule for 20s and 22s, an 8X is eminently practical for any smaller size hook. During the past four seasons I have been experimenting with tippets down to .003, which tests a bit more than ½ pound. An "honest" .003 or 8X is not marketed as a fishing item, but it has various industrial uses, notably in making eyelashes for toy dolls. This diameter is fine enough to swim a #28 artificial without a drag, and it's virtually invisible in the water. In fact, I can't even poke it through the hook eye without magnifying eyeglasses.

I have yet to take a large trout on 8X (my best was about 17 inches long), but it's pointless to expect trophy trout on many of my favorite rivers where a 2-pounder is bragging size. The important thing is that 8X is practical when it's needed. Most of my breakoffs are simply due to bad casts that fall in the grass or clip a stray tree limb. With balanced tackle you can actually "coax" a trout to the net in the ultimate sense of playing a fish. You can't really apply much pressure to use the full bend of the rod no matter how delicate its tip. If a fish is running strong, it's much safer to *point the tip* in his direction. Forget the concept of keeping a tight line and play the fish directly off your reel against the click. The friction of a fly line as it runs through the guides of a bending rod is often sufficient to break a 6X. I must admit this doesn't allow much control over the situation, but there is no safe option. Assuming that the fish doesn't dive under a stump or plow into a cress bed, your chances of recovery are comparatively good.

I never use a landing net when fishing at 3X or 4X. I find it much easier to release a trout with wet hands, after plucking my hook free with a pair of short-nosed pliers. However, it's impossible to snub a slippery fish on a gossamer tippet long enough to get a gentle grip across its back. And the flies are so small that tweezers are easier to use than pliers.

Commercially tied artificials are dressed on hooks with both turned-up and turned-down eyes. I use both, but after many seasons of microfishing I'm convinced that the turned-up eye has better hooking qualities as its *rake,* or direction of penetration, is downward; furthermore, it provides more *gape,* or clearance, than the turned-down style, and this is critical with #22s and #24s. In Bavaria and Austria, specially made double hooks are very popular, as their points are clear of a turned-down eye.

It's most important to use the right knot on either kind of hook and what's best is *not* always the strongest. Knot strength has been emphasized to the extent that many anglers don't recognize the dual function of both strength and purpose; whether one tie is 10 or 15 percent stronger is not the sole criterion. In the case of micros, for example, we need a knot that is secure, but it must also form with minimum bulk and cause the hook to be *pulled in a straight line,* thus tipping the point downward on contact. The bulk of the knot should be located behind the eye, not in front of it, and for this purpose the Double Turle knot is hard to beat. An Improved Clinch knot, for example, is marginally stronger, but it creates a bulky weight forward and does not pull in a fixed direction if the hook is turned up or turned down. The mere act of casting often causes a micro to articulate in an Improved Clinch (or any of its variations) so the fly doesn't even ride in a lifelike position. Anything gained in knot strength is worthless in the jaws of an adult trout.

Generally, it's easy to recognize a micro situation. For one thing, the trout will ignore or only take a polite interest in flies of more orthodox size. The fish hang suspended in the current and rise in a regular rhythm, making small whorls on the surface, yet there are no visibly floating insects. Or those that do appear drift with immunity. If you study the water in front of you taking a long, close look, you'll see diminutive insect forms floating awash in the surface film. They may be aquatic or terrestrial in origin, a mixture of chironomid or midge larvae, caddis pupae, the so-called jassids or leafhoppers, several kinds of very small beetles and ants, or the tiniest mayfly duns and spent-spinners drifting on top. At times a veritable carpet of food will cover the river.

Some of the aquatics, particularly the midge, continue to emerge during the coldest winter months and are known as "snowflies" in our Western states. The midge is also a dominant food item for trout in many high mountain lakes where a #10 dry fly looks like a powder puff in that transparent water above the timberline.

I don't believe that there is any need to stock many midge patterns, although they are easy enough for an amateur to tie. The basic colors, red, green, brown, and black, encompass most species, but minute differences in size can be important. Fish will usually refuse a #20 when a #26 matches the natural, and at times the difference is even more critical with fewer strikes being obtained on a #22 than on a #24. Back in 1952 when my book, *The Practical Fly Fisherman,* appeared, I introduced four midge patterns—the Dun, Ginger, Speckled, and my own version of the Black (with an olive-brown silk body), and I still stock these in #20 to #28. When a pupal imitation is necessary, one of these fished vertically on a dead drift will usually catch fish—not only trout but also the microloving whitefish and grayling. Actually, the pupa is the most important stage of a chironomid emergence as it hangs vulnerably in the surface film for a long distance. The "instant" adult takes off so quickly that trout ignore its departure.

Ordinarily, there is a variety of insect life on the water, and unless you have been fishing a river on a daily basis, it's sometimes difficult to see a micro opportunity developing. My wife, Patti, and I spent a June weekend on the Vermont side of the Battenkill, arriving late one Friday. We managed to get about two hours of fishing before dark, and despite numerous rising trout, neither of us could make out what they were taking. Some very tiny *Caenis* duns were on the water as well as several larger ephemerids and caddisflies. I didn't see a fish hit any of the visible insects, but I assumed one or the other was bringing them up, so I floated an Adams in the #14 then a #18. I tried matching a large bluish mayfly that looked like a proper mouthful although there were comparatively few of these to be seen. Then I panicked and knotted on pattern after pattern for an hour and a half of steady casting. I finally managed to hook the village idiot—a brown trout of about 9 inches. This didn't even require an autopsy. As I removed the hook, a gob of green midge pupae was still visible in his mouth. It was too late to continue, but we were on the river early next morning anticipating some fast action.

I have never counted the Battenkill as an "easy" stream,

and that Saturday morning it was absolutely dead. Evidently there had been a spinner fall during the night, but only a few chubs gulped the spent mayflies. We caught four or five smallish trout on a Dun Midge, casting blind. About noontime a few larger trout began feeding in the main current, and after dropping my fly over the first good rises, there was a swirl, and I was fast to a fat foot-long brownie that made two beautiful leaps. The apple-green bodied midge at #22 was a perfect imitation of the natural and despite all the pullouts and breakoffs that followed, it was like casting in a hatchery. Patti took a brightly colored 16-inch brown—half the size of her Alaskan rainbow, but twice the trophy on a 7X tippet. The feeding activity was not as great on Sunday, but I managed to lose a fish of about 2½ or 3 pounds below the rock ledge in Buffum's Bridge Pool. It was a very memorable angling weekend.

Fishing major hatches like the Michigan Caddis, Giant Salmon Fly, and the Green Drake are rewarding experiences for any angler. In one lucky season, I managed to hit all four (including both the Eastern Green Drake or *Ephemera guttulata* and its Western counterpart *Ephemerella grandis*), but we can lose perspective. These hatches are big, the rising fish are often big, and the imitative flies are big at #6. To think small after meaty-winged emergences have passed is not easy. Yet equally awesome in terms of potential are the *Tricorythodes* hatches, which occur with much greater frequency over a longer period of time. These are not as diminutive as *Caenis* mayflies, but they still require #24 and #26 dressings to be matched successfully. Compared to our Western stonefly, it's like a hummingbird versus a 747 jet.

Tricos occur on rivers across the United States and dependably bring an audience and sometimes a thundering rise of fish, but also the echoing question, "What the hell are they feeding on?" It's hard for many anglers to believe that trout are actually taking food from the surface. The bodies of some naturals are no more than 1/10 inch in length, which is virtually out of sight.

There are a number of terrestrial insects that are seasonably important and in addition to midge, mayfly, and caddis patterns you should stock standards like the Letort Beetle, Red Ant, Black Ant, Green Leafhopper, and the deadly little Jassid, all on #20 and #22 hooks. Ants are especially attractive to trout, and the double-humped body form is easy to imitate on a tiny light-wire hook and 6X tippet. You don't want those heavy varnished versions that sink, but rather hair or fur-bodied ties that will float like a natural—flush in the surface film. While fishing with Jim Nelson in Oregon's Crescent Creek some years ago, we caught trout after trout on a Red Ant pattern. Jim finally hooked a brown of perhaps 6 or 7 pounds. It looked like a black-spotted whale. Brother Nelson never has a chance in that deeply undercut and willow-bordered pool, but the fact that so large a fish would even take a #20 is a pleasant reminder that in microfishing, big profits may be earned with a small investment.

[1975]

9

Catching McClane with His Pants Off

Wading a river and falling in is at best inconvenient and uncomfortable; at worst, fatal. And with that I hope to emphasize the first point McClane makes in this story: that wading know-how should be basic fishing knowledge for everyone. A novice fisherman in brand-new waders facing a big river for the first time faces likewise a real potential for disaster, which the advice in this chapter can help to avert.

Wader technology has improved dramatically in the thirteen years since this piece was first published. Stocking-foot waders, for example, can now be had in lightweight versions of urethane-coated nylon (but still not impervious to barbed wire) or in body-hugging neoprene, the insulating value of which is a real plus in very cold water. And the makers of many chest-high, boot-footed models seem to be paying better attention to sizing, so it's easier now to find boots with the appropriate in-seam. Improvements in equipment, however, won't help your technique, and proper technique can save your life.

The fact that a man can drown while fishing is obvious, and although it's important to know how to cast or match the hatch, the very first lessons every young angler must learn are the techniques of water safety. Proper boat handling is the sphere of our boating editor, but I am more concerned with the number of people who literally jump into a river without the foggiest notion of how to wade.

Paul Butler and I were sitting on the bank of the Madison River one morning, discussing our plans for the day, when an angler stepped out of the willows on the opposite shore and disappeared. He didn't make a splash. He simply vanished, and his hat went floating downstream. Before we could even figure out how to get to him, his head emerged; the current had pushed him down to a shallow gravel shingle, and he was on bottom again but minus his fly rod. Why anybody would step off a deep, undercut bank is beyond explanation, unless he assumed that the water was shallow—which it was both above and below that run. On the Madison, nothing can be taken for granted. For the most part, it's a brutal stream to wade, even for an expert. This river has all the mantraps, from slime-covered tilted slab-sided rocks between which you can wedge a foot, to deceptive gravel bars that run out to a channel of no return. Many a hearty soul has abandoned the Madison forever, after taking a daily bath.

The Klamath, Snake, Yellowstone, and other Western streams are as dangerous in whole or part, but our Eastern states have some bad ones too, like the Housatonic, the Delaware, and the Connecticut. There have been a number of fisherman drownings, not only among amateurs, on these waters in recent years; Al Reinfelder of the Garcia Corporation disappeared in the Delaware's currents, and although there was a canoe involved, Al was a pro. The most ludicrous near-miss happened to fly tier Harry Darbee who was wading the Delaware, working downstream, when a canoe rammed him in the back. Two youngsters were at the paddles and neither one could control the craft. By the time they realized their predicament, it was too late to warn Harry, who was only bruised—but it could have been fatal to lesser men. Canoes have become a real hazard on the trophy-trout waters of Michigan, such as the Au Sable and Manistee, where squadrons came by last fall with all the direction of a fire drill on a Chinese gunboat. Sometimes they run three abreast, and blessed be the angler caught in midstream around a blind bend.

I have been wading trout streams for forty years, and while I consider myself competent, I've had my share of hairy moments, always from the same mistake—misjudging the strength of a current. Now that's a basic error, one that you would think anybody who has spent most of his life in and on water would never make. Nonsense. We all get careless, and I'm no exception.

I nearly cashed in my chips on the Green River in Wyoming late one autumn, when I waded into one of those slick currents above a long, deep pool. I knew it was powerful flow, but it wasn't much over knee-deep and I'd managed such currents a thousand times before. The idea of getting a fly to the far side of the river was uppermost in my mind, so I didn't bother to analyze the bottom, a sloping shingle of loose gravel—and that made a difference. Once committed, there was no way back. I tried to turn around and in that fleeting instant lost a couple of yards to the current as the gravel rolled like ball bearings underfoot. By this time I was hip-deep, and the harder I leaned against the flow, the faster the gravel spun, until it was like riding a down escalator. The next thing I knew I was in water over my head. I had a belt secured tight around my wader tops, and though it delayed the escape of air, it also prevented me from shucking several layers of clothing, which now felt like a ton of lead. All I could do was lie on my back and go with the Green, sometimes under it, but surfacing often enough to gulp free oxygen.

That I finally made shallow water was a miracle. The river dumped me at a half-frozen moose bog, and after stumbling like a drunk for the next few hours in nothing but my underwear, I arrived at a nearby ranch. It took some fancy explaining to get in the back door.

The important thing that you can learn from my stupidity is that in wading a trout stream, there are always two factors at work that must be considered as one—the speed of the current in relation to the stability of the bottom. Had the bottom been firm—bedrock or bouldery—it would have been safe for me, marginal perhaps for a beginner; but the very shape and slope of the gravel should have rung an alarm bell. It didn't because I had big trout on my mind and was overconfident in my wading ability—a fatal combination. Dumber still was fishing that water without a flotation vest, which I had left at camp because it felt too bulky over my wool sweater. Anybody who fishes strong rivers by wading should wear one, as it's the "safest" investment you can make.

The first rule in wading is to know where you are going. Some people get so intent on their fishing that they have no idea where the next "exit" might be. It's easy to find a safe place to enter the water, but after an hour or two of casting, you might be a half-mile downstream in a cul-de-sac of rapids and perpendicular banks. Actually, it becomes reflexive to survey the visible part of a river and to know immediately just how far one can wade. Bear in mind that you want to combine this with access to the best casting positions without walking over the fish. Often as not, beginners wade where they should be fishing and cast where they should be wading. But as with so many sports, the whole technique of covering a stream starts with footwork. It isn't like strolling down a street. The expert wader is, above all, methodical.

If you are a beginner, stay in the shallows and enter any hole much over knee depth cautiously until you get the feel of the stream. Move slowly, placing one foot ahead of the other, but always keep your weight on the rear, or anchor, foot until the front, or lead, foot is planted firmly on the bottom. However, when wading across a modest or strong current (and this is where most dunkings occur), keep your feet spread apart and, with knees slightly bent, proceed in short, shuffling steps.

The actual technique is similar to the footwork of a fencer in the *en garde* position, although not so exaggerated of course. No sport demands a keener sense of balance than fencing. In assuming the basic guard position with the foil or épée, the fencer stands with heels together and feet at right angles, so that his lead foot points at his opponent; then he moves the lead about 1½ lengths forward, bends both knees, distributing his weight evenly on the legs, and keeps his body erect. From that position a fencer is able to advance (lead foot first), retreat (rear foot first), jump forward or backward, and lunge and recover smoothly. It takes years to do it well, but you don't need to be Errol Flynn to negotiate a river. It's the principle of balance in motion that is important here.

Let's say that you are crossing a current coming from the left. To keep your balance, your left foot, or lead foot, should be pointed in the direction you will travel and your right, or anchor, foot pointed at right angles from it; in other words, with the current coming from the left, your left foot is pointed cross-stream while your right foot is pointed downstream (the anchor). By sliding your left foot forward about 1½ lengths, then bringing your right forward the same distance, and repeating these half-steps so that your anchor foot never passes your lead foot, you can move rapidly in this fast-water shuffle without losing your balance. Of course, if the current is coming from your right, the foot positions should be reversed.

This may sound goofy but it works. I fenced for many years in high school, college, and in the army, and I found myself "attacking" rivers automatically. If you try to walk flat-footed across a strong current, you will be off balance each time you take a step. The same principle applies in wading with or against a current: Always keep your anchor foot at right angles to the flow; and shuffle along the bottom— don't take long steps.

What happens if you take a spill? Hip boots just fill with water and become a drag, but they will *not* pull you under if you lie back, head up, with arms outstretched. Don't panic and grope for the bottom with your feet, because with your body in a vertical position you'll go down like a sash weight. By floating on your back downstream, feet first, you have the best chance of getting out of trouble. It's the shock of a sudden plunge in a cold river and the fear that boots will pull a man under that actually cause most drownings. The victim gets in a vertical position in those first few frantic seconds, wasting his energy and swallowing water. Sooner or later you will touch bottom; and unless you already know where the shallows are, stay in a horizontal position until you float to them.

If you are wearing chest waders, the same rule applies, the only difference being that presumably you had the good sense to wear a belt around your wader tops, whether it has a pucker string or not. The belt keeps air in and water out, not for long, but long enough to get out of trouble in most dunkings. With waders you can hold the trapped air a minute or so longer by raising your legs as high as possible. This will pull your belt tighter and delay seepage. Of course, if you are wearing a flotation vest, you can just lie back and relax. Modern vests of this kind are made with bellows pockets to hold fly boxes and other equipment, so the garments offer both adequate storage space and safety.

Both from a comfort and safety standpoint, when you buy a pair of waders make certain they fit properly. Most important is that you have the freedom to move your legs naturally. You'd be amazed at how many wader wearers can't raise their knees without straining a seam or a muscle. The thigh shouldn't bind when you squat. Assuming that you are not wearing brogues, the boot toes should be reinforced to prevent bruising, because it's easy to get a foot wedged between rocks. Bear in mind that if your waders are not comfortable, they are not completely safe. If you are an odd size in the legs or butt, it's well worth the cost to have your chest waders custom-made.

I haven't found a totally satisfactory pair of waders yet. Despite all the progress made in other kinds of fishing equipment, nobody has solved the riddle of "if they're lightweight, they puncture, and if they're tough, they're heavy." I paid eighty-odd bucks for a pair of superlight waders two seasons back, which lasted all of a month. In this day of miracle materials, one would expect something that can stand up to a brier bush without giving the angler a hernia. On another pair of waders the felts didn't wear out, they simply "walked off" after a few days of fishing.

Nevertheless, chest-high waders of some kind are essential for anybody who plans to fish big streams, and these waders come in two types: the stocking-foot kind that requires a pair of brogues or suitable wading shoes, and the boot-foot type that is a complete unit with boot feet attached. The stocking-foot wader is essentially made of thinner, lighter, more flexible material, so you can slide your feet in the shoes. However, the material must be of good quality, such as double-faced cloth, and you'll have to wear socks between your feet and the brogues to prevent abrasion. This is something of a nuisance because the shoes and socks have to be dried out after each trip. Many anglers prefer brogues for the "stability" that a heavy shoe offers. On the other hand, the boot-foot-type wader can be slipped on and off quite easily and may be dried by being turned inside out, or simply turned upside down and suspended for a time to catch warm air.

Most hip boots and waders come with cleated rubber soles. This is adequate for sandy streams or gravelly bottoms and slow currents, but not many trout waters can be negotiated on rubber cleats. At one time or another I've tried every nonskid device from hobnails and chains to ice creepers, and the only materials that suit me are felt, or outdoor carpeting, and aluminum. Felt soles already built on waders are not cheap. However, felt wading sandals are reasonably priced and can be slipped on and off as needed. If you can find swatches of outdoor carpeting and glue these on over the cleats, they work just as well and don't wear out as quickly. Either one gets a good "bite" on algae in slick-bottomed streams. For general rock climbing, I prefer sandals made of soft aluminum bars. For most conditions, you can get along with two pairs of sandals, one soled with felt and the other bottomed with some aluminum.

Dampness always collects inside boots and waders to the point that sometimes it feels as if the material has sprung a leak. When you are wading in cold water, the warmth of your body causes condensation inside, which is nothing to be concerned with except that the temperature of your feet is going to drop rather quickly. Water removes heat about twenty-seven times faster than air does, so wool socks are essential for comfort. The maze of wool fibers forms tiny air cells that delay the passage of heat from the body. In really cold weather it's smart to wear a pair of light wool socks inside a pair of heavy ones, because the air space between them provides additional insulation. For this reason your boot size should run a bit larger than your shoe size to allow extra room for heavy socks. In warm weather, some hearty souls wade "wet," just wearing old pants and sneaks, but mountain streams can be bone-chilling even in August, and after a few hours quite uncomfortable. But if you do wade wet, remember to wear a sandal of some kind. Plain rubber soles are the kiss of death on slippery or moss-covered rocks.

I have never found a wading staff necessary, but some anglers wouldn't venture into a big stream without one. The truth is that I probably could have spared myself that cold plunge in the Green if I had been using one. The staff is as good as a third leg when maneuvering in fast water, and the steel-pointed fiberglass kind is light to carry.

Wading staffs always remind me of a raw October day when I was steelhead fishing on the Stamp River in British Columbia with Charlie Ritz and General Charles Lindemann. The general was a top British intelligence officer during World War II, but in the winter of life, nearing the age of eighty and still fishing, he was extremely absentminded. Early that morning I waded out into Money Pool to begin fishing and I heard the general wading behind me, mumbling about why we didn't have enough sense to sack and how blasted cold the water was in the Provinces. I didn't look at the old boy until he waded downstream from me, while I began stripping out line to make a cast. There he stood, leaning on his staff, almost hip-deep in the Stamp River with his wading shoes over his long johns. He had forgotten to put his waders on.

[1975]

10

Across the River
and
Under the Trees

*The theory is generally simple: If you can cast your fly
or plug into a place that someone else can't, you'll
wind up catching fish that they won't. As usual,
McClane has some solid advice on casting techniques
here that will enable you to do just that. It's worth
noting that this* Field & Stream *piece was published
in 1970, before graphite came into general usage as a
rod material. Fiberglass rods prevalent at that time
had a softer, easier-loading action than found in
many contemporary graphite casting rods. Remember as you practice that an underhand cast as described in the text will be most easily accomplished
when using a casting rod with a relatively soft tip,
whether made of graphite or any other material.*

*Roll casting, that seemingly most easy of fly
casts, is often a real bugaboo for beginners. The key
is combining some forward thrust with the downward stroke that produces the roll. A downward
stroke alone—which is a common fault—will simply
produce a roll that piles up on the water in front of
you. The correct stroke is commonly compared to the*

forward and downward motion needed to plant a cleaver in a waist-high chopping block.

The first time I went bass fishing in a Southern river, my host cut the motor next to a botanical nightmare that hung over the water and announced that it was a good place to start. It looked like a Maine woodcock cover. I tossed my plug in the opposite direction.

"No, not out there," said Abner Coots. "In *here.*" With a quick flip of his rod tip, he shot the plug through a narrow tunnel of branches. The lure sailed about a foot over the surface and made a *plat* next to the bank. It sat there bobbling like a frog. Nothing struck it, but I was impressed. Having cut my eyeteeth on a casting rod in mountain country, where the banks are uncluttered and every stroke is upright, this underhanded method was a revelation. I immediately copied Abner and whipped my plug over a treetop. He caught a stringer of bass while I was still trying to get the feel of upside-down casting—which is what the underhand amounts to. Back home I never gave the technique a serious thought, although one Delaware bass more clearly demonstrated what Brother Coots had skillfully come to terms with.

There was a deep pool in back of the Todd farm on the East Branch, and below the suspension bridge a rusted oil drum lay on the bottom. This was the home of a certain smallmouth for several years. I doubt if the bass ever grew to 4 pounds, but he was larger than most river smallmouths ever get to be. I was going to Cornell Agricultural school then, and during vacation months I helped the Todds draw their hay. I always straddled the load when the wagon crossed the bridge, hoping to get a look at this bronze hermit. Once in a while I'd see him lying over the gravel a few yards behind the oil drum, and when the hay rigging clobbered overhead the fish would dash into the open end. These brief glimpses never resolved the problem of how to catch that bass, short of finding the right-size lid.

After two summers of futile attempts, my canned bass became a local curio. Friends would come by simply to look at the drum and speculate on the size of its occupant. Finally, a heavy flood scoured the riverbed, and we found the battered drum on a bar far downstream. I have no idea where the bass holed up after that.

Nearly all gamefish of any size live undercover. Cut banks, roots, boulders, even bridge foundations (of which large brown trout are especially fond) provide protection with a path of escape, and in rivers, a minimum current at a safe depth. Nowhere is this truer than in southern bass waters where largemouths hug the wooded shores. Much of our lake fishing is really on inundated streams or swamps where bass can burrow back in trash piles that would confuse a beaver. Getting a plug under the trees by orthodox overhead casting is a hit-and-miss proposition at best. The underhand cast is the hallmark of a real craftsman on the hush-puppy circuit.

Although the northern bass angler may not have as much reason to perfect this technique, it would be the one shot that nails a prizewinner. The way to learn this cast is to use it when it's *not* necessary to use it. Spend an hour or so flipping the plug over open water until you get a flat trajectory. Bear in mind that the bugbear in all accuracy casting is in thinking about mechanics and not concentrating on the target. If your eyes focus on the tree limbs instead of that open spot back next to the bank, you are going to catch tree limbs. An underhand cast can be made with a bait-casting or any type of spinning outfit. Naturally, with the latter it's much easier, as there is no chance of a backlash. The secret of the cast in either case is to supply energy to the rod by making a quick, smooth upward lift, then instantly reversing direction with a sharp downward push. After the tip has completed its backward swing in toward your feet, the plug is released. This won't result in long distances, but you'll be amazed at how far the plug will go when you get the feel of it. Too, it is an accurate cast.

The thing to remember in the beginning is that the rod tip makes the cast through its recoil power; you simply set it in motion. You will accomplish nothing by adding greater speed or more force. Buck-brush specialists in the Old South prefer the shorter rod lengths as a rule, 4½ or 5 feet for a bait-casting outfit and no more than 6 feet for a spinning rig. Regardless of how stout the rod might be, don't confuse its ability to horse a bigmouth out of the stumps with its action. For smooth underhand casting, the rod should bend almost down into the corks. This provides the lever length for fairly long accurate casts.

When practicing on the lawn, assume your stance by facing the target. Then take a quarter turn to the right— which is opposite from the stance you would use in an overhead cast—so your left shoulder is pointed toward the target and the heel of your right foot is opposite the ball of your left foot. The feet should be spread comfortably apart, with your weight shifted largely to your left foot. Left-handed casters can reverse the whole procedure. Extend the rod parallel to the water at waist level so that it points directly at the target. If you are using a spinning reel, free the line from the pickup mechanism; with a bait-casting or closed-face reel, make sure your palm is downward and the crank handles are facing up.

Start the cast from the horizontal rod position with an upward motion by bending your elbow but not your wrist, until the rod tip is at about eye level. Just a quick upward flip. Without pausing, bring the rod back down to your starting position, using a positive push on the handle as you do so. When the starting position has been reached, stop abruptly. These combined upward and downward movements provide the necessary casting energy to your rod tip, and when the downthrust is stopped, the lure will flex the rod in toward your feet. As the tip recovers toward horizontal again, release the line from your finger or the thumb pressure from button or spool. The lure will sail outward in a low, flat trajectory.

There is an initial tendency to release the lure a bit late, which results in sending the plug almost straight up in the air. However, when you hit the correct release point just as the tip begins to recoil, it should feel like an overhead cast.

Aside from the common tree problems, there are other opportunities for the underhand caster to catch fish beneath docks, low bridges, and even culverts. I once hauled a husky trout out of a road drain by flipping a spinner back into his den. Culverts are amazing. Some years ago our local golf course was flooded when a tarpon of 40 or 50 pounds became wedged in the outlet pipe from one of the water hazards. In some types of saltwater fishing, such as snook, red drum, snapper, and baby tarpon among the mangroves, the underhand cast is a tremendous advantage. Snook are especially prone to forage way back among the roots where a slowly fished surface plug is seldom ignored. Naturally, a great many fish are lost to the barnacled limbs, but it's a fascinating game just the same.

Staying out of trees is a universal problem not only for the spin and bait casters, but the fly caster as well. Placing a fly back up under tree limbs requires considerable experience, mainly with the side cast, swishing the line low and parallel to the water. Sometimes a carefully aimed overhead cast will do the trick. But in fly fishing, the real migraine to a beginner is keeping the back cast out of the woods.

Fly casting requires considerable space, and there are many occasions when an overhead stroke can't be used at all. Some streams with long stretches of forest and sheer rock wall can't be fished without roll casting, and strangely, many anglers never take the time to learn the only stroke that might salvage the situation. A good roll caster can lay forty or fifty feet of line across the river, and many experts can reach greater distances. Personally, I much prefer a double-tapered line for roll casting, and in the tight places where this technique is in greatest demand, a weight-forward line doesn't have any advantages.

When executed correctly, the line will not travel more than ten or twelve inches behind your elbow. What makes the roll cast possible from a mechanical standpoint is the water tension against the line—so you can't practice on a lawn.

Assuming that you are standing in the stream with trees at your back, work out about fifteen feet of line by using a horizontal cast in any free direction, or even by stripping line from the reel and shaking it out through the rod. Then pull more line off the reel, which you can drop on the water for shooting. Next point the rod forward as you would in making an overhead cast. Now raise the rod slowly, until your hand is behind your eye and the rod angled back slightly over your shoulder.

When the rod has reached this position, with the belly of the line slightly behind your right elbow, pause, just as you would between back and front strokes in the overhead cast. The forward stroke of the roll is made by driving the rod sharply downward with a stiff wrist and forearm. The impulse given the line that is clinging to the surface causes it to travel forward before the leader and fly have left the water. If you pull the outstretched line *off* the surface before making your downstroke, it won't roll very far. To get more distance, shoot your slack as you would in the overhead cast and repeat the rod movements. Remember, as more line is added, you must put additional emphasis in the forward stroke.

If a crosswind is blowing from your right side, which can cause the loop to tangle in itself, raise the rod to the left of vertical—at about an eleven-o'clock position—so the line drops from the tip to the left side of your body and makes the downstroke. If the wind is blowing from the left, bring your rod to the right of vertical at about the one-o'clock position. This will compensate for any deviation by slanting the loop so there's no tendency for the line to unroll against itself.

The roll cast does make considerable surface disturbance when you're fishing in very calm water—enough to spook a trout if the fly is aimed directly at him. Ideally, you want to cast across the river and let the fly swim down to the fish's position. Despite this technical handicap, when there's no other way to get a line out, a few scared fish are not very significant.

Actually, if you use a light line, the percentage will be very much in your favor. For example, one day I hiked in to a cliff-bordered run on the North Platte River. Len Benson had showed it to me on a previous float trip, but we'd skimmed through it so fast because of the chute of white water entering it that I didn't have a chance to work it carefully. It just isn't a boat pool, so I went back to see how much of it could be waded.

One side was bouldery but reasonably shallow despite the granite wall that rose vertically, perhaps a hundred feet up. Balancing in the current was hard work, but I found that by wading in the back eddies from boulder to boulder I could manage fair roll casts across the river. I wanted to use a big Marabou Muddler, but big flies have too much air resistance for smooth rolls unless you swing a heavy rod and line, and I was fiddling with my #4 outfit. So I knotted on a fur-bodied Gray Nymph, fishing it as slowly as possible. At about the third boulder, after the fly swept around and came to a stop in the current, a brown trout took it right out in midstream.

The fish bored for the far side of the river and the frail bamboo quivered in a tight bow. Then the trout raced below me and began tugging frantically at the straining rod. The fish was down in the backing when I crabbed out of the water and eased along the cliff to get below him. The trout sensed this shift in pressure and continued into faster water, which still left me bringing up the rear.

I splashed along, cranking the line and trying to slow the beast down. Not once did the fish jump. It wasn't until we covered a hundred yards that the trout turned to fight the current. Maybe it wasn't a spectacular show, but I finally released what looked to be about 4 pounds of brightly colored male. This was the only large fish I hit all day. However, the nymph produced plenty of action, including a dozen better-than-average browns.

The roll cast has other uses. You will be amazed, for example, how often it can pick a snagged fly out of a sunken branch or limb. The reverse direction pull of the loop is usually all the force necessary to free a hook. A roll cast is also useful in bringing a deeply sunken fly line to the surface without the danger of an uncontrolled back cast because of water tension. In fact, it's standard procedure with heavy lead-core shooting heads.

The roll can be put to further advantage in handling a wet or dry fly after the cast has been fished out. It is sometimes difficult to lift a line smoothly from the water and get it in the air for a back cast. Perhaps a fish followed and you gathered slack practically down to the leader butt, or the line was caught in conflicting currents and bellied out in the wrong direction. In either case, if too little line is lifted from the water, the fly will simply hover overhead until the rod is given more weight for proper flexing. As a rule of the thumb, you need a minimum of two rod lengths of line extended from the tip to make a proper back cast. However, any length can be rolled from the surface, then with a slight left-hand pull turned into a smooth overhead stroke.

Neither the underhand cast nor the roll cast are difficult to learn. They do take considerable practice to master, but these techniques are well worth spending time on.

[1970]

11

Casting Clinic

Fly casting isn't easy. I know it looks simple. And I know that lots of tackle manufacturers tell everybody how easy it is to learn, thereby promoting new customers. I've been fly casting for more than thirty years, yet everytime I cast with masters like McClane or Joan Salvato Wulff I learn something new and helpful. The road to fly-casting success includes both teaching in print, of which McClane's piece here is a good example, and personal instruction.

In this particular piece, McClane describes teaching casting at the old New York Sportsman's Show. In recent years, many of the old-time big-city shows have suffered a decline because of high operating costs and all the logistical problems associated with downtown locations. Many of the better shows are now in more suburban locations, and these are also attracting the better fly-casting instructors. Shows in Suffern, New York; Worcester, Massachusetts; South-field, Michigan; Denver, Colorado; and San Mateo, California, are just a few examples.

You can go, with or without your own tackle,

> *and get on-the-spot instruction from such modern masters as Joan Wulff, Jim Green, Leon Chandler, Lefty Kreh, or Steve Rajeff. Many of these excellent teachers and others are sponsored at these shows by manufacturers who want you to improve your casting just as much as you do. So don't be bashful or embarrassed. Go introduce yourself to Joan Wulff or one of the others, from whom ten minutes of instruction is worth ten years of fumbling on the stream.*

On February 17, and continuing through February 26, the wraps will be uncovered from an army of fly casters we had the privilege of working with one year ago, when *Field & Stream* conducted its first Fisherman's Clinic at the New York Sports and Vacation Show, held in Kingsbridge Armory, the Bronx. We have been limbering up for this second clinic for months, because the pace during the first was, to put it mildly, hectic. In nine short days, a total of 1,800 rank beginners was checked out by an assemblage that included some of the best casting talent in the country.

It isn't often that we get the opportunity to study the problems of such a large group. Those of us who were teaching came to the conclusion that eight out of ten people can be whipped into expert form with just a modest amount of coaching. This was especially noticeable among teenagers who had never held a rod before. They had no bad casting habits to overcome. Adults with considerable fishing experience often lapsed into the very rod movements they were trying to correct. As a result, we will probably have a higher percentage of advanced students this year among the youngsters.

Spreading the salve of enlightenment was of mutual benefit. Instructors caught in the seething vortex of this piscatorial twister found themselves scrambling for the right answers. Some were scholarly, some essentially commercial, and some clearly the result of desperation. One thing stood out clearly: John Public would make a hell of a good caster if he could just learn to restrain himself.

Ellis Newman and I were discussing teaching methods

over our coffee and toothpicks one morning, and he pointed out that most instructors fail in not emphasizing the fact that fundamental rod movements do not necessarily apply to distance casting—which nine out of ten people want to learn. But the basic strokes must be understood absolutely before the pupil can adapt himself to any distance style. What Ellis had in mind was that after learning the motions of ordinary casting, the student would return for advanced instruction and find that he was being taught what appeared to be a new set of rules. Actually, the motions involved in distance fly casting are an adaptation of fundamentals. For the benefit of casters coming to the second clinic, I'd like to go over the points that you should be familiar with before shooting at the other end of the tank.

When you take a rod in hand, you must be relaxed. Proper relaxation is at least half the secret of good fly casting. Most of the adults we coached "froze" as soon as their lines were in motion, and this feeling of uncertainty was transmitted to the rod in quick, jerky movements. I must admit that learning to cast in the vicinity of several thousand people isn't conducive to fluid rod work, but the real problem is that people are wrist benders. As the wrist is bent, so the back cast is lowered. Paradoxically, the dropping back cast seems to signal that more wrist bending is necessary, and when casting becomes an effort, the student is no longer relaxed. We solved this by the ancient device of holding the rod just above a beginner's hand and casting back and forth very slowly, dropping the line on the water with each forward cast, thus forcing the caster to keep a "dead" wrist. Remember this, should you be charged with instructing a beginner: the value of dual performance should not be underestimated. There is a feeling in fly casting; it cannot be put into words, but it can be conveyed by actually casting with your pupil. Within ten strokes he has confidence; ten casts later he is completely relaxed.

Before you can ever become a distance caster you must understand the role of your line hand. Actually, you should have some knowledge of what is involved in line-hand control before tank time, if you want your instructor to get you over the ninety-foot mark. It's just too complex a subject to cover, even superficially, there on the spot. So, if you want to empty your reel, pay heed.

Let's assume that you are right-handed. In casting, the left hand always holds the line, keeping it taut at all times to provide the maximum power in delivery. Your right hand moves back and forth while your left hand follows in a parallel path, almost as though you were swinging a baseball bat, except that in casting the stroke is vertical. The analogy is not precise, but I think you get the idea. If your line hand remains stationary, the distance between right and left will vary, tightening the line on your back cast and throwing it slack on the forward cast. There must be tension both backward and forward, because with this control you can add extra speed to the line whenever it is needed. Having a method of adding speed, you can (1) correct casts that are affected by the wind, (2) get greater distance because the slightest pull on a line while under tension will shoot it much farther, and (3) correct your own errors in timing. Thus, the line hand has a positive role—and a very important one—in maintaining a tight line.

I think the best example of what your left hand can do for you is in lifting line from the water. Nearly every caster who came on the platform made his lift for the back cast by pulling line directly off the surface. If forty or fifty of taper was extended on the water, this direct lift was traveling at about half the speed required for an easy back cast. Yet a short pull with the left hand to start the line moving simultaneously with the raising of the rod was enough to send the cast high and fast to the rear. Why put an extra burden on your rod by fighting surface tension against the line? This simple motion of pulling as you lift becomes more pronounced when reaching for long distances; but first, get in the habit of casting with both hands.

If you attend the clinic this year, I suggest you take the time to watch Bill Taylor. Bill is a master of the minimum pull. He just barely nudges his line to shoot out a 100-foot cast, and all of his handwork is in the belt-to-ear zone. Ellis Newman, by comparison, is a high-hand stylist. Both men cast over 160 feet with tournament tackle, and Newman, if you recall, tosses a full double-taper with no rod at all. Either of these gents will be glad to show you what your left hand can add to a cast in yardage.

The instructors were unanimous in their postmortem reports last year on how they got the best results in a condensed period. On busy days a pupil couldn't get more than ten or fifteen minutes of tank work at one time. Thus, necessity cut the ground from under the belief that you have to teach a complete cast. What really counted in these quickie courses was teaching a man to throw a high back cast. Forward casts come easily and naturally. We know that any complete cast is a combination of several movements blended together in what appears to be one movement. This same combination of strokes may have to be executed at different angles and with varying speeds under fishing conditions. Therefore, the logical way to start is by learning each motion separately until they are automatic, and then combining them in rhythm. By dropping the line on the water after each forward cast you have an automatic timing control, and by watching the line extend in the rear you have a back-cast timing control. Our students found that it was possible to cast a long line without wrist bending or swinging the rod below a two-o'clock position. I really was amazed at how quickly the average man and woman absorbed the principles.

You can cast modern-day fly lines their full length, provided your left hand is educated. There is no need to resort to heavier rods or monofilament shooting lines in actual fishing; either device is a crutch and an obstacle in the path of good casting. If you are working on distance at the clinic this month, bear in mind that the longer you keep your line in the air, the less chance you have of getting maximum line speed. The ideal is to get the rod at full load in about five motions—pickup, layout, speed forward, speed back, and shoot. If the rod is not at full load on the fourth motion, drop it on the water and start over again. We had some severe cases of "caster's elbow" at the last clinic, because people who hadn't held a rod since the previous summer were trying to conquer the pool by pure muscle. Although the tackle weighs less than 16 ounces, the muscles you use in casting don't get much of a workout in the course of a year. We figure that it takes about 100 hours to build them up to normal efficiency, 200 to get them at peak.

Another tiring habit that beginners get into is pulling the line violently when making a double haul. Line pull must be smooth, not fast. We had one fellow actually rip the back of his shirt while making a forward pull. Ironically enough, his cast didn't go ten feet farther than the distance he previously made with just an ordinary cast. Line speed must be applied with smooth progressiveness and without jerking or vibrating the rod. I pull line on the pickup, on the forward cast, and each time the rod is flexed in false casting. Aside from speeding up the line, it speeds the rod turnover.

I think this sums up the points we worked on last year. If you have mastered the fundamentals since our last session, there's no reason why we can't put some distance into your casts now. Let me remind you that the clinic is open to everybody, including fly tiers, spin addicts, and bait casters. We had some mighty fine talent on deck last year: Joan Salvato, Reub Cross, Helen Newman, Jack Guinan, Bill Taylor, Ellis Newman, Lew Oatman, and many others, including representatives of the major tackle companies. This year we expect to have more instructors. Just bring along your tackle and cast with the experts. We all look forward to meeting you.

[1956]

12

Streamer Magic

For some unknown reason, for all that's been written about flies and fly patterns in the last thirty years or so, less has been written about streamers than any other type of fly. The mystery is why something that's so exceptionally effective in trout fishing should find so little room in print. Streamers were the fish flies I fished with as a young boy because in many ways they were the easiest to work effectively—and they worked, which I suppose is something to keep in mind if you have a young angler to indoctrinate.

The word perspective *as it pertains to the American angling scene is a word that Al might have invented; he has certainly helped to define it. Consider his observations in this story as to how many "big" trout are generally found in American trout streams—basically, not very many, all of our illusions notwithstanding. After several years of fishing Montana's Big Hole River—a good "big" fish stream —it finally sunk in that my average catch was about 12 inches long, and this after several fish in the 3- to 5-pound class. Streamers, however, as Al once put it, are for big-fish dreamers. The payoff can be very handsome.*

It's funny how we always expect that, in the wilderness, innocent fish will pounce greedily on any fly. It does happen, of course, but in my experience there have been just as many occasions when I had to eat humble pie.

It took two and a half days to reach Río Dos from the village of Futalaufquén in the hindmost part of Argentina. The first leg was by truck, the second was by boat, and where logs blocked the river we began hiking. Fred Cushing and I had to backpack all the camp gear because our guide Erick claimed to have a bad case of arthritis. He led the way, pulling a smelly sheep on a rope leash. The sheep and whatever fish we caught were to be our food the next five days. It was April, late fall in the Andes, and there was an ear-biting wind moaning in the peaks. But when we came out of the ceiba forest, the sight of that river was incredible. No more than 70 or 80 feet wide, it was deep and slick, with a volcanic crazy-quilt pattern of dark blue and pink pebbles on the bottom. We could see trout balanced in the current and, from a high bank, I counted maybe twenty fish that would weigh more than 4 pounds in one pool; a few appeared to be 10 pounds or better. A lethal mixture of rainbows and landlocked salmon waiting to explode.

Fred and I went through the local routine that afternoon . . . streamers, . . . Woolly Worms, nymphs, wets, and even dry flies, though Argentinian rivers with few exceptions do not produce well to floating patterns. We caught a few smallish trout but the important fish only tolerated our presence. Now and then, one would swing behind the fly and make a few quick passes, as though groping for a lost shirt-collar button and deciding the heck with it, I have another one. Erick watched us for a while, then crawled into his sleeping bag. I finally connected with an 8-pound landlocked salmon on a Spruce streamer. At least we wouldn't have to eat the sheep. A few minutes later I dropped my back cast onto a gravel bar and snapped the hook off. It was the only Spruce I had.

We covered another mile of water, shuffling flies until we

were both bone-tired, then headed back for camp. Yup, there was Erick at our starting point, beaching what looked to be a 6- or 7-pound rainbow. Evidently, his casting arm wasn't affected by arthritis. He said it was his third trout, but he'd only been fishing a short time. What was our informative guide using? A bare long-shank hook with three plain-brown rooster hackles tied on each side, curving outward, "breather style." It looked like one of Herman's closeout specials. This is perhaps the most ancient form of a streamer fly. Aelian in his Book XV described trolling chicken feathers that "wiggle in the water" when fishing for Mediterranean tuna in A.D. 22.

Erick had a box full of home-tied plain browns that he doled out like teaspoons of caviar during the rest of our trip. The fishing was sporadic—probably due to the weather and the approach of spawning for salmon—but there were daily bursts of activity when we could take a dozen or more good fish. The salmon, now bereft of their silvery coloration, resembled old buck brown trout with their red spots and hooked bills. I photographed and released one of about 12 pounds. Erick, who is hardly prolix prone, said that the pumping action of the wing suggests the swimming move-ment of a freshwater crab. These crustaceans are extremely abundant in Andean rivers and have no counterpart in North America. We didn't find anything but crabs, a few crayfish, and bits of weeds in the stomachs of the fish we killed for camp. Erick's skinny fly certainly didn't resemble a crab in shape, but who could fault its success? Fred and I kept testing other patterns but the plain brown outscored everything by at least 20 to 1. In all my years of angling, I have never seen such selective fish—and in the middle of nowhere.

Statistically, a streamer fly will take more large trout than any other kind of fly, simply because most big fish eat little fish. However, it is not your everyday or everywhere reliable method for taking trout consistently. Follow an elec-trofishing crew doing a stream census, as I have done on many occasions, and you'll realize that on a per mile basis in most U.S. rivers, big trout are mighty scarce. To define "big," let's say a fish over 3 pounds in the East or over 5 pounds in the West. I faithfully wade streams every season that probably don't even hold more than one or two such trout. Yet, for me, such streams produce a most satisfying sport by virtue of their wild beauty. Here, the insects are the dominant food form and the nymph or dry fly is a prerequisite. In fact, the appearance of a streamer will often send the fish running for cover. However, angling wouldn't be much fun if it was predictable.

I recall a summer afternoon on the Saranac River in New York, when the trout were feeding steadily on midges, ordinarily a selective performance, yet we caught numerous risers on a little Blacknose Dace bucktail. The same gentleman who told me to try that, Ray Neidig, also advised swimming a Mickey Finn whenever rising water began to pearl in a heavy rain, a tip that has paid off on many wet days. All streamer-fly specialists have a bag of tricks, but there is often more logic than magic in their origins.

Jim Poulos of Wheeling, Illinois, is a streamer-fly specialist. He spends part of every summer and fall looking for trophy trout in Montana, mainly in the Beaverhead, Jefferson, and Big Hole rivers. Jim usually plans his day around the hours when big ones are likely to feed, which is before dawn, at dusk, and often into the night. He knows that large trout don't feed as frequently as small ones, so he's content to put in long hours for less in terms of quantity. Tom McNally and I fished with Jim last season, on a day when the Jefferson was rising fast from an irrigation release; it was a torrent when we arrived, though the water was fairly clear. We all caught some fish on nymphs and streamers, but Jim took a pair of heavy browns in a weedy, silt-bottomed backwater off the main stream. I had passed it by because it looked like a pickerel puddle. From years of experience, Jim has found that big Jefferson trout will move out of the flow on rising water levels and forage in what is essentially minnow territory. It's local knowledge of this kind that specialists collect like rare stamps.

Jim anticipates that period in late September, when the aspens turn to gold and the prespawners leave their dens for the chilling riffles. This is when the streamer fly really pays off. The Missouri is probably the best-known river for this kind of fishing. It produces trout of 10 pounds or more, and there have been reported scuba sightings of browns in the 20- to 30-pound class below Toston Dam. But let's get down to some streamer and bucktail basics.

There are more than 200 species of true minnows in North American waters. This includes the shiners, dace, and chub, and at least 200 additional species that belong in other families, such as the darters, killifishes, silversides, and sculpins that are considered "minnows" in an angling sense. Although many baitfish, especially the widely abundant shiners, can be described as olivaceous dorsally and silvery to white on the ventral surface, most of them become very colorful during their spring to summer breeding period. At that time they acquire splashes of rose, lavender, orange, and yellow. Others such as the bleeding shiner, warpaint shiner, and fire shiner have bright red markings throughout the year. The seemingly implausible colors in many streamer patterns often find a counterpart in nature. Conversely, simple barred-rock hackle-wings closely simulate the body markings of all killifishes, while a badger hackle-wing, with its pronounced dark and lateral stripe, could represent almost the entire shiner genus.

There are plenty of tying materials that will suggest, if not imitate, the naturals. In any one river system there is always a dominant forage species that trout consume with some frequency; a familiar example is the mottled sculpin or "bullhead" found in Rocky Mountain streams, which has inspired the many Muddler patterns, or the abundance of darters in the hill country of our Southeast. What's important for the angler to know about sculpins and darters is that they find protection by lying quietly between stones, then hop or dart erratically along the bottom when feeding or disturbed. They do not swim freely like the true minnows. This is the basis for two generally effective techniques with streamers— the swimming retrieve and bottom- bouncing. They have a corollary worth noting, too. The free swimmers are mostly silvery in color, while the bottom-dwellers are camouflaged, dark in color.

Under normal water conditions, with a floating line, the

fly is cast across or slightly upstream. As it drifts with the current, a regular movement of rod and hand gives it a pulsing motion spaced at short intervals to simulate a minnow struggling in the flow. Don't be in a hurry to lift for a new cast. Even after the line has made its full swing, let the fly rise and fall in the current for five or six seconds at least. A "helpless" minnow is tantalizing to big trout. The important thing to remember is that you should hold your rod tip close to the surface during a retrieve—almost in the water. This eliminates that critical few feet of slack between the tip and surface and accomplishes two things: It permits you to give the streamer a positive swimming action when stripping with your line hand; and, equally important, you will feel the strike in your fingers and can tighten instantly. Streamer flies draw a very high ratio of missed strikes in running water because of the slack factor, as the trout is now attacking food instead of "accepting" a drifting insect.

The other technique is to get a deep swim with a fast-sinking line. Some anglers prefer high-density shooting heads with monofilament running line, but this has no advantage except on the largest rivers. The weight of the line should be matched to the depth of the water you are fishing. A #7- or #8-weight-forward fast sinker will serve most purposes. This demands a short leader of 3 or 3½ feet, because precious seconds will elapse while the sinking line is pulling the fly down, and the longer the leader the greater the delay. The standard 9-foot leader will buoy a fly near the surface even when your line is fully submerged. The angle of your cast must be judged against current velocity, but normally you will aim diagonally upstream, then delay drag by mending line until the fly has settled near bottom. As in a swimming retrieve, the rod should be pointed at the water and the fly worked with your line hand. It takes practice and a delicate sense of touch to steer a streamer at the correct level in foot-long hops, but once this is mastered you will be able to cover the deepest pools effectively.

During the summer, streamers are generally more productive at night. Big browns are especially cautious about chasing minnows in bright sunlight. In the protective cloak of dark, or in roily water after a rain, they will cruise the shallows looking for baitfish. A few years ago, I saw an old hookbill, in the New Fork River in Wyoming, swimming with its back out of water while trying to herd smaller trout toward the bank. At a distance I mistook it for a beaver crossing the stream. There was a terrific rumpus under the willows, then a pair of 6- or 8-inch rainbows skittered in the air and disappeared in a churning surface. I worked the area for an hour but never saw the fish again.

Daylight feeding of this kind is unusual, yet on various occasions I've hooked small trout on a dry fly and, while the fish splashed wildly at the surface, had a dark shadow shoot out from under a ledge or cutbank and grab our mutual victim before I had sense enough to slack off. Once I stood eyeball to eyeball with a big Delaware River brown that held my little trout crosswise in his jaws, as though daring me to pull it loose. Trout are keenly predator-conscious, but as they grow into double figures the need for vertebrate food is essential to their survival. I once watched an angler dress an 8½-pound Gods River brook trout, out of which he pulled a partially digested burbot or "ling" that weighed almost 2 pounds. It's a wonder that the trout had the stomach to pounce on a wobbling spoon, no less ingest a freshwater cod of that size.

There are times when a streamer fly fished right in the surface will score consistently. It would be a mistake to regard all patterns as baitfish imitations. Sparsely tied dark dressings on #8 to #12 hooks fished with fine tippets do a very good job of simulating many nymphs. Apply a little silicone floatant to a small Muddler, for example, and you can drift or skim it on the surface as grasshopper, stonefly, or dragonfly imitation. And there are undoubtedly situations where a top-water streamer not only suggests baitfish, but is just what a diffident trout is looking for. I recall one trip in the Western Bays of New Zealand's Lake Taupo, fishing with guide Ron Haughton. We had camped on a gravel beach, and when I crawled out of the tent at dawn there appeared to be a great rise in progress. Rainbows of 5 and 6 pounds were popping all along the shore, yet there wasn't an emerging or fallen insect in sight. I cast one dry fly after another in the paths of cruising trout who left the feathers bobbing in their wakes. After a frustrating hour, I finally noticed a few silvery fry hanging almost inert in the surface film. These juveniles were buoyant and the trout were taking them in suction rises, as though inhaling fat mayflies. I tied on a small, lightly greased brown-and-white bucktail with a silver tinsel body and fished it in nervous twitches just in the surface. This earned three big redsides before the feeding activity ceased in a brilliant sun. Then it was back to deep fishing with Muddlers, which is a rewarding game in New Zealand's lakes.

I have a number of favorite streamer flies. For general trout fishing I stock basic bucktails in two- and three-color combinations, mostly Keith Fulsher's Thunder Creek series that suggests many shiners, dace, and darters. In feather-wings, I'm partial to the Nine Three, Black Ghost, Gray Ghost, and Supervisor. In a fluffy stork-feather wing, I use the White Marabou for clear water and the Black Marabou in roily water. For a breather-wing, get both the Dark Spruce and Chappie patterns. For Western trout fishing, Dave Whitlock's Sculpin and Multicolored Marabou are the two deadliest designs I know of for deep fishing. Throw in a Mickey Finn and a Muddler Minnow and you are pattern prepared. These flies should be stocked in a good range of sizes, from #12 in the simpler dressings to a #1/0. Trophy hunters often go to 3/0 on Western rivers—which would create shock waves on the Beaver Kill, not to mention countless cases of elbow paralysis, a terminal condition to habitués of the Antrim Lodge.

[1979]

13

Dem Dry Bones

Somehow, McClane often seems to have a ready answer for the usual question about what they'll think of next. In this case, it's bonefish on dry flies, and he was the first (and so far only) person to cover this topic to my knowledge.

Unfortunately, there is no good, up-to-date book in print about bonefishing, although the sport is becoming increasingly popular. Al tells me he has a bonefish book in the works, and so we can all hope for a ready reference in a year or two. Until then, no one has covered bonefish so well in magazines as McClane, and what follows is the very latest wrinkle.

My last fish of the day was a sunset loner who came tail-wagging across the sand like a hound dog looking for a long-buried bone. The water was little more than ankle-deep. Staring into the smoky blue and gold reflections, waiting for him to come in range, I had that old squirrels-in-the-stomach feeling, wondering whether he would turn, trying to guess when he would be most vulnerable.

No fish is more humbling than a big tailer who ventures

into glass-calm shallows—a mere presence that dares you to make the first move. I've forgotten how many *myotomes,* those explosive elastic bands of muscle, are contained in that torpedo-shaped body, but once spooked, an old forktail can take off like a Ferrari Testarossa from a standing start.

Although the fish was zigzagging, when he was about forty feet away I got down on my knees and began working out line, then dropped the fly—a dry Salmon Irresistible—on his incoming path. The fish stopped to poke his head in the sand, about five feet short of the fly. The squirrels pounded in my rib cage. When he resumed swimming I gave the Irresistible a twitch, and 9½ pounds of bonefish dashed at it in a splashy rise. He streaked away with that stunning acceleration that throws spray from a disappearing fly line, and was down in the backing before I even got on my feet.

Until 1982, I didn't realize that bonefish could be caught on dry flies. Over the years I had hooked a few fish on the surface with a bucktail wet-wing pattern that didn't immediately sink, and even a few on top-water plugs intended for barracuda. But I was conditioned to the belief that bonefish are strictly bottom feeders, and I couldn't think of a logical reason for them to deviate from that behavior. As every student knows, most of their food consists of benthic or burrowing mollusks and crustaceans, prey probably located by "hearing" and "smell-tasting," senses that must be highly developed in the albulids. The fish literally stand on their heads as they root in the bottom, with tails waving seductively in the air. But bonefish also enjoy a bounty of alpheid and penaeid shrimps, crabs, and other mobile food forms that are flushed in panicky flight, and the tailing activity you see then is in quick, jerky movements as the food is pursued visually.

The most productive way to use the dry fly is on tailing fish. Exactly what a floating pattern represents, I have no idea, but presumably when twitched on the surface, it suggests a crustacean of some kind, such as the snapping shrimp or the miniature pitho, ornate, or spider crabs that will, in mere inches of water, pop to the top when disturbed. Although the vast majority of anglers pursue their quarry from a skiff, going after them on foot with the floater is a totally different adrenaline-pumping game—both a physical and a mental exercise.

For my part, stalking bonefish by wading is the ultimate method. It can't be done everywhere in bonefish country because it requires flats with a fairly solid substrate—preferably sand or firm marl with a minimum of grass. This is far more common to the Bahamas than Florida, where soft marl bottoms are dominant, especially on the bay side of the Keys. When wading soft bottoms in Florida, our resourceful Saltwater Fishing Editor, Bob Stearns, wears his boat sneakers bolted to a pair of plastic snowshoes, taking big fish in water so shallow that they jet off the flat in a contrail of mud.

According to Stearns, snowshoes slide easily through water. However, in the Bahamas there are places like Ambergris Cay, the Joulters, Deadman's Cay, Santa Maria Point, French Wells, and the many excellent locations near Deep Water Cay such as Big Mangrove, Little Harbour, the Bird Bar, Brush Cay, and East End Creek, which offer miles of easy wading.

Sight fishing from a poled skiff is often more productive of numbers, as you can cover a greater area and find more targets. But when there's visible feeding activity, it's more exciting to go after bonefish on foot. The advantage of wading, and indeed the real thrill, is that you can get much closer to the fish and also take them in the shallowest water, where a skiff would go aground. Tailing incomers will sometimes swim within ten feet before spooking, provided you get down on your knees when casting. In a sense, it is comparable to the matador's classic *pase de rodillas* (literally a pass at the bull while kneeling), as the fish almost blindly charge the fly.

The polite position of simply bending at the waist or crouching is little better than standing upright like a scarecrow in a berry patch with eyeball-to-eyeball encounters. And there's a vast difference between an angler standing on a bow platform looming eight or nine feet above the surface in the bonefish's cone of vision, and the kneeling caster with his derriere flat against his heels. I have squatted perfectly motionless without casting and had tailing bonefish come so close that I could almost reach out and touch them; when the school exploded, it was like taking a shower bath. In the thirty- to thirty-five-foot range, I can sometimes make as many as a dozen dry-fly presentations before hooking, or spooking, a tailer. Bear in mind, the floating fly doesn't make a splash, and you're not throwing yards of fish-frightening taper across the sky.

I've been fishing with my old friend Gilbert Drake for twenty-five years. Our system is to park the skiff at the edge of a flat, then go our separate ways, keeping about a fifty-yard interval. Depending on the sun's glare, I can often spot fish working in Gil's direction and signal him, or vice versa. Starting our stalk on the downtide side of the flat, if ebbing or flooding, and wading toward the flow, we sometimes meet a constant parade of incoming pods and singles. Even when no tails are showing, there are some flats that invariably hold feeding fish, and we follow the same routine—watching for surface disturbances and bottom sign. The bottom sign, incidentally, is a visible trail of excavated sand or marl. These bluish-gray holes in a marl substrate, individually somewhat triangular in shape, are fresh "digs" made by the bonefish's pointy snout. They will disappear with the next tide. If there is any marl in suspension, and a dig looks like it holds a little puff of smoke, you are within casting distance of fish—or about to step on one.

Inevitably, there are many frustrations in this kind of angling, especially when you follow a big bonefish swimming uptide in the "wrong" direction for about 200 yards, tailing but staying just at the outer limits of a cast, only to have him spooked by the shadow of a gull passing overhead. I have followed individual fish for a half-hour before finally getting close enough for a cast. Bob Stearns stalked one for forty minutes on his plastic snowshoes and finally nailed it—a 10-pounder. This kind of fishing doesn't add up to large scores at the end of the day, but there's a tremendous satisfaction in a one-on-one contest. Those are the parameters of our game.

To me, top-water strikes are always much more exciting, whether I'm casting for trout, salmon, bass, or any other gamefish. Under the right conditions, ladyfish, baby tarpon, and even small creek snook can be taken on dry flies. But there are three distinct advantages to the dry-fly method on bonefish. First, you always know where the fly is in relation to the fish—a critical factor on tailers who often move randomly, slowly changing direction a few feet left or right. With a sunken fly, it's easy to misjudge exactly where the feathers are, or when to give the fly some action. Second, a floating pattern won't hang in the bottom. Even reverse-wing and keel hook wet patterns will get stuck in turtle grass or pick up weeds when cast in what is often little more than ankle-deep water. The third advantage is that the fish has a much better chance of seeing a dry fly when you are casting over humpy bottoms. Bonefish will often feed in places where patches of substrate are almost emergent on a falling tide; they literally squirm from hole to hole, and often a wet fly will sink out of sight on the opposite side of a slope.

I took one fish of about 8 pounds recently on a turtle-grass flat bordering a channel near Jacob's Cay. Even when the tide has almost fully ebbed, individual bonefish will often linger until what seems like the last drop of water, as long as a safe, deep channel is nearby. When I spotted this bonefish, his back was out of water and he was rooting like a hog in lush pasture, slowly finning from one pocket to another. By the time I waded into casting distance, he was about to ease over another slope, so I dropped the fly in the next hole. There was no hesitation. I twitched the Irresistible and he swam directly for it, poking his head half out of water at the take. In the same situation with a wet fly, I almost invariably get hung in the bottom, or the fish doesn't see the fly at all.

The ideal outfit for bonefish on the dry fly is an 8- or 8½-foot graphite rod calibrated for a #6 line. When fishing from a skiff on windy days, I prefer a 9-foot rod with a #9 line, and regardless of calm morning weather conditions I bring along both, as sight fishing while wading becomes impossible when the wind rises. For lines, I prefer a standard weight-forward, or triangle-taper; I find saltwater tapers with the more terminal, heavy belly section much too splashy for spooky fish. A 9-foot leader tapered to an 8-pound-test tippet is standard for bonefish and provides enough rigidity to turn over #4 and #6 dry flies, which have more air resistance than wet patterns.

So far, I've had my best results with the Irresistible, the Bomber, the White Wulff, the Gray Wulff, and a dry Muddler. I don't think pattern is too important in a surface fly—giving it a few slight twitches is usually what triggers the strikes. Although I spray the fly with a floatant, salt water is more dense than fresh water and thus helps flotation. On the negative side, salt water also rusts lightweight, bronzed-wire dry-fly hooks, so washing them in fresh water at the end of the day is essential.

How effective is the dry fly on bonefish? Well, my neighbor, Ed Reddy, whom I now count as a pioneer in this new dimension (I haven't met anybody else who throws dry patterns on the flats), took eight consecutive bonefish with a floater before getting a refusal, while fishing with Captain Sammy Collins at Bush Cay north of Deep Water Cay. That would be hard to duplicate even with live shrimp. I haven't done half as well as Ed, because I always manage to spook a few between takes, for one reason or another. I still get an awful case of buck fever when fish are working all around me, and my casting goes to hell. And so far, I haven't found the dry fly very effective on cruising fish in water much over knee depth, especially when they are traveling in compact schools, "window-shopping" rather than actively feeding. The wet fly is still the ticket for deeper water.

After almost four decades of emptying conch shell out of my wading shoes, I've learned that making positive statements about *Albula vulpes* is fatuous. Like Winston Churchill's classic description of Russia, the bonefish remains "a riddle wrapped in a mystery inside an enigma." But I see no reason why the largest fish will not surface-feed in shallow water. The problem is, of course, that we don't meet trophy fish every day, and as in all new angling methods, we will learn from collective experience.

[1986]

Book Two

PANFISH TO PIRANHAS

McClane is a trained (Cornell University) ichthyologist who's devoted a lifetime not only to catching both fresh- and saltwater fishes, but also in studying them. In this section you'll find a combination of his in-depth knowledge of fishing tactics with his understanding of the fishes themselves.

We start here where most people start—with the sunfish, perch, and other common panfishes. The information here is anything but common, however, as the marriage of effective tactics and knowledge of fish behavior will almost certainly increase your catch. The same approach is applied here to more glamorous fishes such as Atlantic salmon, and I've also included what I feel to be the best article on bonefishing ever written.

14

All About Panfish

Bluegills are delicious! That might sound like heresy in this catch-and-release era, but they are and I can't bear to let an eating-size one go. Happily, and this is true with most panfishes, keeping a few probably improves the relative dynamics of the whole population, so the bluegill fillets and I approach the pan of hot oil without guilt. Would I rather eat a bluegill (or yellow perch or white perch or crappie) than a traditional fresh trout? In general, absolutely!

For a lazy summer afternoon, as Al points out in this story, when the trout are tough and you can't find the bass, there is no better or more entertaining event than panfishing, as long as your tackle (bait, spin, or fly) is matched to the quarry. We once used one eighteen-foot Old Town canoe—with myself, two brothers, and two parents aboard—year after year along a shoal off Nudists' Rock in Connecticut's over-populated Candlewood Lake to harvest that lake's outsize bluegills, and the aftertaste, with many other things, lingers comfortably in the remembering. It's something I work now to share with my children—as you may with yours.

One of the more generous provisions of nature is that panfish can be angled for on a hot August afternoon. Perhaps the trout are hugging bottom in the spring holes, and the bass are glassy-eyed from staying up all night chasing frogs. But at least ten other species of fish are wandering about in a day that's stupefied with sunshine.

These providential hot-weather fish are found throughout North America in all kinds of waters, from city parks to more than 1 million farm ponds dedicated solely to their culture. Although no panfish is capable of a prolonged struggle against ordinary fishing tackle, the long-promised day that I have been writing about since 1947 has come to pass. We now have ultralight spinning equipment, ultralight spin bait-casting gear, and ultralight fly-casting tackle. These refinements not only make our panfish weighty opponents, but, more important, permit the bubble-gum set and expert alike to profit from the mechanics and lore that surround their development.

I suppose if one item were to be singled out as the pivotal invention it would be the flat Prince Albert tobacco tin that first put the worm in small boys' Sunday pockets. Like a magic lantern, that can materialized the redwings cackling in the cattails and squirrels racing along oak limbs, and bonnets vibrating like drumheads with the sound of crappie chomping on fry. Next to the height of August corn, the most amazing sight was a string of perch ringed in yellow and black with transparent vermilion fins—and the way a granddaddy bream could stare at you through his purple mask. There were then, and there always will be, many things to learn with a cane pole, things that escape modern philosophers.

All panfish can be caught on worms, minnows, grasshoppers, and other insect baits. If we were to take a vote, probably the manure worm, cricket, and roach would win in that order. Ever since the Alleghenies began leaking into farm ponds, the rearing of crickets and the trapping of roaches have become a considerable business in our southern states. Such specialist items as catalpa worms, bonnet worms, and the mealworms, or golden grubs, that gave winter bluegill fishing a jolt in the Midwest are also locally important.

But live-bait fishing for panfish is a simple mechanical

process. As a rule, the line is run through an adjustable float and two small split shot are added just above the hook. The angler estimates where his fish are located and starts to work. If nothing nibbles within a few minutes, he may vary the depth of the bait or move on to a new location. This pursuit of a large school is enough to satisfy any angling appetite, and it requires a devotion hardly less concentrated than that of a hairline caster working with artificial lures. Yet the real art rests on how much the angler has absorbed about the habits of his quarry.

Panfish generally inhabit the marginal areas of a lake, but the larger specimens are likely to be found on shoals that rise from deep water, or over submerged weed beds. Much depends on the season, the character of the pond, and the available food. In lakes where thermal stratification occurs, large yellow perch are usually most abundant just above the thermocline (about twenty to thirty feet down), but in some waters they frequent the stagnant area *below* the thermocline, where there is little or no dissolved oxygen. By comparison, bluegills are unable to venture into deep water, where oxygen values are too low. The sunfish isn't as rugged as the perch, and this fact, fortunately, keeps its schools within easy reach.

White perch, on the other hand, generally move according to the light, seeking deep water during the bright hours and schooling in the shallows toward dark. For this reason, the best fishing is usually in early morning and again in the evening. But the feeding places of panfish also depend to a large extent on the abundance and type of food. Our casual panfisher might assume that all small fish can be taken on any small lure; however, it's not that simple. The individual species adheres to a well-defined pattern in each locality.

For example, Reid, in his report on the food habits of black crappie in Orange Lake, Florida, observed that the consumption of minnows is seasonal; stomach contents revealed that the amount varied from 90 percent in the fall and early winter to a low of 65 percent in the summer months. Furthermore, during the spring breeding season male crappie consumed 33 percent fewer minnows and 33 percent more crustaceans than females.

There are three different types of modern panfish tackle. Most specialists will want to own at least two—a panfish fly rod, a spinning rod, or the newer ultralight spin bait-casting rod. I can't describe all the various models, but let's begin with a typical fly outfit. This consists of a 4-foot, 4-inch fiberglass rod that weighs exactly 1 ounce. Its matching reel is a single-action aluminum job with silent click that weighs 2⅜ ounces. A custom-tapered fly line fits the rod; depending on skill, casts up to 50 feet or more can be made. The assembled outfit feels featherlight, and it provides plenty of thrills against the pull of a fat bluegill or crappie. This covers all fly-fishing situations that the panfisher is likely to encounter; so the second outfit should be calibered to toss baby jigs, spoons, spinners, and live bait.

The ultralight spin bait-casting equipment now on the market isn't made for hairlines—that is to say, monofilaments testing less than 1 pound. The manufacturer told me that what he wanted to create was a miniature enclosed-spool-reel outfit that would handle 2- to 4-pound-test lines. This, of course, is most practical and should appeal to the great majority of panfishers. The thumb-controlled, top-mounted spool is ideal for beginners. Inasmuch as the 5-foot fiberglass rod and reel weigh just 7½ ounces complete, a husky perch can make the drag buzz merrily.

Experts who want to go down to very fine lines of ½- and ¾-pound test will probably choose one of the many rods and reels in the orthodox ultralight field. One popular outfit consists of a 4-foot, 6-inch fiberglass rod that weighs 1¾ ounces, matched with a precision-built 6-ounce reel. The mill is designed for lines testing up to 4 pounds, which should satisfy everybody. Even with large panfish available, it's rarely necessary to use anything heavier than a 4-pound test and smaller diameters are preferable for casting the tiniest lures. But between these two types of spinning outfits you should choose one to supplement the fly rod.

Of all the panfish—white and yellow perch, rock bass, sunfish, white and black crappie, white and yellow bass—

most anglers will be catching some kind of sunfish this month. There are five hybrid sunfish in addition to the eight species, of which the bluegill is the largest and most highly esteemed among panfish specialists.

The bluegill, distinguished by long, pointed pectoral fins (equal to almost one-third of its body length) and black ear flaps, is usually a dark greenish blue on the back and yellowish to orange on the belly parts. It also wears six to eight dusky vertical bars on its flanks. But the coloration of bluegills is more variable than that of other sunfish, and only the fins are a reliable gauge.

The redear sunfish also has elongated pectorals, but the red margin of its opercular flap is distinctive and not to be confused with the black "ears" of a bluegill. Although widely distributed throughout the United States, the bluegill is of prime importance in the Midwest and the South. However, the redear, better known as the shellcracker because of its ability to crush and grind mollusks, often weighs from ½ to 3 pounds in the Swamp Belt, and is seasonally popular during the spring bedding period.

Taken in their native water, either sunfish is no slouch on light tackle, and both can be extremely fastidious about your choice of lures.

LaMont Albertson once told me about a canal that harbored some platter-size bluegills that were so mean that they should have been wearing muzzles. The place hadn't been fished in years because hyacinths and water moccasins had taken over, but last winter a prolonged period of winds pushed out the floating mats of plants. Under the circumstances I expected to catch bluegills.

We hauled a skiff over miles of sawgrass to get at LaMont's sunfish factory and to work. I began with a black featherwing bug. The bluegills assembled and studied it like brain surgeons about to perform a lobotomy. For every fish that took a poke at the bug, twenty swam away laughing. LaMont was casting a bug called the Queen Bee, and he was catching bluegills—great big coppery-purple fish with bellies as orange as the sun on a hot summer evening. I didn't have a Queen Bee, so I shuffled through my box trying other bugs that looked something like it.

"You dasn't use anything except a Queen Bee," cautioned LaMont. "I have some extras."

"Thank you, no," said I.

By the time I had reshuffled the complete box and caught my fifth bream, LaMont had twenty-five. A Queen Bee might be just another bug pattern in your neck of the woods, but it suits the bluegills of Big Mound Canal just fine.

A few miles west and a few weeks later I fished with Mark Challincin at South Bay. For our first three hours on the water we had six bluegills in the ice chest. Then we met Bill McLeod and Dick Wollin. These local bream specialists had almost limited out, which means fifty fish per man. McLeod grunted when I told him we were using the super-duper Queen Bee.

"It's no good here," he said. "You've got to use an all-white bug, or one with red body and yellow wings. Ninety percent of our fish are taken on the white pattern, though."

Mark and I changed to white bugs and continued fishing. Things began picking up right away. We soon found a school back in the bonnets, and for an hour we literally caught a bluegill on every cast. I don't recall ever seeing so many big bream slashing and flopping at surface bugs.

The point is, panfish are discriminating; taking an occasional one doesn't mean that you are using the correct lure or method. On the way back to Mark's landing that evening I found a number of large white caddisflies crawling around the boat. I don't know why we didn't see them in the air—but McLeod and Wollin had supplied the answer from experience.

Just as the overall rule for panfish tackle is lightness, the best method of fishing is slow. It doesn't matter whether you use a spinner or a fly—all panfish are more readily caught at minimum retrieve. The exceptions are rare. Panfish are comparatively slow swimmers when measured against a trout or a bass, and it's apparent that quick motions frighten them.

Sunfish, for example, usually study a surface lure for some time, finning toward it and backing off as though waiting for it to explode. Occasionally one will strike immediately if the school is actively feeding, but their normal approach to a bait is cautious. I have seen many a day when big bluegills would flee at the faint sound of a popping bug. Yet they would hit the same lure if it was left on the water for a considerable period without being popped. All things considered, I don't think that poppers are ordinarily as effective for bluegills or other panfish as quiet swimming bugs of the old-fashioned moth design or the sponge-rubber crickets and spiders.

The ideal lure seems to be one that looks completely helpless and just barely disturbs the surface. And it must be small. You can hardly poke your finger between the rubber-tire lips of a big bluegill, and for this reason his lures must be dressed on the correct hooks. Although an occasional sunfish becomes fastened to a bass bug, this is the exception. Stay within the limits of #8 to #12 hook sizes and you won't miss many bream.

It's interesting to note that many of the larger sunfish caught today are either natural or man-made hybrids. Of these, the bluegill x redear is gaining widespread popularity. Hybrid sunfish not only grow more rapidly but are generally infertile, and for that reason do not tend to overpopulate a pond. Eastern and Western anglers should be seeing more of these hybrids in the future, along with the more familiar pumpkinseed. This gaily colored species sometimes reaches a weight of over 1 pound. The biggest pumpkinseed I have ever seen were in the salt-marsh ponds of Long Island and Cape Cod; these ran up to 1½ pounds. I'm told they grow equally well in some warm-water lakes of Washington and California.

There's no mistaking the pumpkinseed; his dark blue ear flaps terminate in a red border, and his body, which shades from a coppery brown on the back to a yellow or orange on the breast, is brilliantly marked with a thatching of powder blue stripes and orange spots. This sunfish is easier to catch than either the bluegill or the shellcracker, and he'll hit any small wet fly, nymph, dry fly, or panfish bug.

Yet the rule of fishing slow still applies—in fact, the only thing that will discourage a pumpkinseed is fast or erratic retrieving. The spinning-rod fisherman suffers most on this count because many lures are not designed for really slow work. If a spinner blade is too thick, or the lure body too heavy, the angler must reel quickly to activate the lure or keep it from snagging bottom.

The ideal spinning lure for most panfish is an ordinary weighted spinner. There are countless hundreds on the market, but the one you're looking for should have a blade about 1 inch long. It must be free-swinging, slender rather than oval in design, and thin enough to spin at the slightest pull. It shouldn't weigh more than ⅛ ounce, and preferably about ¹⁄₁₀ ounce. I prefer a brass finish to silver, but like most people I can't give a satisfactory reason.

Although the bare spinner is usually effective, it sometimes helps to add a tiny sliver of pork rind. You can now buy the rind in paper-thin 2-inch strips; this is labeled as a fly-rod size, but it's ideal for decorating ultralight lures. It wiggles enticingly at slow speeds. The spinner should be cast out and left to sink near a school. Being light, it seldom snags in weeds; so when it gets near the bottom, retrieve *very* slowly with just the faintest hopping motion.

The second most popular American panfish is the crappie. Although we fondly think of him as a native of Florida, our "speckled perch" feels equally at home in the Colorado River or the Saint Johns. One or both species of crappie are found nearly everywhere today. The white crappie and the black crappie are very similar in appearance. Their general color is a silvery green or olive drab on the back fading to a silvery white, or pale yellow on the belly. The dorsal and caudal fins are spotted with darker green, and the flanks of the white crappie are marked with dark vertical bands; the black crappie wears irregular dark blotches.

Generically, the speck is a member of the sunfish family, but he's temperamentally different from the bluegill. A school doesn't often roam in the open—crappie have a passion for getting under things, such as fallen trees, pad beds, or sunken brush.

One of the best methods of catching speckled perch on big Southern creeks is to troll the buckbrush. This is done by throttling down the outboard until it purrs and trolling a live minnow along the deep banks, pushing through overhanging limbs where necessary. The crappie under the brush will swim out to see what's making the commotion and find themselves a minnow.

The live-bait-trolling method vividly explains why crappie addicts go to such pains to find sunken brush piles. A dedicated speck fisherman will build one if he can't find one. Willow mats are anchored in many midwestern lakes for that reason. Nearly all Western and Southern impoundments have natural brush heaps, created when the land was inundated.

The secret of crappie fishing is to find these areas where the fish school, and once you have a hot spot the rest is easy. My favorite lure is a miniature yellow jig for the spinning rod, but many small spinners and spoons, worked slow and deep, will pay off. Crappie are not consistent surface feeders, but like the voracious white bass, they school periodically to feed on clouds of forage fish, notably the threadfish shad. At such times fly-rod lures of the feather-minnow type, bucktails, and even top-water bugs will take fish.

The chief reason that most casters go after the pan species is to collect a mess of eating fish. With the liberalized bag limits of today (which is sound conservation) I can think of no finer way to spend an August afternoon than catching the makings for a fish fry. Although some mighty fancy recipes have been concocted for cooking panfish, my favorite method is the old-fashioned deep frying.

Try our bream chips the next time you get a string of bluegills. Fillet the bream by making a crosscut just above the tail with a sharp, flat knife. The blade should just touch the backbone. Then, holding the tail with your free hand, run the knife along the backbone toward the gills. Now, with the knife angling in toward the head, make a slice from behind the pectoral fin, lifting that side free. Lay the fillet, scaly side down, and, holding it in place at the very end with one finger, cut through the fillet to the skin. Again run the blade forward, separating the skin from the meat.

Although you may waste a little, it's better to trim out the rib cage; then you can just forget about the bones. This will leave you with a solid piece of white fillet. Cut the fillet in 2- and 3-inch-long strips.

While the cooking oil (which is 1 inch deep in an iron skillet) is reaching a heat just short of smoking, roll the fillets in some good cornmeal. Yellow cornmeal is all right, but the white water-ground, unbolted, unsifted kind is what we prefer in the South.

Some people drop the fish in a beaten egg before dipping it in the meal, but I'm strictly against it. Eggs are for batters that you might use on large chunky fish, but they don't add a thing to panfish fillets. All you want is a light coat of meal.

Assuming that you have all the fixings on the table and the guests seated, drop the meal-powdered fillets into the hot oil, one by one. With the oil at the correct temperature, the fish will get a crunchy jacket almost immediately, which keeps the oil out and the succulent flavor in. Don't overcook. As soon as one side is golden, flip each piece over and stand by with the spatula.

When they are finished, drop the cooked pieces on a sheet of absorbent paper and sprinkle them with salt and pepper. Onion salt or, if you prefer, garlic salt adds a point of flavor. Serve immediately. You can also make chips of other panfish, and if there's any trick to getting mouth-watering results it's frying at the correct temperature. By the thermometer that would be 425° F.

[1960]

15

The Little Fish Who Eats People

Everybody's seen or at least heard of piranhas, or so it would seem. The stories about men and horses being devoured in seconds by schools of these rapacious South American fish are part of every schoolboy's folklore.

But like other things you're likely to read, it ain't necessarily so. Incredibly, McClane has collected, waded with, caught, photographed, cataloged, and even slept with *(see Chapter 38) his share of piranhas and is uniquely qualified to debunk some popular myths about these fish, while unfolding a fascinating tale at the same time. Should you ever find yourself in piranha country, you'll also find here directions on how to catch them!*

Two years ago, a young boy fishing with his father in a canal outside of Fort Lauderdale caught a "funny-looking bluegill." Its teeth clicked like Spanish castanets, but somehow the lad managed to juggle his prize into a bucket of water to take it home, his father meanwhile insisting that it was just another "brim" with a very red belly and a dental problem. The fish was soon identified as a red piranha.

Several months later, an off-duty Florida highway patrolman went fishing in a barrow pit that joins the Snapper Creek Canal west of Miami. The trooper was still-fishing with minnows and after being mysteriously cut off several times, he finally landed what he believed was "that little fish who eats people." A positive identification was made by the Game and Freshwater Fish Commission—another red piranha.

At both locations the waters were poisoned with rotenone over an extensive area by Florida biologists. No more piranha were found. Nevertheless, these isolated events confirm the necessity of present state regulations that strictly prohibit their importation.

Like so many exotics, piranha can survive in Florida's climate and certain species might readily live in more northerly water. The illegal release of aquarium fishes is a problem that extends all the way to Wyoming and Montana, where tropicals such as the swordtail, guppy, and platy form reproducing populations in thermally warmed pools and streams. These live-bearers have the same temperature tolerances as the piranha. So the ban in Florida recognized a very real danger. Dumping piranha in the village pond is not the act of a rational citizen—as this characin is not a very rational fish.

The popular conception of piranha is that they are small, aggressive, occur in vast, water-churning schools, and that they eat man and beast alike. The facts are that at least two species reach a weight of 8 pounds, some are so shy that they seldom take a natural bait (much less an artificial), and a few species are almost solitary in habit. All are potentially dangerous to man, particularly the capaburro, dusky, and black piranhas, as many fingerless and toeless men can attest. Yet throughout tropical South America primitive people bathe, swim, and freely wade in piranha-infested waters. The trick is knowing where and when—a knowledge that brings forth a flood of speculation but little else. During the past twenty years I have waded among piranha for hundreds of hours while fishing and pulling seine nets in tributaries of the Orinoco, Amazon, and Paraguay rivers. I am a devout coward, however, and the only thing that gives me confidence is when an unscarred, all-extremities-accounted-for, local Indian (preferably over eighty years old) says "Ho-kay" and jumps in first. Even then, I wait to see if he comes up with a smile on his face.

Piranha (pronounced "peer-ahn-yah") is the name given by the Tupi speakers of Brazil and literally means "tooth-fish." Throughout most of Spanish-speaking South America it's known as *caribe,* the origin of that tribal name being the Carib Indians who were cannibals. Other Indian appellations such as *pana, perai,* and *piraya* are used in the Guianas and eastern Peru, but piranhas were first imported by tropical fish dealers from Brazil, so the Tupi name stuck.

Scientific literature is not clear on how many different piranhas exist. An educated guess would indicate about forty species in five different genera. The common names of piranha are practical descriptions translated from Indian dialects into Spanish or Portuguese. For instance, the caribe *pinche* or "kitchen boy" caribe is perhaps more friendly than most in that several species of piranhas serve as automatic dishwashers for the Indians. The old lady simply leaves her plate in the river and the fish clean the food residue, slick as a whistle. Actually, another characin called the "bucktoothed tetra" does the same job, if you hold the dish under water, he will also shave the hair off your arm.

The white piranha is often called caribe *mondonguero,* which means "dealer in tripe," and by some stretch of the imagination the allusion is to this piranha's abundance around village slaughterhouses where offal is regularly tossed in the stream. It's an unforgettable sight. You'll give up swimming forever. The caribe *capaburro* or "donkey cas-trater" is, oddly enough, known by that name over a wide range (from Venezuela to southern Brazil) in several lan-guages, so it may well deserve its reputation. Capaburro often weigh 4 or 5 pounds, and one glance at this snubnosed piranha is enough to intimidate any jackass.

The dentition of a piranha is more wicked than a casual examination reveals. Although its canine teeth look like uni-cuspids with a single sharp edge, if you depress the gums and expose a complete tooth, you find a tricuspid—three cutting edges that come into play when the fish clamps its powerful jaws shut. The piranha doesn't bite and chew in the manner of a shark, but literally shears out chunks of flesh like an animated scalpel. People who have been bitten by piranha often say they weren't even aware of it until they saw blood in the water. The sensation of pain is delayed as it is with a razor cut. A poultice of tobacco is the usual Indian remedy for minor wounds, which leave deep semicircular scars.

Nobody has ever presented a definitive explanation as to when and under what circumstances piranha become man-eaters. There is ample evidence that they are dangerous in deep, swift, or turbid water, which bears out the natives' belief that they are most aggressive during the rainy season, and on any occasion when there is blood in the water. The latter is a common situation in the simple act of releasing or cleaning fish. However, it is possible to wade in piranha-filled rivers where the water is clear and slow flowing in the dry season. I have never seen an Indian do this where the capaburro, dusky, or black piranhas abound, but in areas where the ruddy, white, or Wimple's occur, they enter the water with no hesitation. Wimple's piranha is an exception in having comparatively weak jaws—which may be why it's ignored. This is purely a personal observation, and certainly not a valid rule, but it would appear that knowing which species is present plays some role in deciding where and when. On numerous occasions we have been wading in a particular location and later, just a few miles away, been told to stay out of the river.

Piranha species distribution is probably not only a matter of habitat preference as to bottom type, depth, and current velocity, but also a seasonal condition. After extensive periods of collecting specimens in one Orinoco tributary, we found that our nets had taken only adult fish of a particular species and never any juveniles. This would seem to indicate a migration from the main river. It's possible that when streams flood in the rainy season the larger, more dangerous species occur in areas that the Indians otherwise consider "safe." Language is, of course, a barrier, but even on trips when we had an accurate interpreter along, with biological training, the explanations were predicated on the *acceptance* of what happened rather than any understanding of it. The sun comes up, the moon goes down, and you don't ford the Rio São Lourenço at Brown's Farm, although it's perfectly all right to wade at the village two miles upstream. Provided the water is clear. And you are lucky.

The well-publicized film demonstration of a piranha school stripping a cow to a skeleton in a matter of minutes is factual, but it's provoked in the same manner that one can create a shark "attack" by towing a tuna carcass behind a boat. I watched a French TV crew try to set this up in Venezuela. The piranha took no interest in the deceased for two hours, despite bloodying the water. When everybody started to pack up and go home, the bashful cannibals suddenly went berserk and ate the cow so fast that the cameraman barely had time to get in focus. This was a school of Natterer's piranha, which are about as unpredictable as any I've observed. I doubt if the "dealer in tripe" or white piranha would hesitate, but then, fish that hang around slaughterhouses have conditioned appetites.

The fact is that cattle wade South American rivers with impunity. On rare occasion an animal with running sores on its legs will get nipped. However, in common with the shark, piranha evidently respond to panic situations. It is virtually impossible to catch an undamaged fish on rod-and-reel in piranha-infested waters. From the instant a fish is hooked the piranha go to work chopping off its fins and finally slashing chunks out of its flesh. Sometimes you'll land nothing more than the victim's head. Obviously, a struggling animal triggers the stimuli through well-defined underwater vibrations. How this differs from a quietly wading man is apparent, but the occasional piranha attacks reported in South American newspapers are probably augmented by the more numerous "drowning" resulting from accidents that are frequent in countries where all the main highways are rivers. The basic native craft is a dugout, one of the tippiest boats I've ever had the misfortune to travel in, and rollovers are commonplace.

Several years ago, I talked with an Indian on Venezuela's Cinaruco River who lost his little daughter and her dog. His dugout turned over one evening and in the commotion that followed, the child and dog disappeared. Not a trace could be found of either victim despite the fact that the river was in an almost currentless dry-season stage. Even if we assumed that his daughter drowned, the father's reasoning was that the dog could swim and, therefore, both had been lost to the piranha. This is fairly typical, although there are reliably documented cases of actual attacks on wildly splashing people. Dr. Alvaro Aguirre of the National Museum in Rio de Janeiro told me that when they were laying railroad track along the Amazon, one of the laborers jumped in for a noon swim and his enthusiastic hand splashing turned him into an armless corpse bobbing in the current. It just happened to be the wrong time, the wrong place, and the wrong piranha.

One would imagine that such an aggressive fish would be easy to catch. At times you can cast endlessly and not get a touch—despite the fact that they will apple-core any other fish you hook. Surface lures as a rule won't even interest piranha, except for a flashy silver plug. A deeply fished jig is perhaps the most effective lure, but even then certain species like the white piranha are as shy as any brown trout, and Wimple's piranha *never* to my knowledge takes an artificial (and seldom a natural) bait. The dusky, ruddy, Natterer's, red, black, Holland's, and blacktailed piranhas are easy marks most of the time. They are not spectacular gamefish although the larger fish of 3 pounds or more put up a fast bottom-boring fight. Piranha are one of the better food fishes in South American rivers, particularly when deep-fried to a golden crisp. The meat is very white and delicately flavored. It's easy, just close your eyes and bite.

[1973]

16

Salmon Don't Lie

Many trout fishermen eventually evolve into salmon fishermen, first as a dream or a goal, and then as a matter of practice. The advice is plain and simple: Forget what you know about trout fishing and learn salmon from a salmon fisherman, because salmon are for you the ultimate paradox. They neither hold where trout do in a stream nor do they act like trout when they respond—or don't respond—to your fly. So for your first-time salmon trip, photocopy *this chapter and take it with you.*

In this 1987–88 salmon season, the picture is very bright. The Canadian Maritimes are having their best season in a decade. Maine's big Penobscot is worth the trip for a shot at the "king of fishes." Inshore netting is now being phased out in Norway, which should *mean that long-empty and once salmon-famous rivers such as the Laerdal will once again host their June bonanzas. Icelandic rod catches have been on the upswing for the past couple of years. The bottom line is that in this decade more people will be going Atlantic salmon fishing than ever before, as the effects of overharvesting and pollution are dimin-*

*ished and rod returns increase correspondingly. For
the neophyte salmon fisherman, Al and I share some
brief advice: (1) Reread this chapter and take a copy
with you. (2) Read our mutual friend Lee Wulff's new
edition of* Atlantic Salmon Fishing *(New York: Nick
Lyons Books, 1983). (3) And go salmon fishing!
There's plenty available and the relatively low cost of
some of it will surprise you.*

Albert Lyons pointed at the gravel shingle on the far side of
Homc Pool and said we should "wade just about six feet from
where the gravel dropped off and cast exactly twenty feet out
in the main current, letting the fly swing around first in front,
then behind the boulder." We would go in turns, Bill Briggs,
Carl Tillmanns, Peter Verstopen, and myself. With four anglers assembled and about to descend on a spot the size of a
bathtub the attack seemed hopeless except for the first guy to
put a fly in the water. However, Mr. Lyons is not only an
astute game warden on the Miramichi of New Brunswick,
but a master of salmon psychology. To complete the concert
he had each of us tie on a fly that resembled a frayed cigar
butt, one of the most unlikely looking salmon patterns I have
ever seen. Furthermore, he announced, glancing at his
watch, salmon never "take" in Home Pool during hot weather
before 9:00 A.M. or much after 11:00 A.M., so we had a half-
hour to enjoy a cup of coffee. Nobody argues with Albert
Lyons. If verbal persuasion isn't enough—he is built like a
bull moose. We had three miles of water to wade and friend
Albert wanted to make certain we each caught a salmon
before he buckled on his gun and departed camp on his
appointed rounds.

There is a certain inevitability about salmon angling,
and after thirty years of minor successes, and major failures,
it did not surprise me that (1) we all caught a salmon precisely as specified, and (2) when Albert wasn't around somebody would sneak into Home Pool after hours and *not* catch
a fish. Oh, there was a legal evening taking-time also, which
I recall was from 8:00 P.M. until dark; we couldn't beat that
either. We tried for five days, and although fish would move
toward the fly or even bump it, they did not actually strike.

According to Mr. Lyons it was a matter of air temperature exceeding water temperature in these critical hours. With the same unerring accuracy he predicted *where* poachers would be setting their nets at 10:00 P.M., 2:00 A.M., or 5:00 A.M. "because they won't risk a sweep in empty water." He collared netters fifty miles downstream with the precision of a Swiss railroad making a local run. I still don't believe that anybody can absolutely say when a salmon will rise, but for a man who fishes the same river season after season under varying conditions, the odds in accurate forecasting are much more favorable.

With more and more Atlantic salmon fishing becoming available to the general public in the Maritime Provinces of Canada, the number of tourist anglers has increased greatly in the past few years. But the ratio of success is likely to be in favor of the individual with no preconceived notions about fly fishing. Experienced trout anglers suffer most. I recall my first trip back in 1948 to the Humber River of Newfoundland. I had read a few books on salmon, bought some mighty expensive flies, and although my casting ability was better than average, I wasn't in the least prepared for what I found.

Wally McKay, publisher of the *Western Star* at Corner Brook, an expert salmon angler, introduced me to a guide who volunteered no information. We drove in awkward silence to the river, and after I staggered hip-deep in currents for a mile or so, casting a long line in every likely looking hole, Donald finally suggested to go "back up and fish that first pool again because that's where all the salmon lie." That sounded ridiculous. His so-called pool was nothing more than a shallow eddy below a riffle and directly against the bank. I figured the old boy just wanted to sit on a stump and meditate. To complete this blasphemy he thumbed through my fly box, a treasure trove of Hardy's Jock Scotts, Blue Charms, Green Highlanders, and Silver Wilkinsons, and snapped the lid closed.

"Here, try this," he said.

Donald extracted a black glob from his pocket. At first I thought the lining of his pants had shredded, but it was a bunch of moose hair wrapped around a hook. Donald stationed me in about two inches of water and, pointing to a pale yellow stone on the bottom of the eddy no more than thirty feet away, he told me to cast so that the fly would swing precisely above it, at the same speed as the current. I made eight or ten casts, none of which drew a murmur of approval from my guide. Finally, Donald said "he moved for it" and I was about to ask *who* moved for it when there was a splash at the surface and the rod was nearly jerked from my hand. The fish only weighed 9 pounds, but a first salmon is perhaps the most important one in an angler's career. In retrospect, Donald actually caught that fish because he knew that salmon don't "lie" in the received sense of the word but reveal themselves as creatures of habit. They are absolutely honest with their anglers—to the point of frustration.

If there is a circadian rhythm in the taking times of salmon, it's variable. In Arctic latitudes, especially northern Norway and Finland, the "dark hours" are considered more productive and the usual procedure is to fish at night, say from 6:00 P.M. to 4:00 A.M. Naturally, it's still more or less daylight in these latitudes and, if nothing else, it induces a good case of jet lag in the angler. Of course, if you can't get the legally required guide to trot along in midday hours, it's a difficult theory to refute. During a month's fishing in Norway one season we caught most of our salmon around noon and in the early afternoon hours. In Iceland, with a banner day of eighteen salmon, all the activity was between 11:00 A.M. and 3:00 P.M., yet we often fished late at night. Once Arnold Gingrich and myself went around the clock in the Haffjardara for the full twenty-four and the only salmon taken was at around 4:00 P.M. But Albert Lyons made his predictions under unusual circumstances; the Miramichi last July was extremely low, the water was actually hot (in the seventies), and the sun as bright as a furnace. Long and similar experience had taught him exactly what to expect under those conditions in that one lie.

There is no universal rule concerning the visible characteristics of water that create a lie—it exists in many forms. A salmon needs to hold in the currents with an economy of effort, as it will remain almost motionless for long periods in its upstream journey, and the water must be of a tolerant temperature with enough movement to supply the right amount of oxygen. In very hot weather, for example, a logical place to find salmon is at the mouth of a cold tributary stream. However, a lie may be nothing more than a slight depression below a log cribbing, the bulkhead of a bridge, a minor channel off the main current, a string of boulders in midstream, or just a projection of grassy bank. There are a few that come to mind—places where there is a change of flow usually where a weak current and a strong current converge.

As other fish move upstream they follow exactly the same paths. These lies never remain vacant for very long, for even if a salmon is caught or the fish continue traveling, a new tenant or even a school will choose the identical position to rest. Trout, on the other hand, cavort in places where there is an abundance of food and position themselves in feeding lanes that are easier to "read" than the lie of a salmon. Some of the most unlikely looking water (to a trout fisherman) is often the only spot to find salmon. So casting blind is seldom productive without that all-important local knowledge of where the fish will hold. Quite often a half-mile or more of river may be consistently fishless in that the salmon, finding no suitable lie, pass through quickly on their migration. And as water levels drop from high to low during the season, the *exact* location used by the fish within a lie may change and indeed even be abandoned in feeble currents.

Few Americans, except those who live in northeastern Maine, have the opportunity to observe a salmon river's metamorphosis day by day, being limited as most of us are to perhaps two weeks for a trip, and we arrive on the scene like toothless tigers. Frequently, weather conditions are "abnormal," and the lies that produced last year are not holding fish now; the salmon may pause but not long enough to be "taking" fish as they hurry along on their journey. It's all very confusing to the beginner, particularly when he can clearly see fish stacked about like so much cordwood.

The only thing salmon have in common with trout is that they are both members of the same family. A salmon, or even a dozen, will hold in plain sight, ignoring cast after cast until the weary angler decides the whole procedure is hopeless. Then, the next man will come along, make one or two casts, and a fish snatches the fly so fast that you'd believe it had been waiting just for that pattern to appear. Salmon fishing is an exercise in patience. There are days, wonderful days but too few, when salmon rise with abandon, yet more often it's a matter of "throw and throw," staying with the fish beyond any normal period of time that you'd devote to other species. On countless occasions I have worn my arm to a nub, and at the last moment of sanity the water exploded and a salmon streaked away with an awesome pounding of its tail, covering the pool in flashing leaps, setting up an electric circuit through my rod. That moment is worth waiting for, although cause and effect is not easily explained.

If we accept the premise that salmon do not feed after entering fresh water, their bodies containing sufficient nourishment to survive the rigors of spawning, then fishing with any kind of lure or bait is not a very logical game. How can anyone expect to hook a fish that has no appetite? Yet salmon are caught on nightcrawlers, herring, spoons, plugs, and prawns where they are legal, and of course on artificial flies. Many theories have been offered concerning their behavior, but the most plausible one is that habit patterns are hard to break, and memories of feeding at sea, or even some dim recollection of hungrily rising to insects as a young parr is sufficient to trigger a feeding response. Judging by some of the big copper spoons used in Norway, it's difficult to believe that the fish are simply curious. Many anglers, myself included, have seen salmon rise to natural insects, but such events are indeed rare and triggered by some unique circumstance. During a veritable "snowfall" of spruce budworm moths on the Miramichi several years ago, we saw fish take them in head-and-tail rises like trout coming to the mayfly. I have heard of similar phenomena, but these are about as frequent as the appearance of Halley's comet. However, fishing for salmon with the fly is not without some direction.

Before examining fly-fishing techniques, bear in mind that salmon fishing requires constant casting, and the lighter your tackle the less tiring it will be. But no rod is suited to all rivers. I had marvelous sport on my last Miramichi trip using a 7½-foot, 1½-ounce graphite rod; the fish were not running large, and small flies were essential in the very low water. I did bring along a 9-foot graphite of 4 ounces, expecting larger salmon in a normal flow. At the extremes, let's say you are going to the Alta or Namsen in Norway, where 40-pound salmon are an everyday possibility, requiring a sinking line and big flies in deep water. Most of this fishing is done by boat, incidentally, and very little casting is even allowed. The guide maneuvers your trailing line into the lies and woe betide the angler who steers his own course. Here, heavy tackle is necessary. On the other hand, if you are going to Iceland, I wouldn't hesitate to use a 7½-foot rod of 1½ to 2½ ounces for two reasons: There is very little opportunity of hooking a large fish in the treeless barrens; and the island is fissured by sparkling streams of an ideal character for light tackle.

Although some of the Canadian rivers are still fished with big two-handed rods, the general trend today is toward 8½- and 9-foot lengths on most streams. I have taken several salmon of over 40 pounds in weight on a 9-foot rod when the conditions were suitable, and except in a few of the world's torrents, I believe that that length is perfectly adequate. Casting with a heavier outfit becomes wearisome—and quite unnecessary. Our European Editor, Arthur Oglesby, took nineteen salmon up to 36 pounds in one week last July, using trout tackle and small flies on the Spey in Scotland—a river that is normally associated with two-handed rods.

The tactical concept is to use big flies, possibly 3/0 and 4/0 sizes early in the spring and swim these deep. As the water warms at the approach of summer, you can use smaller flies, say #4 or #6 wet patterns, fished within a few inches of the surface. Most experts agree that the distinction between fishing on the bottom and at the top occurs when the water temperature reaches 48 to 50 degrees. Should the river become very warm, then trout-size flies in #10, 12, and even 14 fished wet or dry are often most productive. Autumn is an uncertain season; you may have to continue with summer methods if the river is low, but if early rains have raised the level, then larger sunk patterns should be your choice. Of course, what is cold or warm, or high or low is all relative. Arctic rivers can be a frigid flow even in summer, and at low level, torrential enough to handle tugboat traffic. The rule I rely on is visual: *select the size fly that swims at the same speed as the current.* A small, lightly dressed pattern will always swing around quicker than a large one in any given stream velocity. You must control its speed and depth to get a good presentation, and there's a whale of a difference between water resistance on a fly of a ½ inch in length and one 3 inches long.

The usual procedure is to cast a wet fly across and downstream, with the angle depending on the speed of the current. In very slow water this may be directly toward the other bank, in a very fast current aimed more nearly downstream. The line should fall reasonably straight to bring the fly under immediate tension, then form a slight belly so the current will swing the fly over the salmon. If the cast falls slack, the fly may just sit there while an arc forms in the line, which suddenly drags the feathers over the salmon at an exaggerated speed in a boomerang effect.

It's important to keep the fly from lagging behind the line as it swings around in the current. A poor cast can be mended by rolling or lifting the line clear of the surface in an upstream direction without disturbing the swim of the fly. But some skill is required in this maneuver that might otherwise frighten the fish if exercised poorly. The experienced angler fishes with his eyes as well as his hands. In slow water, for example, it may be necessary to lift the rod and strip the line to put the fly under tension and keep it moving at the correct speed. Conversely, fast currents may require lowering the rod to pay out a few yards of line to decrease it. What you want to avoid is accelerating drag, which ends with the fly whipping around out of control. At the end of the drift, the usual procedure is to retrieve the fly in short jerks and pauses. If this doesn't produce a strike, increase the fly's return speed on each playback. Occasionally, when working over fish that have been in the river for some weeks, a very fast retrieve will trigger solid strikes, especially in slow currents. In any event, if a salmon indicates some interest by moving toward the fly, no matter how brief, the fish will probably take if you duplicate that cast without altering its angle or length. If the fish doesn't respond after a reasonable period, rest the lie for ten or fifteen minutes before trying a different pattern or fly size. Bear in mind that while a #6 Butterfly may have achieved instant success in the pool above, as you progress downstream into new water, possibly into faster or staler currents, it may require a #4 or even a #10 in the same pattern to maintain a controlled swim.

I seldom use the traditional featherwing salmon patterns. Some of these are real works of art, but except for admiring the tying skill, they are overdressed for most of the rivers I fish. The simpler hairwing salmon flies popularized in the Maritimes such as the Cosseboom and Rat series, Hairy Mary, Black Bear, Red Abbey, and the British tube flies dressed on double hooks are less expensive and more effective.

I don't believe that the color or pattern is very important to a salmon. After all it's not a feeding fish (except in the late winter and spring when spawned-out "black" salmon are migrating seaward), but certainly the amount or quantity of dressing is significant. Size for size, a sparsely dressed pattern will sink quicker than a bushy one, which results in their swimming at different speeds. While fishing in Finland some years ago, it was the morning ritual of our guides to shuffle through the fly box and after finding an appropriate pattern, tie it on the leader, then carefully trim it, feather by feather, while testing its drift in the current. My old friend at surgery, Carl Tillmanns, dubbed this hour "The Cutting of the Flies," and it would send shudders through Michael Rogan or Megan Boyd to see a Fiery Brown or Torrish reduced to something out of Donald's pocket. But these guides were commercial fishermen who use flies as well as plugs and spoons, and each lure was evaluated for its swimming speed. How it looked didn't matter. The idea was to catch fish, and as one old man said, "A salmon doesn't care what it's caught on." That's not a very romantic observation but it's worth remembering.

[1975]

134

17

To Beat
the Drum

*Channel bass, redfish, red drum—they all spell the
same copper-colored gladiator that's one of the most
popular saltwater gamefishes in an area extending
southward from Virginia all the way around Florida
to include also the Gulf Coast states.*

*The late Van Campen Heilner, for many years an
associate editor at* Field & Stream *and a widely read
author on saltwater angling, was an outspoken advo-
cate of channel bass fishing. In his 1937 book,* Salt
Water Fishing, *he quoted an old anglers' tune as follows:*

> *Oh, the weakfish am good*
> *And the kingfish am great,*
> *The striped bass am very, very fine;*
> *But give me, oh, give me,*
> *Oh, how I wish you would!*
> *A channel bass a-hangin' on my line!*

*From the Hatteras's high surf to the gentler waters of
Florida and the Gulf Coast, here's McClane's guide to what
thousands feel is the finest fish in the salt.*

"Lord Almighty, can these fish pull!"

This pronouncement coming from lesser anglers would be laudatory, but from Frank Mather, whose entire scientific career has been punctuated with spine-jolting giant bluefin tuna, it was the highest praise indeed. Four times he had skillfully pumped an obviously "spent" fish within netting distance, and on each occasion that redfish went running off again, shaking its head like a bull elephant. A 10-pounder on light spinning tackle is in every way comparable to a 40-pounder on heavy surf gear.

If there's one verb that describes the red drum, alias the "redfish" or "channel bass," it's *pull.* He's not speed-crazed in the sense of a bonefish, or violently acrobatic like the tarpon, but if you want a tug-of-war, *Sciaenops ocellatus* is your boy. As our second-most-popular saltwater gamefish in the entire South Atlantic and Gulf region, from the Carolinas to Texas, it provides millions of pounds of angling enjoyment.

Frank and I were wading a sand flat in Turtle Bay, south of Gasparilla Island, with my old friend Bill Cameron. There are countless "off the highway" settlements along the west coast of Florida that tourists bypass; Placida is one of that genre—a grocery store, gas pump, and a house or two set back in the pine and palmetto scrub. Here you'll find a marina with a "one-dollar put-in and one-dollar takeout fee," and from the ramp you can run southward to Turtle Bay or Bull Bay along well-marked channels. Cameron, who has retired to the water-oriented community of Punta Gorda Isles, said that it would take him another lifetime to fish all the bars, passes, and islands.

Although a trailered skiff is essential to reach the actual fishing areas, the fact that much of this angling can be done by wading is a tribute to the unspoiled nature of the terrain. Great fish-food–generating turtlegrass beds, which have vanished in many coastal towns through dredging and filling, run here for miles in all directions, and the water under normal wind periods is clear enough to spot swimming schools at long distances. Over the years I have fished for red drum throughout most of their range, and although it's always an absorbing game, fishing for red drum comes nearest to its potential when you can literally choose your weapon and "sight fish," whether with fly, plug, or spoon. Frank and I, for example, switched from spinning and bait-casting rods to a fly rod late in the afternoon when we found an island where the redfish were working the banks right up among the mangrove roots. Occasionally, a snook or spotted seatrout would wolf our lures.

That kind of fishing can be enjoyed in many areas outside of Florida, and in fact about 30 million pounds of redfish are harvested annually in Louisiana and Texas alone. There is plenty of good wading water in bays and on offshore banks, where just wearing old shoes and rubber-soled Top-Siders, you can wade out and cast for cruising schools. It's prudent, however, to shuffle your feet even on fairly solid bottoms, as there are always stingrays present and they'll flutter away provided you don't take normal steps and pin one to the sand. Redfish can be caught the year-round in some areas, but the larger prespawned "bulls" begin concentrating in the passes by late August. From September through October is the peak period everywhere as the drum feeds and fattens inshore. In the warmer waters of southern Florida and other Gulf states, good fishing may last well into December.

The drum family, which encompasses about thirty-five species in North American waters, including such familiar quarry as the weakfishes, white seabass, silver perch, corvinas, and various croakers, has as many or more representatives in Central and South America, and at least a few more in Africa and Australia. But they are all sciaenids, or fish with a specialized "drumming muscle," which by rapid and repeated contraction against the gas bladder produces an audible sound. Geographically, every angler beats a different drum; however, the redfish has been a celebrated source of food and pleasure ever since our early Colonists followed in the southerly wake of Captain John Smith.

It must be said in all fairness to the red drum that while he rates a second place statistically, such figures are based on state to state "creel counts" and do not necessarily reflect the anglers' preference. Our number-one fish, the spotted sea-trout, is, if not more numerous, certainly an easier fish to catch, and in fact schools are almost suicidal at times. The "trout" of salt water is one of the finest eating fish and supports the very foundations of those Gallic halls of gastronomy in New Orleans. This distinction is made even by callus-thumbed guides such as Ray Bradley who will advise a client, "If you want some fish to eat, we'll catch trout—but if you want a hell of a sore wrist, let's go after redfish."

Ray's statement always brings to mind the words of Van Campen Heilner, longtime associate editor at *Field & Stream* and certainly one of the most experienced marine anglers in our time: "I've caught them all, but there's only one bulldog in the sea!"

Van wrote words of praise to *his* channel bass. In his mind's eye there was a lonely wind humming in the crackling dune grass, black ducks were settling in the marshes behind, and the surf was booming with the promise of a first northeaster. That was a sentimental appraisal, which is every angler's right.

In appearance, the red drum is a chunky fish, coppery red in color, and usually with a single black spot, or ocellus, at the base of its tail. But don't bet on it. Some populations are very silvery in color, and I have seen many redfish with two to four spots on the caudal peduncle. Perhaps a freckled record is the one taken by Joel Arrington at Pamlico Sound, North Carolina, last summer; that fish had *fifteen* spots scattered along its sides.

One of the annual migraines in our Field & Stream Fishing Contest is separating potential winners in the red drum and black drum categories. The black drum, *Pogonias cromis,* attains weights of over 100 pounds (as opposed to an 83-pound record for the red drum), and besides being black to silvery gray in color, it lacks even a single black ocellus and has barbels or "whiskers" on its lower jaw. In amateur photography, the category under which most of our entry photographs would fall, the ocellus can be lost on a true red drum, but at least he's clean-shaven.

The large red drum—fish of 50 pounds or more—are caught from Chesapeake Bay southward to North Carolina. There is no hard evidence but only supposition on the part of researchers that these big fish represent an overwintering population that migrates out into the canyon when cold weather begins. In other words, the smaller "puppy drum" might drift north from southerly nursery areas, and after feeding along the beaches attain some growth and remain in the area. The biggest redfish taken in such locations as Assateague Island on the Maryland and Virginia border, or down the coast to Hog Island, Smith Island, and Cape Charles obviously follow an inshore to offshore migration route. On the other hand, a "big" red drum in Florida is a 15-pounder on either the Atlantic or Gulf coasts. The Gulf fishery from Florida to Texas (the red drum has been caught as far south as Panama) appears to be independent and doesn't contribute to the more easterly Atlantic populations. The state record in Texas, for example, is 51½ pounds, and 20- to 30-pound drum occur often enough in northerly Gulf water to indicate that a similar benthic migration takes place here.

During the last century there has been some change in the overall distribution of the redfish—at one time, for example, the fish was numerous around Long Island, New York. The fact that it occurs in fresh water, brackish water, and salt water, or from 0 to over 30 parts per 1,000 salinity, shows a parallel with the unrelated striped bass, but more is known about the striper's migrations and the contributions of different breeding areas to the overall picture.

When we speak of "tailing" fish on saltwater flats, the bonefish and permit automatically come to mind. There are occasions when even very large tarpon will stand on their heads during the so-called Spanish worm hatch, a really awesome sight that some knowledgeable anglers anticipate like the salmon fly emergence on the Madison. And at random periods big mutton snappers will tail also. The fifth or out-tailing species is the red drum. Again, this is not an everyday occurrence but evidently related to the cyclic abundance of a particular food. Over the years I've had maybe a dozen days on tailing redfish schools, but for guides who are on the water constantly it's less a rarity. While fishing out of Big Pine Key with the late Joe Brooks and Harry Snow one afternoon, we ran into schools of tailers consisting of hundreds of drum in the 5- to 10-pound class. We could see the fish at perhaps a half-mile distance with their coppery black-spotted tails flashing in the sun. From low water well into the flood, our fly rods were bent in an almost continuous arc. I killed two drum and their stomachs were crammed with juvenile blue, or finny, crabs and it's probable that a coincidental migration of these crustaceans triggered a feeding orgy.

On another occasion I was fishing with my wife, Patti, and Ray Bradley out of Goodland, Florida (another of those little bypassed towns), in the Ten Thousand Islands region. We were drifting and spin casting one of the outside passes at flood tide, taking fish so regularly that often all three of us were tied into a fish simultaneously. It was almost unreal. As the water level dropped, the redfish began tailing along the sandy banks. I grabbed my fly rod and went wading into the schools. That we continued to catch fish was no surprise, but the thing that really startled me was at dead low water whole *islands* of pink fiddler crabs emerged above the surface, uncountable billions of noisily scrambling crustaceans that obviously had no intention of staying in the depths as long as redfish were on the prowl. Although most of us think of fiddler, or grapsoid, crabs as terrestrial or shallow-water crabs and white in color, some are fully marine forms and pink as any milkmaid's cheek.

Pink is certainly an effective and popular color in saltwater fishing lures, as it was on this particular occasion, both in the form of a ¼-ounce leadhead jig for Patti and Ray and a pink bucktail on my fly rod. Ordinarily I don't find pink as effective as some other colors, especially when fish are selectively feeding on shrimp. Our most common penaeid species along the Atlantic seaboard and in Gulf waters are the brown shrimp and the white shrimp. These common names are not necessarily indicative of the actual "natural" color, as the pink and brown shrimp species are frequently very similar in color (brown) in Gulf nursery areas, and the white shrimp is very often blue-gray or lemon-yellow color. For strictly shrimp-imitative lures I would favor mixtures of brown and yellow or white and yellow with Mylar strips for "flash," not unlike Bill Curtis's famous Bluetail pattern (essentially a yellow fly with blue Mylar strips). Many live shrimp have rusty-red, blue, and purple shading, especially on the tail and legs. The only reliably "pink" shrimp is a *cooked* shrimp, which is not what a gamefish is apt to see. I think the Pink Shrimp fly pattern was created at a cocktail party, but we will take this up in some future discourse.

The kind of tackle to use for red drum—with the exception of, say, Hatteras surf casting, where conventional 10- to 12-foot rods equipped with standard multipliers or spinning reels are essential to long casts over the breakers for truly big fish—is for the most part any type or caliber of gear you prefer. On northerly beaches cut bait impaled on 5/0 and 6/0 hooks is pitched skyward with a 4-ounce pyramid sinker; most casters prefer monofilament lines in the 30-pound-test class. On a day with a strong undertow, even this can seem light when 40- to 50-pound bass are cavorting beyond the farthest comber. But over the greater part of the redfish's kingdom, where light tackle is the rule, a standard 7-foot spinning rod with 10-pound test line, or a comparable bait-casting rig, or any fly rod with a #10 weight-forward line is the common denominator you need.

Local conditions may require minor adjustments, such as narrow mangrove passes where even a small drum can burrow under the oyster-covered roots on his first run. There I'd feel more comfortable with 15-pound-test monofilament. It's also advisable to use an 18-inch wire leader with the spinning or bait-casting outfits, and a 40-pound-test shock tippet on the fly rod. Red drum have very abrasive scales; in fact, they are so tough-skinned that even filleting one is a job. They often get a line over their "shoulders," so a leaderless rig is worthless.

Red drum feed on a variety of foods including other fish, shrimp, crabs, and mollusks. Over the years I've found in red drum stomachs less evidence of a fish diet than one comprised of crabs or shrimp, but I suspect this is both a seasonal and a geographic condition. During spawning migrations of mullet or anchovies, redfish will literally tear the schools apart. Some of our most exciting top-water plugging occurs in winter months when forage fish are concentrated in huge numbers.

Generally speaking, the popular lures in most areas are

wobbling spoons, leadhead bucktails, any of the flashy-mir-rored gold and silver "jerk"-type plugs (either floating or slow-sinking models that can be worked in a whip retrieve), and the new legion of plastic baits that come in shrimp, grub, and tail-wagging designs. For the fly rod, I prefer yellow-and-red and yellow-and-white combinations and the shrimplike Ruff Necks in brown-and-yellow and red-and-white. Both popping and skipping bugs bring good results when you can see moving fish. Redfish will strike many different kinds of baits *but,* and that's a big qualification, there are definitely days when one lure is superior to another. Experienced an-glers never become stylized. The redfish is both a scent and sight feeder and can locate a cut mullet in a muddy surf just as readily as a wobbling spoon in a clear-flowing pass or river. However, the fish is seemingly myopic, so casting close to its nose is more likely to score with artificial lures. Accu-rate casts really pay off for this species.

When I first moved to Florida years ago, I had fabulous red drum fishing almost at my doorstep. Patti and I could wade the shell beds near the Burnt Bridge or the turtlegrass flats at the mouth of Earman River and catch redfish with regularity. Those coppery gamefish were always ready to do battle. More than a decade ago these waters silted to the point that a wading angler could disappear under ten feet of mud. The oysters, the grass, and the redfish have vanished com-pletely. True, we still have wonderful sport in more pristine waters nearby, but the ecological requirements of the drum are absolute. Marine gamefish populations decline cyclically for various reasons, and these are not always because of man. In this case I believe careful estuarine management is essential to the future abundance of what we so easily take for granted—or marching to the red drummer will be a very ragtag army indeed.

Dredge and *fill* are two dirty words that every child should become aware of in 1975.

[1975]

18

Mayhem in the Mangroves

The doorman at the Breakers in Palm Beach spotted my rod case as I checked out, and from then on the service improved substantially. He was a snook fisherman, and the stars still showed through his bleary eyes as he recounted last night's 20-pounder. By the time my ride showed up, I'd sold him a big graphite fly rod that I didn't want to lug back to Vermont, we'd swapped some fly patterns, and were forever friends.

I thought about that on a recent trip to Boca Paila on the Yucatán's Caribbean coast, where the snook were so numerous that on several days I quit bonefishing altogether and fished for snook instead. It was often total frustration. Small groups of snook—including some very big ones—were basking in the sun around the edges of numerous mangrove islands. They'd follow a streamer right to the boat—nose to the feathers—then turn and leisurely take up station again next to the mangrove roots. You could almost hear them laughing. It finally turned out that red and yellow was the only combination that worked, and I was almost out of luck after losing my

last one. A small collection of red-and-silver swim-
ming plugs saved the rest of the week.

Snook are plentiful in this area and on south
through the east coast of Panama, where most of the
record-class fish have come from in recent years. Un-
fortunately, and although snook are still a popular
gamefish in Florida, overfishing and declining quality
of spawning habitat have reduced snook populations
in the southeastern United States substantially. Start-
ing in 1982, snook gained some protection in this area
through bag and size limits plus a closed season dur-
ing the fish's summer spawning period.

The red-and-yellow feathers of the big streamer were still
dry, so it floated on the brown-stained water for a moment.
I pulled the line sharply, fluttering the long saddle hackles,
and it sank from sight. I worked it back toward the boat and
about halfway out from the mangroves the surface bulged
and broke with a loud *wompf.* Suddenly, my fly was fifty feet
upstream and going away; despite the pressure of my rod, the
line sizzled through the water until the snook decided to
jump. He wasn't a big one—snook always feel heavy at first.
This one jumped three times, and for ten minutes I tried to
keep him out of the mangroves.

Just when I figured I had him whipped, the fish shot back
under the rod and snapped my leader. That snook probably
didn't weigh an ounce over 6 pounds, but at times he per-
formed like 18 pounds. But then, snook are never as big as
you think—they have more impact than most fish.

There are at least nine species of snook (no one knows
exactly how many) and the one thing they have in common
is a complete contempt for anglers. We have four species in
Florida, but periodically a snook is captured that doesn't look
like the others except for his sneering lower lip. The common
snook *Centropomus undecimalis* grows 4 to 5 feet long and
weighs up to 50 pounds. It gives the impression of being
slender but its shoulders are thick, and the older one gets the
more muscular it becomes. Snook are usually a shade of
patinated brass but they also turn silvery when foraging in
the sea.

The family hallmark is a jet black stripe that runs from the gills to the middle of the forked tail. Snook jump when hooked, and make one or two pile-driving runs.

Dedicated snook fishermen are nocturnal in habit. You'll find them pacing back and forth across bridges at two o'clock in the morning, dragging a plug under the spans, or skulking along seawalls and breakwaters, or hanging over the end of a pier doodling figure eights on the water with a plug, mullet, or cardboard lure attached to a wire line and a clublike rod. True, other angling-type citizens do the dusk-to-dawn routine, but the difference is that snook fishermen are compulsive sleepwalkers.

Of course, fish are caught in daylight, but the big ones are more active after dark, and to rack up your legal three in the 15- to 30-pound class, the night is best. I like the hours from the crack of dawn to about nine in the morning, although fly-rodding in the backcountry seems to be productive at all hours of the day.

Tourist fishermen usually compare snook to bigmouth bass. There is a certain similarity and an experienced plug caster will catch some snook if the conditions are right. But it takes a lot of savvy to take them with any consistency, and the game is quite different in all respects from bass fishing.

Snook are found not only in the surf but up rivers in brackish and fresh water. They also go pussyfooting through canals and drainage ditches, prowl near spillways, and lurk in the shadows of mangrove islands. Snook love to hide below bridges and under boathouses. It's not unusual to find a hundred or more of the crafty fish loafing under a pier, but catching them is something else.

Snook range from the Atlantic coast of Florida through the Gulf of Mexico and as far south as Brazil. Two, possibly three, species range from Baja California down to the northern border of Peru.

Florida snook are most abundant in the southern half of the state, with the biggest fish in the inlets and lagoons around Stuart, Palm Beach, and Boynton Beach. However, these hot spots are seasonal; for year-round fishing, the lower west coast from Whitewater Bay north to Naples is more reliable. In Lake Worth, which is one long cast from my

145

home, the game consists of plugging on the flats during the late spring and summer months.

In September the action swings to the inlet and surf when the big mullet migration takes place. There is sheer bedlam when the big fish chop up block-long schools of bait-fish. They get into a windrow of mullet and send great, silvery clouds showering in the air.

With the first northeaster, our snook addicts look for sport in the mangrove creeks and bays, particularly in the southwest corner of the state. I much prefer this backcountry fishing—casting to jungle shorelines where a 12-pound snook or a 20-pound tarpon can bust the next cast. If the weather cooperates, a specialist guide, such as Ted Smallwood in Everglades City, can always find a few fish for you, even in January. However, prolonged high winds or cold weather will knock the fishing out completely.

Snook are caught on nylon, feather, and bucktail jigs, especially when they're in deep holes. They also take spinners and spoons at times, though we don't use metal baits very often in Florida. Virtually all the big snook (20 pounds or more) coming out of our east coast waters fall for a plug or live mullet. I have been lucky enough in the past ten years to take six snook of over 30 pounds with plugs, and there's no denying that the casting rod produces the heaviest fish.

Whether you prefer bait casting or spinning there are several things both methods have in common. The rod must have a stiff tip. A limber rod just won't handle the plug correctly, nor will it have enough backbone to set the hook. With a willowy stick you can't make the lure get up and dance, and when an old snook wolfs the plug, you want to hit him hard. All synthetic lines are elastic, and if the tip doesn't have some backbone the barbs won't penetrate. The ideal bait-casting or spinning rod is somewhat heavier and a bit longer than you would use for freshwater bass. This gives you better control over the lure. Remember a lot of snook fishing occurs when strong breezes are blowing, and it's difficult to keep slack out of the line in a crosswind unless you can get elevation. A 6½-foot casting rod or a 7- to 7½-foot spinning rod is about right for open water and big surface plugs.

146

Back in narrow mangrove creeks, where short, accurate casts are the rule, you can switch to ordinary bass tackle. The reel should be a heavy-duty spinning mill, or one of the service bait-casting jobs designed for lines in the 18-pound-test class. It must have a smooth drag and an ample cranking radius so you can wind at top speed. Those little freshwater reels will do the job, but not comfortably.

When casting in shallow water on open flats or along the mangrove banks, most anglers favor surface-disturbing plugs. These are mainly cigar-shaped with or without a propeller aft, and have no inherent action of their own. Darter plugs are probably second in popularity, and various kinds of poppers are next. These are worked a bit faster and more erratically than for bass.

For deep-water casting around bridges, channels, and inlets, a plug with a metal lip to make it dive and wobble is very effective, as are straight flashing plugs retrieved with snappy jerks of the rod tip. These lures are usually silver-colored, with some red, blue, or green trim generally suggesting a mullet or menhaden.

Speed of retrieve is most important. After the cast is made, the angler "whips" his lure back, causing the lure to dart erratically over the water. You can sometimes catch snook by reeling slowly with a darting plug, or popping a hollow-nosed bait at medium speed, but the whip retrieve accounts for more fish than any other. A crafty snook caster gets his cigar-shaped bait swimming rapidly with a rolling, side-to-side motion, so that it barely pauses with each jerk of the tip. Underwater plugs can be retrieved somewhat slower, but they should achieve that same dart-pause-dart sequence. Lure manipulation is the key to the game and the best way to learn it to watch a veteran snook caster.

Casting from bridges at night is quite different because of the tide flow and depth. You should know where the pilings are, and then cast your plug "upstream," or against the tide. Always fish from the side of a bridge that faces the flow. The cast should be made at an angle that allows the plug to swim downcurrent and swing under the span somewhere near the pilings. The tide gives the plug its motion and speed, and you only have to retrieve fast enough to keep slack out of the line and lead the lure to the snook. Bridge casting requires heavy tackle. Even with a 30-pound-test line a man can lose a lot of snook because they have to be walked off the span and beached.

An important factor in plug manipulation is the leader size. It would be ideal to eliminate wire entirely; however, a length of stainless steel or carbon steel is necessary to hold big fish. The edges of a snook's gill covers are razor-sharp, and they'll cut a braided or monofilament line instantly. Also, the snook lives and feeds around oyster bars and shell-encrusted roots, where 18-pound-test casting line pops like thread. Even with a wire leader you'll still lose fish because some of them will burrow way back in the mangroves.

On Lake Worth the regulars prefer a #6 stainless steel (58-pound-test) in a 24-inch length. This is for big snook—the 25- to 35-pounders. In the Everglades, where snook do not often run as heavy, we use a 10-inch length of #3 stainless steel (32-pound-test).

I don't add wire to my fly leaders except for scissor-mouthed species such as the Spanish mackerel, bluefish, and barracuda, but other casters do. I'd rather gamble in the mangroves because I feel the action of a fly or bug is most important for snook and tarpon. I use 9-foot leaders tapered to .016 (14-pound-test) or .014 (12-pound-test) most of the time, but will go lighter or heavier as the conditions demand.

The ideal in snook fishing is to have visible targets. Sometimes you'll see snook cruising the flats or in canals, making visible humps in the surface as they push water. Or you'll see them smash into schools of baitfish. But most of the time you fish blind—casting at the mouths of creeks, back in the mangrove pockets, into the holes on the downtide side of sandbars and oyster bars, and the deep spots at the edge of a current. The shelving points of islands are often productive. The critical thing is that you must know the water.

Tide stages have a great deal to do with snook success. Again, it requires exact local knowledge. Generally speaking, I prefer a high tide in the backcountry only because it makes travel easier in the shallow mangrove creeks. As a rule, though, a high, falling tide is considered best for both snook and tarpon around river mouths and along coastal shores, and a flooding or rising tide most productive at the creek heads. I try to arrive at the fishing grounds one hour before high tide and look for my best fishing during the first two hours of the ebb. I think falling water sucks baitfish out of the roots and into holes where big snook can get at them. A dead low tide might be productive for the same reason in areas where channels and cuts are deep enough to hold gamefish.

Creek heads, on the other hand, are usually quite shallow, and the fish will move in on the rising water for a feast of crabs or mullet, then drop back. It all seems to boil down to the availability of cover and food; in shoreline casting a high, falling tide provides optimum conditions. For this reason a competent guide will keep his client on the move fishing the "holes" in a pattern corresponding to the tidal flow. It's not unusual to cover twenty miles in the course of a day—and enjoy fast fishing at each stop.

[1963]

19

The Hide-and-Seek
Perch

*I watched the mink grab one perch head after an-
other, making trip after trip to some secret cache
along the shoreline. He seemed as anxious to save the
white perch remnants as we had been to save the
fillets. From the hemlock grove I could hear the fire
hissing and the quick, sharp spatter of the fish against
a hot cast-iron griddle.*

*There had been a few landlocked salmon that
day, but we'd released them in anticipation of white
perch that evening. They rose finally across the evening surface of our little Maine cove, and we took
half a dozen easily on the dry flies we usually reserved
for trout. Although it was one of the finest meals I can
remember, it wasn't repeated often during the Maine
years because the perch, unless rising in the evening
calm, were difficult to locate. A white perch, like gold,
is where you find it—which isn't always easy. In typical McClane fashion, the find-the-fish key has been
recognized in this instance, and he offers here some
advice on finding a fish that can be as baffling as it is
delicious.*

One of my earliest recollections of freshwater angling was a Thanksgiving Day when my father took me to Fort Pond at Montauk, New York, to fish for white perch. It was a double-purpose trip, because while I waded the sandy shores he picked cranberries that grew in profusion in the adjacent bogs. That part of Long Island is no longer a wilderness; the ruby-red berries and the silvery-black perch have been absorbed by land developers and other sponges of civilization. Not long ago I was reminded how important panfish are to children and how quickly we forget angling fundamentals when I spent a day with Stanley Leen, who runs a deluxe Maine fishing camp when he isn't organizing a perch expedition for the kids. Naturally, parents are invited along, too.

That day Papa Leen divided our small fry into a well-equipped flotilla on Third Machias Lake, after holding a seminar on the problems of perch fishing for the benefit of the kids. His final words were an inspired tribute to the species and an assurance that the adults would catch enough fish for the cookout, so the young needn't worry about their inexperience. Needless to say, if it hadn't been for a pair of ten-year-olds, we would have starved. Bud Leavitt, Leen, and I anchored in all the wrong places, which is catastrophic in white perch angling, while our unsophisticated heirs, unhampered by years of piscatorial adventures, walloped them good.

The white perch is a master at the game of hide-and-seek, and unless somebody blows the whistle he can be as elusive as a tax return. But perch are caught by adults from time to time, and they are probably one of the most interesting panfish in the eastern United States by virtue of size, distribution, and susceptibility to various angling methods. The white perch *(Morone americana)* had become more widely distributed than it was when I was a youngster, and modern spinning tackle has made fishing for it more popular. These fish frequently feed below fly-rod range, and my Fort Pond days were productive only during those periods when the fish came topside or inshore. We didn't have small spinning lures and fine lines to get down to schools during bright daylight hours.

The white perch does not look like the yellow perch.

151

Oddly enough, it is sometimes confused with the largemouth bass, and more often with the striped bass. Actually, the white perch and the striper are both members of the sea bass family, and there is a general similarity between the two. The white perch resembles its relative in the number and outline of its fins and its deep caudal peduncle. But the perch is about 2½ to 3 times as long as it is deep (not counting the tail) and is more flattened. There is no space between its two dorsal fins, although they are separated by a notch.

The perch has about forty-eight rows of scales between the gill cover and the base of its tail, whereas there are sixty or more on the striped bass. The first dorsal of the white perch has nine spines and the second dorsal fin has one spine and twelve rays. The anal fin originates under the second dorsal, and the ventrals, which are armed with one stout spine on the forward margin, are located slightly behind the pectorals.

The most apparent difference between the two species is coloration. When very small, a white perch may have pale longitudinal stripes similar to the striped bass, but they aren't present in perch of the size usually caught. The back, or dorsal surface, varies from olive to a blackish green, shading to a pale silvery green on the sides and a silvery white on the belly. White perch taken in saltwater or brackish-water ponds are likely to be lighter in color.

The average white perch is 8 to 10 inches long and weighs a pound or less. In the more fertile Maine ponds fish up to 15 inches and weighing about 2 pounds are not uncommon. Perch of over 2½ pounds are rare; although 3-pounders are occasionally reported. But the fish is active for its size, and wherever it occurs it is abundant. Catches of fifty or sixty in an afternoon are not unique.

As the state of Maine biologists point out, perch populations have cycles like grouse, but they aren't affected by angling. The annual production from a single pair of large white perch can more than replace all that are caught by fishermen. This rabbitlike characteristic can create problems when a population is on the upswing, resulting in many small and stunted fish.

Ironically, the white perch is a careless spawner. The schools migrate into tributary streams, and without pairing off, the females release thousands of tiny eggs (150,000 in the case of a 1-pound fish) that adhere to anything they touch, and immediately afterward the males release millions of sperm. Haphazard as this spawning is, the ratio of hatched eggs is enormous in comparison to that of other fish. The only critical factor is a temperature change of four or five degrees; however, the fry ordinarily hatch within a few days instead of the fifty-odd days it might require to produce a trout, for example. Furthermore, white perch have a long life span. Fish of twelve years are common, and Maine has recorded at least one in its seventeenth year. So everything works in favor of the white perch—including its sometimes whimsical attitude toward the angler.

White perch inhabit salt, brackish, and fresh water from Nova Scotia to North Carolina. They occur inland as far as the Great Lakes. Actually, their range has increased in recent years because of environmental changes made by man. The seaward distribution of the white perch is more restricted than that of the striped bass. Although perch are caught in pure salt water, sometimes as deep as twenty fathoms, they are much more plentiful in ponds connected to the sea and in brackish bays and estuaries. Even though schools of perch in salt water wander about in search of food, there are resident populations in any area they inhabit.

In the spring and early summer the saltwater perch that migrate into rivers from Massachusetts south to Chesapeake Bay constitute an important sport fishery. However, the strictly landlocked perch populations are becoming more numerous along the Atlantic seaboard. Maine biologists found white perch in 295 of 780 lakes and ponds surveyed in 1957.

Like most fish, white perch will eat in large quantities whatever food is available, and their diet varies according to the season. For example, in winter and early spring the fish grub larvae (mostly midge) out of the pond bottoms. As the weather warms and large burrowing mayflies emerge from the mud, they gorge on nymphs. In the months when temper-

153

atures reach their peak and crustaceans and water fleas become abundant, as do small fish of many kinds, so the perch schools change their diet once again. By fall any young fish present in most lakes are too large for the perch to eat, so they concentrate on insects and crustaceans.

White perch seldom venture into shallow water where minnows are numerous. Usually the schools remain in comparatively deep water by day and move close to shore at sundown. In salt water they forage on small fish of all kinds as well as squid, crabs, and shrimp. Here they bite freely on any natural bait and are readily caught with spinning lures or streamer flies.

The standard technique is first to locate a school. Talk with a local resident, look for a collection of boats, or simply try various locations.

The prospecting method is fun. You can begin by checking areas that are from fifteen to thirty feet deep with a firm mud bottom, where burrowing mayflies and midge larvae are most abundant. Drop anchor, then lower a worm or minnow to the bottom. If you don't get a nibble within a few minutes, raise the bait four or five feet, until you've checked all levels. Sometimes the perch will be very close to the surface over deep water. If nothing happens after a reasonable trial, move to a new spot fifty or a hundred yards away and repeat the procedure. Once you find a school the action will be fast, but it can stop abruptly as the school wanders off to another area.

You can troll with a small spinner-and-worm combination until the fish are located, then drop anchor and still-fish. If it's a windy day, just let the boat drift as you work the spinner close to the mud. In the evening a trolled streamer fly is often productive, as are small wet flies with or without spinners attached.

I have experimented religiously with small jigs, but leadheads are frequently disappointing. On rare occasions a jig will excite white perch, but this probably happens when a school is particularly dense and ravenous. A spinner, however, is invariably effective, but you don't want to use a blade more than one inch long. Regardless of its shape, it must be thin enough to spin at the slightest pull. With a fly rod or a spinning rod the spinner should be cast and allowed to sink to the bottom, then moved very gently to the surface in slow, short strokes. My favorite, which I use with ultralight spinning tackle, weighs $1/10$ ounce. I reel it just fast enough to keep the blade fluttering, and because the hooks are small it rarely gets snagged in weeds. The addition of a worm isn't ordinarily necessary, although there's no denying that the combination gets more perch, and faster.

The pinnacle of perch fishing usually occurs in the evening, when the fish come to the surface to feed on insects. White perch will hit a small bass bug now and then, and at times you can catch them with very small poppers from #8 down. But nymphs and dry flies that represent the naturals are usually far more effective because perch can be quite shy. As a rule of thumb, floating patterns like the Light and Dark Cahills, Black Gnat, Black Ant, and McGinty are greedily accepted. Almost any brown, black, or straw-colored nymph will work, and like the dry flies should be dressed on a #10 or #12 hook.

Of course, there's no problem in locating surface-feeding perch, as they'll dimple the water over a large area. The rise generally begins at sundown and continues until dark. However, when ants, bees, and other terrestrials are abundant you may get a good rise during bright daylight.

There is no finer fish to eat than the white perch. It has firm white meat and makes a delectable fish chowder. Perch fillets can be fried in the usual way by coating them with cornmeal, bread crumbs, or just plain flour. The best method I know is to cut the fillets in 2- to 3-inch "fingers" and dip them in a batter called One-Two-Three. However much batter you make, the ingredients must be in the following proportions: one part egg, two parts *ice* water, and three parts self-rising flour. One raw egg is generally equal to $1/4$ cup, so the formula is as follows: Break one cold egg in a mixing bowl, and add $1/2$ cup of ice water then $3/4$ cup of self-rising flour. Stir but do not smooth the mixture, which should remain slightly lumpy. It is of paramount importance to keep the batter absolutely cold (we add ice cubes to the water) and the fish cold until the instant it is placed in hot (over 400° F.) cooking oil. It's a good idea to keep the batter and the perch fingers in the freezer compartment of your refrigerator until you're ready to cook them.

When the oil is bubbling hot, dip each piece in the batter and drop into the pan. The difference in temperature will prevent the oil from penetrating the batter and cause the fish inside to steam and puff under the golden-brown crust. There is a magic in this simple ritual that befits an art which Izaak Walton found a "calmer of unquiet thoughts."

[1963]

20

Jack the Giant Killer

They aren't the most glamorous fish in the sea, and they aren't very good to eat. But the jack crevalle and his many cousins may outdo any other fish that swims when it comes to pull power. On a day when the tarpon or bonefish aren't cooperating, you can do a lot worse than to hunt up a school of jacks ready for action. As the late Joe Brooks once put it: "I've heard a lot about the 'pound-for-pound' business, but although I'm a great admirer of the smallmouth black bass . . . Well, Dr. Henshall certainly called that one wrong."

Not long ago, I spent some time with an ultralight spinning rod and a few small jigs, working some holes and cuts between Mexican bonefish flats just to see what was biting. Of the numerous small fish— runners, bonefish, assorted snappers, and small jacks—I landed, even the smallest jack crevalle out- pulled them all. As an update to this chapter, the International Game Fish Association now does recog- nize jack crevalle within its record categories, where the current all-tackle record exceeds 50 pounds.

157

Shortly after moving to Florida I met a man who knew all the snook hot spots for miles around. Until that time I had never caught a snook, so the first day we went fishing together, I watched how Sammy Sharp worked his plug, and generally tried to absorb those nuances of technique that were strange to me. I used a silly little spinning rod that was vastly under-calibered for the job, but since I had no idea of what I was supposed to catch, it really didn't matter.

I'd walked a long distance down the beach, looking for a hole or a channel, when I saw something pushing water. I cast my surface plug in front of the wake and began to re-trieve. The lure swam about one foot before it was taken in a tremendous swirl. The fish charged across the flat, leaving a muddy trail, and I turned the brake tighter to slow him down. Nothing happened. For almost fifteen minutes I cranked and pumped, increased and decreased the drag. Eventually the fish showed signs of tiring and I led him back toward the beach. When I saw the cause of all the rumpus, I couldn't believe my eyes. The fish didn't weigh more than 2½ or 3 pounds—it was without a doubt the strongest little fish I'd ever caught up to that time.

Five minutes later I hooked another fish and my line snapped. From then on my luck was bad. Monofilaments were unreliable in those days, and before long I had lost four plugs. Sammy finally came down the beach and waved me out of the water. "Nothing but jacks," he said. "Let's go."

"What's the matter with jacks?" I asked.

"Are you kiddin'?"

I have probably heard and been guilty of the same sin a thousand times, but now I make expiation because the cold truth is that jack is a giant killer—yet nobody wants to admit it. Pound for pound the crevalle is one of the toughest fish in the sea. For sheer brawling power, old *Caranx hippos* is a heller, and probably one of the most underrated gamefish in U.S. waters.

If all this seems implausible, then you have never tangled with a jack. The crevalle is a blunt-headed, beady-eyed bar-room fighter who humiliates tourists by busting their tackle. Jacks don't jump when they're hooked; they just pull your arm out of its socket, and when you finally whup one he grunts piglike. And they're not much good to eat; you can cut off the tail and bleed them, which helps some, and they can be made tolerable on charcoal with a lot of barbecue sauce, but nobody really fishes for crevalle as food. In short, the jack doesn't give you much reason to pursue him. But his swift, slashing strike at a surface plug is electrifying. At that moment he has the style of a champ.

When we talk about jacks we're splitting a large and diverse family fish. In fact, the crevalle has twenty close relatives around North American shores, such as the green jack, yellow jack, socorro jack, blue runner, Atlantic horse-eye jack, bar jack, Mazatlán jack, cottonmouth jack, and many others. This doesn't even include seven other family groups with forty-eight more species that are also carangids.

These jacks have more aliases than the Cosa Nostra. Some of them, like the permit, the roosterfish, the greater amberjack, and the California yellowtail, are by now legend. What the jacks have in common is their strong, fast swimming. I think the bar jack, for instance, is about as tough a little gamefish (they seldom go over 4 pounds) as you'll ever see.

Nobody really knows how many jacks exist throughout the world. I have caught huge bluish-colored ones near the mouth of the Congo (they were tentatively identified as lyrefish) and small brown ones off Brazil (which were probably black jacks). One important reason why science has not learned too much about the carangids is that many species undergo drastic changes in body shape and fin structure, not to mention coloration, as they grow older. The jack is a puzzle to everybody.

The crevalle—or jack crevalle, cavally, horse crevalle, and toro—is believed to occur almost around the world in tropical and subtropical waters. In the Atlantic it ranges from Uruguay to Nova Scotia, with the chief center of abundance in the Gulf of Mexico, around Florida and north to Georgia. In the eastern Pacific the crevalle is found from Peru into the northern Gulf of California and around the outer coast of Baja California. One of its many look-alike relatives is the spotted jack of Hawaii. In the islands there are about a dozen species called ulua, and fishing ulua is the most important form of inshore angling. A big Hawaiian jack in a running surf is plenty of *pilikia,* but trouble is the jack's middle name in any language.

The crevalle is usually bluish green on the back, fading to a golden or silvery underside. There is a prominent black spot on the gill cover and a more obscure one on his long, scimitar-shaped pectorals. The Atlantic form has twenty-six to thirty-five scutes at the tail end of its arched lateral line; the Pacific form grows a few more. A crevalle's body is as rigid as a steel bar. When you grab one to pull a plug loose, you think that rigor mortis has already set in.

Not much is known about the crevalle's life history. The clan is believed to spawn in offshore water sometime from spring to fall. This jack does have a tolerance for brackish water, however, and is occasionally caught far inland in rivers of very low salinity. Probably more crevalle are taken in shallow bays, creek mouths, and inlets than anywhere else, but they appear in the surf quite often with tarpon, bluefish, and snook.

It's the jack's proclivity for getting mixed up with larger or perhaps more desirable gamefish that bugs the veteran angler. Common is the lad who zeroes in on a lunker snook and hits a big jack instead. You might have to play tug-of-war for an hour. In the meantime the snook has romped out of sight. I have seen people cut their line and lose a good plug rather than go the limit with a heavyweight.

Guide Willie McKoosh calls the jack his "money fish." When we get an unseasonable blow in winter, and the more delicate species are lying around on the creek bottom in their fur-lined underwear, the crevalle are almost as busy as the tourists. Jacks are not bothered by cold weather. If anything, it stirs their appetites. Willie, like a lot of other people in town, knows a hole where the fish congregate when the mercury dips. We ordinarily avoid it because the touted fishing is for snook farther upriver. But in cold weather Willie makes a beeline for Jacks Pool, and after easing the boat into position he tells his sport to cast. If the man is a real greenhorn, McKoosh gets a pained expression on his face the instant the plug hits the water.

"Stop!" says Willie. "It's a school of jack!" Then he shivers like a bird dog, and if the sport looks bewildered he gives him the fast one-two.

"You don't want to hook a jack on *that* rod," warns McKoosh. Of course, no man will ignore such a challenge, and before he can properly turn the spool his rod is bent in a quivering hoop. The fish won't weigh more than 4 or 5 pounds, but by the time the poor snowbird gets back to the dock he feels as if he'd shot a herd of elephants with a BB gun. The McKoosh charade invariably works.

Willie is doing anglers a favor. After all, what makes a gamefish? Must it jump? The bonefish doesn't. Must it be edible? The tarpon isn't. Must it win a beauty prize? Most fish are homely. The definition of gamefish is "an unyielding spirit," and that fits the jack like his scales. But even the International Game Fish Association, which lists such unlikely subjects as the codfish, flounder, and sea bass, ignores the jack. A crevalle could eat all three, including the lead sinkers, without a burp.

The fact of the matter is that the jack never has been fashionable, and McKoosh in his own way is setting the matter straight. One of several things in the crevalle's favor is the fact that he's a first-class light-tackle fish that can be caught on fly, plug, or spinning. He'll even wallop a bass bug around the mangrove knees just for laughs.

Small crevalle up to 6 or 7 pounds travel in schools. As they get older the big jacks occur in pods, and sometimes you'll see a single or a pair belling along at top speed. Crevalle seldom linger in one spot. When food, such as mullet, is abundant, several schools apparently join forces to execute some of the fanciest maneuvers since the Fourth Armored Division hit the beach. Jacks run the mullet right up on the sand, against seawalls, or into a boat. In open water they herd the baitfish into a compact mass, then plow through it from all sides.

The individual crevalle takes his dining seriously. Here and there a mullet will rise above the surface, doing front and back flips, then leaping madly in all directions, with a telltale swirl countering each shift. If the hapless baitfish is lucky, it may elude the jack for two or three jumps, but sooner or later it'll land in the crevalle's jaws. You can drift through acres of frantic mullet and actually observe this single-minded pursuit. They'll chase a lure into the tip-top of a rod.

Ordinarily we catch jacks where we find them, and with whatever tackle we're using at the time. Plugging is probably the ideal method for most people, but live bait, such as mullet or pinfish, is deadly for the noncaster. Streamer flies tied on #2/0 and #3/0 hooks are the usual fly-rod fodder. Incidentally, I always bring along a casting outfit because there are days when fish don't visibly show, and after I have located them with a plug I can use my fly tackle. This is a generally sensible procedure for most types of saltwater fishing except, of course, on tailing fish. The characteristic feathering slash of a jack at baitfish can be seen for a long distance, so there's usually ample time to decide whether or not you want to fight him with the fly rod.

The thing to remember about jack fishing is that whatever lure you use should be retrieved progressively faster. A crevalle may slam a plug, for instance, the instant it hits the water, or take it within the first few feet. But if a fish merely boils under it, then speed the plug along. A lure that tops or just doodles along is invariably refused. The faster you pull the bait through the water, the more strikes you'll earn. Besides, you'll miss a lot more fish on a slow retrieve, perhaps because of the jack's relatively tough mouth or the speed with which he raps the lure.

When a school is excited and feeding wildly, the rule is even more inviolable. A whip retrieve is ideal. When fly fishing, you are bound to get into trouble because it's difficult to keep the feathers moving fast enough to get a strike, a situation you find with many other dynamite-charged saltwater gamefish, such as the dolphin, king mackerel, and the cero, to name a few. With a little practice, however, it's possible (because you have a visible target) to put the fly in front of a jack, then strip line in hard pulls, though the strike nearly wrenches the rod out of your hand.

One of the silliest performances ever put on by fishermen occurred the day that Johnny Dieckman and I ran back and forth along a seawall, trying to hook a crevalle on streamer flies. The jacks had the mullet in a cul-de-sac against a one-hundred-yard stretch of cement. Although we were four or five feet above the water, we both got soaked every time the fish drove the mullet into the wall. It was impossible to cast to them, simply because the fish were boiling directly below our feet. Dangling the fly did no good because it wasn't moving. Then I discovered that by running along the narrow ledge and dragging the streamer across the surface the jacks would hit it.

Of course, in our excitement it was inevitable that we should run into each other, as we had to sprint while looking to the rear. At least a hundred 10- to 12-pound crevalle churned the water to a froth. The jacks would make a wide circle at the edge of the channel, then chase the mullet straight into the wall with a wet *thwack.* Between running, jumping off the end of the wall to play a fish, climbing back, and doing a *pas de deux,* we were exhausted. Finally we both hooked a lunker jack that emptied our reels of backing. The lines just went out and out without a pause, and the fish hadn't slowed down one bit when the leaders parted.

I once played a jack for a little over two hours in the Palm Beach inlet. I'd hooked him while casting with 8-pound-test spinning gear. I guessed that the fish weighed between 35 and 40 pounds. If we hadn't been able to follow him with the skiff, he'd have busted off on the very first run. In common with the permit, large jacks always seem to have an extra ounce of energy in reserve. Their tactics are dogged and unrelenting. It's not uncommon to play a 20-pounder for an hour or more on light tackle.

The maximum size of the crevalle isn't really known. Since he has only recently gained recognition in the new Saltwater Division of the Field & Stream Fishing Contest, no authoritative records have been available on the species. The maximum weight has been given as 36 pounds by some authorities, but this is misleading. The six top crevalle taken by members of our local fishing club in the past six months are a 45-pounder caught by Bryant Hilliard; a 42½-pounder by Jimmy Branch, Jr.; a 40-pounder by Fred Mewbown; a 40-pounder by John E. Leg; a 38-pounder by Edward Kelly; and a 36-pounder by Carlton Smith.

One of the all-time greats was a 55-pound jack caught by Lake "Pud" Lytal, Jr., in 1959. In a gesture reminiscent of the mighty Bobby Jones, who penalized himself one stroke and thereby almost lost the National Open, Pud proved his manhood. Though he stood to win a $1,000 prize, young Lytal disqualified himself after realizing that his catch involved a minor violation of the contest rules. In the excitement, a well-meaning friend had reached over and grabbed his line to halt the wild rush of the crevalle. Lytal, today a law student at the University of Florida, withdrew his entry when he learned that nobody may touch the tackle except the angler—inadvertently or not. This purely voluntary gesture cost the lad a lot of dough, but the funny thing is that while we can't remember who *did* win the contest, everybody remembers Pud. In our eyes, Mr. Lytal is already qualified for the Supreme Court.

Among the smaller jacks, the Atlantic horse-eye, the Pacific horse-eye, and the bar jack are topflight gamefish. Generally speaking, this trio runs from 1 to 2 pounds, but occasionally a school of larger fish appears in channels and around the edges of bonefish flats. The bar jack doesn't have the real blunt profile of a crevalle, and its gray-blue body has a dark-blue or black stripe along the back. Both horse-eyes are distinguished by their comparatively large eyes, and their generally dark coloration rapidly fades when the fish moves over a sandy or light-colored bottom.

Horse-eyes have a characteristic black-tipped dorsal fin that, during the period when their sale was banned in West Indian markets because of suspected poisoning (ciguatera), the commercials would cut off to conceal their identity. But the bar jack is one of few carangids that is an excellent food fish. I built a smokehouse at Deep Water Cay several years ago and experimented with a number of possible gourmet items, such as the houndfish, needlefish, bonefish, porgy, yellowtail snapper, and bar jack. The latter was by far the most delicious; unlike the red-meated crevalle, the bar jack has firm white flesh and can be pan-fried, broiled, or smoked.

Admittedly, there is a tendency to play favorites in angling, so the tarpon, bonefish, permit, and a few others will be the monarchs of the flats. The crevalle isn't likely to be fitted for one of their crowns, but come a day when the TV antenna moans in the wind and all the glamour-pusses shamelessly snooze in their aquatic playpens, you'll find brother jack cutting capers with the tourists.

That's what I call a real gamefish.

[1964]

21

In Search of
El Dorado

*South American dorado fishing by its nature con-
notes adventure in the wilds. No U.S. agents that I'm
aware of book dorado fishing with regularity on the
Paraná, for example, although a couple of inquiries
revealed that bookings could be had "by special ar-
rangement." Leander McCormick, to whom McClane
refers below and who in the 1930s compared the
fighting qualities of dorado favorably with those of
Atlantic salmon, noted also that the Paraná tended to
be the color of watery coffee with insufficient milk,
which points out another problem.*

*I'm told by a couple of South American guiding
friends that a two-week stay on the Paraná, preferably in October, is necessary to have any assurance of
hitting relatively clear water conditions and the best
fishing. I'm also told, however, that the dorado fishing is still excellent, and some anglers may eventually
find it worth their while to make the trek after one of
South America's premier gamefishes.*

In 1937, when Leander McCormick published his delightful
book, *Fishing Round the World,* it was fashionable to make

an expedition by launch up the Paraná River to fish for dorado. When Gil Drake and I made the trip twenty years later,
there were no launches for hire and by the time we reached
Posados, about a thousand miles north of Buenos Aires, we
were like two beached whales. There was only one red-dust
road going anyplace we could find on the map, and that ran
out of the Hertz littoral. I don't recall who told us about
William James Jack, but we met him in the bar of our flea-
bag hotel. The pixie-faced son of a Scottish missionary, who
ministered to the Chaco Indians on the Paraguay side of the
river, WJJ spoke Spanish, Guarani, German, and English.
More important, he had wheels. WJJ couldn't imagine why
anybody would want to go fishing voluntarily, least of all on
the upper river "where funny peoples live," but his chauf-
feuring was for hire. It must have been a chain built by some
sadistic entomologist because we finally ended up at another
buggy hotel in the town of El Dorado.

After a brief reconnaissance, WJJ produced a guide who
could double for Peter Lorre—in a blue serge suit with an
accent like a glockenspiel. There was a lot of serious palaver
between WJJ and Peter, or whatever his name was, which I
gathered had something to do with visiting Americans. I
think he wanted formal résumés. Their conversation was
going nowhere until I took a wild shot and announced *"Meine
Grossmutter war Deutsche."* That did it. All Germans love
grandmothers. Peter rolled his poached-egg eyes and nearly
kissed me. I ducked. To be accurate my maternal grand-
mother was Alsatian, and if he had pushed the subject my
German verbs would have spawned French nouns in a hurry.
Anyhow, I *ja*-ed and *nein*-ed and stood beers all around.

That night we were invited to see a home movie of Peter
in action, which I figured was going to be a fishing film—and,
Geez, the picture opens with this guy riding a camel in North
Africa wearing an SS collar flash and shoulder boards befit-
ting a general. In 8-millimeter at 16 frames per second, it was
like an out-of-sprocket Mack Sennett comedy with our *Gruppenführer* shaking the hands of happy Arabs and saluting
companies of *Schutzstaffel*, while humping around the pyra-
mids. There was maybe a dozen of Peter's friends at the
movie, and after we got our noses in the schnapps, they began

167

singing *Ich hatt' einen Kameraden.* WJJ whispered to me. "Nazis," as if I needed a diagram. In my lifetime collection of psychopathic safaris—this was shaping up to be a classic.

The next morning when Gil, WJJ, and I stumbled down the almost vertical cliff to the Paraná, there sat Peter in his skiff with a hangover. His face was as blue as his suit. The suit bugged me for some reason, but I didn't figure that out until later. Our Gruppenführer was vibrating so bad that I thought he'd come unglued. Well, he did manage to get us a few miles upstream near some rapids and cut the engine. The Paraná is not very wide at this point, maybe 200 to 300 yards, but it's deep and has some giant whirlpools that have sucked huge cargo vessels under. These aquatic booby traps, at the vortex 3 or 4 feet below surface level, are marked by the spindrift that piles in dirty red clots along the shore. Gil and I rose to the occasion with our bait-casting rods and began tossing plugs in every direction. Nothing happened for a while. We had a couple of bumps at our lures as the boat drifted willy-nilly all over the place, whacking the lower unit on a few boulders. Peter wouldn't tilt the engine because he wanted to be ready with his starter cord in case we got in trouble. Geez, a camel jockey for a guide. WJJ clung to the gunwales in silent terror. Then, in front of a rock pile in the main current, my Pikie minnow was ambushed. I gave the rod a hard yank and it was nearly wrenched from my hands. The plug flew out of the water like a Polaris missile. Its treble hooks were mashed flat. Gil scored the first visible strike when a dorado swallowed his plug within a few feet of the skiff. In clear water, we watched that golden whale swim off, then circle back, while the old maestro hit him again and again. As the dorado passed by, it simply opened its maw and the plug popped out. Gil's hooks were as straight as arrows. Before the day was done, we lost a dozen fish. It was obvious that our bass-oriented lures weren't going to do the job. A couple of fish even bit our plastic plugs in half. Peter offered no advice. He was glassy-eyed. WJJ, who had been tongue-tied for hours, finally blurted out, "*Why* are we doing this?"

I asked myself the same question.

If there is a secret to successful fishing, it's learning not to let what you know keep you from finding out what you don't know. Fortunately, Gil and I proved that we didn't know anything about dorado fishing, so we could start from square one. When a sober Peter turned out the next morning with a stout casting rod, I wasn't really surprised. What did boggle my mind was the 6-inch-long, jointed wooden plug mounted with two single hooks that I judged to be 8/0s—big enough for sailfish. WJJ said he had "seenus" trouble and a deck chair on the *Titanic* wouldn't improve his problem, but our Gruppenführer was going to explain how dorado are caught. *Achtung!* We were lectured in German/Spanish, which WJJ translated, and for a while I thought we were going to get haircuts. Somehow, *barb* became *barber* in English. WJJ began our discourse with "one barber is better than three, and he must be a big barber." Sorting it all out, what Peter said made a lot of sense. The strike of a dorado is viselike. Pulling at a lure to set the hook is comparable to yanking a bone out of the jaws of a bulldog. Either object is immobilized. One barb of a treble hook may catch soft bone or cartilage, but invariably two hook points are engaged and the dorado can straighten both simply by opening its mouth. The crushing power of its jaws can also flatten a treble engaged in the area of bite. A large, heavy-gauge single hook, on the other hand, will slip into a soft spot and hold. You may catch the odd fish on trebles, but when big dorado are on the prowl, the number lost can be phenomenal.

Well, we took off in a cloud of oily smoke, downriver this time, skirting whirlpools with our Gruppenführer playing the throttle like A. J. Foyt coming off the wall at Indy. I suddenly had sweaty armpits. When we came to a wide place in the river, Peter nosed the skiff into the current and handed me his rod. With the outboard barely keeping headway, I let the plug swim out about fifty yards and we began slow trolling in a zigzag pattern. I could feel the big jointed lure working in the tip as it wiggled and dove over the bottom. Peter goosed the engine now and then to compensate for a quickening current. There are huge piles of sandstone in midriver. Some of these are submerged and others form little islands. It is around these current breakers where dorado disport themselves while waiting to pounce on innocent schools of passing sabalo.

For sheer voracity, the dorado has no equal in South American fresh waters. From the time it is two weeks old and two inches long, it will eat any fish smaller than itself—including other dorado. In the practice of cannibalism, baby dorado grab each other by the tail and swim around in circles until one or the other is too tired to continue, or its tail is bitten off. You will seldom see a dorado with its tail completely intact. As an adult, it is a formidable predator, with massive jaws and short but wicked canine teeth, which are double-rowed frontally. Its favorite food, the sabalo, is a pound-size fish that it gobbles like a kid eating popcorn. Waterfowl and even that giant rodent, the capybara, have been found in dorado stomachs. In a life span of twelve years, it may reach a length of 4 feet and a weight of 75 pounds (the rod-caught record is 34 kilos, 100 grams, from the Bermejo River, Argentina, 1975). Though the average fish is closer to 15 pounds—30- to 40-pound dorado are not uncommon. Its spawning migration, or *piracema,* occurs during the rainy season, when some tropical rivers have a 40- to 60-foot rise in level, leaving a peculiar flotsam of Indian dugouts in the tops of tall trees. The ripe fish enter tributary streams where the female digs a redd, similar to the salmon. The male guards the nest until the fry are free-swimming, then proceeds to eat those he can catch. Fortunately, the bluish gray ovaries of a large female contain from 1 million to over 2.5 million eggs—so at least a few fingerling get a running start in life.

That morning, we worked around three or four rock piles before a dorado struck. The fish jumped in slow motion, head wagging, gills rattling, body shaking, a blooded gold demon in the early sunlight. My drag was screwed down, yet the fish made a powerful run and came out of the water again with a resounding splash, and bucked violently against the rod before doing a long belly whopper. During the next half-hour that dorado vaulted over the river at least a dozen times between thumb-burning runs. When Peter finally gaffed my fish (dorado will tear a landing net to shreds), we had

170

beached about a mile downstream, on an island where hundreds of parakeets whirled and screeched in the jungle canopy. The alarmed birds triggered a chorus from a band of red howler monkeys—a jetlike roar from a thousand throats. I could hardly hear what Peter was saying. I understood that my fish was at least 20 kilos, which called for a celebration that night. I prayed it wouldn't be another dromedary documentary. Gil and I rotated with the trolling outfit and finished the day by catching more dorado. We didn't lose one fish. That big single hook held like the ultimate magnet (I subsequently had Creek Chub mount, on special order, a pair of forged 8/0s on their 6-inch-long jointed Pikie, which at 1½ ounces handles perfectly on a stiff bait-casting rod). I didn't realize at the time that we were fishing perhaps the best of all rivers, and over the next two decades I made a lot of interesting, but sometimes disappointing, trips in my search for gold.

Dorado are a geographic conundrum. These characins, related by family to the tigerfish of Africa, are found from the Magdalena River of Colombia in the north, west to the muddy Ucayali River in Peru, and as far south as the Plata River in Argentina. However, their distribution is spotty, and the number of trophy waters can probably be counted on both hands. There are four known species of dorado and the smallest, which seldom exceeds 4 pounds, is common to northern South America; it is called the tabarana, *Salminus hilarii.* I have caught tabarana in swift mountain streams of Venezuela, and unlike other dorados they are more slender and silver in color—reminiscent of a bright steelhead at first jump. The other three species are look-alikes and differ only in scale and fin ray counts. The word *dorado* means "gilded," and, indeed, they are an unbelievable yellow-gold in color with brilliant orange fins, except for the midrays of the tail, which are a deep, velvety blue. The dorado's body is marked by narrow transverse stripes, giving it a speckled appearance. The most isolated dorado is *S. brevidens,* which is found mainly in the São River system of Brazil. It is said to reach a weight of 40 pounds or more. I have never fished this watershed but I did fly beyond it, and camped on the São Lourenço River, where *S. brevidens* has been reported. However, we caught nothing over 5 pounds in size. Here, some of the piranha were bigger than the dorado. The third dorado species, *S. affinis*, is found principally in northeastern South America, from the Magdalena and Cauca rivers of Colombia to the Santiago River of Ecuador. It also attains good size, although the biggest I have seen was about 20 pounds. It was hand-lined by an Indian on the Cauca.

The giant dorado species is *S. maxillosus*, which is found primarily from the upper Amazon, south to the Plata River at Buenos Aires. Though it occurs in many smaller, remote waters, the Paraná in Argentina, the Mogi-Guaçu and Paranaíba in Brazil, and the Paraguay and Uruguay rivers are the accessible places for trophy fish. In fact, today there is a fancy hotel overlooking Iguaçú Falls on the Paraná—in convenient juxtaposition to some of the greatest dorado fishing on the continent, and there is now a paved road along the upper river. The best location I have found is at Paso de la Patria, where guide Luis Oscar Schulz operates a hot line with his peers. They keep each other posted on the peregrinations of dorado schools following the sabalo. All the upper river ports hold dorado fiestas in July and August. Whole towns turn out for a contest, followed by the nightly fun and games that end with a dorado *asado*—or barbecue—with the fish crisping over hot coals, while the wine flows to infinity.

It was an *asado* that our Gruppenführer had in mind for the "celebration." About fifty or sixty people turned out at the barbecue pit in back of our hotel. Even the mayor was present. WJJ made an emotional speech after a few drafts of the local poteen. I don't know exactly what he said, but with the fervor of a missionary, he described whirlpools and ravenous fishes, while waving his arms and stamping his feet. It must have been a cliff-hanger because he got *oohs* and *aahs* from the audience. My little thank-you speech, which WJJ translated with the solemnity of an emergency meeting of the UN, was anticlimactic. Peter was there looking gloomy, but his suit was freshly pressed.

I remembered then, a long-ago day when we took a town somewhere across the Rhine and after a perimeter was secured, my squad, ever allergic to foxholes, flopped on the floor of a reasonably intact brauhaus. We met the owner hiding behind the bar. He gave us bread, sausage, cigars, and did everything but kiss us good night. In violent times bodily functions are collective, and when we woke like a bunch of groundhogs at dawn, there stood our now clean-shaven host at rigid attention in an immaculate black uniform bearing the skull and crossbones of the SS. With a click of his heels, he withdrew his holstered Luger and offered it butt out. We had to jump off again in a matter of minutes, so we told him to go surrender somewhere else. In the flickering light of the barbecue pit, Peter had the same bewildered expression of a weary marathon runner who sees the finish line in the distance but knows that he will never make it.

After the speeches, Peter joined Gil and me for a drink. Although we had a week of dorado fishing left at El Dorado, Peter wanted to be paid off now. *"Ich muss jenseits des Flusses gehen."* He didn't explain why, but he had to go across the river, into Chaco country. I suppose he was taking his movie along.

With a click of his heels, he bowed, and then was gone.

[1983]

22

Panama Paradise

*Twenty-five years later, the Panamanian fishing re-
sort built by the late Ray Smith goes by the name of
Tropic Star Lodge, and the fishing—having had its
ups and downs over the years through the vagaries of
ocean currents—is currently extraordinary. As was
the case in 1963, when this* Field & Stream *piece
appeared, extreme southwestern Panama may offer
the world's best shot at a single (or more) black marlin in a week's fishing.*

*Blacks from 400 to 600 pounds were relatively
common here during the 1986 season, with fifteen
having been taken during one week in January.
Striped and blue marlin are also on the bill of fare,
in addition to Pacific sailfish (forty-seven during one
week in 1986) and a wide variety of lighter-tackle reef
fishes. Several U.S. booking agents now handle
Tropic Star, including Frontiers International in
Wexford, Pennsylvania. The lodge is very popular
and thus hard to book. Call early.*

When a Texan by the name of Ray Smith built a $500,000
resort at Piñas Bay last year, he put an end to the safari-style

174

expeditions formerly required for fishing that area of Panama. It will take a legion of anglers to get Smith off the nut, but the laconic Dallasite figures that even if he goes broke he'll have one hell of a fishing hole all to himself.

Ever since Zane Grey discovered the big sloping reef fifty to two hundred fathoms deep, twelve miles northwest of the new Club de Pesca, adventurous anglers have cruised from the Canal Zone, with an overnight stop at Cocos Point, looking for fabled giant marlin said to roam the belly of the sea, the great depths of the Gulf of Panama. Although no one has yet engaged that spooky billfish in combat, the quantity of other marlin taken in the gulf is impressive. Recently Mr. and Mrs. Ross H. Walker of Richmond, Virginia, tallied forty-seven black marlin out of seventy-eight hookups in less than a week of trolling.

Over at least two months a staggering number of marlin were jumped, the heaviest—796 pounds—falling victim to Mrs. Helen Robinson of Key West, Florida. Blacks in the 400- to 600-pound class were numerous. But *Makaira indica* is a temperamental critter, and the man who expects to find the same conditions every day can also reasonably expect to find a ten-dollar gold piece in front of St. Patrick's Cathedral each morning of the year. Piñas Bay may harbor a never-ending supply of billfish, but the wise man always goes on a marlin junket with the idea of catching *one*. True, a lot of people spend weeks trying to accomplish that elsewhere, without success. But the odds are heavily in the angler's favor at this tropical outpost. If he's looking for a better-than-average shot at a black, the practical certainty of boating one during a short visit, and the chance of hitting a wild week such as the Walkers encountered, let him hie to the Club de Pesca, just 8 degrees north of the equator and 15 miles from the border of Colombia. No devotee of billfishing could expect more than the prospects I've outlined above. Add a bonus of Pacific sailfish, dolphin, yellowfin tuna, striped marlin, an occasional blue marlin, huge amberjack, brown, hammerhead, and mako sharks, plus the several runs of corvina and snappers inshore, and you have your work cut out for you.

"You" embraces a multitude. Piñas (pronounced "peen-yas") Bay is one of the few places where the average citizen can find black marlin in quantity. This billfish is almost entirely a species of the Pacific and Indian oceans. Its eastern range is from Mexico to Peru, with a few fish straying as far north as southern California. In the western Pacific it ranges from Japan south to New Zealand and Australia. It is scarce around Hawaii, whose waters teem with the equally corpulent blue marlin. In the Indian Ocean, the black ranges from Sumatra to South Africa. Commercial fishermen report catching fish up to 2,000 pounds, and the rod-and-reel record, a black taken at Cabo Blanco, stands at 1,560 pounds. But fish in excess of the half-ton mark have been boated by longliners in the central Pacific and at Capetown, South Africa, which is the only place where black marlin edge into the Atlantic Ocean.

It's barely possible that in the right season, when water conditions are favorable, giant blacks may occur anyplace within their range. Possible but unlikely. Extensive migrations, if any occur, have never been observed. All evidence indicates that the fish exist as local populations; some are so well defined physically that they can be identified one from another.

Blacks are distinguished from other marlin by their rigid pectoral fins, which extend stiffly at right angles to the body and cannot be folded flat without breaking the joint. The black is a slab-sided fish with hide like a rhino's, and it develops a prominent shoulder hump when it achieves 500 pounds or more. Body color varies from black to a dark slate blue dorsally, with an abrupt change to a silvery white below the lateral line. In some populations, vertical pale blue stripes can be seen on the flanks of a live fish, but they quickly disappear after death.

Black marlin have color phases—bronze and milky white—particularly in the waters around Taiwan, where the Chinese refer to it as the *pu-pi,* or white-skin fish. The Japanese, who transform more than 1 million pounds of black marlin into fish sausages each year, call these fish *shirokajiki,* which means white marlin. But no matter whether black is white, or vice versa, this marlin is one potent gamefish.

The pulse of the sea was slow that first morning we went

176

out at Piñas. Ray Smith felt that the action was over, but it's still a little early for even the bossman to know the rhythm of the local seasons. And Smith, who is the archetype of the big-game angler, and has a Texas sombrero full of tackle records (he fishes marlin with 12-pound-test), freely admits that he's still learning the where-and-when of Piñas Bay.

The very word *Panama* means "abundance of fish," and it takes several years to learn the habits of even one species with any certainty. It's apparent now that black marlin fishing is at its best from December through most of February, and sailfish are at their peak in July and August. We came in the between-time period, so Gilbert Drake and I hoped for the odd billfish and no more.

We could, and did, plug-cast for dolphin on the reefs, and we worked the rocky shores for corvina and snappers with leadheads, and took to the Jaqué River with flies. With artificials we collected odd species like the triggerfish—something we'd never seen done before. But mostly we went exploring in the countless bays and coves, hoping to find a snook called *Centropomus grandoculatus.* Our search proved fruitless, perhaps because of the season, the tides we fished, or the locations we selected. We did find a reef fifteen miles to the southeast that held not only an abundance of sailfish but small yellowfin tuna in the 20- to 30-pound class as well—fish that could be caught on plugging gear.

On our way out to the Zane Grey Reef the mate rigged a pair of 4- or 5-pound bonito New Zealand style with the hook in front. This bait size almost precludes the possibility of hooking a sailfish or a dolphin; however, both species would knock the chunky bonito from the outriggers once in a while—and make a gallant but futile attempt to swallow them.

Marlin fishing is a one-way street. To catch sailfish you must troll feathers or strip bait; at times the spindlebills hit the little jigs we trolled on a short handle to take bonito. The system of fishing for black marlin at Piñas Bay differs from that used at Cabo Blanco. For one thing, outriggers aren't necessary at Cabo. Here the best results are usually obtained by trolling in the boat's wake, and at Cabo it's primarily sight fishing. You can see those Peruvian giants finning at the surface, and although blind strikes occur from time to time, the opposite condition is true at Panama.

The bow of the *Babe Smith,* a 31-foot Moppie, dripped jewels in the rising sun. The mountains stood tall on the horizon, their brows cloud-covered and wrinkled with mahogany forests. The grumble of the surf had long since disappeared when we raised the first flock of booby birds about ten miles offshore. The boobies were screaming and diving at hordes of rainbow runners, which exploded and scattered like shrapnel before piercing the wall of a swell. The flashing emerald-and-yellow forms of dolphin bombed the baitfish from all angles. Great hammerheads and brown sharks feathered along the surface with their dorsals out—and it crossed my mind that a man could put a lot of time on one of these monsters, time that could be better spent on marlin. Although Captain Archie goosed the *Babe* whenever sharks showed behind our baits, they occasionally chopped our bonito in half, and twice took us out of action for almost an hour of grunting and sweating for no reason except to save the terminal tackle.

My marlin strike came in midafternoon. We had just washed down ham sandwiches with cold bottles of Balboa beer when the bill showed behind my bait. It was no crash strike. The line snapped out of the outriggers and I let it go away slowly, free-spooling with the click on. There was only the barest indication of a fish. Captain Archie put the *Babe* in neutral so we could wait and watch. For a long minute it seemed as though the black had dropped the bonito, but then the spool started to turn again and as it accelerated I threw the brake on while Captain Archie gave the *Babe* full throttle. We were off in a cloud of exhaust.

The marlin shot out of the sea a good ten feet into the air and fell back with a mountainous splash. A dozen jumps later the fish settled down to short runs punctuated with rhythmic thuds as he banged at the leader with his bill. He had two more jumps left before he wallowed to the transom in a creamy wake. It was all over in twenty-seven minutes. I told Archie before we even started that whatever we caught was to be released, so he grabbed the sandpaper bill (which is like holding a mule by the teeth) and yanked the hook free. Then we all stood around for a while puffing and staring at each other. It's easier to put a flying gaff in a marlin than to bill one for a release. An empty Balboa bottle rolled around on the deck.

On the way back to the club we stopped over an indigo reef for some plug casting. The shoreline around Piñas Bay is precipitous, sheering straight down to ten or fifteen fathoms, which makes plug fishing difficult. To find corvina, Captain Archie ran the boat among the jagged niggerheads, which were hidden one moment and bared like fangs the next by the retreating ground swell.

The idea was to cast at the rocks, then turn seaward with a fish in tow. The great tide in this area, which varies from twelve to twenty feet, according to season, creates such a suck of conflicting currents near rivermouths that at times an estuary can be hidden below the thundering surf.

One of the native guides elected to run the Jaqué River entrance with his piragua while we maneuvered the boat into the narrow rivermouth. He was swamped. Two Indians in their cockleshell *cayucos* came to his rescue through the pounding waves with such speed that the mahogany hulls fairly hissed across the surface. In the way of the jungle, even a remote catastrophe had an unblinked Morse. The Chocos had a line on the sinking piragua before the high-chined fishing boat could get on plane. And the Moppie is probably the swiftest hull afloat.

Club de Pesca has facilities as fine as a wilderness resort can offer. Beginning with your flight down on a Braniff 707 Jet or DC-7C out of Miami or Dallas, and with shuttle service via Grumman Mallard from the Tocumen airport to the club, the journey is smooth and comfortable. If you arrive at night in Panama, there's a modern motel that makes a good stopover until morning. The Mallard departs about 8:00 A.M., to assure clear weather and calm water for the fifty-minute flight to Piñas Bay. Thus, it's entirely possible to get a full day of fishing on the day you arrive.

The Braniff people have dispatched platoons of anglers

to the Smith headquarters, so even the desk people can keep you oriented. The resort itself consists of a spacious palm-frond–topped lodge and bar, and five separate duplex cottages that are scattered over a hillside banana grove facing the bay. The rates, and this should surprise, are $20 a day per person, including meals, and $90 a day for the boat. The boat tab has become virtually standard everywhere, and in some billfish ports is a bit higher, so the room and board charge represents a big buy when you add nature's largess to the Gulf of Panama.

The floating equipment of the club consists of eight brand-new diesel-powered boats, all equipped with fighting chairs, outriggers, flying gaffs, gin poles, two-way radio equipment, and depthometers. Their tackle is in the 50-pound- and 80-pound-test class, so it isn't necessary to bring along your own outfit unless you prefer lighter equipment.

The normal run to the Zane Grey Reef is less than an hour away, so you don't have to waste a lot of time getting to and from the fishing. All things considered, the Club de Pesca has been conceived with you in mind.

[1963]

23

Shedding Light on Shad

Although Atlantic-salmon restoration programs have gotten considerable publicity on northeastern rivers in recent years, the programs have also been aimed at other anadromous fish. So far, shad have been the real winners. The press for new fish ladders on the Connecticut River, for example, has resulted in excellent shad fishing as far upstream as Bellows Falls, Vermont, and even beyond. The Merrimack River in Massachusetts also now has excellent shad fishing. Connecticut's Enfield Dam, for decades the epicenter of northeastern shad fishing, has been increasingly eroded by spring floods, and the current hot spot is now farther upstream, below the dam at Holyoke, Massachusetts, on the Connecticut River.

About twenty years ago, as a very junior fisheries intern on my first summer job with Connecticut's Department of Environmental Protection, I spent the better part of a season seining shad from the big Connecticut, to be trucked around a tributary dam for a spawning habitat project. Invariably, a few were injured in the process, but the result was a happy one—

*ice-cold beer and chunks of smoked shad on a spring
evening, together with informal lessons on shad biology from Bob Jones, who eventually succeeded the
late Cole Wilde as Connecticut's Chief of Fisheries.*

According to legend, the shad arrives when the shadbush
blossoms in clusters of white flowers and a mottled brown
caddis, or "shadfly," emerges in great clouds to dance in a
warming sun. But unlike the ancient prophets, modern-day
computers hold an arcane finger in the wind and provide
statistics. Next month some 750,000 shad will appear in the
Connecticut River, according to Cole Wilde, the astute chief
of fisheries in the Nutmeg State, and with the benefit of conducive weather, it will be the largest and perhaps most productive run in the past five years. In terms of cycles, this
should mean that dozens of major shad streams all along the
coast will enjoy a similar bounty.

But go forewarned. Shad are notoriously susceptible to
changes in water level and temperature, and sometimes the
best angling is had when comparatively few fish are in the
river, and conversely, bank-to-bank schools can be totally
disinterested in a well-cast lure. The water may warm to just
the right range for taking fish, then a sudden cold snap
knocks the game dead. Or a late spring rain puts the river in
flood, and that wild action of yesterday becomes a muddied
memory. The angler works on a critical balance—measured
in Fahrenheit and cubic feet per second, a combination that
only the shad understands; but at least we can grope for the
principle.

Shad are members of the herring family. They are anadromous, like salmon, maturing in salt water and spawning
in fresh water. Essentially there are three species in the genus
Alosa that are of interest to fishermen—the American, or
white, shad, the hickory shad, and the Alabama shad. Related
species occur elsewhere in the world such as the Allis shad
of Europe and the hilsa of Southeast Asia, but the only sport
fishery of any consequence exists in the United States. The
American shad *(Alosa sapidissima)* is the largest member of
its genus and the most widely distributed on our continent.
This shad will average 3 to 5 pounds, and though fish of 13

pounds have been netted, the rod-and-reel record is 9 pounds, 2 ounces, from the Connecticut River. In the southern portion of its range the shad rarely attains 6 pounds in size, an environmental limitation predicated on ambient water temperatures.

All white shad are four to five years old when they appear on their first spawning run, and as many as 30 percent will become repeat spawners in rivers from Chesapeake Bay north—living eight to nine years. The biggest fish, of course, are the older second-time migrants and, in lesser numbers, those fish on their third or fourth spawning run. In recent years, of those fish authenticated to weigh 8 pounds or more, all were caught from the Wicomico River in Maryland, north to the Palmer River in Massachusetts. South of Cape Hatteras, postspawning survival is virtually unknown and the entire population dies after reproducing at the latitude of Florida's Saint Johns River. These deaths are correlated with energy demands at higher stream temperatures; adult shad, like the salmon, are nonfeeding fish while in fresh water. ' After a long migration and a tremendous loss in body weight, often as much as 40 percent, the fish simply lack the fat reserves to return to the ocean. In the colder northeastern rivers and those of the Pacific Coast, a substantial number of shad are able to make the downstream journey.

American shad are found from the Gulf of St. Lawrence to northern Florida, and on the Pacific side, from southern Alaska to southern California. The top Pacific Coast shad waters arc California's American, Russian, and Feather rivers. On the East Coast, popular white shad streams are Connecticut's Salmon, Scantic, Eight Mile, East, and Connecticut rivers; New York's Hudson and Delaware rivers; Maryland's Susquehanna, Gunpowder, Patuxent, and Middle rivers, and Octoraro and Deer creeks; Virginia's Pamunkey, York, Chickahominy, James, Appomattox, and Rappahannock rivers, and many small feeder streams of the James and York rivers; North Carolina's Cape Fear, Tar, Neuse, Pee Dee, and Roanoke rivers; South Carolina's Cooper, Edisto, and Combahee rivers; Georgia's Ogeechee, Satilla, and Altamaha rivers, and Florida's Saint Marys and Saint Johns.

The best time of the year to fish in any of these rivers

depends again on latitude. While at sea, shad remain offshore in deep water at a temperature range of 55 to 65 degrees, which causes the schools to travel in a northerly direction in spring and a southerly one in the fall. They have been caught by trawlers at distances over 100 miles from shore and at depths below 400 feet, so these movements occur over a wide area. When spawning time approaches and the colder coastal rivers begin to warm, the fish seek their natal waters, entering the currents at about 55 degrees.

Like salmon, they return to their "home" streams, oriented by light intensity and an olfactory ability to taste/smell the familiar chemical substances of individual rivers. In their extreme southerly range this is a reverse phenomenon, as rivers there normally run over 65 degrees throughout most of the year, so shad begin entering Florida's Saint Johns, for example, when the river becomes "cool" after the first chill winds of late November. Thus, the farther north the shad stream, the later its run begins. The peak migrations, when shad are most abundant, occur in the 62- to 67-degree temperature range. Broadly speaking, the best fishing is in January at the latitude of the Saint Johns, during May in Chesapeake tributaries north to Massachusetts, and in late June around the Gulf of Saint Lawrence. This has a parallel on the Pacific Coast where California's Feather River peaks in late May, while the Columbia River far to the north is shad-filled during the first week in July. Small "buck" shad dominate the earliest catches, with the percentage of roe, or female, shad increasing as the season continues to progress.

The second important shad is the hickory *(Alosa mediocris),* which is considerably smaller than the American shad and not as widely distributed. Hickory up to 5 pounds have been weighed, but they average 1 to 2 pounds, and a 3-pound fish is a trophy. Nevertheless, the hickory is a high-jumping acrobat when taken on light tackle. Although the hickory shad is found along the Atlantic Coast from Florida to the Bay of Fundy, it's common only in the mid-Atlantic states. The most productive waters would include the Susquehanna, Potomac, Maryland's Deer and Octoraro creeks, Choptank, Northeast, Patuxent, Pocomoke, and both the east and west

Wicomico rivers. The Pitchkettle and Grindle Creek are very popular in North Carolina.

In the thermal cycle of a season, hickories migrate into fresh water when the river temperature is 50 to 52 degrees, usually preceding the run of white shad by about two weeks. And unlike the larger species, which remains to spawn in the main stream, hickory shad prefer small tributaries. The migrations of the hickory are not wholly understood; those entering streams that drain into Pamlico Sound, for example, whereas the stocks coming into Chesapeake tributaries evidently reproduce in brackish water even though they densely school in what appears to be a spawning run. Nevertheless, the hickory shad invades much shallower water than does the white and provides excellent fly fishing. Invariably, you will get three or four jumps out of even a small hickory, and inch for inch, it's more spectacular than most freshwater gamefish. A 2-pound, 18-inch hickory is dynamite. In those rivers where the hickory occurs with the white shad, the two species are easily separated; the hickory has a long projecting lower jaw, while the American shad's lower lip is entirely enclosed in the upper jaw when the fish's mouth is closed.

The third shad species of any angling consequence is the Alabama shad *(Alosa alabamae).* This fish is smaller than the hickory, averaging ¾ to 1½ pounds. The Alabama shad is not widely distributed, being limited to Suwannee, Apalachicola, and Alabama river systems. There is no major sport fishery for this shad, and, in fact, it's so similar in appearance to the skipjack, or river herring *(Alosa chrysochloris),* which is abundant in these same waters, that most anglers assume that they've caught a large skipjack. The Alabama shad is taken mainly in the tailwaters of big impoundments on small jigs, and when you're casting a tandem rig, it's not unusual to catch them two at a time. However, as a gamefish it's not in the same league with the white and hickory.

Shad fishing with artificial flies is a very old game. Henry William Herbert, who wrote under the pseudonym Frank Forester, was already praising fly fishing for shad with a "powerful trout rod" in 1849. In northern rivers, shad fishing is most productive early in the morning and again in the evening rather than during bright, daylight hours. The fish seem to be inspired by dank weather, and a light spring drizzle will often provide a full day of taking shad. This is particularly true of the hickory, which is inclined to quit when light intensity reaches the sunglasses stage. But for whatever this rule is worth to a Yankee fisherman, the southern shad strikes freely in bright light. Slightly turbid water is a plus, as opposed to clear or muddy water.

Fly fishing is most effective in small, shallow streams. It is possible to take a shad with flies from big, deep rivers such as the Susquehanna, Connecticut, or Saint Johns, but you need normal to below-normal water levels and the ability to handle long casts with a fast-sinking line. By fast-sinking, I mean "instantly," as shad hold bottom in ten to twenty feet of water. Although small streams may have fewer shad available for that reason, you will often find long stretches where a fly can be presented in a proper swim. Even here shad prefer the deeper pools, and wet patterns must invariably be bounced on the gravel to produce any number of fish. I don't know of another area where shad are caught on dry flies (although I'm sure it exists), but at times the upper Delaware offers excellent surface fishing. I've enjoyed some fast action in the late season, particularly when flying ants appeared on the river. Every rule seems to have an exception, and while white shad are essentially a nonfeeding fish in fresh water, they will suddenly sample floating insects in a general rise. As a matter of fact, two of the larger Delaware shad that I've scored on in recent years came to a dry pattern while casting for trout.

From a practical standpoint, big rivers, which hold the main body of fish, are invariably crowded with boat traffic and shore-based spin casters, lending a festive air to the occasion, but it does make fly fishing difficult at times. This brings to mind a trip that Fred Cushing and I made several years ago to the Saint Johns. Fred is a New York–based publisher and a "nut" fly fisherman. After striking out on Florida bass fishing due to a prolonged northeaster, we decided to try for shad; the falling thermometer had sent a silvery horde upriver. We launched our skiff at Sanford, which is located on Lake Monroe just two miles north of where the Saint Johns enters. The river from Lake Monroe south is better known as largemouth-bass water, but it's also a prime spawning ground for the white shad. There are small islands and sharp bends in the river, long sloping sandbar shoals, and endless grass beds. It follows a serpentine path all the way to Lake Harney, and in its faster sections the shad mass for courtship. Although most Saint Johns anglers use spinning tackle and troll for their shad, Fred and I anchored near shore and went to work with our fly rods. Nothing happened for the first half-hour, and the fleet of patrolling boats seemed to be working over one spot some distance away. Then I hooked a shad.

My fish made one wild jump, which probably sounded a general alarm, because Fred hooked another shad, which ran across my line, and before we could maneuver ourselves free, a small armada descended on us. Fred's shad soon fouled in somebody's lead-core trolling line, while my fish ran under another boat and was promptly netted by a very kind old gentleman in a plaid shirt. In spite of the confusion, both shad ended in our live well.

Throughout the rest of the day we caught fish by anchoring over sandbars and drifting our flies. But at times it was like watching an accident about to happen, as we had a number of double hookups, and even 2- to 3-pound shad can't be steered to net very quickly. Among other things, these fish have "paper" mouths, and a hook will tear free if you apply too much pressure. A gentle hand is the rule regardless of size. Not all shad jump, either in southern or northern rivers, and certainly the larger Yankee fish taken in faster currents provide more sustained play, but frequently you'll hook one that rockets skyward or even greyhounds across the surface. Shad often hang broadside in running water and a 3-pounder can give the illusion of weighing twice its size in a strong flow.

The fly rod for shad should be 8½ or 9 feet long and calibered for a #8 line. It has to be powerful enough to handle a sinking line on long casts. Remember, also, that shad are relatively large fish and extremely strong. Because the fly must be worked deep, the standard approach is to cast quartering upstream. The fly, ticking the pebbles, drifts down with the current. Occasionally short twitches or jerks should be imparted to the fly, especially when it swings wide in the current at the end of a drift. It's important to keep a taut line. With any appreciable amount of slack it's difficult to detect a strike, which is usually nothing more than a light tap and sometimes repetitive taps. If the current isn't running too fast, you may be able to work a school from the upstream side by making a short cast, then paying out line to ease the fly back among the fish. When it drifts near the shad, gently raise and lower your rod tip to impart an enticing action in the fly.

Shad can be fussy about patterns at times, preferring one color to another, but as a rule white or yellow are reliable in a sparsely tied wing with Mylar strips for flash when dressed on #2, #4, and #6 long-shank hooks. Some anglers use conventional streamers such as the Black Ghost or White Marabou, and many Western anglers take shad on their standard steelhead patterns. I've often found the little hickory more selective than the white shad. For hickories the hook size should be somewhat smaller, preferably #6, #8, and #10. The important thing really is *where* the fly is fished; it has to swim at shad level; not 2 or 3 feet over their heads. I am a long-leader exponent for most kinds of fly fishing, but a 7½- to no more than 8-foot length is much more effective, as the fly will sink quicker. This should be tapered to a 6- or 8-pound-test tippet.

Spinning tackle is by all odds the most popular gear for shad fishing. A 6½-foot rod calibered for 6- or 8-pound-test monofilament line is the standard-bearer, although more and more anglers have been flirting with lighter equipment in recent years, using 4-pound-test line; this refinement is not only sporting, but the wispy line helps to sink tiny baits fast, an advantage when seeking bottom-hugging fish. When cast across and upstream, the lure swings down over gravel, and despite the occasional hangup, it puts the bait where white shad hold. These fish follow the channels, so deep fishing is the name of the game. However, light tackle is not practical everywhere; in the swift water below Enfield Dam on the Connecticut River, for example, where large shad are a possibility (10-pounders are *not* rare and a 12-pound shad was taken by commercial net) the chance of success with 4-pound test is slim indeed. So line test should be matched to prevailing conditions. Three basic lures are widely used: a small silver spoon, a thumbnail-size spinner, and the "shad dart," a leadhead offspring of the venerable Quimby Minnow. More shad are probably caught on red-and-white darts than any other lure, but the popularity of baits is cyclic among fish and fishermen, and it pays to stock some metal teasers.

Between now and the end of May there will be many shad derbies along the Eastern Seaboard. These gala occasions usually include parades, canoe races, a fishing contest, and the inevitable crowning of "Miss Shad Festival." This has been a spring ritual since before the arrival of the white man on these shores. The culmination of such social events is, of course, a shad cookout. The chief reason most people go shad fishing is to enjoy them at table. In this respect the female shad is more desirable than the buck, not only for its roe but also because it's a larger, fatter fish. There is a great similarity in flavor and texture between shad and bonefish, incidentally. But it's the roe of both the white shad and the hickory that really becomes a gourmet item when fried crispy brown and splashed with lemon. Even canned roes are now astronomically priced in supermarkets, so the angling dividend is considerable. When selecting fish for the stringer, it's easy to distinguish a roe shad; the vent of the female is reddish and protrudes slightly, whereas the vent of the male is white and does not protrude.

[1959]

24

What the Bonefish Eats

There is relatively little current information in print on bonefishing, which creates a real problem for the growing number of fishermen taking up the sport. Bonefishing, especially with a fly, is in my own limited experience every bit as subtle and demanding as the most difficult brown trout, if not more so. Certainly I, like most people, need all the help I can get.

Given the relative scarcity of good information, the following chapter is worth its weight in airline tickets to any bonefisherman—neophyte or otherwise. Can bonefish be selective? They certainly were last spring, when McClane and I fished together at Deep Water Cay, where some of the area's big bones set my teeth to grinding with refusals to my flies. At least some of the answers as to what next are in this story.

Anyone who has mucked the bonefish flats until his toenails curled has experienced one of those rare days when he could do no wrong. Tails and dorsals seemingly beckoned forever in that dimensionless glare of sky and water—a theater so hushed that you could hear a coconut drop on some distant island. But every good cast shattered the mirrored silence as your fly line went swishing away in a great curving spray with an audible *bump* at the backing. The bonefish accelerated faster and faster, running to infinity. By sundown it had all been so easy. It was just a matter of how long your wrist held out. On the very next day, at the perfect tide, bonefish swam over, under, and around the fly, leaving it rocking in their wake.

In one ego-deflating morning, while wading the Big Mangrove flat near Deep Water Cay, I cast to eleven bonefish without provoking a strike. On the following day I released sixteen fish—a score that I haven't equaled since in Bahamian waters. I don't know what was wrong in the first instance, or what I did right in the second. After thirty years of pursuing an enigma, I have more questions than answers. Trophy bonefish, over 12 pounds, always elude me, for one reason or another, and their behavior is no less erratic. My last hookup at Chub Cay was pure burlesque.

Austin Pinder was poling us slowly across a mangrove-studded flat. I stood ready in the bow with shooting line coiled at my feet. After a futile morning without a target in sight, I turned to ask him about lunch, and there, not thirty feet behind our stern, was one of the biggest bonefish I've ever seen, following the puffs of marl made by his pushpole. Reflexively, I slapped my fly on the water. That fish took it in a gulp and kept right on swimming. I struck hard several times as the chrome-plated specter slowly finned past our skiff. It was long seconds before the fish responded, then my line knifed through the water, singing like a cable in the wind, followed by 200 yards of backing. I was certain the fish would come to a halt but it didn't, and when the spool was bare my rod bucked in an agonizing arc. The fly popped out. We could still see that bonefish pushing water for another hundred yards or so before it disappeared. Austin said it would have gone 14 pounds—easy.

Why a fish with at least twelve years of predator experience suddenly acts like the village idiot is no less explicable than the countless times a craftily worked fly is refused. You can make a perfect cast to an incoming tailer—the easiest shot in the book—and see the fish swim up to the fly, then turn away. You give the fly a few more inchy twitches and the fish circles back again, head down like a bull with his tail working jerkily as he gets ready to pounce. Pause and twitch. The bonefish follows, nose to feathers, as you ease the fly enticingly over the bottom. And there you crouch, shorts in the water, with sweaty armpits and steamed Polaroids wondering what the hell is wrong. Finally, the fish turns away, again uncertain, then bolts off the flat in a sudden terror as though he recognized a bomb with a burning fuse. If this happens often enough—and Lord knows it does—you are forced to the conundrum. Can bonefish be selective? If so, to what degree and what are the parameters?

One of the more revealing physical features of the highly specialized bonefish and perhaps the key to what I am about to set down is its adipose eyelid. It doesn't have a naked eyeball like a trout or bass. If you run your hand over the head of a bonefish, you will find that its eyes are protected behind a smoothly tough transparent sheath, a sort of face mask. There is a tiny pinprick opening centered over the pupil. A bonefish can literally bury its head in sand without being blinded and when "mudding," its vision is not critically obscured by sediment. Some scientists have postulated that the same fatty tissue polarizes light, thus accounting for its keen eyesight. There are comparatively few other species having an adipose eyelid; it is modified in the mullet (another mudding fish) with a vertically elliptical opening at the pupil. It also appears on a few swift-swimming species such as the wahoo and jack crevalle. Hydrodynamically, the sheath reduces water turbulence around the eyes when swimming at maximum speed. The unerring aim of a wahoo leaping at a trolled bait in a rough sea is awesome. I once saw a wahoo nail a 3-inch-long nylon jig that was accidentally left astern when the boat was roostertailing at twenty-five knots. Bonefish may tolerate an angler's presence, even taking a fly almost at his feet, but its adipose eyelid suggests that sight is not an albulian problem.

There has been very little spadework done on imitative fly patterns for bonefish. True, effective dressings exist but as in trout fishing—no single pattern will produce day after day, in all seasons and all regions. Generally speaking, we know that bonefish feed actively in the brightest sun and calm water at temperatures from 75 degrees to 88 degrees. In the 69- to 74-degree range you will see a few to many fish with their number and activity progressively increasing as the water approaches 74 degrees. Below 68 degrees (the temperature at which corals cease to grow and within the definition of a tropical sea), bonefish disappear from the intertidal zone. Chilling water, strong winds, and an overcast can produce good trout fishing from the Beaver Kill to the Madison, but it's a negative condition on the flats. Most bonefish foods are invisible to the angler. They are mainly discrete or burrowing animals that the fish must flush or root out. School-oriented, bonefish advance in a loose aggregate, poking, digging, and blowing their food free. A bonefish "breathes" in normal fish fashion by drawing water into its mouth, then closing it while contracting the gill arches and raising the rear edge of its operculum, which forces water through slits between the oxygen-absorbing gill filaments. But when a bonefish suspects the presence of a crustacean, worm, or mollusk, hiding just under the substrate, it instantly reverses the flow by a powerful adduction of its gill covers and jets a stream of water from its mouth and exposes the food. A foraging school leaves a telltale trail of excavated sand on the bottom where the bluish-gray marl has been disturbed. In a lush pasture, individual bonefish may spook a number of crustaceans simultaneously, which escape for a short distance in panicked flight and gradually the school scatters. Their feeding is a leisurely process when compared to a bluefish or striped bass school, for example, so we must assume that shape, size, movement, and color of various food forms are critical factors in angling success. All shallow-water fishes have developed color vision; they can distinguish twenty-four different narrow spectral hues. The bonefish is a hunter when stalking the flats. In human terms, he is not unlike a reflexively conditioned bird shooter walking through a cornfield, who responds to the sudden flight of an anticipated target. The man doesn't actually see his prey in detail, yet he instantly separates by color, a hen from a cock pheasant or any other kind of bird that may be smaller, larger, faster, slower. The brain accepts or rejects the target before it is even in focus.

For sheer gustatory enthusiasm, the bonefish is in a class

by itself. Equipped with powerful clam-busting pharyngeal teeth on its tongue and palate, it's an ultimate predator with a smorgasbord complex. In addition to bivalve and gastropod mollusks, such as Venus clams, nut clams, ark clams, pectens, cockles, tellins, turbans, marginellas, cone shells, limpets, olive shells, snails, and tulip conch—I have found squid, spiny lobster, mantis and snapping shrimp, swimming and grass shrimp, spider crabs, numerous swimming, walking, and mud crabs, cusk and snake eels, sea horses, sea anemones, annelid worms, brittle stars, sea urchins, and the remains of various fishes in bonefish stomachs. This is only a partial list. However, the number of foods that we can suggest or imitate with an artificial fly is limited.

A dominant forage by frequency, among Florida and Bahamian bonefish, is the banded snapping shrimp. This burrowing crustacean of the family Alpheidae looks like a tiny lobster with one large claw. When disturbed, it makes a sound like one of those "crickets" that kids used to bring to school It's a metallic *click,* not loud but puzzling if you happen to be wading where these crustaceans are abundant. For a moment it may sound as if you're standing in a bowl of Rice Krispies. The noise is made by the shrimp's wrist joint. Just the sound of water lapping against a skiff can send bonefish running off a flat, so the audible snapping shrimp must be an easy prey. These alpheids have a light brown or orange-brown body banded on black, but some species are white, banded in greenish brown. Most of those I've found in bonefish stomachs are about 2 inches in length. Snapping shrimp dart rapidly in a few short bursts before hiding again, and I suspect that when bonefish tail in quick starts and stops—this is what they are feeding on.

Another favorite food of bonefish is the mantis shrimp. It doesn't resemble a shrimp at all but looks like a freshwater hellgrammite with a fan-shaped tail. Mantis are members of the order Stomatopoda, encompassing about 200 species. In our waters, the false mantis, which are pea green to dark green in color, with seven thoracic segments, each edged in bright yellow are most common. Those that I find in bonefish stomachs are usually 2 to 3 inches long. Some of the larger mantis or squillids may exceed a foot in length (if you plan to collect any, beware, as they are armed with multitoothed raptorial claws and are painfully known as "thumb busters"). A dark green Woolly Worm palmered with yellow hackle makes a workable imitation. Mantis are burrowers and not as active as snapping shrimp. Fish the artificial dead, or in very short pulls.

The swimming shrimp family, Penaeidae, is the one most anglers are familiar with, when found on a leaf of iceberg lettuce awash in a cocktail sauce. There are three common penaeids in Florida waters, the so-called pink shrimp, pink-spotted shrimp, and the brown shrimp. While the traditional Pink Shrimp fly pattern is effective at times, especially in dim light over weedy bottoms, it's probably fished more than most dressings and wins an occasional hurrah by sheer popularity. It's a poor imitation at best. Color is a geographical character-istic among different shrimp populations. The pink species is most often light brown to reddish brown and may even be lemon yellow; those in the Tortugas area achieve a "rosy" tone with reddish-brown marking. Except for the sea bob, which turns black, shrimp become pink only after death. The pink-spotted shrimp differs in having a prominent reddish-brown spot on both sides of the tail. And the brown shrimp is reddish brown suffused with blue or purple on the tail and legs. In living color then, penaeids are dominantly brown, and basic brown mixed with some other shade is in my experience most effective. These shrimp are uncommon in the highly saline environments of the Bahamas, where smaller "grass" shrimps of the families Palaemonidae and Hippolytidae are abundant. Grass shrimp are more slender, usually 1 to 2 inches in length and are a translucent brown, gray, green, blue, or lavender with minute dark spots. One species, the red-backed cleaning shrimp, resembles the Mickey Finn fly pattern with a bright yellow body and a band of scarlet.

I have caught several large bonefish in years past while casting for barracuda with a top-water plug, and in fact the camp record at Deep Water Cay of 14 pounds was taken on a ⅝-ounce Heddon Zaragasso. This lure could hardly suggest anything but a fish. Nevertheless, plugs are seldom attractive to bonefish. In stomach samples, vertebrate food forms rank extremely low numerically, considering the large abundance of small fishes available on most flats. It appears that bonefish are piscivorous by chance or necessity, rather than choice. One can discount the popular Cayman Island method of chumming with anchovies or sardines. Chumming with any food form simply creates an abnormal condition—effective though it may be—which doesn't reflect food habits. In both seine and rotenone collections that I made in isolated tide pools over a three-year period, the numerical abundance of vertebrates has always been high, but compared to stomach contents low. The exceptions are the snake eel and cusk eel, which are minor in occurrence yet frequent in stomach count, suggesting a preferred food. While a typical fishlike streamer has never been especially productive for me, a long, thin eellike dressing is often very effective; this may also suggest many marine worms.

Among the brightly colored bonefish food are the segmented worms or annelids of the class Polychaeta. The polychaetes of flats importance are mainly burrowing forms found in sand, marl, and coral crevices. Some species are blue or brown in color and others are iridescent red or orange. These worms emerge partially or wholly from their dens when searching for food. One polychaete, which is common to the Florida Keys, known as the palolo worm, creates a feeding orgy even among tarpon during its brief breeding period when the worms swarm near the surface. Actually, the swarm does not consist of whole palolo worms but individual segments from their posterior ends called epitokes. This segment breaks off and swims to the surface where it literally explodes and releases its eggs or sperm. The mass epitoke phenomenon is triggered by warming water temperatures near the end of May and the beginning of June within three days of a full or new moon tide. A "hatch" may occur as early as April and into July at other locations in the extremes of its Western Atlantic range. It occurs in November and December in the South Pacific. The palolo epitoke is comparable to the trout angler's Green Drake in stirring fish to feed, and both bonefish and tarpon can become extremely selective as these hatches progress. Palolo worms attain a length of 2 feet or more, but the epitokes are only 2 to 4 inches in length.

There are four basic food forms in the bonefish's diet, which fall within the scope of artificial flies: these are shrimp-like, eel- or wormlike, fishlike, or crablike in shape. In a broad sense, the distinction is comparable to the mayfly, stonefly, caddis, and minnow categories of freshwater fishing. An effective crab imitation has long been a challenge to fly tiers, largely because of the permit, a fish that has a demonstrable preference for these crustaceans as opposed to shrimp. Even a live shrimp makes a lousy bait for permit. Back in the 1950s, that celebrated permit specialist, Johnny Cass, was experimenting with a variety of crab patterns and when I last fished with him several years ago, he still hadn't found one that worked. He even had a trimmed deer-hair dressing that looked like a natural, right down to the claws. It's probable that some flies and certainly leadhead jigs simulate crabs by the way they are retrieved, scuttling over the bottom. A parallel can be found in South American trout fishing where freshwater crabs *(Aegla spp.)* are an abundant food form and greatly resemble many small marine species, which are the size of a quarter. A fatly dressed Muddler fished in short, quick jerks is concomitant to Andean rivers. Not surprisingly, the Muddler is an excellent bonefish pattern and has taken its share of permit.

A Paramachene Belle syndrome exists in saltwater fly fishing as red, white, and pink clearly dominate every catalog and seaside tackle shop. This is grossly magnified by the tendency to use large flies, in the 0 sizes, an extravagance that has its roots in the "big is best" concept of marine angling. In my experience, the effective range is from #2 to #10. Considering the fact that a great percentage of bonefish foods are only 1 to 2 inches long, it pays to use small dressings, especially when you are in a run of refusals. A #6 fly with a 1¼- to 1½-inch wing is a reliable standard.

The following ten patterns are my guidelines for "shrimp" imitations. Chico Fernandez, who ties these flies commercially (11450 S.W. 98th Street, Miami, Florida 33176, telephone 305-596-4481), uses light-reflecting polypropylene to get a wing and dubbed body of just the right intensity. Whether you prefer an upright wing, inverted wing, Keel hook, hackle or no-hackle design, the suggested colors and sizes represent these important bonefish foods. The Banded Snapping Shrimp pattern accounted for more than a thousand released last season according to Chico, so maybe it's time to bring order to the disorderly world of *Albula vulpes*.

BANDED SNAPPING SHRIMP
(Alpheus armillatus)

HOOK: #6
HACKLE: Brown
WING: Orange, brown, 5–6 black bands, 1½ inches long
HEAD: Orange
BODY: Brown

BROWN SNAPPING SHRIMP
(Alpheus armatus)

HOOK: #6
HACKLE: Mottled brown and tan
WING: Light brown, red underwing, 1½ inches long
HEAD: Tan
BODY: Brown
BUTT: Bright red

YELLOW SNAPPING SHRIMP
(Synalpheus brevicarpus)

HOOK: #6
HACKLE: Yellow
WING: Mixed green and yellow, 1½ inches long
HEAD: Red
BODY: Yellow

GREEN MANTIS
(Gonodactylus oeratidii)

HOOK: #4
HACKLE: Green
WING: Dark green, 2 inches long
HEAD: Emerald green
BODY: Pale blue

GOLDEN MANTIS
(Pseudosquilla ciliata)

HOOK: #4
HACKLE: Yellow
WING: Golden yellow, green spots
HEAD: Emerald green
BODY: Pale green

PINK SWIMMING SHRIMP
(Penaeus duorarum)

HOOK: #2
HACKLE: Mottled brown and pink
WING: Dark brown, pink underwing, 2¼ inches long
HEAD: Brown
BODY: Pink

BROWN SWIMMING SHRIMP
(Penaeus aztecus)

HOOK: #2
HACKLE: Mottled tan and purple
WING: Reddish brown, pale blue underwing, 2¼ inches long
HEAD: Brown
BODY: Beige

GRASS SHRIMP
(Tozeuma carolinensis)

HOOK: #8
HACKLE: Pale blue
WING: Dark blue, pale blue underwing, 1 inch long
HEAD: Black
BODY: Pale green
BUTT: None

NOTE: Standard hook 2X stout, 1X improved Sproat; also, hackle not necessary when tying inverted dressings, but should be used in conventional wing styles.

BUMBLEBEE SHRIMP
(Gnathophyllum americanum)

HOOK: #6
HACKLE: None
WING: Underwing brown bucktail or synthetic hair, overwing 2 grizzly hackles dyed brown
HEAD: Brown
BODY: Dubbed brown and yellow bands

CUSK EEL
(Parophidion schmidti)

HOOK: #4 Keel
HACKLE: None
WING: Brown with yellow below, 3½ inches long
HEAD: Brown
BODY: Beige chenille

Chico Fernandez tells me the Bumblebee Shrimp pattern took some unusually large fish after the last Islamorada Bonefish Tournament (won three times by the Banded Snapping Shrimp pattern). I have found only a few bumblebee naturals in stomachs, but have an idea that has to do with my limited sampling, rather than the frequency of occurrence. They are difficult to collect, as they live in grassy areas where sea urchins are numerous. The bumblebee feeds on the tube feet of urchins, a neat trick in itself. In any case, this suggests the kind of bottom where the pattern might be most effective.

[1981]

25

Spotted Seatrout

Fly fishing for southern seatrout is just one of several successful methods described here by McClane for the South's most popular marine gamefish. Most people with whom I visit assume this method to be relatively new to tidewater, but intrepid fly rodders have been taking seatrout (and other fish) around Florida and the Gulf Coast for at least a hundred years and perhaps longer.

In 1876, Forest and Stream carried a report by one angler of catching several species—including seatrout—on flies in Florida's Homosassa region. And no less an authority than Dr. James Henshall, best known for his writings on bass fishing, noted his capture of a 10-pound seatrout on a fly in 1878, also in Florida waters. In one hundred years, however, the fun hasn't diminished one bit. There are still 10-pounders (and larger) waiting to be caught, and in this particular story McClane offers some tactics especially for the big ones.

Spotted seatrout are not smart in the clever way of a snook, although a big one will get behind your plug forty yards out and come back with the retrieve, making halfhearted passes at the lure, then stop at boatside and stare at you before wandering off to contemplate a crab hole. The trout doesn't have the wild speed of a bonefish or the endurance of a jack or the acrobatic bent of a tarpon of equal size—about all he'll do with any style is splash and throw his head and tail out of the water. On the other hand, you don't have to be a genius to catch seatrout, at least modest-size ones, on any kind of tackle, which is a noble attribute. And few seafoods can match this delectable member of the drum family at the table. Best of all, trout are abundant inshore throughout a long season, offering plenty of opportunity for the beginner to hone his skills on live targets. In every creel count *Cynoscion nebulosus* is our number-one species in southern U.S. marine angling—a status that cannot be denied.

Spotted seatrout belong to the same genus as our northern weakfish or "gray trout," the silver seatrout, sand seatrout, the California white seabass, and corvinas of the Pacific. The range of seatrout and weakfish overlap to a large extent, but the two fish are easy to distinguish; both are marked with black or bronze spots, but on weakfish these are small and appear as undulating streaks that run downward and forward along its back. The spots on a seatrout, however, are large and distinct, providing the fish's most common name, "speckled trout." These spots become less prominent with age and almost disappear on fish of 10 pounds or more. Both species take artificial lures as well as live baits, and they can be rated on a par as gamefish. The real difference lies in their respective habitats, as our southern trout is essentially a very shallow water fish compared to the northern tide-runner. I have caught trout in the 10-pound class in little more than a foot of water, and early one dawn my partner Ed Reddy took a 13-pounder off our favorite oyster bar that was just wet enough to float the fish. That trout humped the surface like a small whale as he poked among the shells. Stalking these spotted monsters can be a kind of excitement in itself, especially on a dead-calm morning when the tide is sucking out and finger mullet gather in holes, which become seething caldrons of food for needle-toothed predators.

Seatrout are sensitive to temperature extremes. They prefer water in the mid-sixty– to mid-seventy–degree range, which probably explains why the best angling occurs in late spring and fall throughout much of the fish's range. During severely cold weather they will move offshore to warmer depths, but sometimes a sharp temperature drop can cause a cold-kill among populations that lingered inshore, leaving thousands and periodically millions of dead fish floating on the surface. Normally, as the water temperature drops, trout in the mid-Atlantic region, for example, will congregate in "holes" and continue to feed. Some of the best fishing along the Core Banks in North Carolina occurs in the winter months from November into February when big schools crowd in deep pockets along the beach. It's not unusual for a late-season angler to take thirty or forty trout with spin gear and small lures from a very small area. Hot summer temperatures have a similar effect in more southerly regions, although the schools will move inshore at night to feed. Much of this fishing is done from causeways and bridges by drifting a live shrimp, needlefish, or small mullet with the tide. Ordinarily, night fishing is best during a flowing tide. It doesn't seem to matter whether it's flooding or ebbing, so long as it's moving. In my experience, however, the very best time for big trout is from first light until about 8:00 A.M. and on a falling tide from two hours before the change to one hour after. Ideally, this should be in a period from the new to the full moon, but it's worth checking elsewhere.

Trout can be highly selective at times, especially when the schools concentrate to feed on shrimp. These crustaceans drift with the tide just under the surface, and the fish make a distinctive splash and "popping" sound as they gobble the shrimp. In calm water this activity is accompanied by rapid, wavy movements on the surface, and there's seldom any mistaking the situation, as trout will boil behind a plug again and again without touching it. They are obviously attracted by the mouth of the lure, which probably suggests another feeding fish. This response is so well known that commercial fishermen sometimes use with deadly effect a "splash pole" or long cane pole with a noise-making bobber rigged just over a shrimp bait. There are many rough-bottomed banks where stop nets or haul seines can't be used by market fishermen, so the practice is an ancient art. However, don't be misled. There are two schools of thought about catching *big* trout with artificials and it's important to understand both.

Many years ago, in fact it was probably my first trip for seatrout, I fished with Ray Harmon at Marco Island in the Ten Thousand Islands area. After a very slow morning with a few fish striking short and boiling under an assortment of top-water plugs, we arrived at an enormous turtlegrass bed. Our skiff was drifting slowly with the tide, and occasionally we could see or hear trout feeding.

"Why don't you try a stinger rig?"

"A what?" I asked.

"A stinger rig. Get one of those streamer flies out of your box and tie it behind that popping plug. Knot about a foot of monofilament to the plug hook, then fasten on the fly."

"What'll that do?"

"More than you're doing now, that's for sure!"

I made the stinger rig as instructed (although I later discovered that 6 inches of stiff 20-pound-test monofilament is better because it is less likely to tangle) and flipped a long cast over the grass bed. After the plug sat for a moment, I began a slow swim-and-pause retrieve, as though I was fishing for bigmouth bass.

"Not that way," Ray admonished. "Get some speed in it. Kick up a fuss until we locate a school."

I cast and cranked eight or ten fast runs over the grass before a trout boiled behind the plug. Then my line tightened as the fish grabbed the streamer fly. A few minutes later I boated a 2-pounder; in the next hour, trout after trout smacked the bucktail teaser after chasing my plug. Several of these fish weighed about 4 pounds. Ray explained that while noise attracts the trout, there are occasions when they will only hit a small lure, too small to make a proper disturbance. This made sense and in fact the stinger rig is an old reliable in the Gulf angler's bag of tricks. But it wouldn't earn you a banana on Banana River, no less a trophy. Let's talk about *big* trout, and this begins with their distribution.

Spotted seatrout are found along the Gulf Coast states, Florida, and up the Eastern Seaboard to Chesapeake Bay, sometimes straying as far north as New York. There's excellent fishing to be had along the coasts of Alabama, Mississippi, Louisiana, and Texas. The Chandeleur Islands, located about 30 miles off Louisiana's southeast coast, are well known for their extraordinary seatrout fishing, particularly for fly rodders. The Texas coast has many miles of prime spotted seatrout shallows. San Luis Pass, at the lower end of Galveston Island, is a top spot for wading anglers, as is the 100-mile-long baylike Laguna Madre. Other fine seatrout areas include Georgia's Cumberland, Saint Andrew, Altamaha, and Ossabaw Sound; Saint Helen South and North Carolina's Pamlico and Core sounds, the tidal marsh areas of the Cape Fear and Newport rivers; and the eastern backwater areas of the Chesapeake Bay in Virginia and Maryland. But year after year the largest fish are taken on the east coast of Florida, particularly around Cocoa, Melbourne, Vero Beach, and south to Fort Pierce. Here, seatrout of 5 pounds are common, 8- to 10-pounders are not unusual, and the world's record of 15 pounds, 3 ounces was taken in this vicinity.

Over on the west coast, 800-square-mile Florida Bay produces consistently good results, but the average fish is small. Actually, there is more angling along the Gulf in a miles-available sense, but for a trophy trout I'd select the Indian or Banana rivers on the Atlantic side. Tagging studies indicate that seatrout populations do not make extensive migrations, so areas where large fish occur are likely to produce quality catches with regularity. In a three-year period at Pine Island, Florida, where 2,538 fish were tagged and 271 recovered, only 1 trout had moved more than thirty miles. In a subsequent study, 5,409 were tagged in two weeks and the recoveries during the next four months totaled 1,349 trout, or almost 25 percent—a very high return.

Spinning tackle is by far the most popular gear for seatrout. Bait casting is just as effective, and indeed for callused thumbs the multiplier has no peer; but in either case, you have to be able to make *long* casts. Don't underestimate the virtue of distance on the flats. Big trout will often follow a plug all the way back to your rod tip before striking. They are notorious window-shoppers, and the longer they have to boil and make passes behind a bait, the more fish you'll catch. A standard 5½-foot bait-casting rod or a 6½-foot spinning rod designed for ¼- to ⅝-ounce baits is ideal. A freshwater-size reel spooled with 8-pound-test monofilament on the spin stick and 10-pound-test line with the multiplier is most effective. For lures, you should stock small spoons in the ¼-ounce size, plastic shrimp, bucktail jigs, and darter and popping plugs. But above all, for big trout, you need a quiet swimmer. Among specialists like Gary Bennett, Reuben Hill, Dick Jones on the Indian River, and Charlie Urban, the rule is "no noise." If you want to watch 2- and 3-pounders, you can make all the fuss you want. Otherwise play it quiet. The eight-, nine-, and ten-year-old trout, or those in trophy sizes, don't feed in schools for the obvious reasons that there aren't many survivors in an old age group. They not only become more wary, but also shy away from the company of smaller trout in the search for food. According to local lore, the heaviest fish are more or less solitary hunters, and my experience indicates that it's true. Noise seems to make these trophy-size trout suspicious rather than arouse their interest.

When big ones are feeding, you can take a fair number by covering a wide area, but like brother Reddy's 13-pounder, these are individual targets, and far more cautious. Charlie Urban scored three 6-pounders, an 8-, a 10-, and an 11-pounder during one tide in the Banana River on an actionless plug—one that comes straight back in the water without wiggling—by stalking surface-cruising singles. The most popular pattern is a needlefish design in green and silver, a slow sinker that can be teased along in spasmodic jerks or left to swim deeper over lush pastures. Another old reliable is a fatter bait that resembles a mullet, but the only action permissible is a bobbing motion imparted by smooth strokes of the rod tip. It doesn't make a sound. Many old-timers who fancy the shape of a new plug's body even remove the metal or plastic lips, which the manufacturer artfully designed—devices to be spurned in the citadel of troutdom.

Seatrout are usually caught by fishing from small boats,

by wading, and in some areas just by walking along a river-bank or beach. There are many places in the Cocoa–to–Fort Pierce area where you only have to drive your car to the waterside and start wading. Gary Bennett and I drove over to Sykes Creek one morning and, before sitting down to breakfast, we took half a dozen nice trout, including two that bettered 8 pounds, on needlefish plugs. We didn't even get our knees wet. Of course, fishing from a skiff covers more area and the usual procedure is to drift with the wind, making blind casts until you locate trout. Then, you can anchor and work the spot thoroughly—or if the bottom is firm, get out and wade. During cold weather, especially in the Gulf, trout move farther offshore and may be found at 10- to 20-foot depths, but here again, the fish are usually first pin-pointed by drifting before dropping anchor. Some of our fishing is done on deep tidal creeks (a population of spotted seatrout thrives in the fresh water of the Saint Johns River), which is not so much a game of blind casting as knowing the areas trout frequent. One east coast river that Ed Reddy and I have fished for many years is typical; there are certain shell beds, points, grass patches, and mangrove islands that season after season produce trout, and these are widely scattered over eight to ten miles of stream. Places that look identical in between the hot spots never hold trout. There are tarpon, ladyfish, snook, jack crevalle, and sometimes bluefish at various locations, but the trout, which are large and rarely abundant, have their own cafeterias. Creeks of this kind are great for fly casting during blowy winter months when shallow bays get churned up by chill winds.

Seatrout fishing doesn't require specialized fly tackle. Any standard bass-bugging outfit will serve nicely. An 8½- to 9-foot fiberglass rod made for a #8 or #9 is perfect. An inexpensive single-action reel with an interchangeable spool is sufficient; although a floating weight-forward line will cover most situations, there are times, especially in winter, when you'll have to swim a fly deeper, so a sinking line or sinking-tip line should be available on that extra spool. Tapered leaders with 12- or 15-pound-test tippets are recommended, as trout have small canine teeth, not sharp enough to warrant a heavy shock tippet, but sufficiently abrasive to cut lighter diameters. These fish aren't skittish, so the leader needn't be any longer than the rod. On windy coasts many fly casters use stripping baskets to store their shooting line, rather than have the free portion blown and tangled on the water. A small plastic wash basin belted at hip level does the job.

Fly fishing for seatrout is not only a barrel of fun but sometimes more effective than other methods, especially when the fish are selectively feeding on small natural baits like shrimp, silversides, and anchovies (so-called glass minnows). Generally speaking, the simplest patterns are effective. Even the most amateur fly tier can turn out a basic trout bucktail. All you need is a #1/0 hook, some white and dyed-green bucktail, plus a few strips of Mylar. Use the white bucktail for an underwing and fasten it so that the hairs extend about 1 inch beyond the hook bend. Tie a bunch of green bucktail over the white and add a half-dozen strips of Mylar for topping. It's not necessary to make a body. This same fly tied with a red-and-white wing, or all pink or all yellow, and the Mylar strips provides an effective color range. Any of the "breather"-type streamer flies with splayed hackle wings are also standard and need be no more complicated than a bushy hackle at the hook eye and a long divided wing. The real migraine is taking trout when they are feeding on the bottom in grass beds. For this you'll need streamers tied on a Keel hook with the bend and barb turning up, or a Ruff Neck–style fly. This is a shorter-winged bucktail, dressed on #1/0, #2, and #4 hooks in 1X Long. Trout can be real fussy about fly size. The wing of the Ruff Neck is fastened behind the hook eye as usual, but then the hair is bunched up at the head and secured again with tying thread, forming a small collar. This collar deflects snags because the buoyant bucktail wing is tied under the shank, causing the hook point to ride up instead of down.

Naturally, popping bugs are deadly on school trout, and any of the saltwater models marketed will take fish. I prefer bugs with an elongated slender body and a bucktail or saddle hackle tail. This design casts easily in wind, which is the criterion of these lures. Highly air-resistant bugs with wings or beer-barrel bodies are next to useless on the flats. Bear in mind that the same virtue of distance applies in fly fishing: the longest casts score more trout. The angler who can reach sixty feet or more has a better chance of success. All yellow, red-and-white, and blue-and-white bugs dressed on #2 and #1/0 hooks are effective everywhere. I must admit, I've never caught a really big trout on the bug, but in areas where fish of 2 to 5 pounds are the norm, top-water fly fishing is great sport for anybody who craves fast action. When the "specks" are popping at shrimp, it's not unusual to hook forty or fifty fish in a day's outing.

The spotted seatrout is an exceptionally fine food fish, which is one of the main reasons for its popularity. However, no fish loses its flavor quicker if not iced immediately after capture. Its sweet and delicate flesh becomes *blah* after a few hours of lying around at ambient temperatures. I have seen skiffs at dockside loaded like Russian stern trawlers with sun-baked trout, an excess that boggles the mind and dulls the palate. The South's number-one fish rates first-class treatment.

[1976]

26

An African
Fish Story

*There are occasions, I admit, when McClane strains
my credibility. This is one such example. First, there's
the small matter of dry-fly fishing for walking fish on
dry land. Not to mention a brief interlude with some
barracuda, while wondering about the possibility of
cannon fire amid a Congolese revolution. And then
there's . . . Well, read for yourself.*

*I know this story to be true for two reasons. First,
Al told me it was true, and he hasn't failed me—or
you—yet. Second, the only person I know who could
make up a story like this is Ed Zern, and he assured
me as to his innocence—at least as regards the following.*

There is an island in the mouth of the Congo River called Ile
de Pecheurs, where on any normal day you can build a fire
on the beach and wait for the fish to walk out of the water.
Actually, if you are in a hurry to eat you don't have to wait.
You can knock some out of the trees and get right down to
cooking. For obvious reasons, I don't believe that *Periophthalmus* will ever appear in *The Gourmet Cookbook,* nor will

the Komodo dragon, four-eyed fish, the capybara, or crocodile feet. Yet in various parts of the world these creatures are as common as a Parisian *omelette aux fines herbes.*

However, the method of smoking a *Periophthalmus,* as I learned it from a banana planter in the old slave port of Banana Point, is worthy of recognition. As a member of the Brotherhood of Singed Eyebrows (I have burned down three smokehouses), I am obliged to state that Africa holds at least one secret that should find a place in civilization's only indispensable art.

In March 1959 I went to what was then the Belgian Congo to learn, among many things, the habits of the *poisson qui marche,* or tree-walking fish. Obviously, it was the wrong time to arrive in Leopoldville, as political upheavals (shooting had already commenced) made traveling rather sticky.

Some die-hard colonists were still arguing as to the source of the distinctive merits of the *quenelles de brochet* at Le Grignotier restaurant, but this was really just a gastronomical symptom of their very peculiar status while waiting for the spear to hit the fan. Elvis Presley was whining from the jukeboxes along Boulevard Albert Ier, street hawkers patinated their freshly made primitive carvings with shoe polish, and a handsome matron plunked her nickel-plated .38 on the counter, while she searched in her purse for change to buy a Coca-Cola. My problem was how to get out of town. I can still remember the skeptical face of the man in the Bureau des Passeports when I announced the tree-walking fish as my reason for going to Moanda. It is a difficult subject for fractured French. I had to demonstrate how fins became legs by thumping across his desk on my elbows. He said something unintelligible and made an upward punching motion above his head—a signal, I had thought, to his *sous-officiers* to bring out the straitjacket. Actually, it was an attempt to describe Moanda.

Moanda is about 250 miles from Leopoldville and 10 miles from the Congo estuary at Banana Point. There is (or perhaps was) a clean modern hotel there standing high on the cliffs overlooking the sea. In that part of the world, where temperatures range from 110 to 150 degrees, any building perched at an altitude of sixty feet is almost alpine in character. So the Mangrove Hotel was a popular spot among colonists who came down from Leopoldville on weekends to enjoy the breeze and to roam miles of uninhabited beach. The patron was a typical *traiteur* or, literally, "eating housekeeper," who was dedicated to the establishment's cuisine. We became friends almost at once when I admired his *jambon à la crème gratinée.* I compared it to Dumaine's in Saulieu, which was a sincere compliment. He immediately took an interest in my search for *Periophthalmus* and said he would arrange for a native guide to take me to Ile de Pecheurs.

"Ah, but first you must meet with Albert Fisher, who is our great angler at Banana Point. He will be happy to take you on his boat. Perhaps you can catch something for the hotel, no?"

"I will be delighted to meet Mr. Fisher," I said.

It turned out that Albert Fisher was one of the Congo *colons* in the Joseph Conrad tradition—as tough as the mahogany of which his vast beach home was built. He was seventy-four years old, and his wife, younger by two years, was on the tennis court having a fast game of singles with a young male houseguest when I met them. At dinner the old man told me that we would troll the mouth of the Congo River early the next morning, then head out for blue water and work south along the coast of Angola. He owned a forty-five-foot diesel, which was like finding a magnet in a bolt factory. Next to the Tonle Sap in Cambodia and the Amazon River in Brazil, the Gulf of Guinea along Africa's west coast is the world's most prolific fishery.

"Don't worry about *le poisson qui marche.* There are millions of them in the river. You will see. First I show you our barracuda!" I have never been one to refuse a fishing trip, so the object of my visit was temporarily shelved.

When we left the dock at Banana Point, Mr. Fisher handed me a Portuguese flag. The Belgian flag was already flying topside.

"What do I do with this?"

"Oh, it's the custom. When I signal with my hand [he

212

made the same motion as the passport official], you will be obliged to raise the Portuguese flag."

"Why?" I asked.

"They may shoot at us from Bulabemba. Angola is on the other side of the river and we must go by it."

"Is there a war?"

"No, but one cannot be too certain," he said, as he advanced the throttles. Before the day was over, I changed flags six times to compensate for Mr. Fisher's zigzag course. My idea of adventure is riding New York's Seventh Avenue subway; but there, smelling the hot breath of unseen cannons, I had a strong urge to swim ashore and look for *Periophthalmi.*

Technically, the Congo River is not muddy, but it's heavily laden with sediment, and the dark stain extends about fifteen miles into the sea. At its mouth, the river is 5 miles wide and, according to the echo sounder, some 1,200 feet deep. Roughly four miles out, and toward the coast of Angola, the sounder spun rapidly and we found a "cliff" where the ocean bottom dropped from 2,000 to 6,000 feet. We trolled from the dropoff into blue water. Fish constantly hammered our spoon lures. These were mostly giant barracuda and jack crevalle, but occasionally we caught a small tuna, a Spanish mackerel, or a kingfish. Within a few hours, the cockpit was filled to overflowing with enough fish to feed the whole village of Banana Point.

The African barracuda is impressive. Of the twenty-odd species roaming the warm oceans of the world, it is probably the largest. The fish range from a few feet to 9 feet in length and weigh as much as 120 pounds. Unlike our giant barracuda, found from Florida to the Bahamas, which is silvery and black-spotted near the tail, the African kind is bronze-green in color and has uniform arrow-shaped bars along the entire body. Barracuda are considered a great delicacy by the local people, and the Mangrove Hotel had them on the menu every day after our trip. In the tropical Atlantic near North and South America, any barracuda over 5 pounds in weight would be suspect, as large fish are known to be periodically toxic due to their feeding habits. However, small barracuda are an excellent food fish the world over.

213

Even if flocks of terns had not marked the schools of feeding fish, we would have had no difficulty in locating barracuda, or they us. Underneath, the ocean boiled with shoals of these razor-toothed giants. It was a simple matter to hook one after another to the point of monotony. We were never able to get our lures down deep enough to discover what species might dwell on the escarpment. Between running back and forth to raise and lower the flags and tending the tackle, I was exhausted. But the real work began the next morning when Mr. Fisher's houseboy, Twombe, was assigned to take me "perch" fishing in a fourteen-foot skiff. Somehow *le poisson qui marche* was becoming a remote fiction.

Twombe was so big that when he sat in the stern of the boat, the bow, with my 165 pounds in it, came about three feet out of the water. His gnarled and widely splayed feet had soles with the texture of an ancient butcher's block. An old British outboard spluttered to life with the first pull, and we left the dock at Banana Point. The roar of the boat's open manifolds and the clouds of dense blue smoke that rolled over us now and then were not conducive to conversation. I asked him if he knew where the tree-walking fish lived, in French, English, and Swahili, and finally gave up. Twombe sat like some great black Buddha in a loincloth, his face appearing and disappearing under the smoke. When we reached a place called Muila Binga, he motioned for me to put a huge red-and-white plug out. With the motor cut down to trolling speed, the exhaust only became worse. The sun got a hot grip on the river and I felt dizzy.

All the mangrove shores in the Congo estuary are the feeding places for what are locally known as "perch." Actually, they are our familiar cubera and gray snappers—with one important difference. They come in weights from 20 to 100 pounds. At home in Florida we would consider a 5-pound gray snapper a big one, and a 15-pound red snapper well out of the ordinary. We dragged the huge plug along the mangrove banks. I didn't know at that point what we were fishing for, or why Twombe clung so resolutely to the overhanging tree limbs. The plug wasn't doing any good, but once in a

214

while I would see the swirl of a large fish ahead of the boat. Obviously we were flushing our quarry from their hiding places before they even had a look at the lure. For an hour I swatted mosquitoes and bathed in suntan oil. I finally made Twombe cut the motor so I could try casting for the perch.

I maneuvered the boat about ten yards away from the thickety mangroves and tossed the big plug close to some undisturbed branches. As my lure hit the surface a great billowing wake rose back under the limbs, and when I started to retrieve the plug the waves got bigger and bigger as the fish came toward it. He nailed the lure before it moved three feet. The fish hit with such impact that he jerked my rod tip almost to the water. The reel whistled for an instant, and the heavy line snapped; Twombe burst out laughing, as though a broken line was the pinnacle of Baluba humor.

"Perche," he announced in French. It was the one word he would repeat over and over again.

I had a plan now. It seemed apparent that if the plug was targeted in mangrove pockets and reeled very fast to clear the limbs before a snapper could strike, I would be able to draw the fish into open water. My system put a premium on accuracy, and the boat drifted at a moderate pace while I was casting. I had nothing but a series of deflection shots from a moving platform. A few minutes later another monster came charging after the plug. The fish hit with a villainous *woof* that sent spray for yards around. African snappers are not jumping fish, but their strike at a top-water plug is savage, and the game of getting them out into the open demands considerable work and luck. The first gray we boated weighed about 20 pounds. I don't recall how many fish we finally caught, but it was easy to get a strike on every cast. Many snappers surged back among the limbs against a full drag and broke off. By late afternoon we had drifted to Ile de Pecheurs. I noticed a clearing in the mangroves where some natives were working over a series of fires. It was then that I saw them—hundreds of fish scrambling out of the water and running across the beach. I had Twombe crank up and head for the island.

To science, the *Periophthalmus* is one of the skipping

gobies, an evolutionary fish that is in the process of becoming a land animal. Their fins have an elbowlike base that can be worked very rapidly; in fact, they move more swiftly on land than they can swim. Their respiratory organs are modified for breathing air, and an unusually thick skin conserves their body moisture even under the blast-furnace African sun. By following individual fish, however, I discovered they take a dip once in a while just to keep damp. Their purpose in running among the mangroves and up the aerial roots is to catch insects, which are apparently their chief source of food. They are small fish, ranging from 4 to 9 inches in length, yet their agility is astonishing. Unlike the walking perch of Southeast Asia (which is a relatively clumsy land fish), the *Periophthalmus* travels faster than a man's normal pace. Nature went all out, as the fish have rotating vision. A *Periophthalmus* can fix the gaze of one eye on an insect in the mangroves above, while the other eye searches elsewhere, much in the manner of a submarine's periscope. The entire island was punctured with water-filled holes or burrows in the mud. This was where the tree-walking fish lived when at home. I couldn't understand why *Periophthalmi* were continually coming out of the river proper, but after examining the stomach contents of those collected by the natives I discovered that they had been feeding on small crustaceans, which are more abundant in the tidal zone.

The native fishermen were not friendly. Twombe said something to them, which probably amounted to "He's a harmless screwball," and they went back to work. They had racks of *Periophthalmi* drying in the sun. The stench was awful. Some racks were placed over the small fires, evidently to reduce the moisture content of the fish in a sort of hot-smoke process. I didn't learn much from watching them, as my every move was observed suspiciously.

The encampment was deserted when I returned the next morning to catch my own tree-walking fish, so I couldn't even swap notes on the game. I caught three-dozen large ones (as requested by Mr. Fisher) on artificial trout flies. Doubtless, I am not the first angler to hook fish on dry land, or in the trees, as most Waltonians are connoisseurs of the eccentric. It was

216

the indomitable Mr. Fisher who provided the final touch, however, in smoking the *Periophthalmi.* To begin with, the climatic conditions are hardly favorable to smoking anything—even a cigarette.

"I have been smoking fish for almost thirty years," Mr. Fisher said, as we examined his mahogany smokehouse. It was a classic example of some cabinetmaker's art. "You will taste none better anywhere. I have a secret. How do you smoke fish *aux États-Unis?*"

"Well, I can't go into the whole process, but basically we leach, brine, air-dry, and smoke. Do you want the temperature cycle?"

"No, no, my friend. You see you are doing it the ordinary way, wasting salt and ruining good fish. We cannot waste salt in Africa. Here, taste this barracuda." He handed me a golden-brown chunk of pungent fish that I shall never forget. The ambrosial delicacy of the flaky white meat with a spicy, aromatic quality was vastly superior to my own results. Mr. Fisher carefully arranged the *Periophthalmi* on wire racks in the smokehouse, while I licked my finger.

"You will say it is our wood that makes the difference, but that is not so. I eliminate leaching and brining. My fish are dry-salted and then hot-smoked. They do not lose all their good juices and absorb water. The only time brine serves its purpose is when you are going to cold-smoke—which, of course, is impossible in our climate."

Mr. Fisher's pronouncement was so simple that I couldn't quite grasp its significance at first. It was like telling Gene Tunney that he never learned to throw a right cross. But many a fish has passed through our smokehouse done in the African way, since that evening at Banana Point, and now I can't go back to the old system. Briefly—and if you operate a smokehouse you won't need any more information—this is the method:

The fish are first split and cleaned, then washed thoroughly to remove all blood. While the fillets are still damp, they should be sprinkled with iodized salt. The amount of salt depends on the thickness of the fish. A thick slab of kingfish, for example, requires more salt than a mullet fillet. As in all smokehouse procedures some experimentation is necessary until exactly the right amount is found. It may be best described as a "liberal coat" of salt. When it is completely absorbed (about one hour), the fish are ready for smoking. Mr. Fisher used two different kinds of wood—one for heat and one for flavor. In America a dry oak provides the best coals and a green hickory makes the richest smoke. However, oak and green maple are also an excellent combination. The smokehouse temperature should level between 160°F. and 180°F. Slabs of fish to 1½ inches thick will require about 5 hours; 2- to 3-inch sections can go for 8 to 9 hours. That's all there is to it.

My final dinner at Banana Point had as its main course grilled smoked *Periophthalmi.* Except for the absence of orange vegetable dye, the texture and flavor were highly reminiscent of Lake Winnipeg goldeye, or a Florida west coast mullet.

I was scheduled to start for Kivu the next day to do a story on the Pygmies. The Fishers and Twombe came out to the Moanda airport with me. The old man made me promise to stop at the Couronne Restaurant in Brussels on my way home and try their sole done with a *sauce cardinale.*

"Ah, c'est magnifique avec un jeune vin blanc et . . ." I think the sight of the DC-3 had made him just a little homesick. As I climbed aboard, Mr. Fisher said he would write to me, but I knew as I looked at the red-dust roads leading down to the sea that I would never hear from him.

[1963]

Book Three

THE GUSTATORY ANGLER

Sharing a meal with Al McClane can be a wonderful education, I've found, although he doesn't—gentleman that he is—press his wide-ranging knowledge of fish cookery unless asked. He has, through the publication of two cookbooks and articles such as those included here, been established as an international authority on fish cookery.

Fish and seafood have assumed a larger role in the American diet in recent years as, I suppose, part of a growing concern with health. The information and tested preparations in these chapters are all designed to give you better results in your kitchen with your fish. I've tried many of them myself. Not only can they be fun, but they work—and the exclamations of dinner guests are more than worth the effort.

27

Fish and Seafood
in a Stew

If you, as I do, happen both to fish and to believe that dinner with friends can be an event unto itself rather than a precursor to the movies, you will find both enjoyment and inspiration in this chapter. McClane makes it perfectly and happily evident here that a rather spectacular fish stew can be built of essentially local fishes, no matter where in the country you might live.

I add from my own experience and fond recollection that some versions of the following instructions can make wonderful and easy meals for a large group of anglers in camp. I can remember as a small boy going to sleep in a tent next to the roaring West Branch Penobscot in Maine, my insides warmed by a landlocked-salmon bourride one of the older men had made during the afternoon.

Were I to nominate one fish stew as memorable, it would be that saffron-flavored bowl served at Colonel Hank Thorne's old Bang Bang Club on Pot Cay in the Bahamas. No classically trained toponymologist would ever make sense out of these place-names. But there was fabulous white-crowned pigeon and pintail shooting in the nearby mangroves where Corey Ford, Ray Camp, Ben Crowninshield, Van Campen Heilner, and other top guns mucked about at dawn and dusk between bouts on the bonefish flats; so between fish *bang bang* was a familiar echo. As for the pot (grass was something you mowed in 1948) the colonel's chef de cuisine, Chico, was famed for throwing anything into one—from conch to iguana—and after a ritual splash of sherry he would by arcane magic produce a meal worthy of three stars in the *Guide Michelin.*

Pot Cay sits in the remote North Bight of Andros Island and the bonefishing was then, and probably continues to be, extraordinary. It's also the only area I know of outside of East Africa that produces 8- to 10-pound ladyfish. Both Thorne and his hostelry are gone, and Chico, who never had a recipe for any dish, left no record of his handiwork. From my own observation in the Bang Bang kitchen, he followed standard procedures for a bouillabaisse using all kinds of grunts, snappers, porgies, groupers, cowfish, porkfish—whatever he could collect in abundance. In the 260-year history of this stew, which originated in the old port of Marseilles, it never required anything more than whatever could be delivered fresh to the stove. There is a formal list of local species—the *roughet, merlan, vive, grondin, lotte, rascasse,* and *congre*— that make a bouillabaisse "authentic," but it's about as valid as the French recipe for fifty-fifty rabbit pie: one horse, one rabbit.

As a young New York editor, I had dinner with George LaBranche, who was one of my boyhood heroes. Pioneer author of *The Dry Fly in Fast Water,* first published in 1914, and *The Salmon and the Dry Fly,* a decade later, he extolled the virtues of light tackle long before Henry built the first Model-A Ford. LaBranche was an eighty-year-old, high-collared dandy when we shared pasta and a bowl of *zuppa di pesce* at Gino's on Lexington Avenue. As a raconteur the man was totally in charge of the interview. I couldn't get him off the Test, Itchen, or Kennet (which he owned a stretch of), or off the deck of his championship sloop *Wee Betty,* or off the golf course, or his pheasant farm. My mentioning Bache Brown ("oh, you mean that spinning fellow") and then applauding Arthur Howald's newfangled fiberglass rod were tactical failures. By the time the soup came I felt like a *banderillero* trying to divert the bull, so I risked pointing out that there was no fennel in our *zuppa.*

If LaBranche remembered me at all in his subsequent years, it was probably as "oh, you mean that soup fellow."

There are so many soups and stews in the lexicon of fish cookery and it's not easy to distinguish one from the other. In theory, if the dish is composed of more liquid than solids by volume and is unthickened, it's properly some kind of soup. However, Mediterranean versions like *zuppa di pesce,* or *sopa de pescado,* which are called "soups," often incorporate six to eight kinds of fish in a velvety stock and qualify as hearty stews. Unlike game stews that are usually singular in content whether squirrel, venison, or pheasant, fish stews are commonly plural.

Bouillabaisse is the granddaddy of all fish stews, and despite a formidable recipe it's really easy to make. The only problem you might find is in getting enough variety of species, especially when limited to what can be caught in fresh water. The checklist in any one inland region is often sparse, although, like Alexander Dumas, who supposedly ate a bowl every day, I'd settle for whatever I can catch or buy. That special flavor comes from saffron, fennel, and garlic. Even our much-maligned sea robin, which innocent Atlantic Coast sinker-bouncers throw back by the bushel (yet it wins praise on Mediterranean tables as the *grondin*), is elevated to gourmet status when found swimming in an herb-and-tomato-flecked pool.

Ideally, you want lean fish and fat fish, large ones and small ones. The largest should be cut into chunks and the very small left whole, scaled and dressed of course. And when you make this noble stew, invite a lot of people, six or eight at least, as you can't economically cook a variety of fish without being burdened by a mountain of leftovers. No flower wilts more quickly than yesterday's bouillabaisse. Unlike a game stew, which can be recycled for days or even frozen, fish stews are at peak when they come steaming from the fire.

Before venturing into the recipe, which calls for 12 pounds of assorted fish, crustaceans, and mollusks, bear in mind that the ingredients can be halved if you are going to serve a small group of not-so-hungry people. Halving does not always work in recipes, as the mathematics of cooking has its own rules. However, it will succeed in this stew. The assortment might consist of flounder, black sea bass, striped bass, hake, halibut, or cod if you live in the East; sole, salmon, rockfish, sculpin, barracuda, or yellowtail from the Pacific; pompano, red snapper, grouper, sea trout, or Spanish mackerel if you live in the South. Don't ignore species like lookdowns, sea robins, silversides, sand launce, monkeyface eels, surfperch, anglerfish, or any of the porgies and grunts. Freshwater kitchens can look for whitefish, yellow or white perch, walleye, catfish, trout, sunfish, and black bass. There is some dissension among iconoclasts concerning the use of crustaceans and mollusks, but I include whatever I can get my hands on because the more textures and flavors incorporated, the better the stew. Jumbo shrimp, lobster, crayfish, and—although usually available in frozen form—lobsterettes (sold as Danish or Icelandic lobster tails) are tasty options. Among bivalves, clams or mussels cooked in the shell make succulent dividends in soups and stews.

The sequence in arranging these various items in the pot is important; you will want large and heavy chunks of lobster, for example, on the bottom and over these the rough-edged clams in order to avoid breaking the pieces of fish when it comes to serving. The more delicate fishes or small whole fish should be on top. Bear in mind that a chunk of Maine lobster will cook more slowly than a fragile fish fillet or shrimp, whereas a halibut steak will be intermediate in timing. Separate the ingredients according to slow, medium, and fast; never add them all to the pot at once, but in sequential order. If the lobster has been at simmer four minutes, then it's time to introduce the halibut, and after another four minutes, the more fragile cuts of fish. Chef André Sarat, who preached the hotchpotch gospel for a period of sixty years, observed that "you must *build* a bouillabaisse."

Sarat was also adamant on the use of fish stock instead of water. While our recipe called for water because it's always on tap and won't ruin a stew, by all means use stock if it's on hand. The stock adds a briny perfume that intensifies the rich flavor.

BOUILLABAISSE

12 pounds assorted fish, crustaceans, and mollusks
1 cup plus 2 tablespoons olive oil
2 pounds onions, coarsely grated
7 garlic cloves, peeled
1½ pounds fresh tomatoes, peeled
2 celery ribs, chopped
Bouquet garni (see Note)
5½ ounces fresh fennel
Coarse salt to taste
White pepper to taste
6 tablespoons unseasoned tomato paste
½ ounce saffron threads
1 French bread (baguette)
⅔ cup grated Parmesan cheese
1½ cups Sauce Rouille (see following recipe)

Dress fish and cut into appropriate pieces. Use a wide, deep, heavy kettle. Pour in 1 cup oil, then the fine onion shreds. Simmer over low heat, stirring now and then, for 15 minutes; onions should be translucent but not browned. Mash 5 garlic cloves with flat side of a knife; quarter the tomatoes. Add these with celery to the kettle. Add the bouquet garni and the fennel ribs to the pot. Simmer 15 minutes longer, until moisture from tomatoes has evaporated. Layer shellfish and fish chunks in the kettle on top of vegetable mixture. Add boiling water to reach 2 inches above the fish. Season with coarse salt and ground white pepper. Add tomato paste and saffron. Simmer 25 minutes, adding the more delicate fish pieces at intervals.

Remove kettle from heat. With a skimmer or flat

strainer, remove fish and arrange each kind together on a warm platter. Reduce the broth in the kettle by one-third; it will thicken. Pour broth into fine strainer set over a soup tureen; remove bouquet garni, and push remaining vegetables through the fine strainer.

Rub the crust of the baguette with remaining 2 whole garlic cloves. Cut the bread into about 6 rounds, and place in a shallow earthenware dish. Sprinkle with the remaining 2 tablespoons oil, and brown in the oven. Sprinkle hot toast with 2 tablespoons or more grated cheese.

Thin the Sauce Rouille with some of the broth, stir in a little grated cheese, and pour over platter of seafood. Serve the soup over toast in individual bowls. Let each guest add various pieces of seafood to his or her bowl.

NOTE

Bouquet garni is a mixture of herbs; fresh herbs are preferable; dried are also fine but result in a sharper flavor. If using fresh herbs, tie together, using string, thyme sprigs, bay leaves, parsley sprigs, and some orange peel (plus indicated fennel). If using dried herbs, wrap 1 teaspoon thyme, 1 bay leaf, 1 tablespoon parsley, and 2½ tablespoons dried orange peel (plus indicated fennel) in cheesecloth and tie with string.

Serves 8 or more.

SAUCE ROUILLE

1 red bell pepper or canned pimiento
4 garlic cloves
½ to 1 cup fresh bread crumbs
¼ cup olive oil

Roast the pepper until the skin is blackened; rub off the skin and remove ribs and seeds. Chop pepper. Peel garlic and mash; add pepper pieces and continue to mash until well mixed. Soak bread crumbs in water, and squeeze dry. Add olive oil to mashed mixture, 1 tablespoon at a time, mixing well, then add as much of the crumbs as needed to make a thick sauce. When diluted with fish broth, it should have the texture of thick cream.

Makes about 1½ cups before dilution.

Cioppino differs from bouillabaisse in being essentially a crustacean and mollusk stew with morsels of fish appearing as dividends. Some of the older recipes are composed entirely of crabmeat. Cioppino has become legendary in California—it's claimed to be an invention of Italian commercial fishermen in the San Francisco area. However, *cioppin* is from the Genovese dialect and defined in the venerable Gaetano Frisoni dictionary as "a tasty stew of various qualities of fish," so the point is moot. What isn't in contention is the meaty Dungeness crab, without which no modern-day cioppino could be labeled "California." Nor is the stew complete without a loaf of San Francisco's sourdough bread to mop up the juices. Dungeness crab is seldom available in Atlantic markets, but I've substituted blue crab with excellent results. If you do make the substitution, remember that the Dungeness is a big crab of 2½ to sometimes 4 pounds, so you'll have to figure on at least 4 blue crabs in this recipe.

CALIFORNIA CIOPPINO

1 medium onion
2 large garlic cloves, or more to taste
6 parsley sprigs
¼ cup olive oil
3½ cups canned Italian plum tomatoes
1¾ cups canned tomato purée
1 cup red Burgundy or other dry red wine
2 tablespoons wine vinegar
1 tablespoon mixed herbs (basil, rosemary, marjoram, and oregano)
½ teaspoon seasoned salt
½ teaspoon black pepper
2 medium Dungeness crabs
2 dozen clams in shells
1½ pounds halibut or rockfish fillets
1 pound large shrimp in shells, split and deveined

Use a Dutch oven or a large pot with lid. Finely chop onion, garlic, and parsley. Cook in oil over moderate heat, until soft but not browned. Add tomatoes, tomato purée, wine, 1 cup water, vinegar, herbs, salt, and pepper. Bring to a boil and reduce heat to simmer 40 minutes. (This sauce may be made ahead of time, if desired, but heat before adding to fish.) When sauce is completed, reserve it in a separate container. Dress the crabs, crack claws, and break into serving pieces. Layer crabs, clams, halibut, and shrimp in the pot. Pour the sauce over all. Cover tightly and cook over low heat 20 to 25 minutes. Serve in large heated bowls.

Serves 6.

Our third classic, bourride, differs from bouillabaisse and cioppino in being a purely fish stew—no shellfish of any kind. It is most distinctive, however, because of an aïoli sauce introduced into the stock, a garlicky napping that is really a kind of mayonnaise. In common with bouillabaisse, a bourride requires a variety of fish but in skinned fillets cuts into pieces. Again the choice of species is a regional option, but we will make some suggestions. Back when Arnold Gingrich and I were sharing a cabin on the upper Beaver Kill, he stayed off the river one day to read galleys of *The Well-Tempered Angler,* which somehow got his creative juices going again. Of all things, he whipped up a jumbo-size bourride made solely of trout. I had been on the river since dawn and the water squishing in my waders was the temperature of Bernard De Voto's classic martini. Maybe it was because I hadn't eaten since breakfast, but his stew kept us at the table until almost midnight. I guess it can be a success in singular form—at least it was on that occasion. He often said if he had escaped the ignominious fate of being a publisher, he would have gone to the hotel school at Lausanne.

BOURRIDE

1 pound fillet of red snapper, rockfish, or black bass, skinned
1 pound fillet of sea bass, cod, or walleye, skinned
1 pound fillet of striped bass or fillets of yellow or white perch, skinned
1 pound fillet of halibut, white seabass, whitefish, or any trout, skinned
1 large onion, sliced into rings
1 large carrot, sliced
4 fennel ribs, sliced
2 leeks, cut in julienne
2 tablespoons chopped parsley stems
1 bay leaf
1 tablespoon salt
Dry white wine
Fish stock or water
4 egg yolks
2 cups Aïoli Sauce (see following recipe)
12 to 16 potatoes, boiled and peeled
chopped fresh parsley

Cut each fillet into 6 pieces. Place in a large deep pot. Add onion, carrot, fennel, leeks, parsley stems, bay leaf, and salt. Mix 2 cups wine and 2 cups stock (or water), and pour in. If necessary, add more wine and stock in equal amounts to cover fish. Bring to a boil, reduce heat, and simmer 12 minutes; remove from heat. Carefully remove fish to a large serving bowl and add just enough cooking liquid to keep fish moist. Beat egg yolks; add 1 cup Aïoli Sauce, and turn into a large saucepan. Strain remaining cooking liquid into the egg yolk–Aïoli mixture. Simmer until the sauce is thick and smooth; do not let it boil. Strain into a second serving bowl. Place potatoes around fish, spoon a little of the sauce over, and sprinkle with parsley. Serve the rest of the sauce and remaining Aïoli in separate bowls. Accompany with toasted slices of French bread.

Serves 6 to 8.

AÏOLI SAUCE

8 to 10 garlic cloves
2 egg yolks
1 teaspoon salt
Dash of white pepper
2 cups olive oil

Peel garlic cloves and push through a garlic press into the container of an electric blender or food processor. Add egg yolks, salt, and pepper. Blend or process at lowest speed for a few minutes. Drop by drop, slowly add olive oil, and blend. Sauce will be very thick.

Makes about 2 cups.

Pensacola Fish Chowder is one of the oldest North American classics, originated with the family of Manuel Francisco Gonzalez during the Spanish settlement of Florida in the 1600s. This hearty stew is a Pensacola specialty, seldom found in other Gulf Coast kitchens. It's singular in form, requiring just one species of fish—red drum for choice (widely known as redfish), with red snapper, or a grouper called the scamp, in that order. Personally, I think it's great when made with black bass, and Pacific cooks can use any of the rockfish—bocaccio, chili pepper, canary, vermillion, or whatever your preference. Unlike the other stews, our Pensacola recipe is a long-simmering process wherein the fish heads are reduced to a fumet before other fish are introduced into the pot. Believe me, it's worth the extra time to prepare this restorative for jaded taste buds.

PENSACOLA FISH CHOWDER

One 4-pound red drum, or two 2½-pound fish
Salt
Ground white pepper
2 large baking potatoes
1 large yellow onion
2 large garlic cloves
6 scallions
⅔ cup celery leaves
2 medium fresh tomatoes
1 medium green pepper
¾ cup tomato paste
2 teaspoons Worcestershire sauce
8 black peppercorns
2 tablespoons minced fresh parsley
2 pinches of dried basil
2 pinches of dried oregano
2 large bay leaves
2 lemons
⅔ cup dry red wine
2 slices of bacon, or 4 tablespoons bacon drippings
4 tablespoons flour
4 cups canned tomatoes
Cayenne or crushed pepper to taste (optional)

When you dress the fish save the head (or heads) with the gills pulled out. If you have an extra fish head or two, so much the better. Cut fish crosswise into steaks about 1¼ inches thick. Sprinkle with salt and pepper and set aside. Put the fish heads in cheesecloth and tie with twine, leaving a loose end for a handle.

Peel potatoes and cut into 1-inch cubes. Peel and chop onion and garlic. Chop scallions, including 2 to 3 inches of the green tops, the celery leaves, fresh tomatoes, and green pepper. Put these last four ingredients in a large bowl and add tomato paste, Worcestershire sauce, peppercorns, herbs, ½ lemon, unpeeled and unsliced, ⅓ cup wine.

If using bacon slices, put them in a Dutch oven or large

cast-iron pot and heat until all fat is rendered and bacon is crisp. Remove bacon, pat dry, crumble, and set aside. Gradually sprinkle the flour into the fat or bacon drippings, stirring all the time. Cook and stir until roux is the color of strong coffee with cream, being careful not to scorch it. Add chopped onion and garlic and continue to cook until onion is translucent. Add canned tomatoes and heat and stir until well mixed with the roux. Add boiling water to within 4 inches of the top of the pot. Add the bowl of chopped ingredients and seasonings, and the crumbled bacon, if any. Tie the bag of fish heads to the pot handle and drop them into the chowder. Bring to a boil, cover, and simmer about 2 hours. Stir occasionally, and add hot water if liquid is reduced too much.

Remove fish heads and let the sack drip into a bowl to save all the juices; add juices to the chowder and discard the sack. Add cubed potatoes and cook for 5 to 7 minutes. Add fish steaks and cook until potatoes and fish are just done—the potatoes should be somewhat crisp and the fish still firm. Add remaining ⅓ cup wine.

Cut the remaining 1½ lemons into slices, and place a slice in each soup or gumbo bowl. Ladle chowder into bowls, giving everyone some fish and potatoes. Add cayenne pepper or crushed hot pepper to taste.

Serves 8.

[1980]

233

28

Black Bass
Cookery

*Imagine, if you will, having to eat a largemouth bass
that has, first, been kicked around in a hot boat bottom all afternoon; second, been caught from a muck-
and-algae–filled pond; and third, been deep-fried as a
warm fillet in rancid oil. I can imagine a few things
worse—like missing the spring smallmouth bass season—but not many. As parts of that scenario aren't
uncommon, however, so bass aren't widely hailed as
prime table fare. It's the sort of situation that brings
sneers from trout fishermen.*

*A properly conducted fish fry—with bass fillets as
the main attraction—can be a wonderful experience,
but a kitchen confrontation with America's most popular gamefish doesn't have to be so limiting. As
McClane amply demonstrates here, a little extra effort with your bass cookery can be more than worth
your while.*

In 1937 Wallace W. Gallaher dedicated his book *Black Bass
Lore* to "The Great Unorganized Brotherhood of Black Bass
Fishermen." Both title and author are now as dimly remem-

234

bered as our jet-propelled brotherhood is brass-band visible. With Ray Scott as the modern Pied Piper, some 285,000 bass addicts form a union that has no peer in angling history. Despite the great leap forward, one aspect of black bass technology remains virtually unchanged—cooking the fish. Bass seldom reach seraphic heights in most kitchens because of a frying-pan syndrome that has been prevalent since before Dan'l Boone cremated one in bear fat. And there are those in the parish who won't even eat bass because they smell funny—a sometimes truth. Yet bass can be spectacular at the table when the same degree of effort is applied to the cooking as to their joyous capture.

Unlike trout, or the Oriental carp for that matter, black bass lack a formal culinary genesis. They were found only in North America and not widely distributed in U.S. waters until late in the nineteenth century. The first mention of bass as a food is in the journals of a French expedition in 1562, when Lieutenant René Laudonière observed that the Indians of northern Florida—Muskogee or Creek speakers—held captive bass in aquatic reed pens.

The Spanish, who settled around Saint Augustine a few years later, evidently ignored bass but thrived bountifully on red drum, mullet, and sheepshead, according to the telltale bones excavated from their kitchen middens.

The popular Muskogee method of cooking was *calo hotupev,* or barbecued bass, served with *safke,* or boiled grits. In Laudonière's time, bass were known as green trout, mountain trout, and swamp trout; these misnomers proliferated long after the French naturalist Comte Bernard Lacépède first described our two most common black bass in 1802. The centrarchids had no exact counterpart in Europe, and early-day nomenclators were adrift in strange waters. The muskellunge was even called white salmon by Ohio Valley settlers, simply because of its succulent flesh.

Elsewhere in North America, the smallmouth bass, or *achigan,* was a food of the Algonquin and Huron Indians of southern Canada, according to naturalist Pierre Boucher. Despite these and other French connections—such as Rafinesque who first described the spotted bass, and Valliant and

Bocourt who identified the Guadalupe species—nobody became bass-addicted, and its cookery remained an Indian art form.

We know that the Muskogees began tossing garlic, or *tafvm pe vhake,* in a bass stew and that the pungent European lily bulb probably arrived with the Spanish, who also introduced oranges to Florida. By the time naturalist William Bartram journeyed into Seminole country, the Indians were steaming fish with sliced oranges.

In brief, nothing much happened to the bass during the two and a half centuries that our pioneers gorged on other fish and game. It rated one hiccup.

The pivotal year in bass history was 1810, when George Snyder of Hopewell, Kentucky, built the first multiplying bait-casting reel. By all accounts, the craftsmen to follow—Milam, Hardman, Talbot, Noel, Sage, Gayle, and other good ol' boys—also knew the virtues of white, water-ground, unbolted, and unsifted cornmeal. At the monthly meetings of the Bourbon County Anglers Association, they dusted their fillets in meal, fried them in rendered beef suet, then served them crackling hot with steamy mounds of golden hush puppies. It was said that their vision of heaven was a fish fry with the Lord presiding over the branch water. Only that autocratic master Ben Meek, perhaps the greatest reel designer of all, had no interest in fish or fishing. Ben just wanted to make things run smoothly.

This booming age of tackle making inspired widespread stocking of black bass and coincided with the opening of the Erie Canal, which accidentally delivered these fish to our eastern states and, inevitably, into the culinary revolution of the late nineteenth century. Thus, it remained for the more opulent generation of Joseph Leiter (Favorite Old Recipes) to create a steamed crown mold made of bass and lobster forcemeat, garnished with truffles and presented awash in lobster sauce. Bear in mind that the catfish of Pass Manchac had long since been elevated to *chaud froid en belle vue* in the French outposts of Louisiana. But where catfish fanciers had sense enough to strip the fish of its skin and plumbing in one dexterous stroke, bass for the most part were being served in-the-round with skin intact. And therein lies the nitty-gritty of bass cookery.

The skin of a fish is quite different from that of mammals; it's made up of living cells as far as the outermost layer. A coating of slime makes it watertight, and with the kidney it plays a role in the excretory function. Freshwater fish absorb water (saltwater fish drink it) and the flavor of their skin is an environmental product. When crisped by heat, it can be fragrantly nutlike or run a gamut of unpleasant flavors. Nobody knows why, but the skin of a snook tastes like soap, yet the meat is so sweetly delicate that in years past it was sold to innocent Florida tourists as red snapper.

The skin of most black bass has a distinctly musty or even muddy flavor and to a lesser extent—but not always—so does the flesh. Black bass from some waters aren't fit to eat. This is not a singular condition, as trout, carp, and catfish are similarly affected. The chief offending agent is a colorless oil called geosmin. Geosmin derives from blue-green algae and also from several bacteria (actinomycetes) found in the organic sludge of polluted water. It is absorbed through the gill membranes and into the bloodstream.

Researchers at Auburn University (Richard Lovelland and associates) found that fish of poor quality are more common in fertile ponds than those with low fertility, and that soft, acid waters produced geosmin only during the spring and fall turnovers. These turnovers coincide with a release of nutrients that stimulate an algal bloom. So the edibility of bass varies according to habitat and season.

The widely distributed largemouth is most often identified with a muddy flavor, yet when taken from a prime lake or river and shucked from its skin, the lean white meat lends itself to many forms of cooking. Smallmouths from the cold, gravelly lakes of Maine—or spotted, redeye, and shoal bass from clear upland streams, like the Halawakee in Alabama or the Ichawaynochaway in Georgia—are all excellent food fish, which to my nose have a faintly cucumber aroma, typical of other delicious sunfishes. Waters that produce gourmet-caliber bass are not necessarily the places where you would go looking for lunkers. In fact, the two concepts are not always compatible.

Our best eating bass here in southeast Florida are found over limestone substrates; ponds of this kind are dwindling now, in a proliferation of housing developments. Perhaps equally as good are the crystal-clear, white-sand–bottomed potholes that are common to the ridge lines of Florida. My late angling pal, Willie McKoosh, used to call them "wade-fishing ponds"—some of them are no more than an acre in size and hip-deep at most. Typically, there will be ten or even twenty within a short cast of each other. The largemouths here are pale green dorsally with snow-white bellies—very different from the darkly colored fish found over muck bottoms in the Everglades drainage.

Wade-fishing ponds seldom produce big bass. One day while I was bugging the pads with tackle maker Len Borgstrom, he caught an 8-pounder, which is a trophy for water of this kind. However, size is a negative factor in edibility. I rarely keep bass over 3 pounds for the table, and 2 pounds is ideal for most cooking methods. Heavy bass become coarse in texture and can be turned into a noble chowder, but they lack the pristine flavor and tender musculature of a plump young largemouth.

Willie, who always drooled like a Roman fountain at the mere mention of a fish fry, spent most of any day releasing bass because they didn't fit his size requirement, which looked like cat food to me. McKoosh was methodical. He would tote his selection from pond to pond, alive on a stringer, and the moment we got back to the jeep he'd cut out the fillets. Then he'd slip each one in a tie-off plastic bag and pack them on ice in his cooler. Bass left at ambient temperatures in the bottom of a boat or creel can defeat the greatest recipe. Willie had only one method: He'd roll the fillets in cornmeal, then chill thoroughly for temperature contrast, before lowering them into bubbling-hot peanut oil. Over a platter of spicy coleslaw, or swamp cabbage, and beer-batter hush puppies, McKoosh consoled himself with the reflection that he could go looking elsewhere for a lunker bass—tomorrow.

When cooked skillfully, deep-fried bass can be a memorable outdoor meal. The best I recall was crisped to perfection on the banks of Arkansas's Buffalo River by Forrest L. Wood, now the uncrowned king of bass-boat builders. Twenty years ago he was probably the most popular guide in the Ozarks. Nobody in those hills made a better camp or set a better table, skills that are becoming rare in these lax times.

The discipline of fish cookery doesn't end in an iron skillet. It begins. When bass are delivered to a kitchen, the true ichthyophile has many options: pudding, pie, pancakes, stew, custard, or, my favorite, bass dumplings. Skinless fillets are required for some dishes, while others demand bass in scaled and gutted form with head and tail intact. With respect to scaling, this should be done as soon as possible. Bass scales are deeply embedded and "pucker" very quickly, making them difficult to remove once a dead fish has been exposed to air. If the fish is to be cooked whole, it's also advisable to leave the fins intact when dressing bass. The pectoral, pelvic, anal, and dorsal fins should never be trimmed off externally, as this simply leaves their sharp basal bones hidden in the flesh. They can be excised with the point of a knife, but it's easier to pull the entire fin structure out (pull forward) after the fish has been cooked. This is true of all sunfishes and is the reason why country boys can eat bluegills like corn on the cob.

BLACK BASS DUMPLINGS WITH CUCUMBER SAUCE

1½ pounds black bass fillets, skinned
2 eggs plus 2 egg whites
1½ cups heavy cream
1 teaspoon salt
¼ teaspoon mace
2 cups chicken broth
2 cups dry white wine
Cucumber slices for garnish

CUCUMBER SAUCE
¼ cup butter
1 large cucumber, peeled, seeded, and diced
¼ cup flour
1 cup reserved poaching liquid
1 cup heavy cream, at room temperature
2 egg yolks
*2 tablespoons chopped fresh dill, or 2 teaspoons dried dill
weed*
Salt
White pepper

Cut fillets in pieces. Place bass, eggs, and egg whites in a blender or food processor and whirl until smooth. Gradually add cream, salt, and mace while machine is running. Turn mixture into a bowl, cover, and chill for several hours.

Pour chicken broth and wine into a large skillet. Bring to a simmer. Shape the bass mixture into rounded tablespoons, and place them carefully in the simmering liquid. Cook 10 minutes, or until dumplings are firm; remove from liquid with a slotted spoon. Arrange on serving platter and keep warm. Reserve 1 cup poaching liquid.

Prepare the sauce. In a saucepan, melt butter and sauté cucumber for 3 to 4 minutes. Blend in flour. Gradually add reserved cup poaching liquid. In a bowl, whisk the cream and egg yolks until smooth, then stir into saucepan. Add dill. Continue stirring over medium heat until sauce thickens, but do not boil. Season to taste with salt and pepper. Spoon sauce over the dumplings, and serve garnished with cucumber slices.

Serves 6.

BLACK BASS PANCAKES

PANCAKES
4 eggs
½ teaspoon curry powder
½ teaspoon salt
1 cup milk
1 cup unsifted all-purpose flour

FILLING
2 pounds black bass fillets, skinned
Salt
White pepper
1 cup dry white wine
½ cup butter
½ cup flour
Reserved poaching liquid with enough half-and-half added
to make 4 cups
1 package frozen chopped broccoli, cooked and drained
⅓ cup grated Parmesan cheese

In a bowl, combine all pancake ingredients and beat until smooth. Let stand for 1 hour. Stir thoroughly, and make 18 crêpes as follows: Spoon about 2 tablespoons batter into a heated, lightly buttered 7-inch skillet, and rotate pan to cover bottom with a thin layer of batter. Brown on one side, then turn out on a piece of foil. Butter pan again and repeat, until all remaining batter is used.

Preheat the broiler.

Prepare filling. Sprinkle bass fillets with salt and pepper. Place in a large skillet and add wine. Cover and simmer gently 20 to 25 minutes. Let bass cool in liquid. Break meat into bite-size pieces. Reserve poaching liquid. In a saucepan, melt butter and stir in flour. Add the poaching liquid and half-and-half, stirring over low heat, until sauce thickens and bubbles. Season with salt and white pepper to taste. Place half of this sauce in a bowl and add the bass pieces and broccoli; use this mixture to fill the pancakes by spooning about 3 tablespoons into each crêpe and rolling them up. Place filled pancakes, side by side, seam down, in a shallow, lightly greased casserole. Spoon remaining sauce over the pancakes, and sprinkle with Parmesan cheese. Place in preheated broiler until sauce is bubbling and cheese is golden brown.

Serves 4 to 6.

BLACK BASS FONDUE

3 egg yolks
1 cup beer
1 cup unsifted all-purpose flour
1 teaspoon salt
1 teaspoon paprika
Dash of garlic powder
3 egg whites, stiffly beaten
2 to 3 pounds black bass fillets, skinned
Deep fat or peanut oil heated to 360°F.

In a bowl, mix egg yolks, beer, flour, salt, paprika, and garlic powder. Fold in egg whites. Cut fillets into bite-size pieces. Spear on fondue forks and dip into batter. Drop batter-coated fish into hot oil and fry 5 to 6 minutes, or until pieces are golden brown and crisp. Serve with one or several of the following sauces.

Serves 4 to 6.

HOT SAUCE

Mix ½ cup chili sauce with 2 tablespoons frozen orange juice concentrate and 1 tablespoon white horseradish.

TARTAR SAUCE

Mix ¾ cup mayonnaise with 1 tablespoon lemon juice, 1 tablespoon drained capers, and ¼ cup well-drained pickle relish.

CURRY SAUCE

Mix ⅓ cup mayonnaise with ⅓ cup sour cream, 1 teaspoon curry powder, and ⅓ cup shredded peeled green apple. Add salt to taste.

MUSKOGEE BASS STEW

⅓ cup corn oil
3 onions, finely chopped
3 garlic cloves, chopped
4 slices smoked bacon, diced
1 green pepper, chopped
½ pound mushrooms, sliced
1½ cups chopped celery stalks and leaves
4 large tomatoes, diced
½ teaspoon dried oregano, or 6 branches fresh oregano
½ teaspoon dried sage, or 3 clusters fresh sage
1 bay leaf
One 13¾-ounce can chicken broth
1 cup dry white wine
1 cup tomato purée
1½ pounds black bass fillets, skinned
Salt
Coarsely ground black pepper

In a large saucepan, heat oil and sauté onions, garlic, bacon, green pepper, mushrooms, and celery 5 to 10 minutes, or until lightly browned. Add tomatoes, herbs, bay leaf, chicken broth, wine, and tomato purée. Cover and simmer 15 to 20 minutes, until vegetables are tender. Cut bass fillets into bite-size pieces, and add to stew. Cover and simmer another 15 minutes. Remove herbs, if fresh are used, and bay leaf. Season to taste with salt and pepper. Serve in large bowls with slices of crusty bread.

Serves 6.

BLACK BASS PUDDING WITH SAUTERNE SAUCE

One 2- to 2½-pound black bass, whole, gutted, and scaled,
fins intact
Salt
Sauterne
¼ cup butter
2 tablespoons each chopped green pepper, chopped
pimiento, chopped celery leaves, chopped chives
4 cups plain croutons
3 eggs, well beaten
1 teaspoon Worcestershire sauce
2 cups half-and-half
Fine dry bread crumbs

SAUTERNE SAUCE
¼ cup butter
¼ cup flour
1 cup reserved poaching liquid
1½ cups heavy cream
Salt
White pepper

Sprinkle bass with salt inside and out. Place fish in a skillet or poacher and add enough sauterne to half-cover fish. Simmer, covered, 20 to 25 minutes. Let bass cool in liquid. Remove fish and reserve 1 cup poaching liquid. Skin bass and pluck out fins, removing the basal bones. Break meat into small pieces. Heat butter in saucepan and sauté green pepper, pimiento, celery leaves, and chives 5 minutes. Scrape mixture into a bowl and stir in bass pieces and croutons. In a separate bowl, beat eggs with Worcestershire sauce, 1 teaspoon salt, and the half-and-half. Stir into bass mixture. Let stand 15 minutes.

Preheat oven to 350°F.

Heavily butter two 3-cup fish molds and sprinkle inside of molds with dry bread crumbs. Shake out excess crumbs. Fill molds with bass mixture and bake in a preheated oven 40 to 45 minutes.

Prepare the sauce. Melt butter in a saucepan and stir in flour. Gradually stir in reserved poaching liquid and cream. Continue stirring over medium heat until sauce thickens and bubbles. Season to taste with salt and white pepper.

Loosen edges of the pudding with the tip of a knife and unmold on a serving platter. Top with Sauterne Sauce.

Serves 6.

[1979]

29

The Caliph
of Caviar

The big rainbow cartwheeled over a moss bed, landed on the 7X leader, and was gone. Cursing with a thick Swiss accent, friend Arthur Frey returned to our bench on a northern California spring creek, from which we'd watch for another rising fish. In addition to his angling skills, Art is the beneficiary of a very civilized Swiss education and, from his experience as the longtime manager of a leading club in the San Francisco area, sometimes does yeoman duty as one of my epicurean gurus.

"Say, Arthur . . ."

"Hand me another of those little yellow flies."

"What does an ounce of malosol beluga *sell for these days?"*

"You got any more leaders?"

"Caviar, Arthur."

"You don't want it."

"Why not?"

"In San Francisco right now . . . a good restaurant . . . maybe thirty-five dollars for a one-ounce portion. There's some Chinese stuff coming in now,

too. Not too bad. Maybe a little cheaper. Where's my fly?"

I duly delivered what proved to be the correct pattern, thinking to myself that it wasn't that I didn't want it. With total disregard for J. P. Morgan's classic advice, I simply had to ask.

This McClane piece will tell you everything you ever wanted to know about caviar with his usual combination of exhaustive information and entertaining anecdote. I note herein yet another sad fact of inflation, as McClane cites a 1965 caviar price of only three dollars an ounce.

The Volvo diesel tractor whined through the dark toward the Russian border. A fierce wind coming out of the dark forest slammed waves of snow on the road ahead, but the driver fishtailed his seven-ton trailer expertly over the ice. The big man next to him hunched toward the dashlight and looked at his watch. "It's twenty-three thirty. We should be at Finnish control now," he muttered. The driver remained silent.

Two white flares suddenly arched across the sky, hanging like halos behind a veil of whirling flakes. The Volvo stopped at the sentry box, and now there was nothing to do but wait. The big man kept glancing at his watch and thinking about his cargo. Time was running out. At 11:50 P.M. a pair of red flares shot into the air about a mile away. The driver hesitated, but the big man's bullhorn voice prodded him into action. "That's the signal. Let's roll!"

At precisely midnight the Volvo crawled across the border. Two Russian soldiers leaped onto the truck steps, and a pistol waved the cab window open. *"Gospodin Beyer?"*

The big man took a deep breath. *"Da."*

The gun examined him carefully. After a long minute the soldiers jumped back into the night. Leningrad would be alerted.

The truck pulled into the city at 4:00 A.M. on December 21, and by ten that morning the cargo had been switched to another truck for a $250,000 payoff. The big man checked into the Europskaya Hotel and slept until four in the afternoon.

He caught the evening Aeroflot to Helsinki, lucked onto a Pan American jet, and was back at his New York headquarters on West Fifty-fourth Street on the afternoon of the twenty-second.

This real-life James Bond type was not delivering a secret weapon—or even a truckload of wastepaper from the CIA. He had just hauled three tons of caviar into Russia. And not even good caviar. It had the mossy flavor of old sweat socks. This reverse twist on the world's costliest food is no less remarkable than the man who engineered it. Malcolm K. Beyer is a tough, mustached brigadier general, retired, of the U.S. Marines Corps—not the stripe of man that you would expect to find wandering around the backroads of Russia. However, thirty years of active service, including almost every major campaign from Guadalcanal to Korea, amply qualify him for the physically demanding business of being the "Caliph of Caviar." A huge batch of spoiled caviar, for example, was delivered to him in New York on December 18, and after getting a sneering cable from the shippers when he asked to return it, Beyer phoned Moscow direct and boomed, "I'll damn well sell it, and *that* will be the end of Russian caviar in the United States." This stopped their clock. But only for minutes.

"They made a deal," Beyer reflected, "and they figured to have me by the short hairs. Some logistics-minded comrade suggested that if I could get the caviar back to Leningrad by midnight of the twenty-first they'd refund my money. They said it could be marketed in West Germany. So I *had* to make the deadline. Getting a three-ton cargo out of the States in the Christmas rush looked impossible to Moscow, and delivering it to Leningrad within seventy-two hours—well, that's rocket time. But it was take it or leave it, so I chartered most of the cargo space in an ancient DC-6 bound for Stockholm, then transferred the caviar to an even older C-47 for the ride to Helsinki. Getting through all the red tape in Finland was a nightmare. But in this crazy business a man could go broke with one snafu, so I used Marine sign language and got the boys in formation. Actually, when I think of it, everybody was very cooperative—including the Russians—because the border is officially closed at that time of the year."

The roe of fish has long been one of man's choicest foods. The shad, Pacific barracuda, flounder, mullet, bluefish, whitefish, mackerel, and dolphin provide some of the finest roes on the gourmet's list of cooked items. So-called white roe, the testes of a male fish (usually salmon or mullet), is no less delectable. Certain roes are poisonous; those of the puffers, gars, and Pacific rockfish have killed more than one dining adventurer—so a little knowledge helps. Among roes served raw, and this commonly includes those of carp, whitefish, salmon, paddlefish, and sturgeon, only the latter has achieved world renown as caviar—the delicacy that Russians call *ikra.* The word *caviar* is a corruption of the Turkish *kavayah.* It is the product of a sturgeon, and the eggs range in color from a pearly gray to pale brown.

Caviar has been described as "fishy marmalade" and "salty mush," but it is neither. Real caviar eggs have the firmness of ripe huckleberries; in fact, the individual egg is known in the commercial trade as a "berry." It crunches between the teeth, leaving a taste that is unique—faintly salty, slightly nutty, but definitely not fishy. To the connoisseur, caviar is better than gobs of ice cream. Yet there are people who will convulse like snakebite victims at the mere mention of the word—and with good reason.

Until quite recently, any fish roe that could be colored black was called caviar. The whitefish, carp, and paddlefish supplied large quantities of roe for the American market, and some of this "caviar" stained the customer's mouth a bilious green because of the dye added. Then the Food and Drug Administration people got busy and defined the product, limiting it to sturgeon eggs. But even within the legal definition of caviar there is a wide variation in quality, since there are at least twenty-two species of sturgeon in the Northern Hemisphere from which the roe is taken, and the eggs are processed in many different ways.

According to Beyer the best caviar is made from the roe of the yellow-bellied sterlet. "Only a few people in the world have ever tasted these pearls beyond price. This delicacy was once known as the "golden caviar of the Czars," and was reserved exclusively for the Russian imperial court. Even if you could find it today, it would cost a fortune.

"The finest grade of caviar exported from Russia now —in sufficient quantities to supply the restaurants of the world—is made from the roe of the beluga. The beluga is the largest sturgeon, so it produces the largest berries and commands the highest price. First-quality beluga caviar is packed as *malosol,* which in Russian means "little salt." In other words, *malosol* is not a brand of caviar but a type distinguished from caviar that has been heavily salted and that eventually finds its way into the jars on delicatessen shelves. Salt, of course, tends to shrink the egg and change its color, so the art in making caviar is knowing just how much salt to use, and then keeping the product at exactly the right temperature. In round figures, 1 pound of salt is sufficient for 1 *pud* of caviar, a *pud* being a Russian weight unit approximating 36 American pounds.

The grotesque source of Beyer's product is a primitive fish that probably lives to be a hundred years old. Despite the precise methods of ichthyology, accurate gauging of sturgeon age is a fairly recent technique. The *annuli,* or growth rings, on a fish scale can be interpreted in somewhat the same fashion as the annual rings of a tree trunk. Unfortunately, sturgeon do not have scales, their covering being more like armor plate, to protect a soft, cartilaginous skeleton. So to determine age, early researchers used cross sections of the sturgeon's *otoliths,* or ear bones. This method has a limitation: in really old sturgeon the bones crystallize and become difficult to read. Then the Russians found that the first bony ray of the pectoral fin could be cross-sectioned and analyzed with a great deal more accuracy, and this is the method used today.

The beluga has been recorded at the century mark. The white sturgeon of the United States apparently has the same life span as man; fish 14 to 16 feet long live from sixty to seventy-five years. There's no doubt that sturgeon are the largest fish to enter fresh water, yet this great size is sustained by the barest essentials. Beneath the sturgeon's snout is a protractile, toothless mouth with thickened lips that operate much like a vacuum cleaner in scooping insect larvae, mollusks, crayfish, and plant life off the bottom.

There are seven species of sturgeon found in the United States. Among these the white sturgeon of the West, ranging from Alaska south to Monterey, California, is the largest, reaching a weight of 1,800 pounds. In the Pacific is found the green sturgeon, which is hardly edible, being dark-meated and disagreeable in both taste and odor—although it is a source of caviar. Then there's the Atlantic sturgeon, which ranges from Maine into the Gulf of Mexico, and the lake sturgeon of the Great Lakes watershed, the flesh of which Beyer rates as superior to any Soviet fish. The shortnose and pallid sturgeons are freshwater species of the Atlantic seaboard, and the shovelnose inhabits the Mississippi valley.

The largest sturgeon in the world, reaching a known weight of 2,500 pounds, is the beluga. It ranges through the Caspian Sea, Sea of Azov, and the eastern Mediterranean as far west as the Danube River. The beluga differs from other sturgeon in eating quantities of fish, such as carp, bullhead, and the herring, and even young seal. Most sturgeon are anadromous and spend part of their life cycle in brackish or salt water, and the really big ones taken from the Snake River in Idaho, the Columbia in Oregon, the Apalachicola in Florida, and the Fraser in British Columbia are marine migrants.

Sea sturgeon still puncture the nets of Hudson River shad fishermen not far from the George Washington Bridge. These rancid adolescents—locally known as "pelicans" or "hacklebacks"—are mere ghosts of a horde that once existed next to an island now surrounded by sewers. The flavor of roe is adversely affected by pollution, or even by basic plant changes in a river system. But back at the turn of the century it was a common sight to see Hudson River barges loaded with 100 to 150 large sturgeon on their way to Albany, where the meat was sold under the name "Albany beef." The sturgeon brought 1½ cents a pound, and the supply seemed limitless. Caviar was so cheap that free lunch bars could afford to give it away. Nobody then realized that the virgin sturgeon need urgin', because the female does not mature until at least fourteen years old. A crop that grows so slowly demands careful management.

Because of the need for good management, sport fishing for sturgeon has had a cyclic history in America. Some of the principal states concerned, such as Oregon, Idaho, California, Wisconsin, and New York, have had periodic open seasons, with some closures as long as eight or ten years. *Maximum* size limits have been the rule for most of the last two decades. Oregon, for example, restricts the catch to sturgeon of 30 to 72 inches in length, in order to protect the big females.

Though necessary, these laws have had a diminishing effect on the art of sturgeon fishing. It's such a long time between bites! When a legal season is declared, anglers rush en masse to the river; then, like absentminded professors, they mill around trying to remember what they're supposed to do. Among a few old-timers, such as Willard Cravens of Nampa, Idaho, the word *sturgeon* recalls Homeric battles, and he regards 50-pound-test saltwater spinning tackle as a sporty proposition. Craven holds the rod-and-reel record in the United States with a 360-pound white sturgeon he took from the Snake River. To many pros his choice of gear borders on the ultralight; a grownup sturgeon is a powerful gamefish capable of busting quarter-inch rope and perfectly able to tow a skiff full of fishermen down the Columbia.

Cravens caught his big sturgeon on a shrimp, but pieces of meat, slabs of fish, clams, crayfish, and even river algae dried in the sun to form a ropelike mass are all worthwhile baits. In sturgeon fishing you have to make up your mind that heavy tackle is essential, and that the longer you can keep the bait lying on the bottom, the better are your chances. Sometimes this requires a 10-ounce sinker, and you'll lose a lot of rigs. Sturgeon are a pool fish but not in the sense of a quiet-water pool. They hold and feed in the strong, deep places of stream; frequently they are caught in turbulent stretches below hydroelectric dams. Setlines are legal in some states, and there is a winter spear fishery in the Midwest, but taking sturgeon on rod and reel is an exciting sport. Unfortunately there just isn't enough of it to go around. Nobody regrets this more than Beyer.

There is no doubt that the number of sturgeon entering

the Soviet fishery has declined in the last twenty years. Industrial pollution and hydroelectric dams in rivers tributary to the Caspian Sea (which itself has steadily dropped in level) have reduced the runs by 50 percent. Faced with the inevitable, Russia has not only accelerated its sturgeon hatchery program but also researched the possibility of a "synthetic" caviar. Professor Grigory Slonimsky of Moscow's Academy of Sciences has produced a chemical "caviar" that the Soviet paper *Nedelya* declares to be identical with the real thing. While lunching with a top Russian diplomat recently we posed the question of ersatz caviar. After a studied silence he observed—diplomatically—that his nylon shirt is a synthetic but he would not want to eat his shirt. The shirt analogy is appropriate for the Caliph of Caviar, because he regularly stands to lose his shirt.

"One bum shipment could wipe me out," Beyer says matter-of-factly, "but that's what makes the exotic-food business exotic."

As president of Iron Gate Products, an affiliate of New York's renowned restaurant, the 21 Club, Beyer is a fast-moving trader. He has a profound knowledge of fish and game, not only as an ardent sportsman but as one of the world's largest purchasers of more than twenty items in the exotic-food field. He spends six months each year junketing around the globe, buying smoked reindeer tongues in Finland, red deer and wild boar in Australia and New Zealand, saltwater brook trout in Denmark (they are later smoked in Brooklyn), and sole and turbot in England, then journeys to the Highlands for Scotch grouse and on to Sweden for ptarmigan, snow grouse, and hazel hen. Beyer purchases quail by the thousands from farms in the southern United States, and salmon in the Northwest. His imports of rock lobster tails from South Africa run eight to ten tons per shipment. All this requires a keen knowledge of quality, prices, and sources. But of all of his purchases, none is riskier or more difficult to bring home than caviar. Beyer makes at least four trips a year for it—all the way to the Caspian Sea.

A barrel-chested, six feet, three inches, General Malcom Beyer is one of those robust men who look even taller.

Though the Corps has abolished the swagger stick, he carries an invisible one, and as an acquaintance observed, he has "a hell of a temper when aroused."

Years ago, when Beyer was new to the caviar business, he presented five pots for the critical inspection of one of New York's most temperamental restaurateurs. A "pot" is 1.800 grams, or close to 4 pounds, of caviar and is worth about $200. The restaurateur, Pierre (that is not his name), is esteemed by his clients as a sort of demigod. He spooned a bit of caviar out of each pot and tasted it, and finally at the fifth pot he announced, *"Theese* is for Pierre!" and walked away. Of course, the four other opened pots couldn't be sold, but Beyer took his $800 loss stoically.

"It was a great prestige account, and even if it cost me money, I had to get started somehow. The trouble was that after a few months of sampling I realized that the Great One was giving me the shaft. There wasn't that much difference between one pot and the next. Then, just before Christmas, which is always our big season, I delivered some of the finest beluga we ever imported. Maybe it was the holiday spirits or the fact that I was getting sore, but after he muddled his spoon in all the pots and made a crack about my integrity, I picked up a pot, slapped it in his face, and said, *'Theese* is for Pierre!' You might say he had egg on his face that day, but I never had any trouble with him afterward. Today he's one of my best clients."

The Russians have been in the caviar business since the thirteenth century—at least 500 years passed before other countries learned about the delicacy—and the method of making it has always remained the same.

"Anybody can make caviar at home," Beyer said cautiously, "provided, of course, he can catch a sturgeon. It's important to remove the roe from the fish as soon as it is killed. The eggs should be washed on a fine screen with a mesh size larger than the individual eggs, permitting the eggs to fall into a tub or bowl underneath as you *gently* stir the roe to separate the eggs from the tissue and sac. The eggs are then tenderly washed in cold water, changed three or four times, and drained for not more than ten minutes, removing any froth. After draining, the eggs are salted. You use 5 ounces of very fine grained salt to each 10 pounds of eggs, a 32:1 ratio. Immediately afterward, the caviar is placed in a slip-lid tin or a jar, with *no* air left in the container. The caviar must be held under refrigeration at a temperature of 27 to 30 degrees Fahrenheit. It will reach its peak flavor in one week, and should be served within six months, for after that it may lose its delicacy and eye appeal very rapidly.

"The best caviar is generally eaten plain," Beyer continued, "on a thin piece of freshly made toast, without butter. The caviar itself should be fat enough not to require butter. Caviar that is more heavily salted than the best grade can stand a few drops of lemon juice, or may be sprinkled lightly with some finely chopped egg white, egg yolk, onions, or chives.

"The crowning achievement of an epicurean sportsman is to serve caviar with the breast meat of cold roast pheasant minced extremely fine. It must not be ground, but knife-chopped. Each guest heaps as much caviar as he wants on a piece of dry toast or very thin black bread, then sprinkles the minced pheasant meat over the caviar. The meat shouldn't be piled on the caviar—use just the amount that will adhere to the surface."

In an age when caviar brings three dollars an ounce, a man who buys in lots of three to fourteen tons is living on the edge of an abyss. Unlike any other food product, its critical storage temperature may vary only 5.5 degrees (26.5 to 32 degrees). From the time Beyer departs with his shipment from Astrakhan, on the Volga, until he reaches New York—a distance of 8,000 miles by boat, rail, and plane—he lives with thermometer in hand, checking the caviar every four hours.

Beyer tapped the lid of an elaborately decorated blue tin well known to gourmets throughout the world. "It has to be packed in slip-lid tins—never sealed. The prime test besides the berries' being whole is that each one is glistening in its own fat. The fattest part of the caviar rises to the surface of the can during transport, so a conscientious shipper has to make certain that his tins are turned frequently to keep the fat well distributed. I designed this tin myself, and one thing the Russians didn't notice at first, aside from the fact that I'm a Marine general, is our label."

He shoved the tin across his desk. Stamped in the scroll is the proud brand name: Fidelis.

[1965]

30

Dining on
Fish Roe

*Shad roe starts to appears on the menus of our north-
ern New England restaurants by mid-May and is as
much a part of spring's arrival as the blooming shad
bush and hatching "shadflies" that often signal the
start of both river-running shad and trout fishing.*

*If you're lucky enough to catch a large roe shad,
you'll find here detailed directions on how to make
the most of it. But not just shad, for as you'll see the
roe of a variety of fishes will all serve the purpose in
a variety of ways.*

When I first moved to Florida, thirty years ago, we used to
hunt quail on the Lykes Ranch west of Lake Okeechobee. One
of the most popular dishes among the cowboys back then was
a breakfast of pan-sautéed mullet roe served with grits. Delicate, nutlike, orange-colored roe in melted butter with crisp
bacon bits is one of those supernal dishes in fish cuisine. At
that time, there was no market for the ubiquitous mullet, and
I remember offering fresh-caught roe to friends who politely
refused it. Then came the invasion of astute Japanese buyers
a decade ago, and mullet roe shipped to Tokyo immediately

commanded some fifty dollars a pound—and the price has since gone out of sight. Reexported to the United States in the form of *karasumi,* it is now regarded as a Japanese delicacy. With the recent boom in sushi and sashimi bars, mullet roe is back in our markets; and along with cod roe (*hon-tarako*), pollack roe (*momijiko*), and herring roe (*kazunoko*), it is responsible for the coming of a new lexicon for the trendy Madison Avenue chopstick trade.

History does repeat itself, of course. The now-popular American caviar had no market until 1873, when Henry Schacht of Chester, Pennsylvania, began artfully salting the eggs of Delaware River sturgeon and shipping his product to Europe. Part of Schacht's output eventually returned here in the form of "Russian" caviar. The Delaware provided a phenomenal 670 tons of sturgeon roe in one season; yet it wasn't widely appreciated until the fishery collapsed at the turn of the century. For years it had been dispensed on free-lunch bars in New York saloons.

The gonads of fishes are ancient food. Even the milt sac of the male, known as the soft, or white roe—or more succinctly in medieval Britain as the fish's "jolly"—was consumed raw like an oyster by Indians of our Pacific Northwest and cherished by the kings of France when baked in tartlets as *laitances en caisses.* The promise of virility on the half shell may be a fable, but when you dine on shad roe, you are, depending on its size, consuming 25,000 to 150,000 oocytes, or immature eggs—a polyunsaturated wallop of protein that's far more satisfying than the hairy horn of rhinoceros.

Millions of ripe shad enter rivers from Nova Scotia to Florida and from the Sacramento River in California to southeastern Alaska. A standard-bearer in American cuisine for more than two centuries, shad roe has dominated the kitchen by sheer numbers. Nonetheless, whitefish, cisco, carp, striped bass, flounder, weakfish, spotted seatrout, Atlantic mackerel, Spanish mackerel, corvina, bluefish, haddock, cod, halibut, alewife, pompano, and dolphin (the fish, not the mammal) also produce fine roes. Dolphin, the famed *mahimahi* of Hawaii, which is even more abundant

in our Gulf Stream, offers a roe that is equal if not superior to shad. (The roes of puffers [blowfish], Atlantic barracuda, trunkfish, and freshwater gar are not marketed, because they are toxic. I mention this as a caution to those
anglers who may be tempted to conduct kitchen experiments.)

Roes vary in flavor and texture according to protein (granu-
lar yolk), oil, and water content and range in color from pale
yellow to bright orange, with some blue-gray and even green
roes, as in the lumpfish. The size of the eggs varies according
to species, generally from ½ millimeter to 5 millimeters in
diameter, with a few inedible, rubbery spheres reaching the
size of a golf ball. However, the dimensions of the eggs bear
no relation to those of the fish: the huge giant tarpon (popular
in Mexican and Central American kitchens) produces eggs
that are about the same diameter as those of a shad. Diminutive oocytes are typical of most pelagic spawners, which produce immense numbers; a big cod, for example, will scatter
9 million tiny eggs in the open sea during the course of a
season. From a culinary standpoint, we have to make a distinction, because large eggs tend to explode like popcorn
when heat is applied. The eggs are ideal when they're about
the size of a small bird shot (7½s or 9½s, if you're ballistically
oriented).

Cooked fresh roe is entirely different in texture from the
salted kind. It can be baked, broiled, poached, pan-sautéed,
or turned into creamed soups, casseroles, pâtés, and soufflés.
Roe are enclosed in two sacs connected by membrane and
together are called a set. A set can weigh as little as ⅛ ounce
in a herring, to more than 5 pounds in a tuna. If the set
exceeds an inch in thickness, it should be gently simmered in
water with 1 tablespoon lemon juice for about 5 minutes
before sautéing; otherwise it will burn on the outside before
cooking through. This also firms the roe and prevents it from
falling apart in the pan.

Of all preparation methods, I'm still partial to the old
Florida cowboy method of sautéing roe of any kind in butter.
The following ingredients are for an average 6- to 8-ounce set.

259

Optionally, you may want to add 1 or 2 cloves garlic, finely chopped, as I do.

SAUTÉED ROE WITH BACON

2 tablespoons flour
¼ teaspoon salt
⅛ teaspoon pepper
One 6- to 8-ounce set roe
2 tablespoons clarified butter
1 tablespoon finely snipped chives
2 slices bacon, crosscut in threadlike strips
2 toast points, buttered
1 tablespoon butter
1 tablespoon minced parsley
Lemon wedges

Combine the flour with the salt and pepper. Dust the roe lightly with this mixture. In a small sauté pan, warm the clarified butter over low heat and add the roe. Rotate the roe in the butter, then sprinkle with chives. Add the bacon bits. Cook over medium heat until the roe is browned on both sides (the interior of the roe will become opaque) and the bacon is crisp. Place each set on toast points. Quickly brown the additional butter in the pan drippings, then scrape and pour over the roe. Sprinkle with parsley and serve with lemon wedges.

Theoretically, a 6- to 8-ounce set should provide one portion; however, I never find it quite enough.

[1984]

31

The Ugliest Fish
in the Sea

*Increases in the American consumption of fish and
seafoods have been making newspaper headlines for
the past couple of years, which is partly, I suppose, as
a result of a new and national concern with personal
health. This at least partly explains the new popularity of some fishes on the plate that not too long ago
were sold simply as mink food to commercial ranch-
ers or otherwise disposed of. The goosefish, as cited
here by McClane, is a prime example.*

*Not long ago, the National Marine Fisheries Ser-
vice was a headline feature in the august* Wall
Street Journal, *which article described its efforts at
renaming some fishes—especially so-called ground
(bottom) fishes that make up the bulk of draggers'
catches—to improve their marketability. As
McClane points out here, goosefish by its name
alone just doesn't sound appetizing. A goosefish,
however, by any other name . . .*

It is perhaps to soothe innocent palates that many seafoods
must bear a foreign, and sometimes misleading, label before

261

they become popular. Historically, the witch flounder was a commercial disaster until it became the "gray sole"; the delectable grunt, a Keys staple back when Henry Flagler built his Florida railroad, never made the big time until two years ago, as "white snapper"; the truly superb walleye sounded like a barstool candidate for AA until it became a "yellow pike." In fact, these and other fish deserve applause under any name.

The American Fisheries Society, the august body that assigns common and scientific names, uses eighteen criteria other than menu niceties when christening a new species. Few diners would order a ratfish, batfish, horned whiff, long-spine combfish, slippery dick, gag, leatherjacket, or a scorpion fish, although the latter, for example, is the venerable *rascasse* of bouillabaisse fame. Until recently, the goosefish—aka monkfish, anglerfish, allmouth, bellyfish, frogfish, and sea devil—was a total flop in the American marketplace. When my *Encyclopedia of Fish Cookery* was first published in 1977, the goosefish was one of the cheapest seafoods available. At times, New England and Canadian draggers couldn't even give it away. Then George Morfogen, the astute buyer for Grand Central's Oyster Bar in New York, substituted its French name, *lotte,* and *voilà!*—a star was born. Some purveyors still use the name *monkfish,* but it doesn't sell as quickly as the Gallic version.

Fortunately, only the edible skinned tail portion of the goosefish appears at market. Fainthearted buyers would run screaming into the streets if they were to lay eyes on the whole fish. It has a huge, flattened head with its eyes on top, a cavernous mouth, and a short tapering body—a kind of tadpole shape, but 3 to 4 feet in length and weighing up to 50 pounds or more. The scaleless skin is so loose that it reminded some nomenclator of a monk's cowl. Its mouth is slanted upward, with its lower jaw projecting so far beyond the upper jaw that the multirowed curved teeth are exposed even when its mouth is closed—the ultimate underbite. Probably the ugliest fish in the Atlantic, the goosefish is literally a mouth that swims, and like the fowl, constantly stuffs itself, consuming anything with or without fins. Its diet consists of flounder, skate, squid, starfish, lobster, eel, herring, cod, sea bass—also ducks, cormorants, auks, gulls, loons, and sea turtles. Never one to pass up dessert, the goosefish will eat inanimate objects such as the buoys from lobster pots, beer cans, Coke bottles, light bulbs—even cigarette lighters and sunglasses have been excised from goosefish stomachs.

Even in sedentary periods, the fish doesn't quit eating; it lies camouflaged on the bottom, wiggling a long, rodlike spine that projects from the snout over its open mouth. This spine has a fleshy "flag" at its tip that lures curious prey into the creature's jaw—thus the name anglerfish. A large goosefish at Westhampton Beach, New York, grabbed a woman bather by the foot some years ago and attempted to tow her seaward. I recall trying to remove a hook from the mouth of a 20-pounder with a carbon-steel knife, and when its jaws clamped down, the blade was not only bent into an L-shape, but couldn't even be pried loose. How the lady got her foot out is a mystery to me; it would be like escaping from a bear trap. But if Nature in her bounty designed a bizarre creature, she overcompensated in the form of a truly delicious fish in its docile rear end.

The abundant goosefish roams the Atlantic, from the Grand Banks to North Carolina, and from coastal Norway through the Mediterranean in shoal water and deep. The dressed tail section that is now marketed from coast to coast is as firm and flavorsome as lobster meat, to which it is often compared. There is only one, easily removed median bone running through its center. The whole tail can be poached or steamed, but I prefer to cook it in the form of boneless medaillons by slicing the tail across the grain as though making veal cutlets. The medaillons can be pan-sautéed, then served with various sauces or butters. Indeed, the *lotte* is such a versatile fish that it will tolerate just about any whim of the chef.

My favorite is Medaillons of Lotte with Grape Sauce. You can use bottled pure-white grape juice in the recipe, but it doesn't take long to squeeze or process enough of the fresh fruit to make 1 cup, and a more velvety and fragrant sauce.

MEDAILLONS OF LOTTE WITH GRAPE SAUCE

½ cup sugar
2½ pounds white or green seedless grapes
1 orange
1 teaspoon chopped shallots
1 cup dry red wine
1 teaspoon cognac
1 tablespoon heavy cream
12 medaillons lotte, cut 1-inch thick
1 cup milk
3 eggs, beaten
Flour
¼ pound clarified butter
Salt and pepper

Dissolve the sugar in 1½ cups hot water. Poach ½ pound grapes in this simple syrup for 5 minutes, or until they're plump and tender, then drain. Slice the orange into 6 rounds, and cut these into half-moons. Set aside.

To make the sauce, combine in a saucepan chopped shallots, wine, and 1 cup juice extracted from the remaining grapes. Over low heat, reduce the liquid by half. Stir in cognac and cream; simmer about 2 minutes and reserve.

Moisten the fish in milk, then dip in beaten eggs and lightly coat in flour. Melt clarified butter in a large skillet and sauté the medaillons over medium heat until golden in color, or about 2½ minutes on each side. Season with salt and pepper to taste.

Arrange the medaillons in a row on a warm platter with ends overlapping. Tuck a slice of orange between each medaillon, so the bright rind is visible. Sprinkle with poached grapes. Reheat the sauce, and drizzle over the fish.

Accompany with crisp shoestring potatoes and a salad of Bibb lettuce with vinaigrette dressing. For a wine, either a California Chardonnay or Sauvignon Blanc; of Chardonnay, I recently enjoyed Robert Mondavi's 1981 Reserve, and of the latter, a Château St. Jean la Petite Etoile 1982.

Serves 6.

[1985]

32

A Not-So-Common
Perch

*As in the previous chapter, the walleye is another fish
whose unappealing—albeit accurate in terms of a description—name belies its wonderful role as table
fare. As McClane points out, the walleye is the peren-
nial basis for the famous shore lunch prepared by a
skilled guide/cook on a lakeside, north-country ledge.
This is a grand tradition in the northern Midwest and
in midwestern Canada as well, where walleyes are
common enough to be counted on for lunch before
they're even in the landing net.*

    *I live in trout country, where the nearest walleye
is at least two hours away by car, but as McClane
suggests here the method given for* crêpes de poisson
*also works well with a variety of other fishes, includ-
ing weakfish in the North and the ever-popular
Southern seatrout. Weakfish are usually included in
my northern saltwater excursions, and so will these*
crêpes *be henceforth.*

In fishing camps throughout Canada—from Quebec to Al-
berta and north to Hudson Bay—there is a ritual called the
shore lunch, which gives rise to an accumulation of smoke

that on a clear day can probably be seen at the North Pole. No matter which gamefish is being sought in the some 6,000 camps in that region, the one that is always delivered to the frying pan is the walleye. The fact that it has become a daily habit is a tribute to this bucolic perch with the nearly opaque light-reflecting eyes that look like a pair of moon marbles. A freshly shucked fillet, dipped in egg wash and rolled in crushed cornflakes, them steamily crisped, is the set piece by which a guide's culinary skills are judged. Yet the walleye is also found from sections of New England to Montana and south to Tennessee, where a record 25-pounder was caught in Old Hickory Lake. Millions of pounds are taken in our Midwest and South, especially in the spring, when spawning fish are migrating in the shallows.

The name *walleye* never excites unfamiliar taste buds. It's a *Zander* in Germany, a *smud* in Yugoslavia, and the name *kukka* does nothing to improve its image in Finland. The French name, *doré,* is more euphonious and less misleading than the American market label, yellow pike, that essential ingredient to a classic gefilte fish. Some anglers still use that old sobriquet walleyed pike, which isn't much better than *smud.* It isn't a pike, despite the fact that it frequently appears in restaurants as *quenelles de brochet.* But more important, it is one of the most versatile species in fresh water, the counterpart of an ocean sole, with sweet, snowy white meat that can be cooked by any method. It is easily filleted and has no pin bones or floating ribs to defeat an amateur's knife. In the myotomal structure of fishes, the walleye can be classed among those having the lightest flake. When bought at market, they are usually sold in fillet form, and the flesh should be firm to the touch, not mushy, despite that fragile texture.

As with other delicate fish, the simplest preparations are the most popular. I remember days spent fishing around Baltic islands where the shore lunch was *zander med pepparrot*—a gently poached fillet napped with melted butter and freshly grated horseradish—an old Swedish favorite. In Hungary, a broiled fillet was basted with butter and sweet paprika. My *smud* in Yugoslavia was quickly fired over a scorching heat in an oiled pan, skin side down, with the lid on the pan so that the flesh partially steamed while the skin almost burned—a most peculiar method of cooking, yet the dish was surprisingly tasty when doused with lemon butter.

The walleye is superb in any of the well-known sole recipes, but one of the most elegant ways of preparing it is in a crêpe. I have served this at small dinner parties on many occasions with great success. The recipe doesn't require any exotic ingredients; in fact, if you can't find yellow pike at market, you can try any mildly flavored, white-fleshed fish, such as sole, pompano, weakfish, grouper, snapper, or one of the quality Pacific rockfishes. Species with a robust flavor—mackerel or bluefish—are not suitable in a *crêpe de poisson.*

CRÊPES ZANDER

4 eggs
½ teaspoon curry powder
Salt
1 cup milk
1½ cups unsifted all-purpose flour
2 pounds skinless walleye fillets or other mild, white-fleshed fish
Fresh lemon or lime juice
½ pound sweet butter or margarine
1 cup dry white wine
3 cups half-and-half, approximately
Pepper
½ pound cooked chopped broccoli
⅓ cup grated Parmesan cheese
Capers for garnish

In a bowl, combine eggs, curry powder, ½ teaspoon salt, milk, and 1 cup flour. Beat these ingredients until smooth, then let the batter stand for 1 hour.

In the meantime, sprinkle the fillets with fresh lemon or, preferably, lime juice and dash them lightly with salt. Heat a 7-inch crêpe pan or skillet and wipe it with butter. Stir the batter thoroughly, then spread about 2 tablespoons in the pan and rotate it, spreading a thin layer over the entire bottom. Brown the crêpe on one side, then turn it out onto a piece of aluminum foil. Butter the pan again and make another crêpe. You have enough batter to make about 18 crêpes, which allows 3 stuffed crêpes per person—a dinner portion—for 6 people.

Place the walleye fillets in a large skillet and add white wine. Gently simmer, covered, 12 to 15 minutes; thin fillets will cook quickly and you don't want them to shred. Let cool in the liquid, then remove and break into bite-size pieces. Add enough half-and-half to the poaching liquid to make 4 cups. In a saucepan, melt ¼ pound sweet butter or margarine and stir in remaining ½ cup flour. Add the poaching liquid mixture and stir constantly over low heat, until the sauce thickens and bubbles. Add salt and pepper to taste. Pour half the sauce into a bowl; add the pieces of walleye plus the broccoli. This is your crêpe filling.

Preheat the oven to 350°F.

Spoon about 3 tablespoons filling into each crêpe and roll it up. Place them side by side, seam side down, in a lightly greased oblong casserole. Spoon the remaining sauce over the crêpes, and sprinkle them with grated Parmesan cheese. Bake in preheated oven 30 minutes, or until lightly browned. Garnish with capers.

To accompany the crêpes, I would serve a pear-and-watercress salad with a light oil dressing. A Chardonnay or a full-bodied Gewürztraminer would be my choice in wines.

Serves 6.

[1985]

33

A Shrimp by
Any Other Name

*Shrimp are perhaps more commonly ruined in cook-
ing than any other seafood. Overcooking here is the
cardinal sin—whether in a simple steaming or in a
more complex version as presented here.*

*I have made the following version of shrimp
scampi for guests several times, with all due credit to
McClane of course. The most memorable was one
evening when—more by good luck than good management—the pasta and the shrimp were ready in
exact sequence, all to the astonishment of our friends,
who recognized the impossible when they saw it. I
haven't done this dish for them again, not wishing to
press my luck!*

I don't know what happened to the original concept of the
fish called scampi, but the popular restaurant version has
become an insipid plate of shrimp mummified in a beurre
blanc with a splash of lemon. Gone are the days of old
Nando's in West Palm Beach, when the scampi was served
en cotte sizzling with enough herbs and garlic to stun a water
buffalo, a dish so addictive that the landed gentry of neigh-

boring Palm Beach ventured across the lake for a regular fix.

Of course, the very name is a conundrum, as a scampi and a shrimp are two different decapods, or ten-legged crustaceans. The authentic scampi are actually lobsterettes, unique and diminutive members of the lobster family. A scampi doesn't resemble a shrimp; it has the heavily armored body of a Maine lobster but with pencil-thin, virtually meatless claws. Although they are often identified with European waters—they're known by such designations as Norway lobster, Danish lobster, Dublin Bay prawn, the French *langoustine,* or the Spanish *cigala*—lobsterettes are found on all the continental shelves of the world's oceans to depths of 6,500 feet. Unfortunately, most of these populations in North American waters are benthic (bottom-dwelling) species and not as readily caught as the lobsterettes dwelling in the shallower waters of the Adriatic and North seas. Biology aside, our familiar penaeid shrimp of the western Atlantic not only make a delicious "shrimp" scampi but a celebrated party dish that can be prepared in advance, requiring nothing more than a final ten minutes in the kitchen.

Pasta is the perfect mate to a well-turned-out scampi. Ordinarily these are served separately, but individual courses don't have the eye appeal of a grass-green mound of linguine verdi surrounded by pink crustaceans, nor are they as palate-pleasing as when the two are handy to the fork. At large dinner parties this also cuts down on the dishwasher load, which, I must confess, is why I created the recipe many years ago while surviving in a Manhattan apartment with a kitchen the size of a phone booth.

For this dish you want "extra-large" fresh shrimp, which in commercial grading come 16 to 20 to a pound, heads off. If these are not available, settle for the large (21 to 30 to a pound), but don't go any smaller than that. They should be firm and smell fresh. Stale shrimp have an offensive ammonia odor; don't hesitate to use your nose when buying if the crustaceans appear to be separating from the shell. There are at least seven different penaeid shrimp in our market, and they vary in shell color according to species, so this is no criterion of quality; it's simply a reflection of seasonal abundance and distribution.

SCAMPI WITH LINGUINE VERDI

36 extra-large shrimp
¾ cup clarified butter
¼ cup olive oil
2 tablespoons minced garlic
2 tablespoons lemon juice
½ teaspoon dry mustard
1 teaspoon Worcestershire sauce
¼ teaspoon crushed dried hot red pepper
1 teaspoon minced fresh oregano
1 teaspoon minced fresh basil
1 teaspoon minced fresh tarragon
¼ teaspoon salt
2 tablespoons minced parsley
½ cup Chablis
1 pound linguine verdi
Freshly grated Parmesan cheese
Finely chopped parsley for garnish

The first step, and the only time-consuming one, is to cut each shrimp ventrally, so it can be fanned out piggyback style. With a sharp-pointed knife, slice the shrimp from end to end on the underside without cutting through the shell. With the pressure of both thumbs on the dorsal side, pop the meat up so it sits on the carapace, which is now bent slightly upward in the middle. If a blue or black filament is visible and is aesthetically displeasing, pluck it out. This intestine is perfectly edible, though, and may add a dollop of vitamins in the form of consumed zooplankton. Don't remove the legs. The object of piggybacking is to loosen and expose as much of the meat as possible to the sauce; when split in ordinary fashion, the cooked meat will stick to the carapace, and if you remove the shell completely, it'll look like cat food when composed with the pasta.

There are two other things to know about this recipe. I have a year-round herb garden outside my kitchen window, and there's no question that fresh is best, but if you do fall back on dried substitutes for oregano, basil, and tarragon, you can simplify by using the ubiquitous Spice Islands Italian

Herb Seasoning: 1½ teaspoons in total. And although 2 table-spoons minced garlic may sould like an overdose, it becomes mild when cooked in liquid for 10 minutes. Indeed, lovers of the bud may well use 3 tablespoons for like-minded guests.

In a saucepan, melt ¾ cup clarified butter. Add olive oil, garlic, lemon juice, dry mustard, Worcestershire sauce, crushed dried hot red pepper, oregano, basil, tarragon, salt, and parsley. Mix well and simmer over low heat until the garlic is blond. Turn off the heat.

Take each shrimp by the tail and dip into the mixture so that each is well coated, and arrange them side by side, flesh side up, in a shallow foil-lined baking pan. Add Chablis to the saucepan and bring to a boil, reduce heat, then simmer 10 minutes. Spoon all of the sauce over the shrimp, making certain that garlic bits and herbs cling to the meat. (At this point you can set the pan aside if dinner is an hour or two away, or place it in the refrigerator for longer periods. For that matter, this can all be done a day in advance.)

When ready to cook, preheat the oven to 400°F. and simultaneously bring salted water to a boil in your pasta pot. The shrimp will take exactly 7 minutes and the linguine 8 minutes for both to be *al dente*. Drain the pasta and fork a small mound in the center of each warm plate, leaving a margin for the shrimp. Arrange the crustaceans, with tails pointing outward, at equal intervals around the linguine. Spoon the remaining sauce over the pasta and sprinkle with freshly grated Parmesan. Anoint both pasta and shrimp with finely chopped parsley, and serve. The crustaceans can be taken by the tail and eaten with the hands; if you do it this way, provide a communal bowl for the shells.

I usually accompany scampi with a spinach or water-cress salad with a simple vinaigrette dressing. As for wine, you want a *light* red, if red is preferred, for this I suggest a Chianti Classico Riserva (by Castello di San Paolo Rosso) 1978, or for a white, Gavi dei Gavi 1983. A mint sorbet is a fitting climax.

Serves 6.

[1984]

34

Angling for Trout

As trout fishing and trout eating are often inseparable both in winter memory and summer supper, I'm delighted to pass along a brief guide to the latter. Among other things, McClane offers here a unique approach to the famous Truite au Bleu *(Blue Trout), which in this instance doesn't taste like "trout with vinegar" as the traditional preparation might better have been called.*

For the angler, and as Al points out, eating a trout is inextricable from the memories of many catches. My own eating fish are trout from the dashing mountain brook by the house. I shoot grouse and woodcock along its banks in the fall, and play with my children in its summer pools. The sound and taste of cooking trout always brings such things to mind.

One of the dividends of a Catskill boyhood in the 1930s was a chill, fern-fringed brook that tumbled off the mountains through dark hemlocks and windfall tangles. On those rare days when the chores of a dairy farm were not demanding, I could jump along the mossy rocks in Rider Hollow Stream, probing its currents with a dry fly to catch the brilliant little jewels that sparkled and danced in the sunshine. Sometimes I'd just sit on a ledge and watch the trout. Against the pale amber bottom they looked like jade butterflies, speckled with crimson spots, as they swayed and swooped in some stylized dance. Even the sounds of the forest were ethereal. A chipmunk would whistle, or a band of hummingbirds would tune the bells of the daylilies, but the compelling sound was flowing water, so cold that it would hurt my teeth to drink it on a summer day.

At the top of the mountain, there was an infant waterfall that formed a deep greeny pool shouldered by gravel bars where I could build a fire and cook my trout. Early in the game I stashed an iron skillet under a granite ledge, which must be an oxidized artifact today. As in all Pleistocene-epoch streams of the Appalachian chain, native brook trout have a brief life span, with a climax size of about a foot in length. Nature designed them for the frying pan; three little trout could be tucked in my skillet, allowing room to curl and sizzle until the crisp skin popped, exposing moist, pink flakes. After a half-century fishing career in over a hundred countries, I admit to more superlative fish at table, but the flavor of a wild brook trout in its prime, foamy with butter, hits the synapses of my brain like that two-dollar Big Ben alarm clock on a school morning.

Nobody but an angler can ever know the joys of these trout at table. There are more than twenty North American species of trout within the salmonid complex, of which only three are cultivated in commercial hatcheries. These "factory" products are uniformly good—indeed, some are excellent—but the nuances of flavor among wild trout from disparate environments is comparable to those of Pinot Noirs or Chardonnays from a hundred microclimates. An astute oenophile can muster at least forty different terms for describing a wine, but, traditionally, there has been little flexibility, or even accuracy, in describing the six organoleptic properties of fish: odor, flavor, texture, color, fat content, and moisture content.

Only among ancient fishing cultures such as the Inuit (Eskimo is a derogatory Cree Indian term) does a single species of fish have a dozen or more different names according to their culinary value. When my wife and I tented at an isolated Inuit village one summer on Ungava Bay in northern Labrador, we dined mainly on seal, caribou, salmon, and Arctic char—a generic clone of the brook trout. The char that we caught in one location were called *irkaluk,* at the next *ekaluk,* and at another *ivitaruk.* Having minimal Inuit at our command, we did not at first realize that our neighbors were describing migratory or nonmigratory char, their sexual maturation or fat content, and flesh color, which can be white, pink, orange, or crimson. The white-fleshed char were simply fed to the sled dogs, but the prime sea-run *ilkalupik,* made crimson and fat from a diet of amphipods and capelin, are to my taste the finest of all fish food in the world. The very best come from northern Baffin Island, in northeastern Canada, near Pond Inlet. However, char is an Inuit subsistence food and rarely comes to the United States. If you can't buy it, you must catch it, and I can think of no better reason for a fishing trip.

High in the Spanish Peaks of Montana there are two isolated lakes within a few miles of each other that hold populations of brook trout. Whenever my craving for a real taste of the wild requires a fix, as it periodically does, my wife and I literally bounce up by four-wheel drive to an altitude of about 8,000 feet where the rocky trail ends; then go by shank's mare past an elk meadow to the east lake basin. In the lake to the west, the fish are white-fleshed, vapid in flavor, and in the other, fiery orange, where in the words of Izaak Walton, "I can compare them to nothing so fitly as to cherries newly gathered from a tree." Although these environments seem identical, the better lake to the east has an abundance of scuds (a shrimplike amphipod), which the trout gorge on, while the other lacks crustaceans of any kind. Flesh color in salmonids derives from fat-soluble carotenoids found in shrimp, crayfish, and various amphipods, copepods, and euphausiids. In both Chile and Argentina, where the rivers literally crawl with freshwater crabs or *cangrejos* (unique to South America), the rainbow trout achieve a brilliant red and a sweet almond flavor. Some commercial hatcheries, both here and abroad, add carotene to their trout food, which produces a good imitation of a wild fish's color, but the flavor difference is like the difference between a barnyard Muscovy duck and that noble canvasback grown fat on a diet of wild celery.

Some fish, such as the sole, remain bland in flavor no matter what they eat; as a result, the sole has inspired a galaxy of what hotelier Charles Ritz has labeled "historic kitchen apologies" in the form of multifaceted sauces. But the best trout require no such adornment.

Charlie Ritz and I once made a trip to a dozen different rivers in France, seeking the perfect brown trout. Our test was uniform in that each sample was cooked in simple *au bleu* style (recipe on page 278), to highlight the essence of trout flavor. Some of the fish we sampled were almost as mossy as those from our Delaware River and had to be salvaged with hollandaise sauce. One sample was so sodden with geosmin (a by-product of algae) that it couldn't even be retrieved with a garlicky sauce provençale. We finally voted for the white, sweet-fleshed fish, with a hint of cucumber, from Normandy's Andelle River. (Many lake and sea-run populations in western Europe provide delectable pink-fleshed brown trout, which has given rise to that contradiction in menu poetry "salmon-trout" or—as I discovered last summer at several Norwegian restaurants, obviously with management's eye to the kroner—simply "salmon.")

But for me the best brown trout are the ones from the crayfish-rich waters of the upper Missouri River in Montana, specifically, those fish of 4 pounds or more. Like a grand cru Burgundy, they require aging—and more than average skill to catch. The juvenile fish are mainly insectivorous, gorging on mayflies, and it isn't until they develop jaws like a nutcracker that crayfish become dominant in their diet, and their meat a deep, sweet pink.

In my search for the perfect trout, I once had an uninvited expert provide the ultimate accolade. A few years ago, while exploring some remote rivers by helicopter on the western shore of Hudson Bay, I found myself standing eyeball-to-eyeball with a polar bear. The pack ice had melted and the old bruin was foraging inland. Fortunately, I had piled a limit catch of big brook trout on the bank to supply our camp, and for the longest sixty seconds in my life, I watched that hairy monster licking his chops, obviously trying to decide which was the daily special. The fact that he selected a classic, rather than nouvelle cuisine, is reason enough to sing the praises of trout and, perhaps, polar bears. He ambled off with a conciliatory burp.

TROUT GRENOBLOISE

1 cup all-purpose flour
½ teaspoon salt
¼ teaspoon freshly ground pepper
Two 8-ounce trout, gutted
½ cup peanut or cottonseed oil
2 tablespoons clarified butter
2 tablespoons capers
1 tablespoon diced lemon pulp
1 teaspoon fresh lemon juice
Lemon wedges and parsley sprigs for garnish

In a shallow bowl, combine flour, salt, and pepper. Wash trout under cold running water and drain thoroughly, but do not pat dry. Dust each fish with the seasoned flour while still damp so that it's lightly coated; shake off excess. Place on a cooking rack and refrigerate 3 to 4 hours, or overnight, for a crisper skin.

Pour oil into a heavy skillet large enough to hold both trout and place over moderately high heat. Add trout and cook, turning once, until crisp and well browned, about 5 minutes on each side. Remove trout to absorbent paper, then transfer to a warm serving platter.

In a small skillet, combine clarified butter, capers, lemon pulp, and lemon juice over high heat until warmed through; pour over fish. Garnish platter with lemon wedges and parsley.

Serves 2.

Virtually all blue trout recipes require that the fish be cooked in what amounts to vinegared water; this inevitably results in a trout that tastes like vinegar. To retain a delicate flavor, I prefer a two-step procedure, which produces instant blueing and more aromatic poaching.

Traditionally, a live fish is used for *truite au bleu;* at the least the fish should be killed and gutted as soon as possible before cooking to retain the characteristic blue color and curled shape of this dish.

BLUE TROUT (TRUITE AU BLEU)

1 cup dry white wine
1 tablespoon fresh lemon juice
2 celery ribs, cut into ½-inch pieces
½ cup celery leaves
1 large carrot, sliced ½ inch thick
1 medium onion, quartered
6 parsley sprigs, plus additional sprigs for garnish
1 tablespoon chopped fresh tarragon, or 1 teaspoon dried tarragon
3 bay leaves
6 peppercorns, bruised
¼ teaspoon salt
2 cups tarragon vinegar
Two 1-pound trout, gutted

In a noncorrodible pan with a lid, large enough to poach the trout, combine wine, lemon juice, celery, celery leaves, carrot, onion, 6 parsley sprigs, tarragon, bay leaves, peppercorns, and salt with 2 quarts water and bring to a boil. Boil 30 minutes, then strain through a fine mesh sieve, discarding the solids. Return court bouillon to the pan; bring to a boil.

In another large noncorrodible pot, combine vinegar with 1 quart water and bring to a boil. With large kitchen tongs, grasp one trout by the lower jaw and, tilting the pot, lower it into the hot vinegar mixture. Boil 30 seconds to 1 minute; when trout is properly bluish-gray, transfer to the boiling court bouillon. Repeat the process with the second fish, leaving the first fish in the court bouillon. When the court bouillon returns to a boil after adding the second fish, remove pot from heat and cover. Let stand 15 minutes, until trout are cooked.

Remove fish with a large spatula. Drain, and serve on a warmed platter. Garnish with parsley sprigs.

Serves 4.

TROUT PORTUGAISE

1 trout (about 1 pound), gutted
3 tomatoes, quartered
3 green bell peppers, cut lengthwise into eighths
4 tablespoons unsalted butter, melted
¼ cup olive oil, preferably extra-virgin
Salt
Pepper
1½ teaspoons chopped fresh oregano, or ½ teaspoon dried oregano
1 stuffed green olive, sliced
3 black olives, halved
6 anchovy fillets
1 teaspoon grated lemon zest

Preheat oven to 350°F. Lay trout in a large baking dish and arrange tomatoes and peppers around it.

In a small bowl, combine melted butter and oil. Pour about half the butter-oil mixture over the fish and vegetables. Season with salt and pepper to taste, and sprinkle with half the oregano. Bake, uncovered, 15 minutes.

Remove from oven and, with a fork, gently lift off the top skin of the trout. Place a green olive slice on the eye. Arrange the black olive halves and anchovy fillets on the trout in a "backbone and rib" pattern. If your anchovies are too soft to make neat "rib" strips, coarsely chop the olives and anchovies and distribute them over and inside the trout.

Pour the remaining butter-oil mixture over the fish, and sprinkle with the remaining oregano and the grated lemon zest. Season with salt and pepper to taste. Return to the oven until the flesh at the backbone is still slightly translucent, about 15 minutes. Accompany with rice.

Serves 2.

SPAGHETTI WITH TROUT MARINARA

¼ cup plus 2 tablespoons olive oil
1 garlic clove, finely chopped
1 medium onion, coarsely chopped
½ pound mushrooms, sliced
Four 12-inch trout, filleted, skinned, and cut crosswise into
1-inch-wide strips (2¾ pounds meat)
3 cups tomato sauce, preferably homemade
½ teaspoon minced fresh oregano, or a pinch of dried
oregano
½ teaspoon minced fresh basil, or a pinch of dried basil
1½ teaspoons salt
¾ teaspoon freshly ground pepper
2 pounds spaghetti
2 tablespoons unsalted butter
2 tablespoons chopped parsley for garnish

In a large heavy pot or flameproof casserole, heat ¼ cup oil over moderate heat. Add garlic, onion, and mushrooms and sauté until the onion has softened, about 5 minutes.

Add the trout strips, tomato sauce, oregano, basil, 1 teaspoon salt, and ½ teaspoon pepper. Simmer gently over low heat, stirring occasionally, until the trout is just opaque, about 10 minutes. Turn off the heat and let the sauce sit until the pasta is ready.

In a large pot of boiling salted water, cook the spaghetti until tender but still firm (*al dente*), 8 to 10 minutes. Drain well. Toss with butter, the remaining 2 tablespoons oil, and the remaining salt and pepper.

Place the pasta on a warm serving platter and top with the sauce. Sprinkle with the chopped parsley.

Serves 8 to 10.

[1984]

35

Smoking the
Best

I recently had the good fortune not only to be salmon fishing in Norway, but also to be on the Gaula River for a couple of days when the salmon were cooperative. We were staying in the small village of Støren, about seventy-five miles south of Trondheim, and the village smokehouse was within a few hundred yards of the hotel. It was a simple matter then, to drop a 25-pounder, still ocean-bright, off at the smokehouse, to be picked up a couple of days later. The extent of this largesse was brought home at the airport in Oslo, where, en route home with my own smoked sides, I noted that smoked salmon was on sale for $25 U.S. per kilo—a tidy sum but still substantially less than our market prices at home.

News of the catch preceded me, and the neighbors were practically standing in line by the time I reached southern Vermont. By the time the tasting and toasting was over, my supply was considerably diminished. The answer, of course, is another salmon trip—but these, it seems, come as hard as the smoked salmon itself.

Wild Atlantic salmon populations are at a critical stage now. The spawning is on both sides of the ocean down 50 to 75 percent, and the West Greenland fishery, which is a common feeding fund for large European and South American salmon, has recently produced some of the poorest catches in history. But there is good news, for salmon farming has finally evolved into a major industry. Norway alone has almost 400 rearing operations, some blocking off entire bays between islands and fjords. Isolated from the rich ocean crustacean diet that colors the flesh of wild salmon to a fiery orange, the domestic kind is pale by comparison. But if it doesn't resemble a rod-caught fish from the Grand Cascapedia, the flavor and texture is undeniably *Salmo salar* at its best. So the future looks bright in terms of supply, but world demand will continue to make salmon a luxury item. With the smoked product costing sixteen to forty-eight dollars a pound, it takes some selection to shop and slice with confidence.

Of the five species of Pacific salmon found along our shores, the coho and chinook (king) most commonly enter the smoked-fish trade. These western salmon are in a separate family from the Atlantic species and have a different myotomal (muscle band) structure, with a higher moisture content. They do not cold-smoke in the firm, elastic style of the Atlantic. But both the coho and chinook are uniquely flavored and make praiseworthy products. During recent years of scarcity, the coho, which more nearly resembles our eastern salmon, was used in British kilns with great success. However, the standard-bearer is undeniably the finely textured fish that appears in the cave paintings of troglodyte man—colorful paeans to that ancestor of all salmons, the Atlantic.

Traditionally, smoked salmon has been identified as Scotch, Irish, Swedish, Icelandic, Nova Scotia, and so on, while some restaurants cling to the Scotch-smoked title even if the fish was a coho from Bristol Bay, Alaska, and was processed in Brooklyn. To me, this is all vague to the point of being almost meaningless, as there is no real basis for comparison. In fact, any smokehouse can turn out perfect (or inferior) cold-smoked sides regardless of its location. If the labeling were to read "Scotch-Smoked by John Ross of Aberdeen"; "London-Smoked by Forman & Sons"; "Swedish-Smoked by A. B. S. Mattsson of Svangsta"; "Quebec-Smoked by Ezio Bera of St. Antoine d'Tilly"; or "New York–Smoked by the Oyster Bar of Grand Central," we would know something of real value.

Each kiln has a "style" predicated on the addition of herbs and spices, sugar, alcohols (some houses use Demeraran rum, Cointreau, or aquavit), the kind of wood used (in barren Iceland the local fishermen burn sheep dung as fuel), and the curing process itself. The basic cure consists of brining or dry salting, air drying, then smoking, but there are so many options in these three stages that perceptible distinctions exist in the final product of various houses. Modern electronically controlled kilns made of steel or tile are in widespread use and regulate the smoking process right down to oven humidity. Still, many old-timers who spurn technology continue to be among the world's best.

Presliced vacuum-packed sides of salmon are more expensive than the uncut fillet, and provided the side is going to be devoured quickly, say at a big cocktail party, the convenience may be worth the extra dollars. But there's no great trick to slicing a salmon. Smoked sides are usually sold with the pectoral fin and girdle (collarbone) intact; these should be cut off. Some curers also leave the rib cage in the fillet, but this is easy to lift out by running a thin-bladed, sharp-pointed knife under the ribs and following their contour downward. The entire cage can be removed in one piece. Begin slicing at the head end of the fillet, cutting on the bias at a 45-degree angle, using a knife with a long, razor-sharp, flexible blade. A serrated twelve-inch, high-carbon-steel knife, such as the Pro 2100 made by Marks, is ideal.

If you want to make really thin slices, run your cut in one direction only—in other words, don't use a sawing motion, but slice, then gently slide the blade back on the reverse stroke before cutting again; that way the myotomes won't shred. As you progress toward the thinner tail end of the fillet, gradually increase the angle of your blade to about 30 degrees, then 20 degrees to create larger slices. It takes a little practice, but if you work slowly with the correct knife, the task is about as difficult as chopping parsley.

Smoked salmon has a shelf life of about two weeks if it's stored in the refrigerator with the skin from any used portion folded back over the fillet. If you still have a leftover piece, cut it in slices, pack loosely in a mason jar, top with extra-virgin olive oil, and screw on the lid—you'll have a modern version of the airless Greek amphora. I've kept salmon this way under refrigeration up to six months with no loss of flavor or texture. Do not freeze the fish, as it desiccates when in an airtight wrap.

When you're shopping, deal with a shop that specializes in smoked salmon and has a rapid turnover. The surface of the fillet should be unbroken; if it shows cracks or fractures, either it was not properly air-dried, or it was smoked at too high a temperature and the flesh is no longer elastic. The surface should also have a glossy finish; this pellicle forms during the air-drying stage of curing and seals in moisture, creating a velvety texture. If you buy a whole side and the tail portion is dry or too salty, it means the fish was not salted skillfully, and the tail end soaked up sodium chloride as the fish "sweated" when hung vertically in the kiln. A quality side has the same delicate flavor and texture from head to tail. Personally, I don't care for salmon that has been too heavily accented with smoke. When curing my own, I use a combination of apple and maple wood, which results in a fragrant rather than a harsh finish.

The salmon should be served fanned out on a slightly chilled plate with lemon wedges, capers, freshly cracked pepper, and, if the fish is lean, a drizzle of olive oil. (If it glistens with its own fat, skip the oil.) The perfect wine for this noble dish is a fruity Gewürztraminer as done in Alsace by Hugel.

[1986]

36

Poaching: Art of the Fish Gourmet

One of the distinct pleasures in working on this book has been the absolute necessity of trying many of the techniques it describes. A recent excursion to northern New Hampshire found us with some stream-fresh trout, an evening fire, and a copy of the following story that I'd brought along just in case. The trout were quickly poached—as described in the following pages—and even more quickly disappeared, eaten by my not-yet-one-year-old son and his grandparents with equal relish.

My mother, for her many successful years in the kitchen, had never poached fish of any sort, and this was a revelation. None of the oils, fats, or salts that her diet restricts is necessarily required in poaching, and poached fish has now become a household staple. We now also carry a collection of cheesecloth "envelopes" sewn at home for the express purpose of poaching trout in camp.

Some years ago, when faced with the task of serving a meal that would best represent American cuisine for Her Majesty

285

Queen Elizabeth and His Royal Highness Prince Philip, who were then visiting New York, chef Claude Phillipe nominated, with historical precedent, striped bass for the royal feast. (William Wood wrote in 1634 in *New England's Prospects*, "the basse is one of the best fishes in the country, and though men are sonne wearied with other fish, yet they are never with basse.") Over 4,500 pounds of stripers, fresh from Montauk Point, simmered on the Waldorf's ranges while Monsieur Claude's crew brewed vats of champagne sauce. Claude Phillipe has since departed for that big kitchen in the sky, but the dinner, which included a South Carolina turtle soup and a fillet of Kansas beef, was a classic based, he told me, "on the integrity of the foods." Fewer than twenty-four hours had elapsed for the striped bass to be delivered from boat to fire—freshness is the secret of all fish poaching. The striper is one of those species that does not require prompt field dressing or rapid transport to be safely edible. Yet, the difference between hours-old and days-old bass is a culinary eternity.

Pike fishing in the Baltic Sea is not high on my list of things I'd rather do than cast for Atlantic salmon, but when Len Borgstrom said he had a craving for *kokt gadda med pepparrot* we abandoned Sweden's Morrum River for the offshore islands. Poached pike with fresh horseradish is a Scandinavian passion. Len deposited me in some soggy bullrushes, then went *pockata pockata* elsewhere. I soon wished I had stayed in the boat—within two minutes I was nearly beaten to death by a pair of nesting mute wild swans. I don't know whether you've ever come face to face with wild swans, but believe me, a 5-foot bait-casting rod is no defense. I used all eight foil parries with suitable ripostes and even did a fairly good flèche before landing on my face in the mud. After disengaging under a cloud of feathers, I found myself peeking behind every bush. However, the little pike were no less frenzied than the swans.

That night Len's wife, Annika, poached our fish in some salted water with carrots, onions, and pimiento. Covered with freshly grated horseradish and melted butter, then served with dill-scented potatoes, it was a memorable meal.

This is the simplest form of poaching. You can even do it in camp with a deep skillet. It doesn't matter whether you use small whole trout, bass fillets, or chunks of pike. Serve the fish hot with melted butter and lemon, or cold with an herb-flavored mayonnaise. Poaching is really easier than pan frying, which requires a modicum of talent to avoid overcooking and moisture loss.

There is another method of poaching, usually called "boiled" fish, which it is not. The salted water churns violently at high heat before the fish is added. It stops boiling instantly and the pot is removed from the stove. Next, the lid is slapped on, and the fish is left to stand in hot water for about 10 to 15 minutes. This is the way we do chunks of freshly jigged cod on the Newfoundland tuna grounds. Slathered in 90-score butter and served with a boiled potato, it's an ambrosial quick meal. This is an old country method of poaching favored by busy fishermen working in small galleys.

All you have to remember about poaching is that it is done at a simmer or about 180°F., so the liquid just bubbles and shakes. As for cooking time, you can figure 10 minutes to the inch, measuring the fish at its thickest point. When done, the flesh will have lost its translucence and become opaque, flaking easily when prodded with a fork. Even in our "serious" seafood kitchen where we might prepare a whole poached striped bass or salmon for the festive board, the method is essentially simple. Although a whole fish of modest size can be simmered in a big roasting pan, the correct poaching utensil is not expensive and is far better designed for the job.

Fish poachers are made in two general shapes: the most common is a rectangular pan for cylindrical-bodied fish and the other is diamond-shaped for flat fishes such as flounders, sole, or turbot. The latter is a specialist item, and if you consider buying a second poacher it's more practical to have two rectangular pans; the popular 24-inch length, which is ample for fish up to 4 pounds in size, and the 36-inch length for fish of 8 to 10 pounds. Larger fish can always be cut in halves or sections and reunited on the serving platter. Remember, a yard-long pan won't fit across the burners of every stove, so there is a mechanical limit.

Inside the poacher you will find a removable perforated rack for lifting the fish out of a hot broth. If you don't own a poacher and are using some other kind of pan, double-wrap the fish in cheesecloth, leaving about 12 inches of cloth at each end. Twist and knot the ends, or tie them off with string and use these as handles. Don't let them hang out of the pan—they can catch fire. I wrap my fish even when using a rack because it makes skinning much easier. You can turn a hot fish in cloth without breaking it, or burning your fingers, and it helps to roll the fish onto a serving platter.

While salted water is perfectly adequate for poaching, the ultimate flavor is achieved by using a court bouillon or short broth. This is made of aromatic vegetables, herbs, and spices simmered in water to which white wine has been added. There is no exact formula. The choice of ingredients is a matter of individual taste, as is the ratio of wine to water. The following is a basic court bouillon and should be made before you begin the poaching.

WHITE WINE COURT BOUILLON

8 cups water
4 cups dry white wine
2 onions, chopped
2 celery ribs with leaves, chopped
2 carrots, chunked
4 tablespoons chopped parsley stems
1 sprig fresh thyme, or ½ teaspoon dried thyme
2 bay leaves, broken up
1 garlic clove
8 cracked peppercorns
1 tablespoon salt
12 thin lemon slices

Combine all ingredients in a large kettle and bring to a boil. Reduce heat and simmer 40 minutes. Strain the broth through a sieve into a fish poacher. With the back of a spoon, press down on the vegetables to express all their juices into the broth. This makes about 2 quarts, which is a minimal amount. Double or triple the recipe according to size of the fish, adding a little water, if necessary, to cover.

After you make the court bouillon, measure the fish at its thickest point to determine cooking time and carefully wrap it in cheesecloth. Place it on the poacher rack and lower into the broth, which is just lukewarm by now. Turn the heat on and bring the liquid to a slow simmer. Put the lid on your poacher. Cook according to the estimated time, and leave the fish in the broth for another 10 minutes. Transfer the fish to your work counter and open the cheesecloth. Remove the skin from one side of the fish by lifting it free with a small sharp knife and peeling it loose by hand. Remove the eye; this can be replaced later with a slice of olive or cherry tomato. The layer of dark-colored meat along the median line, which lies just under the skin and is prominent in some species, can be removed with the point of your knife after the fish has set. When you have skinned one side of the fish, roll it onto a heated serving platter and skin the opposite side. Garnish the platter with suitable citrus slices, vegetables, and fresh herbs. Serve with a bowl of sauce; one of the most simple and versatile is caper sauce.

CAPER SAUCE

4 tablespoons butter
4 tablespoons flour
2 cups strained court bouillon from poached fish
6 tablespoons capers with juice

Over a low heat, make a roux with the butter and flour, and add enough liquid, stirring as you add it, to give the consistency of white sauce. Stir in capers.

Makes 2 1/2 half cups.

At this point many amateurs pour the broth into the sink. This is a total waste. Assuming that you came home with more than one fish and have other uses for the rest of the catch, that broth can be converted into a rich fish stock or fumet that makes a wonderful base for sauces, soups, and chowders. It can be used in any recipe in place of water. All you have to do is add some fish heads and bones to the leftover broth and simmer over low heat for another 30 minutes.

The heads of any kind of fish may be used, but some species are meatier (as seen in the adductor muscles or "cheeks" of cod and salmon, for example) and contain more cartilage, making the stock more gelatinous. Equally rich are grouper, Pacific rockfish, snapper, and striped bass. I throw in fins and skins also (make sure the skin has been scaled) then strain out all the trimmings after cooking. The Chinese classic is shark fin. (In reality, shark-fin soup is a gelatinous stock derived from the radial cartilages that support the fins and, like grouper heads, they have long been the "secret" ingredient of many famous fish and bivalve chowders.) Fish stock is easy to make and keep on hand, frozen in pint- or quart-size plastic containers. As in a court bouillon, there's no exact formula for making a fumet. I usually follow the ratio of 12 cups of broth to each 2 pounds of trimmings. To expedite the cooking of large heads they should be split lengthwise and, regardless of size, the gills should always be removed.

The first time I fished a French chalkstream back in 1948, I was puzzled by the big screened wooden box that local anglers kept floating in the water. I thought they were oversize minnow buckets. However, this piece of equipment was for holding trout alive. Among the classic poached-fish dishes popular throughout Europe is "blue trout." It is not well known in America simply because we don't have the country inns that maintain live tanks near their kitchens. In theory, the fish must be alive until the last instant just before poaching, in order to change color. At least this is the purist chef concept. Actually, you can do it without boxes or tanks by using freshly killed trout a few hours out of the water. The blue color comes from the same lubricant that makes a fish slippery—the slime that keeps it waterproof. A trout that has dried out, been handled too much or frozen, won't turn blue. Trout flavor is subtle at best (or permeated with algae at worst) and poaching enhances that delicate flavor. The fish will run rivulets of stream-born nectar. Small trout of about 10 inches in length, whole and gutted, are ideal for blueing. Allow 1 or 2 fish per person.

To blue trout you need a large kettle or roasting pan (in addition to your poacher) containing a lukewarm court bouillon. No cheesecloth. In the kettle mix 4 cups tarragon vinegar to each 8 cups water. You want enough liquid to cover the fish. Place this on a burner next to the poacher and bring to a boil. With large kitchen tongs, grasp each trout by the lower jaw and drop in the hot vinegar mixture. It takes only a minute or so for the fish skin to turn blue. When properly colored, turn off the heat and transfer the trout to the poacher rack, using the tongs. Turn on the heat under your poacher and when the broth comes to a boil remove the pan from the stove and cover. Let this stand for about 15 minutes and the fish are cooked. Remove the rack and slide the fish onto your serving platter. The trout will be curled in a U shape, which is a myotomal reaction of really fresh fish.

Traditionally, blue trout are napped with hollandaise sauce and served with marble-size new potatoes and garnished with parsley. A side dish of garden-fresh asparagus and a watercress salad are the usual companions. There are countless recipes for hollandaise sauce, but the following is one that I learned from Charlie Ritz on the Andelle River in Normandy, which gives it a kind of piscatorial authenticity.

HOLLANDAISE SAUCE

4 egg yolks
1 tablespoon light cream
1 tablespoon tarragon vinegar
¼ pound butter
1 teaspoon lemon juice
Salt
Cayenne pepper

291

In a double boiler over low heat, beat egg yolks with cream and vinegar, using a wire whisk. Continue beating the yolks until they begin to thicken. Add one-third of the butter, and when melted add the remainder, bit by bit. Beat until the sauce is thick. Should the mixture curdle, immediately beat in 1 or 2 tablespoons boiling water to rebind the emulsion. Add the lemon juice and salt and cayenne to taste. Set the pan in lukewarm water until serving time.

Makes about 1 1/2 cups.

Another poached classic, which lends the final dimension, is a Marguery. This has long been identified with sole but any thin fillet whether yellow perch, flounder, black bass, mullet, or trout will be a winner. Fillets of thin or small fish tend to collapse when poached, but they can be turned into rolls or *paupiettes,* remaining firm and full of flavor. This Marguery recipe is an elegant dish, yet it can be produced in a large cast-iron skillet or even a baking pan and doesn't require a court bouillon. Although the recipe calls for shrimp and mussels, don't let the possible lack of ingredients spoil your fun. At the least you will enjoy a marvelous poached fish with a creamy cheese sauce.

FISH FILLETS MARGUERY

6 thin fillets (4 ounces each)
Water and wine in equal parts to cover fish
1 bay leaf
2 parsley stems
Salt
6 large shrimp, butterflied
24 mussels
Mornay Sauce (see following recipe)
Chopped parsley

Starting with the tail end, roll up each fillet and fasten with a toothpick. If in the 4-ounce size (perch fillets are often smaller), cut each roll in half to make 12 small *paupiettes.* Combine water, wine, bay leaf, parsley stems, and salt to taste in a deep pan. Poach the rolled fillets for 6 to 8 minutes, or until they are translucent but still firm. Remove the fish to a platter and keep warm. Poach the shrimp and mussels in the same broth until the shrimp are tender and the mussel shells open. Arrange the fish fillets on a heatproof serving platter and top with Mornay Sauce. Brown under the broiler. Garnish with mussels and shrimp. Sprinkle with parsley.

Serves 6.

MORNAY SAUCE

2 cups light cream
½ pound Gruyère cheese, grated (2 cups)
Salt to taste
¼ teaspoon cayenne pepper
1 teaspoon white pepper
2 ounces butter
4 tablespoons flour

Combine the cream, grated cheese, salt, cayenne, and white pepper in the top part of a double boiler over a low flame. In a separate pan, make a roux with the butter and flour (melt butter until it foams, stir in flour, and cook 2 minutes). Scald the cream mixture in the double boiler over steaming water, but do not let it boil. Whip in the roux. Cook for 8 to 10 minutes. Adjust the consistency with fish broth leftover from poaching.

Makes about 3 cups.

[1980]

Book Four

RIPPLES AND REFLECTIONS

Ripples and reflections are the afterthoughts of angling; what we find in fishing beyond the fish themselves. Such thoughts for hundreds of years have produced the world's finest angling writing, of which McClane's examples in this section are among the best. He has an inquiring mind, and he inquires well.

Here's the story behind his book, McClane's New Standard Fishing Encyclopedia, *which may be the best-selling fishing book of all time. Or join us for a look at what fishing was like on the island of Manhattan in 1776. And having spent hundreds of pages in this book exploring various kinds of fishing, McClane concludes with a poignant and perceptive look at why we fish in the first place—and reaches a surprising conclusion.*

37

My Most
Memorable Bass

Al McClane, of course, has caught literally thousands of bass in more than fifty years of angling. The editors of Sports Afield *once asked him to single out the most memorable, and the following was his reply.*

I have long believed that bass fishing is a mild form of insanity and the symptoms are first recognized at some point between voice-break, girl-persons, and the latest episodes in the adventures of Roland Martin and his magic worm. There was a time, almost a half-century ago, when my weekly fishing trip was to a place called Argyle Lake in Babylon, New York. I guess the lake and the stream that flowed into it still exist, although they may be under a supermarket or housing development by now. I don't even want to look at the map. Long Island was still "country" in those days and at Babylon railroad cars were switched from an electric to a steam engine for the wild trip east to Montauk, with cinders flying.

It began on a hot summer day, when our train stopped short of Babylon station. Our car halted in the middle of the trestle overlooking the Argyle stream. There was no air-conditioning, so with all the windows wide open I had to lean out and scrutinize every inch of water. Suddenly my heart was pounding in my belly like a blown piston. A bigmouth bass, showing off his black lateral bands of courage, was pectoral pawing and swaying in the current next to an alder bush. The fish was maybe thirty feet downstream from the trestle. I was about twenty feet over the water. This is a dimensional problem you ignore at the age of eleven or twelve. It's just a matter of how quick you can get the tackle together. Fortunately, my three-dollar prewar American Fork and Hoe steel fly rod was *always* at the ready with enameled line and leader strung through the guides and cork bug in place. I merely had to join the rod sections. This foresight always saved minutes of precious fishing time (we even ran from the train station to the lake like our pants were on fire).

In my then brief angling career, I had caught few bass and certainly nothing much over 2 pounds in size. The fish below the railroad trestle was perhaps 3 pounds—a prize beyond my wildest dream. The train was packed and by the time I got my rod waving out the window, a mob was standing in the aisle behind me like Hollywood extras waiting for the big scene. Dapping is what I was doing. I can still see it, a yellow moth-type bug bobbing on the current, headed right down his alley. Then, the train lurched, which meant the electric engine was uncoupled. That bigmouth probably met a thousand trains in his lifetime but he gobbled my bug like he never saw one before.

The struggle was Homeric because I had mastered only one diddly-technique when playing fish—get him out of the water as fast as possible. The passengers began hootin' and hollerin' as I cranked and heaved the poor bass skyward. My rod was nine feet of spastic spring and the fish went up and down past the window like he was stuck in a demented elevator. I couldn't figure out how to swing him aboard. The train made another jolt as they coupled the steam engine and I really panicked. A man behind a big cigar told me to back up and he'd "catch" my fish as it went by. We were trying this method when the train started. I had visions of arriving at the station with my trophy yo-yoing out the window, but the hook, which held fast for five minutes, finally pulled out. The bass bounced on a wooden tie and into the stream. I saw him swim away like he was half-stoned.

Everybody cheered my performance. They should have seen me running back to the lake.

[1979]

38

Amazon ...
Wonderworld
of Fishes

Al and I once passed an evening looking over his field notes from the Amazon trip described in this chapter. Although most people think of McClane only as an angling writer, as I've mentioned, he's a trained and dedicated ichthyologist. And he was frustrated still looking back over those notes, while explaining to me that there were still some specimens here that no one had been able to identify or catalog, including some authorities at the British Museum.

He's interested and thoroughly knowledgeable about fishing, to be sure, but equally interested in the fishes themselves. And as you'll see, there was much about this South American trip to pique his interest.

I rolled over just to drain the sweat from port to starboard and the effort woke me up. It was 2:00 A.M. and still a hundred and something degrees. The stub of a candle was burning in a tin can, and reflected in its pale glow were a dozen luminous red eyes staring at me from the dark. You learn to expect anything in Amazonas because the bizarre is really the ordinary and what would seem ludicrous in Hometown,

301

U.S.A., is just a fact of life in interior Brazil. I watched the unblinking eyes for a while, wondering whether to wake my snoring partner, Vernon Ogilvie; then I reached for my flashlight. Either the rats had been drinking or the bats had conjunctivitis. It was nothing but a bunch of armored catfish standing motionless on their fins. Professor Aguirre had left a gunnysack of them around camp and apparently they'd escaped. The night before, he'd dumped a collection of capaburro under our cots, and I heard teeth clicking until dawn. *Capaburro* as applied to the piranha means "donkey castrater," a conundrum that this jackass pondered on for some hours before getting out of bed. A dog howled in the Indian village across the river, as I lay back and tried to puzzle out whether we were any closer to our goal—or just a month deeper in the 2.5 million square miles of wilderness.

The overwhelming experience in Brazil is the total loss of dimension in space and time. Brazil occupies almost half of South America and all but two of twelve other countries on the continent border it. From its northwest to its southeast corner, Brazil extends the same distance as a line drawn from the Arctic Circle to the Sahara Desert. Beyond the lush forested mountains that surround Rio de Janeiro the land is brown and folded, and the low, barren hills extend for countless hundreds of miles before giving way to a scrubby floodplain. There is no suggestion of jungle until you reach the southern tributaries of the Amazon, which run their northerly courses in oxbows and then abruptly, the solid mass of green begins. From 40,000 feet in the air it looks like an endless mass of steamed spinach. At ground level it is a country unto itself—more mysterious than the fictitious accounts that invade our TV. The 3,915-mile length of the Amazon pumps out one-fifth of the fresh water on the globe, and much of the land behind the riverbanks has never been seen by man. Scores of nomadic, and occasionally hostile, Indian tribes are virtually isolated in patches of a 6-million-acre rain forest. As in nineteenth-century America, the cowboys and land barons are gunslingers, and hacking the Transamazon Road from Brazil's easternmost city of João Pessoa to the border of Peru at times resembles a John Wayne epic.

The most dangerous tribe, the Mayorunas, waits at the end of the road, but FUNAI, the government agency established to protect the Indian, has had a few successes in pacification. It is a hair-trigger balance where a minor incident has started a massacre. One can feel a nostalgic sadness at the progress of the road because it will inevitably bring tragedy to the Indian before any benefits of civilization are realized.

The Amazon is a muddy river and the brown weight of it stains the sea more than a hundred miles from shore. It is of less interest to an angler than the crystal-clear, and blue, and sometimes blackwater streams that feed it from the north and south. The line of demarcation is so absolute that the black current of the Rio Negro after it enters the Amazon looks like a stream flowing in parallel before they finally merge. Some 1,800 species of fish have been cataloged from the Amazon, and even in our own collection unidentified species turned up.

But the *one* fish we wanted was not likely to be found in the mainstream complex. This is a cichlid with no species name and no common name other than the Indian *tucunare* or the Spanish *pavon*, which is applied to the whole family and for our purposes meaningless. We have traced the distribution of six species of cichlae from Peru, Colombia, and Venezuela through the Orinoco watershed south to the Amazon, and heard stories of pavons that were "different." Unlike the common peacock pavon, with three prominent transverse bars on its body, this one was supposed to be a five-barred pavon, or maybe six-barred, or was it nine-barred? It all depended on who was supplying the information. The only remaining area these fish could inhabit would be somewhere between the Mato Grosso in the streams rising in Bolivia and Paraguay and that trackless expanse north to the Amazon. A trip to the moon would be easier to arrange and, in fact, it could be done in greater comfort. After three years of frustrating inquiries, the Instituto Euvaldo Lodi found that the National Museum in Rio de Janiero was equally interested in what these rivers held, and suddenly we were saluting generals, admirals, and assorted brass. Air Force General Moeira Burnier produced our magic carpet in the form of an eroded C-45—a mite slow but capable of setting down on a floodplain 3,000 miles away. I had the distinct impression that nobody expected to see us again. Our pilot, Major Mario Pontes Filho, who was weaned on a Mystère jet, read the manual to our co-pilot for an hour before takeoff. They hugged each other with Latin enthusiasm when we finally lumbered over Guanabara Bay.

My companions in this odyssey were Professor Alvaro Aguirre of the National Museum, former Director of Hunting and Fishing for Brazil's Ministry of Agriculture, who has spent more than forty years in the jungle; and Vernon Ogilvie, fishery biologist for the Florida Game and Fresh Water Fish Commission. Our objective was to collect, photograph, preserve, and bring back a long list of specimens for the museum, the Game Fish Research Association, and the state of Florida. Florida has increasingly become the depository of illegally or accidentally introduced exotics; Miami and Tampa are the pivotal distribution points for the tropical fish trade and more than twenty South American species have been recovered in Florida's waters recently, such as oscars, velvet, and port cichlids, pacu, firemouths, armored catfish, and even a piranha. Ogilvie caused a national alarm in every media from *Time* magazine to "The Tonight Show" several years ago with the discovery of Asiatic walking catfish, which had escaped from a tropical fish farm near Deerfield Beach.

So that controls may be instituted, exotics must first be studied in their native habitat to learn what ecological factors proliferate or destroy a species. But the positive aspect is that some exotics such as the pavon have been introduced successfully into the Panama Canal (where it is now the most abundant gamefish), Hawaii, and more recently Puerto Rico, where it is in the farm pond program. There is always the possibility that pavon will find a compatible role in North America; artificial environments such as the hot-water effluents of atomic generators, for example, are becoming increasingly widespread. Such water could be utilized by gamefish that thrive at temperatures from 90 to 100 degrees. Today there are a total of 300,000 surface acres of hot-water habitat in the southeastern United States. How much more will exist a decade from now and how will it be managed?

I have often studied maps of the remote slopes of the Andean ridge where it spills east from Bolivia and Paraguay. There is no hard information available on this region; Eigenmann and Allen's *Fishes of Western South America,* which is essentially a checklist, more or less stops north of the western Mato Grosso, and although we didn't expect to find pavon in this area, it is the source of some of the largest rivers in South America and the logical place to begin collecting. The Rio São Lourenço, or "Saint Lawrence River," is a tributary to the Paraguay River. Although extremely fertile and containing a great variety of species, these waters are muddy even in the dry season. The primary gamefish here is the mighty dorado, and during a *piracema,* or spawning run, when the rains begin, the Piquiri, Taquari, Aquidauana, and Apa rivers literally boil with 20- to 40-pounders.

So on the off chance that pavon would be found here, we started at the Saint Lawrence and planned to work north. There were no big dorado in residence, but plenty in the 2- and 3-pound fly-rod size, which is a handful of dynamite in fast water. It is a cane-poler's paradise, with 40-pound catfish and piranha so vicious that Fearless Ogilvie—who usually thinks nothing of wading among species we are familiar with—refused to put his toe in the water. Not only are capaburro unnerving, but for years the Indians have been tossing butchered animal carcasses into the river. Our first week's rations consisted of an ancient cow, which the matriarch of the village carved with an ax each morning, and the instant she threw a bone in, the water erupted as though a depth charge had gone off. No matter how far she progressed in her daily chopping, the scrawny animal was inedible, and for six days we ate fish and rice, not aware that our supply plane had broken its landing gear several hundred miles to the south. It was the only camp in Brazil where the cook took a body count before serving a meal.

These were lean yet profitable working days as we filled our barrels with fish that even the professor had never seen. For example, all modern keys to the catfish family include barbels as a distinguishing feature. Yet we found "whiskerless" catfish in the Mato Grosso, several new species of knifefish, a miniature payara, freshwater flounders, puffers, or

305

"blowfish," and even freshwater crabs. Among the more interesting items was the *candiru de cavallo* or "horse candiru."

The candiru is reputedly the most fearsome creature in tropical South America. Malaria and malnutrition are the daily problems of survival but other potentially lethal elements exist nevertheless. This inch-long parasite is invisible except when filled with blood. The fish enters the orifices of the human body and lodges itself by means of opercular spines, and once implanted has to be cut out. Although it has been postulated by some scientists that candiru are urinotropic (attracted toward urine in the water), they feed primarily in the gills of living fish, which would seem to indicate that the attraction is one of motion rather than chemical affinity or tropism. During an experimental tagging program on the upper Orinoco last spring, Ogilvie found a released pavon lying belly up and virtually covered with candiru that had attached themselves to its body much in the fashion of a lamprey. The horse candiru, which grows to 4 inches in length, is said to invade animals much larger than man.

Amazonian Indians use spears, bows, and arrows, and the toxic barbasco plant to catch fish. Barbasco, the source of rotenone, is simply ground in the bottom of the canoe, which is overturned in the appropriate spot. However, aboriginal "fishermen" are more inclined to pursue something substantial enough for a village feast and this requires a spear, as the popular pirarucu must be stalked. In our specialized search it was mutually agreed that "big is not always better" and to spend time chasing a pirarucu would not be rewarding despite the fact that it is the world's largest strictly freshwater fish. Pirarucu (*Arapaima gigas*) are known to grow to 15 feet in length. I have never seen one much over 10 feet, and 8 feet seems to be an average fish. Its maximum weight exceeds 400 pounds, but there are few scales capable of holding a pirarucu in the remote regions where it occurs. To an Indian, it is simply nutritious food when laboriously filleted with a machete. Pirarucu will take live and cut bait, and I have caught three small ones on spoons. It is, however, a fish of the main rivers, and slaying monsters would not only consume our working hours but divert us from the lagoons and small streams where Amazonian pavon thrive. At one camp, our Cajaro Indian neighbors speared an 8-foot-long pirarucu, which took them three days to locate. We bartered for a slice, and the flesh is firm, white, and finely textured, not unlike a red snapper, although the fillet weighed almost 50 pounds.

The aruaná is probably the most difficult fish in the world to hook. Despite the fact that an aruaná will hit almost any lure and with a ferocity that matches its appearance, the fish is a member of the Osteoglossidae or "boney-tongue" family. Its large, oblique mouth is solid bone and making a barb stick depends on the law of averages; hook enough aruaná and eventually one will stay fast. The aruaná occurs only in the Amazon watershed from eastern Peru, through Brazil and the Guianas. Its Portuguese common name is from the Indian *arowana.* Another genus, *Heterotis,* is found in tropical Africa, and a third, *Scleropages,* occurs in the Malay Archipelago, New Guinea, and Australia. To the Aussie angler it is known as the barramundi. This isolated distribution is one of the many links in the continental drift theory.

One day Vernon and I were seining a backwater to get a composite of the forage fish population while Professor Aguirre went off to dunk manioc root bait for catfish. We had been eating deep-fried piranha, and though tasty, the diet was monotonous. Pulling a 60-foot seine is a miserable job in hot weather, but it had been a "two-barrel" morning with specimens enough to catalog for the next year. While we belched over our last bottle of warm beer, Vernon pointed to a group of long, dark shadows traveling slowly along the far bank. My first impression was that they were water boas or perhaps electric eels, as their slender silhouettes moved in serpentine fashion. I grabbed my rod and shot a plug in their direction. Not one, but all of the aruaná pounced on it with such speed that the rod was nearly jerked from my hand. The run that followed was incredibly strong. There was no stopping the fish as it bored for a distant brush pile. When the hook pulled out and I began cranking back for another cast, a second aruaná slammed it, then a third, a fourth, and a fifth. I gave Vernon the rod and the same thing happened. Although we eventually caught several, the ratio of strikes to hookups was astronomical.

Flying east, then north in 500-mile legs, the logistical problem of twelve heavy pieces of baggage that included gallons of formaldehyde and ionol, as well as the nets and 50- to 200-pound containers that held our precious specimens, was solved by using two airplanes. We had just about run out of places to look for the five-barred pavon. Then one day while buying a chicken (God knows what it had eaten; its meat was blue) from an Indian, the professor learned that tucunare were abundant in the lagoons about 30 miles east of the Rio das Mortes. The "River of the Dead" didn't sound too promising, but we borrowed an Air Force jeep on Bananal Island and a precious can of fuel. The Indians had set fire to the gas dump for no particular reason except to hear the drums go boom-boom, and it would be a long wait before more fuel was ferried in. Our map wasn't much help. Bananal Island is the largest riverine island in the world (480 miles long and 136 miles wide), formed by the bifurcation of the Araguaia River, an Amazon tributary. It is dotted by countless swamps and lagoons, and the best we could do was estimate distance and hope the tank didn't go dry. For an hour we crossed a floodplain pocked by giant termite nests; these mounds rise ten or twelve feet high and are shared by swallows who tunnel *their* nests among the termites.

I walked along the bank looking for an open spot to start fishing. Brilliant Morpho butterflies danced toylike on 6-inch-long wings. Aside from the biting kinds (which we gave up counting) the insects of the Amazon are fascinating. In the evening, hatches of huge white mayflies would blanket the streamside like new-fallen snow. Unlike ephemerids of temperate zones, these equatorial mayflies are strong fliers and were almost impossible to hold between one's fingers. The grasshoppers are subaquatic; jumping from underfoot into the stream, Amazonian grasshoppers swim below the surface and cling to weed stems until you pass. At the far corner of the lagoon a great pack of capybara, the world's largest rodent, dove into the water amid the shattering squawks of parrots, and evidently their fright was relayed to the fish, as suddenly a school of pavon came rushing parallel to the shore with their black bars accentuated; like all cichlids their color pattern becomes more intense when they are disturbed. I couldn't decide whether the fish wore five bars or fifty-five, but my plug was already seeking the answer.

Pavon are not the smartest fish in fresh water. The blue-gill has a higher IQ. But pavon are brawlers. They make powerful runs and at times jump themselves into sheer exhaustion. I can't remember the size of my first fish. Each time he flung himself over the surface I tried to count the bars. By the time my pavon was rolling to a halt the school headed back in my direction, so I tossed the fish in the grass and made another cast. The plug hardly touched the surface when another pavon struck. We needed many fish for food, for the museum, and to bring back to Florida and the Game Fish Research Association. I heard Vernon shouting to the professor—they were both obviously into a school—so after collecting a half-dozen I began releasing my fish until we could establish a mutual limit. By noon I quit. It was too easy. A pavon on every cast and my hands were raw from grabbing their jaws. I weighed my largest fish, which was 7½ pounds, and like the others it had five distinct bars. I walked to the other end of the island to watch Vernon struggle with a big one on his fly rod. Then I saw a faint reflection behind the green canopy of jungle.

The lagoon made a sharp bend into the trees and emerged again in a dense stand of ferns and down timber. Small differences in habitat such as the presence of rotting wood (which is the home of the "talking" not walking cat-fish), an accelerating current, or even the consistency of sunlight or shadow over a particular pool is enough to attract or repel certain species. After Vernon released his pavon I mucked my way through sulfurous green scummy puddles to learn what the dark water held. I flipped a shallow-running plug toward the far bank. As it wiggled under the surface something stopped it dead; it was a red-throated pike cichlid, another species yet to be cataloged. A few casts later I was into a pavon again, and while lipping the fish for a release, I suddenly realized it was entirely different—with three faint bars and heavy spotting on the pectoral, ventral, and caudal fins. I quickly deposited it in our barrel at the jeep and went back to the ferns again. The next cast produced a more brightly colored version of the same pavon, evidently a male with an orange underjaw. A matching pair was all the lagoon would allow. I caught fish after fish but no more spot-fin pavon. In a sunlight pool, I hooked an aruaná that broke my plug off, but the tree frogs were telling me it was time to start back for camp.

Professor Aguirre was ecstatic. In the course of our trip we had elevated him from his viciously effective cane pole to a spinning rod, and he bagged enough specimens to fill two museums. Despite the worst dose of ticks I've ever seen on any man, which we probed and painted with antiseptic each morning, his enthusiasm and unfailing good humor kept Vernon and me from going crackers when things didn't go right—which was most of the time. Whether we were picking the fur out of our chowder or the diving beetles out of our drinking water, Professor Aguirre counted small blessings. He is the kind of seventy-four-year-old who thinks nothing of journeying for months by muleback with little more than a sack of rice. His scientific papers on the Amazonian fishes, birds, and reptiles are the product of a man who in another era would have set sail with Columbus.

When we got back to Miami, fishery biologist Bob Lawson met us at the airport. As we headed for Palm Beach along the Sunshine Parkway, listening to Vicki Carr on the radio and seeing the neon lights, I not only felt twenty pounds lighter but a stranger in a strange land. Autos whooshed by, jets screamed overhead, and people stood hosing identical green squares of lawn between starkly white houses. There are some cattailed ponds off the parkway where we go bluegill fishing once in a while. Vernon had been half asleep, but after we passed four or five ponds I saw him staring at the dimly lit water. I had the feeling.

We were home again.

[1972]

39

Fishing with Ritz and Gingrich

Arnold Gingrich and Charles Ritz were both central figures in the evolution of fly fishing after World War II. Gingrich was best known in the publishing world as the founder of Esquire *magazine, at which he helped to develop such then-fledglings as Ernest Hemingway. As a hotelier, Ritz's name was self-explanatory. Gingrich evolved as a spokesman for fly fishing, both in print through such books as* The Joys of Trout *and* The Fishing in Print, *and through his involvement with numerous clubs and national angling organizations. He was, for example, the board president of The American Museum of Fly Fishing at the time of his death. Ritz, while no less an ardent spokesman, was better known as a tactician—casting techniques, rod design, leader formulas, and such were an endless source of fascination and considerable discussion, much of which he recorded in his book* A Fly Fisher's Life.

Both men died within a few days of each other in July 1976. At that time, I was working as an editor

311

at Fly Fisherman *magazine and called Al McClane in Florida for his recollections, which follow here.*

I probably learned more about fly fishing from Charles Ritz than from any other angler who has taken the time to make painful faces at my casting. I first met him in 1947 after an article of mine appeared in the French publication *Au Bord de L'Eau.* He was fifty-six years old then, but as lithe and strong as a man half his age—which I almost was. He could intercept a taxi on the Place Vendôme like a heat-seeking missile. A health nut, he exercised for an hour every morning, doing push-ups and knee-bends and honing his casting muscles by twirling a pair of champagne bottles in each hand. They had more class than Indian clubs and were disposable in travel.

That winter he stayed at my then bachelor apartment in New York because he didn't really like living in hotels, even though he owned the Ritz-Carlton right down the street. I soon discovered that his calisthenics were conducted in the buff, at 6:00 A.M., with all available windows open, including mine. Even under a mound of blankets the ambient temperature left me in a state of shock.

In the summer of 1948, I was in France, which was still emerging from a postwar depression. There weren't any new automobiles around, but we managed to make a two-month motoring tour of Charlie's favorite trout streams from the Risle to the Ain, then into Bavaria and the high valleys of Austria. He had borrowed a French police car, a topless and virtually brakeless relic that didn't even have a horn. At busy intersections he leaned over the door and let out a Swiss yodel. This had the same effect as a rebel yell. I think the car finally collapsed from a nervous breakdown.

He also had a rather unique method of selecting the streams on our itinerary. "You will love the Andelle! It's impossible. The fish are like fat men in a cafeteria. They are not very big trout but they will drive you nuts." This calculated sadism (and there were easier rivers to choose from) was in part the cornerstone of his skill. That first day on the crystalline park water at Radepont, I think Charlie caught ten fish to my one, and it was probably the village idiot, because a hundred trout refused my flies. During the next week he pounded home the importance of getting on a trout fast—loading the rod and shooting the entire line, if need be, with two back casts. As I learned in subsequent years, an instant response to a rising or cruising trout in calm water can be a deadly practice, and for that matter it's fundamental in fly fishing for tarpon, bonefish, and permit; when a big saltwater gamester appears out of the sun sixty feet away, excessive rod waving produces few rewards.

Always the gadgeteer, Charlie brought along his collapsible landing net, collapsible fishing stool, and collapsible fish cage to keep the trout alive—when trout were on our menu. He had a thing about collapsible equipment, probably because he transported so much gear; twenty to thirty rods on an important trip was the norm, as there was always a backlog of experimental models to be tested.

Paradoxically, Ritz took very little interest in fly patterns; the Tups Indispensable was his favorite, but for a long time the only fly I saw him use was an oddball dressing known as the Panama. While we were making a trout-fishing film for World Video on the Risle River in Normandy, he borrowed a Light Cahill from me; after that, I had to keep him supplied with what he called the "superfly." To Charlie, stalking and presentation were the ultimate demands, and the fly had only to be "believable."

When tube flies came along this simplified his salmon fishing; he just carried boxes and boxes of tube flies. But his tremendous skill in painting a fly on the water with a minimum of back cast and at maximum speed (the fly seemingly arrived before a rising trout could close its mouth) explained why he considered pattern almost irrevelant. In his concept "the fish reacts above all to presentation and only a minor degree to the fly." We were not always in agreement—anglers seldom are—but the basic truths of his pontifical utterances were difficult to deny.

Charles was a master craftsman on the river. He was capable of laying out ninety feet of line under the worst winds, or of dropping a fly with teacup accuracy between the

313

weed sweepers of a chalkstream. He had a total economy of motion. In later years, he changed his casting style to something called "High Speed/High Line," a distance technique favored by then world champion Jon Tarantino. It worked for a platform artist like the late Big Jon, but while Charlie preached the gospel of HS/HL, he sacrificed that beautifully flat turnover, which sent his line out like it was triggered from a crossbow—for an underwear-ripping tournament style.

Once Ritz had decided to pursue a mechanical absolute, it was with singular and dogged devotion until he was ready to try something new. The last time we cast together in a practice pond at the Bois de Boulogne in Paris, he had abandoned HS/HL for "Instant Fly Casting" or IFC—which was vintage Ritz at his best. If Charlie had a preoccupation with initials it was out of necessity; he was professionally involved in so many divergent disciplines including ice hockey, wine, food, hotels, shoes (among other things, he invented the après-ski boot), model railroads, children's toys, and women's clothing that every new development required a label. His parabolic rod, a milestone in bamboo construction in 1937, ultimately became the PPP (for "Progressive Pendulate Power")—which was what he meant in the first place. Parabolique was simply a Pezon et Michel trade name.

There was a facet to the urbane Monsieur Ritz that he seldom revealed. He had known tragedy in his lifetime, which he endured in silence. Perhaps this made him especially sentimental. One touching incident that I will never forget was the day I found him picking flowers. We were making a movie on steelhead fishing in British Columbia. Another friend of mine, General Charles Lindemann, was along on the trip. Ironically, the general had spent his honeymoon many years before on the Stamp River, the location of our film. His French wife had been killed during World War II and was buried in Paris.

"Since when have you become a botanist?" I kidded.

Charlie looked embarrassed. I never knew he could blush. "Don't say anything to the general. Promise? I am bringing his wife flowers. She would like that."

I first met Arnold Gingrich in 1955 after his early retirement (he had quit *Esquire* ten years before at the age of forty-three to become a winegrower in Switzerland, but the magazine didn't prosper in his absence), and a year later I introduced him to Charlie Ritz. It was inevitable that they would become fast friends because their appetites for life were so similar. Charlie immediately elected Arnold to his International Fario Club (once labeled the "Gallic Chowder and Marching Society" by Ernest Hemingway because we were the only Americans in the group at that time), which in later years occasioned a magnificent annual dinner at the Paris Ritz for about two hundred of Charlie's comrades in rods from all over the world.

For five seasons, Arnold and I shared the old Jay Gould cabin at Turnwood on the upper Beaver Kill. The river was about ten yards from the house and there was always the smell of waders and wool socks drying on the porch. Gingrich was a flea-rod enthusiast, whether he was fishing for trout or salmon, and his favorite stick was Paul Young's 6½-foot Midge. He was a polished performer; his cryptic angling notes, which he analyzed each time we had lunch in town, showed that in four Beaver Kill seasons with 64 days on the water, he averaged 21.6 fish daily. I was busy tagging fish in those days, and he was not only recatching my current releases but repeating some twice.

A few of these trout apparently wearied of ducking Arnold, as they were eventually recovered fifty or sixty miles downstream in the Delaware.

Ritz called Gingrich "that terrible fishing machine." He carried more fly patterns than William Mills could catalog but his favorites were the Betsy Streamer and the Cahill Bivisible Spider (really a skater). He fished the Betsy as a dry fly upstream and down, using a long, often 18-foot leader tapered to 4X to 6X. He took fish of all sizes, gently releasing each one as though it were a Ming vase. Even the tiniest trout was rewarded with a belly rub and a verbal compliment to his spirited play. Keeping score instead of keeping trout was Arnold's passion—until a pickpocket lifted his wallet-size

315

diary one day in a New York subway. Unfailingly, his comment was pure Gingrich.

"I wonder what the poor S.O.B. will think when he reads it? May 8: 4:00 A.M. to 10:00 A.M.; water clear, 58; Betsy size 10; scored 8; 9 to 14 inches. Geez, I'd love to see the expression on his face!"

Like Charlie, Arnold had the physical stamina of a bull. Twenty years ago in Iceland, with its then unregulated fishing hours and its midnight sun, he was on the river around the clock, banging a dry fly into the teeth of a gale. At one point in our island-circling safari I found myself casting in my sleep, trying to keep up with the guy.

I also recall stumbling through a cold November woods at 4:00 A.M. near his home in suburban Ridgewood, New Jersey. Arnold, who always lived in multiples, was taking 6:30 A.M. violin lessons in Manhattan before opening *Esquire*'s office, so his daily routine was to catch a fish at the Joe Jefferson Trout Club, right down the road from his house, before catching an early bus into New York City.

The logic of our predawn tour had escaped me as my Gucci's crunched on the new-fallen snow, since I had just stopped by for dinner the night before. We were dressed for a board meeting—not a fishing trip. The night was so black that he had to point me in the direction of an invisible pond, where we began to cast into the darkness. And cast. Something in my rod hand didn't feel right. The line wasn't pulling its weight against water.

"Arnold?"

"Hmmm?"

"Something doesn't feel right. I think the pond is frozen over."

"Yeah, I discovered that."

"Then, what are the hell are we casting for?"

"Geez, it's better than waiting for a *bus!*"

Ritz was true to his name in being the personification of elegance. He was always impeccably dressed, even on the river. In the social world Arnold reflected the sartorial splendor of *Esquire*, but when suited up for angling, his

316

wife, Jane, likened him to the fashion editor of the *Hobo News*. Even the wrinkles in his waders had wrinkles. He was a walking tackle shop. With extra reel spools and fly boxes stuffed in every pocket, he clanked down the brook like a Sherman tank.

When Ritz's *A Fly Fisher's Life* (originally *Pris sur le Vie*) was in translation, Charlie asked me to shoot a cover photo for his American edition. I took a picture of Arnold playing a 9-pound tiger trout in one of our Turnwood ponds and sent it along to the publisher. The book finally appeared three years later. Arnold phoned me and said, "Charlie's getting pretty slobby looking."

"I didn't know that."

"Yeah, did ya' see that picture of him on his book jacket?"

"No, I haven't received my copy."

"God, he got fat. He looks like a Sherman tank!"

I changed the subject. It was some time before Arnold discovered that *he* was the angler on the book jacket, not Ritz, and when he did, he laughed so hard that tears streamed down his face. He wrote about the incident in *The Well-Tempered Angler,* but it didn't convey what others could better express. Arnold had a marvelous sense of humor, that wry, self-mockery that only great men can afford and totally enjoy.

He also had that mystical ability of dominating any social group just by being Arnold—or, by choice, to leave doubt whether he had ever appeared at all. After an unprogrammed weekend on an "exotic" estate (for Arnold, one having a trout stream), the hostess said as I departed on Sunday evening, "I'm sorry Arnold couldn't come, dear." I didn't have the heart to tell the lady that not only had he come, but had seen and conquered a 20-inch rainbow, and that his Bentley was still by the brook.

Another *grande dame* who had a real crush on the guy started a silent war by hiding his fishing tackle upon arrival. Poor Arnold stood bug-eyed on the patio like an addict needing a fix as he watched trout rising in the river below. The ploy never worked after that; he would bring junk rods for her to closet, and hide his working tackle in my room. Midway in the preprandial festivities he would disappear faster than the martinis.

I visited Arnold a week before his death, and then went on to the Miramichi River. When the news finally arrived—in that July weekend of delayed confusion—that both he and Charles Ritz had made their last cast, it seemed as though somebody had compounded the one possibility with another message. I had circled a September fishing date with a healthy Charlie.

But it was true and it was too late to say good-bye. To me, as it must be to others, their presence is still as tangible as the nearest river. And so it will for generations to come.

[1977]

40

Drop Those Daggers, Men!

Almost thirty years later the "Great Spinning Contro-versy" is still in full cry. Fly fishermen feel that spin-ning tackle has ruined some of America's better trout rivers, since it allows the spin fishermen to reach fish that the fly boys can't, thereby allowing a stream to become more quickly "fished out."

The fly fishermen seem in general to regard spin fishermen as a bunch of unwashed gluttons who fish with total disregard for what they view as appropri-ate stream manners.

There's something to be said for each side, I sup-pose, and I've seen examples of both the snobbery and reverse snobbery the foregoing implies. But the pres-ent proliferation of catch-and-release and similar restrictions on our better trout rivers has helped moot the question. Many streams are restricted to "artifi-cials only" rather than the once-popular "flies only" in a more democratic attempt at conservation. Cer-tainly a single-hooked spoon will do no more damage to a trout's jaw than a big streamer fly, assuming, of course, the fish is to be released.

319

The Great Spinning Controversy is now in full cry, and nobody knows it better than I do. You've seen some rancorous letters on the subject in the "Cheers & Jeers" columns, and there are others you haven't seen, because they'd set fire to any paper they were printed on. The anti-spinners declare: "A spin fisherman is the lowest form of life—a meat hunter who is ruining the streams for us fly-fishing sportsmen. Spinning should be banned before every last trout is done!"

The spinners retort: "These fly boys are just a broken-down bunch of octogenarians who couldn't catch an olive if they went fishing in a martini. They're just jealous because we get fish and they don't!"

The whole hassle is the damnedest fricasse of biased and baseless opinion that their tired eyes have yet seen. May I suggest that some of our great fraternity may be looking for an alibi? This awesome assemblage whips a vast acreage of water in the United States and bemoans its luck in a score of accents.

Yet most of us know that the efficiency of any method of angling is always subject to fishing conditions at the time it's used. The fact that threadliners make heavy bags while I fumble with my fly rod is, to me, unimportant. In the course of a full fishing year, I find that things have a tendency to even out, and that I'll get fish when a spinner upstream is getting nothing but exercise.

When conditions are wrong for its use, spinning is little more than an excuse to be outdoors. The same is true of fly fishing and bait casting. Not long ago, I worked a river where a 4-pound brown trout on the dry fly was just average. My biggest was 8 pounds, and I lost one estimated at 15, after grounding him three times in ankle-deep water. For three days, with #10 dry flies, I hooked browns that went through the wildest gyrations seen outside the Savoy Ballroom. Several local anglers fishing with spinning tackle caught exactly nothing. Not one itsy-bitsy trout. It was the same elsewhere in the area. On the fourth day I decided to have a try at spinning, and I served the trout a variety of hardware. They held to their belief that such fare invites malaise, vapors, and insomnia.

The phenomenon has occurred many times in the past decade, and I mention it to caution young anglers that learning one method of fishing is not enough.

Once, in Alaska, my wife and I ran into a period of fog and lashing rain. I worked very hard day after day with all kinds of flies and caught a few small fish. When the fog lifted, the wind blew so hard that all I had to do was get down on the bank and let it pull my casts out. After a week of this I rigged up my spinning rod and began having some fun. The salmon and trout knocked the enamel off my wobblers. One day my wife and I caught and released thirty-three fish. Then the sun came out and we went back to fly fishing. Patti caught her first 10-pound rainbow on a Royal Coachman.

That was a great day, but so was the day we banged the salmon with spinning gear. Yet it doesn't follow that spinning will always pay off in wilderness waters. I have seen brook trout and Arctic char that probably had never glimpsed a lure in their lives solidly refuse metal baits. Yet these same fish could be caught one after another on flies.

I have also fished in places where spinning for Atlantic salmon is permitted and had the honor of being high rod with a wet fly while my fixed-spool companions got nothing but stiff wrists. But more important, perhaps, is the creeping paralysis of spin fishing that has been reported in domestic waters during the past three years.

It is apparent that a population of trout can become nearly immune to spinning lures. On rivers that are continually fished with metal baits, the threadliner works under a handicap except for periods when natural insects are scarce or when the stream is in flood. I queried twelve Eastern resort operators on major trout streams this season, and the consensus was that the efficiency of spinning diminishes with the approach of summer. Inevitably the hatchery-reared fish are cropped off and the angler is left to deal with big native fish or trout that have survived their first wild year. In all cases the local experts felt that such trout are more readily caught by fly fishermen.

Some measure of this selectivity is confirmed by my own observations on the pond near our summer house. We let our guests fish the pond in any way they know how. A large part of the population is composed of tagged brown trout that I released last year. The remainder are the old resident brook and rainbow trout that have no intention of becoming extinct. At the very beginning of our season a few of these fish were caught by spinning, but then the take dropped to nothing. Yet a good fly caster can score every time.

Western resort operators report a split decision between fly fishing and spinning, with a slight edge for the fly during August and September. On coastal streams, both steelhead and salmon are taken on hardware during well-defined periods—chiefly during fall and winter runs. Summers runs are much less common and it's no surprise to find fly fishermen in the minority. Inland trouting, however, particularly in the Rocky Mountain area, where rich clear-water streams breed lush hatches of mayflies and caddis, is given over to the fly enthusiast.

I have seen many a spin addict go home skunked from rivers literally teeming with trout. I think the classic example of conditioned immunity occurred on a European chalkstream some years ago. The river was like many of our Western meadow streams, the only difference being that nobody had slapped a blade on its sensitive face in fifteen seasons. Spinning was new to America and to me at the time, so my host offered to demonstrate it. He clipped the barbs off a devon and I sat on the bank like a tourist about to witness the honorable ceremony of hara-kiri. Each cast was followed by a flea-hopping horde of minnows; they, like the devon, enjoyed complete immunity from the trout. Browns were rolling nose and tail over the river, feeding on nymphs, and we found it no trick at all to catch them with a fly rod. But the spin stick got no takers.

The smallmouth bass is another fish that demands switch-hitting. I spent several days one summer casting plugs for them on the Cacapon River in West Virginia. Unfortunately, I caught some bass the first day—just enough to make me think the Cacapon was an overrated river. Then I saw a man wading the flats. After a few minutes he took a beautiful fish on a dry fly. I was not a very accomplished caster then, but I fly-fished the rest of the afternoon and took quite a few nice bass.

The reason I prefer fly fishing now is that most anglers use spoons or plugs, and I firmly believe that river bass (the older ones at least) are fairly well educated. Also, their natural food in the summer months is best imitated by fly-rod lures—streamers, hair frogs, and all dry flies. Late in the fall, river bass go into the deep holes and the casting lures become important again.

Mechanically, the fly rod has advantages that aren't obvious to those who don't cast flies. Last spring, for instance, four of us fished together one morning in two separate boats on a small central-Florida lake. At the beginning, we all caught a few bass, but when the sun came up, the fish burrowed back into the lily pads. The two spin addicts in the other boat had to stay in open water. Lily beds in Florida are usually protected by whip grass, which grows thick and stands like hay. You can't retrieve a weedless lure through that stuff. The way to fish it is with a heavy bugging line and leader. I slam the bug in the open pockets between the pads and let it rest. After a bit, I give the bug a few twitches and if nothing happens I make my pickup with a high back cast and aim for the next opening. With a fly rod, there is no need to retrieve. The heavy-bellied line simply slides off the grass, whereas casting lines drop and tangle when you have to swim the lure out. The lad fishing in my boat that morning used very heavy plugs and the bass weren't in the mood. I caught eight fine largemouths and lost several others. The rest of the party scored nothing.

But Florida bass fishing requires a great variety of tackle and technique, in water ranging from open canals to peppergrass prairies.

There are two different kinds of bass fishing where bait casting still rules supreme. Any man who can take really big Florida bass on light tackle deserves special commendation. Florida real estate in the rough is one part water, two parts stump, and seven parts weeds. When trophy fish plunge into the eternal clutch of peppergrass (which can be as big around the roots as asparagus), you might just as well blow the whistle. Unlike whip grass, peppergrass grows below the surface. Lakes may have one or the other—more often, both. Although you can cold-deck an old bronzeback with heavy line, bass-size spinning reels won't comfortably handle diameters of 12 pounds and up. Not unless you have a heavy rod and plug. Then you are better off bait casting with 36-pound-test line, which is how the cracker boys do it. I have caught many Florida bass under the right conditions, but few big ones, and then only when I was in the right place. The headwaters of the Saint Johns is a right place; here the water is open and you can follow your fish anywhere. The hayfields of Lake Okeechobee is a wrong place unless you get lucky. Canals are a cinch to spin or fly fish because they are relatively narrow and you can control the direction of the play, but there are a few bad ones, where the fishing is really good, and these are better explored with bait-casting gear.

The other type of bass fishing that requires a multiplier is found in the evergrowing system of TVA dams, where heavy, deep-planing plugs are fished on the bottom. The weight of the lure and the work of the rod demand too much of regulation spinning tackle.

The argument for or against spinning is not a matter of ethics, as the current imbroglio suggests. The question most of us are still exploring is *when* to threadline rather than *whether* to.

One thing is abundantly clear—fly fishing is supercharged with mysterious, magnetic stuff. From the passionate prose of Walton to the halcyon days of Gordon, emotional bonfires have been lit by specialists among specialists, men who examined everything from the geometric form of horsehair to the tilt of a hackle. Spinning is a bit too young to compete with tradition, but if in the meantime it brings new sportsmen to the pleasure pools of our nation, I say God bless—it and them.

[1956]

41

The Evolution of Spinning in America

The spin-fishing phenomenon in this country was concurrent with yet another: A. J. McClane himself, whose angling-writing career likewise started during the 1940s. The timing was in many ways providential, as an emerging and major talent was on hand to explain this wondrous new method to millions of readers through his columns and articles in Field & Stream. *Few writers at this time had the international perspective that McClane brought to his columns, and the development of spinning was truly an international event.*

Oddly, and even though it's the single most popular angling method in the country, very little attention has been given in print to the technical or historical aspects of spinning. A simple method on its face, spinning can be subtle as well. And although a recent development in the long history of angling, spinning is not without a unique and entertaining history of its own. No one to my knowledge has written better about spinning in all its facets than Al McClane, which made the inclusion of several chapters on spinning a must for these pages.

No one event during the last century did more to promote fishing as a sport in America than did the introduction of the spinning reel. The number of people who became part of our angling statistics in the 1950s accelerated out of proportion to the normal increment of growth. The reason was simple. Anybody with a minimal complement of fingers could operate the fixed spool, offering a kind of "instant expertise" that our traditional bait-casting reel never allowed. New tackle firms were literally created overnight to supply the demand for spinning gear, which was almost totally international in origin. Yet the fact that the game ever started at all was more a series of coincidences than an engineering feat. Before the existence of hot-stretched nylon and fiberglass, the spinning reel was an anachronism that American manufacturers avoided like the plague. The biggest hangup was that spinning reels had to be mounted below the rod grip and cranked with the left hand. In a nation where generations of bass fishermen have pressed their thumbs against a running spool, the idea of some disembodied thing hanging below the rod held no currency. It was a foreign concept both in fact and practice.

Asking who made the first spinning reel is like asking who put the hole in the bagel. Nearly all concepts in angling evolved over a period of time with each designer adding some new feature to the accepted principle. The idea of throwing line off a fixed object is very old. A device suggesting our spinning reel was the eighteenth-century *bird cage,* a cylindrical frame that could be held in one hand while the bait was tossed with the other hand or with a rod in the general direction of the target. The line was crosswound on the frame and aimed so the spiraling coils passed over the end of the cylinder. Primitive societies quickly discovered that tin cans work just as well—after tin cans became part of commerce. In 1884, Peter Malloch of Perth, Scotland, combined the fixed spool with a revolving spool. When retrieving, his "turntable" looked like our multiplying reel, but in casting, the spool was flipped around so its end faced the direction of the cast. This created as many problems as it solved; each time the spool was pivoted from one position to the other, the angler reeled in all the twists made in the line by casting. The golden egg was still in a field of complicated birds' nests.

In 1905, Alfred Holden Illingworth, apparently inspired by the bobbins used in his family's British cotton mills, eliminated the revolving function by designing a pickup mechanism that rotated around the spool and thus produced the spinning reel as we know it today. There are prior claims by both French and Irish historians, but Illingworth took first place in the 3-gram distance event with his new reel at the International Casting Tournament of 1908. That's when it all began and, for practical angling purposes, stopped for three decades. The fixed spool reel could cast ¹⁄₁₆- to ³⁄₈-ounce weights beautifully, but few lures were made in that size range. And from ³⁄₈- to ⅝-ounce lure range, the spinning reel couldn't match a precision-built American multiplier. However, this was a minor problem.

The first spinning reel was marketed in the United States by Paul Mauborgne—the Luxor. This was distributed by Bache Brown in New York beginning in 1938, but so few rods were sold that the fixed-spool idea remained almost unknown to the American public. Not only were there no suitable rods, but also only two kinds of line were available: braided silk, which clung to the spool like soggy spaghetti after an hour of fishing; and "gut substitute," the ubiquitous Japanese product made from glue that came unglued almost the minute it hit water. Bache Brown had to be a visionary of the supreme order. Cut off from his source of supply in 1944, he went to an American firm phasing itself out of the aircraft parts industry and there designed a new model under the Luxor patent called the Airex. Although metals were scarce because of the wartime shortage, Airex initially produced 25,000 spinning reels and nearly 2 million would be sold in the next six years. This was the first spinning reel made in the United States.

The development that sent it into orbit was nylon. Braided nylon lines were first marketed in 1946 (these were made of yarn, rather than monofilament) and a vast improvement over the more hygroscopic silk, which soaked up water like a sponge. But early nylon had an eerie capacity to stretch. If you hung a lure in a snag on the far side of the river and tried to pull it loose by hand, you walked a long distance before it snapped free with blood-letting velocity. Monofilament was even worse with an elongation of 20 to 35 percent. For eight months Bache Brown closeted himself with the Gudebrod Line Company perfecting a "hot-stretch" process that not only reduced the elongation factor but provided greater strength per diameter. The line was still a long way from caprolactum-based polymerized type-6 nylon, but for the first time that rubber-band effect, so critical when a heavy fish struck, was no longer a problem.

During the postwar hiatus in Europe, Switzerland provided the Fix and Record reels to our growing market. But in 1947, the first American closed-spool reel, the Humphreys, started a new trend. This looked like and was seated in the same position as a fly reel with the line coming out of a hole in the center of the side plate. It was followed by the similar Fre-Line and Good-All designs; although their spools were fixed, the line peeled off at a right angle before escaping through the hole, which increased friction. Paul Mauborgne in the meantime had created the "missing link" with the help of Charles Ritz. As far as I know, there's only one such reel in evidence, the 1946 prototype that I own, and this precision instrument was made from solid aluminum in the basement machine shop of the Ritz Hotel; it combined the first "push-button" concept with an oscillating spool. The button in this design triggered a metal arm that contacted the rim of the spool housing to hold the line preparatory to a cast. Although the spool remained absolutely stationary, oscillation is achieved by the outer frame's moving back and forth. As a commercial item it was a dud, but the button was significant; it just happened to be in the wrong place.

Beginning with the Illingworth back in 1905, spinning-reel spools did not oscillate or crosswind the line. Instead of moving in and out during a retrieve, the spool remained in one position and the line was simply wrapped back coil upon coil, which hopefully slid one off the other. Crosswinding is not important on a large-diameter, narrow-throat spool of say ¼-inch width, such as we find on some modern closed-face reels designed for 10- and 12-pound-test lines. Confined between close-fitting plates, lines of relatively large diameter are less likely to jam. But on a wide, open-face spool of about ¾ inch, the line piles in ridges unless there is a back-and-forth movement, which serves the same function as a level-wind mechanism on our bait-casting reel. Without cross-winding, just one coil can become wedged and bring the cast to a screaming halt—or several coils might peel off simultaneously and throw an endless bird's nest in the rod guides.

Oscillating is accomplished by an eccentric pin on the main driving gear and this motion is synchronized with the rotation of the pickup mechanism, which is turning around the spool's circumference. On one-half turn of the crank handle the spool travels completely forward and on the next half it retreats backward to the original position, thereby completing one revolution. The speed of retrieve is determined by gear ratio and the spool diameter. To use round numbers, if the gear ratio is 4:1, the four coils of line are wrapped on the spool by the revolving pickup—two on the forward stroke and two on the return. Other systems were tried to provide oscillation. At one time we had a "wobbling" spool on the Felton reel, an effect similar to a loose wheel about to fall off an auto and just as predictable. This went the way of the Edsel. Then there was the "swinging" pickup, a double entendre in modern idiom and equally provocative on the first Italian Capta as the mechanism shuttled over a *revolving* fixed spool. This was about as logical as the Rustic reel made in 1903 by the Viscount Henry de France. Henry used what looked like a crocheting needle; the line passed through its eye, which was held by hand against the spool rim preparatory to a cast, then the line was wound back on the needle. A painfully slow process, but what the hell, he was on the right track.

Illingworth's pickup operated manually. All early-day spinning reels had the same device: simply, a roller mounted on a bracket at the edge of the revolving cup. This is reliable because without working parts it's not subject to mechanical failure. The line is lifted from the roller with the forefinger preparatory to a cast, then caught again after the toss is made and pulled inward and dropped back over the pickup. The manual pickup is still popular among a coterie of nimble-fingered old-timers who would have it no other way. With practice, it's fast and foolproof if the line is kept under tension—a subtlety of motion that escapes most beginners. To provide a less dexterous means of catching the line, a metal "finger" was adopted in the 1930 Luxor, a spiral-curved arm extending away from the spool that automatically scooped up the line. The finger-pickup was opened by hand to make a cast, and when the crank handle was turned about one-half revolution, it automatically closed, being tripped by a cam in the housing. Inevitably, a loose coil of line would get wrapped around the finger, so the next logical step was to eliminate the error-prone gap by making a pickup in the form of a semicircle or "bail." One end was set in a socket on the side of the revolving cup and the other attached to the pickup bracket on the opposite side. The bail is spring-loaded so that it snaps closed by turning the crank handle forward; in closing, the bail moves over and around the front of the spool, knocking the line under, which in turn slips into the roller. The bail first appeared on the Hardy Altex and is the most popular pickup on open-face reels today.

With the rise of the Mastereel by 1948, a proliferation of foreign imports arrived in the United States. To satisfy the demand for miniature baits, all kinds of European spinners, spoons, devons, rubber minnows, and plastic eels went swimming in local ponds. A veritable garage industry grew overnight with amateur lure makers casting molds, and while much of it was junk, some of the homegrown variety became classics. The number of reels buzzing with French or Italian accents was staggering. There was Gatson, Meig's Ru series—the Ru Sport, Ru Lac, and Ru Mer—followed by the Cargen and the Alcedo reels imported by the Tonkin brothers at Continental Arms. These vied with George Thommen's Record reel, while the Orvis Company brought in the Ambidex, then the Pelican by Fiat—ancestor of their present model. Charles Garcia, a New York–based silkworm-gut import house under the aegis of Thomas Lenk presented two more

330

French reels—the CAP and Mitchell—while in California the Booth Import Company distributed the big Centaure. A kind of Gallic overkill, the Centaure with its gear ratio of 4.20:1 recovered 36 inches of line per revolution (full spool), and its 300-yard capacity quickly found an audience among surf casters, which moved spinning into the saltwater field. At the other extreme the little Micron with a gear ratio of 5.25:1 and designed for ultralight spinning almost fell on its open face. Despite all the reels available, the rod situation was, at best, mediocre.

It seems almost ludicrous now, but some reel distributors sold long cork screw-chuck handles to which you could attach the tip of a bait-casting rod or the tip and midsection of a fly rod. This produced two actions: rug beater or flyswatter. Imported spinning rods were either expensive and fragile bamboo models or made of tubular aluminum. American builders were still geared for tubular steel and offering beryllium copper as an alternative. After a century of producing bait-casting rods, it was impossible to switch overnight from the draw-down method of making thin-walled metal tubes designed primarily for ⅝-ounce lures to a shaft that would handle ⅛-ounce baits requiring a thickness of .004 inch in steel alloy. Standing in the wings was Dr. Howald who was about to present fiberglass cloth through the Shakespeare Tackle Company, but for almost three critical years spin addicts were in limbo. Tubular-steel rods fractured frequently, while aluminum and copper took spooky shapes "as the twig is bent" so to speak; if you put pressure on a fish with an aluminum rod, it would bend and remain bent until it was straightened out by hand—more or less. Eventually, it resembled a corkscrew. In classic negative advertising, the only thing guaranteed was that the rod wouldn't take a *permanent* set. However, the first "resinated" glass rod made by Fairfax and displayed at the New York Sport Show was gimbaled and harnessed in a big-game fighting chair with a huge weight dangling below its tip. The rod was arced at an alarming angle. When the show was over and the weight removed, the rod remained in the same position. Nobody could unbend it.

The ratio of resin-to-fiberglass was not perfectly understood—an initial bonding problem also encountered by the builders of graphite. But despite these technical bugs, one of the great casting rods of all time was an 8-foot tubular-steel fly rod converted into a spin-stick by adding a long cork grip and suitable ring guides. Harmonically, the metal was perfect without excessive vibration and the long lever length rocketed lures across the river with ease. To this day I think we are overlooking an important feature in spinning-rod design now feasible with new materials in terms of length and modulus. Why an ultralight rod should be just 5 or 5½ feet in length, or a light spinning rod 6 or 6½ feet long is puzzling. The only drawback with tubular steel was metal fatigue. At unpredictable times, a tubular shaft would collapse under very little stress. But fiberglass made its timely entrance on the scene and once again spinning took a step forward.

By 1953 most American reel manufacturers were making open-face fixed-spool reels, and a year later Zebco and Shakespeare came out with the first closed-face models that mounted on top of the rod with a right-hand retrieve. This was the most significant advance in the history of spinning in terms of its growth in America. As early as 1948, Ashaway managed to get the reel topside in an open-face bail-pickup version called the Slip-Cast, which in itself stemmed from Paul Mauborgne's "missing link." Paul realized that his trigger mechanism could be worked up as well as down to hold the line in place before making a cast when the bail disengaged. But the Slip-Cast was bulky and the external trigger awkward. When refined "undercover," so to speak, the closed-face reel was its ultimate simplification. Instead of a pickup, all it required was a pair of pins to catch the line enclosed within the housing. True, the cover is a source of friction against the line, but for the popular ⅜- to ⅝-ounce lures used by the majority of American anglers, it's of no significance. For baits less than ⅜ ounce the open-face reel held its market—as it has in saltwater fishing.

Spinning tackle of one kind or another is the most popular gear in the United States today. It had a peripheral effect on the fishing scene by greatly increasing the numbers of people who are using the fly rod. Once a neophyte had confidence in his casting and discovered the joys of angling, the next step came easy. To some extent this is equally true of bait casting with the traditional multiplier, as the revolving spool of 1976 has benefited from the technical advances made in the spinning reel.

[1976]

42

Meet
Mr. Fish

Al Pflueger, Sr., the famous taxidermist featured in this chapter, passed away a number of years ago, and the business he founded is no longer in family hands. His statement of more than thirty years ago—"I've been experimenting with plastics. That's the future of taxidermy."—has proved to be more true than even he might have imagined.

There are still a number of real artists around the country who work with the traditional full-skin mounts and then paint them with incredible skill. But it's increasingly possible now to catch any popular gamefish and have your wall-hanger without having to kill the fish at all. After catching and releasing a bragging-size Alaskan rainbow a few years ago, for example, I found that given the fish's dimensions and a color photo—something easily done without killing the fish—that a ready-made plastic 30-incher could be painted to my specifications and/or photograph. Not only is this easier than all the work that goes into a full-skin mount, it's also substantially less expensive and the results to my eye are most acceptable.

*True, you may not get the exact physical configura-
tion of your particular fish by this route (and really
unusual specimens will still require at least a full
mold on the spot), but in this era when catch-and-
release is needed to protect trophy populations of
both fresh- and saltwater species, ready-made
mounts can be the perfect solution. Ask your outfitter
or boat captain for information.*

The world center of taxidermy, piscatorially speaking,
sprawls over a forty-five-acre tract of wood lot in North
Miami, hard-pressed by a housing development on the east
side and a boggle of Florida jungle on the west. Since the
rambling ranch-style home of Al Pflueger (no relation to the
tackle company) is an unclassified repository for bird, snail,
snake, and fish collections, and the surrounding lawn is a
feeding station for wild doves and quail, the Pflueger manse
is rightly considered part of the professional tract. The cin-
der-block buildings, where the work of skinning, casting,
sculpturing, and painting is done, radiate from the grove of
trees like tide marks in the flood of a business that poured
over a half-million dollars into the Pflueger coffers last year.
The phenomenal success of this enterprise is based on the
concept that fishermen like to brag, and at a dollar a pound
live weight you can pat yourself on the back all night, while
standing under a 1,200-pound black marlin.

Ordinarily you would expect a taxidermist's shop to be
a somewhat subdued, strange-smelling sanctuary where art
and dissection flourish hand in hand. But the Pflueger acres
are a milling mass of trucks loading and unloading fish, and
they often jettison their cargoes among bewildered customers, who pace the grounds like expectant fathers. From this
frenetic activity, Pflueger cuts himself a wide slice of human-
ity. Like the trio of sports who deliver their catch in an armored convertible. Two of them, with coats bulging under
the armpit, make a quick inspection of the area before the
third man steps out with his prize. "There's somethin' funny
about those guys," Pflueger observed. "They bring me one
reef fish every week. Why one every week?" However, the

335

Pflueger billing runs the gamut from John Smith through Herbert Hoover, Errol Flynn, Clark Gable, Ernest Hemingway, Van Johnson, Gary Cooper, and of course, President Dwight D. Eisenhower.

"Most of our work is on sailfish and bonefish. I just did an order of bones and dolphin for Arthur Godfrey. Dolphin were thick this year; so all our regulars had to have one. But the heavy load is always sailfish," he continued, "and one of these days I'm going to open a separate plant just to handle them. The other fish slow up our production. Get a reef job like the four hundred specimens, and we have to shift help back and forth."

There are artists of big-game animals, like Steve Horne of Jonas Brothers, who can build the heads of great pachyderms from wet cardboard and make the curving ivory from papier mâché. He is that good. In homes that hang trophies of the chase, you feel like a kudu crouched in the tall grass waiting for death when you face one of Horne's shaggy-maned lions. This is one facet of the taxidermist's art, the animal kind, where your host looks less like a butcher in his shop than a hunter of beasts. But as Horne said in his Westchester, New York, studio recently, "When it comes to fish, I tell my customers to send them to Pflueger. We couldn't do work like that here. Taxidermy is a specialized business, and Pflueger is Mr. Fish." Coming from the boss of world-famous Joan Borther, this was no small compliment.

Al Pflueger is a big man with a barrel chest and arms like a blacksmith. He did a great deal of amateur boxing in his younger days, but after fighting Mickey Walker and several other sharp shooters he decided that the fight game held no future for the grandson of a German gamekeeper. Like most boys in south New Jersey around the beginning of the century, Pflueger grew up with an intense love for the outdoors. The now-decimated Newark meadows held thousand of migratory waterfowl at that time, and young Pflueger became an ardent hunter. He began reading books on taxidermy, and by the time he was fourteen had achieved such skill that he went to the Museum of Natural History in New York to apply for a job.

The museum's staff was greatly impressed by his work, ". . . but they couldn't pay me enough to commute from Elizabeth to New York City every day. I wandered from one job to another after that," he continued, "washing bottles in a bottling company, working as a toolmaker; you know, anything that came along. The big thing was that I had time to work at my hobby. Then one day I met Tommy Gifford in Long Branch," he added reflectively, "and that was my real break. Tommy saw the work I was doing on striped bass, and he asked me why I didn't go to Florida, where there were more fish. That was twenty-nine years ago, and I've been here ever since."

To put bragging on a paying basis, Pflueger became a sailfish specialist. Sails make beautiful mounts, and the nimble-fingered Mr. Pflueger not only re-creates the color and muscle pattern, but catches the smoke that poured from your reel when the fish took off. It makes your eyes sting. In an art where the result often looks as if it were done with hay and baling wire, he has accomplished a dramatic movement that nets him $16 a foot FOB Miami. About 3,000 sailfish are mounted by Pflueger every season.

"The Mexican business, from Acapulco alone, is fantastic. I paid one agent down there twenty-eight thousand dollars in commissions last year." Pflueger's agents are charter boatmen and dock operators who get a percentage on each fish they send to the North Miami shop. "We get the same price for barracuda, grouper, and amberjack," he continued, "but real big fish like tuna and marlin go by the pound." It takes mountains of raw material to maintain such a volume of work, however, for the shop consumes 370,000 square feet of lumber, 78,000 pounds of plaster, and over 10,000 gallons of paints and varnishes in one season.

Telephones jangle all day and all night, but most of the after-dark callers want Pflueger to identify an unknown animal prowling in their neighborhood. "Had to take the phone out of the house. It got so that every time a skunk took a walk, somebody'd get me out of bed. Those damn skunks are a real problem, too. If somebody smells one on a warm night, they call the Health Department and tell 'em Pflueger's place is ruining the neighborhood. When the wind is out of the southeast, they might smell the North Miami garbage dump. We don't smell here—not unless you get right inside the skinner's shed."

It is not unusual to find a group of scientists puttering around the sheds with notebooks and calipers, measuring specimens that aren't often available to research. Many of the world's foremost ichthyologists visit Pflueger to get his advice and assistance in solving research problems. Pflueger has had no formal training in marine biology, but in some respects his knowledge of fish is greater than that of the average scientist. When he talks about fish, or birds, trees, snails, or snakes, it is in the Latin terms of order, genus, and species. Years of practical experience and study are reflected in his familiarity with the bottomless pool of systematics.

"You have to be precise in this business. First, because we're collecting for museums and universities; and second, because the common names don't serve my purposes. We have four species of snook right here in Florida, for instance, but they're all just plain snook. I've collected three of them, but I can't get a good snook specimen of the fourth. That's *Centropomus ensiferus* with the long anal spine. His anal fin runs half the length of his body. Quite a few of them are caught every season without anybody ever knowing it."

A world traveler, Pflueger frequently takes off on an expedition of his own, gathering material for museum collections. "I won't get away for a while yet; business has become too big. If I could get it to run without me, I'd head for British Guiana. You should see the catfish down there! There's over a hundred species, and most of them aren't even classified. They have one big yellow-colored cat who feeds in shoals; a school of them surface with their mouths open and drive the baitfish into the bank. Craziest thing I ever saw—all these heads and mouths poked out of the water, making a big semicircle, and the little fish hopping right in their gullets."

Pflueger's bird and tree-snail collection is soon to be donated to a university. The birds represent species found in British Guiana, but the complex snail inventory covers the entire Caribbean area as well as the Florida Keys. Tree snails are an old Pflueger interest, and consequently many of his specimens are of snails that are now extinct.

Pflueger often spends his weekends in the nearby Bahama Islands, fishing with what promises to become a valuable exploratory instrument. "I'm using a gas-operated 16/0 reel now, with a mile of steel cable line. Some of the boys are building them to operate electronically, and some use compressed air, but I think we're going to learn new things in this deep-water fishing," he said. "We used a small crane instead of a rod last spring and, working around Bimini, we brought up silk snappers, cow sharks—they're the ones with emerald green eyes and pale cream skin—and all kinds of thousand-fathom fish. Most of them were Lutianidae, but I know we're going to get some unknown species this way.

"Darndest thing, you know we bait ten or twelve hooks on the cable, and you can hardly get a load of fish back up to the surface. Sometimes a big cow shark will swallow them and pull the boat backwards. The fish pop or swell with the change in pressure, but pressure changes don't bother sharks. They'll follow your fish right up to the surface and snap the cable."

Pflueger has a standing order with the commercial boys working for tilefish in 1,000-fathom water out of the Hudson Canyon. The tilefish, first discovered in 1879, dwells along the outer edge of the continental shelf and represents a highly specialized deep-water fishery. Along with the tilefish, the commercials haul barrels of unidentified trash fish that are iced and sent to the Miami collector. The trickiest bit of collecting is done by daughter Joanne Pflueger, who shoots flying fish from the pulpit of their 40-foot boat. If you have ever seen this jet-propelled sailfish fodder skimming over the Gulf Stream, you will understand how Joanne became Champion of Champions at the famous Vandalia shoot. She downs the blunt-nosed flyers with #10 shot, and a museum group of thirty or forty is just an afternoon's work. Nonflying small specimens are taken on the spinning rod that Pflueger recently adopted for exploring under docks. Sophisticated business associates are astounded to find that a luncheon date in town consists of first jigging for moonfish under a pier to check the tidal influence on feeding and, while the apple pie is still hanging on their chins, driving the back roads around Miami looking for gopher turtles.

It takes Pflueger all day to make his rounds. He usually breakfasts at seven, and a half-hour later he's on the job. After checking the mail in his two-secretary office, Pflueger walks through the workshops to see how any one of 200 or 300 fish is being handled. A few words of obscure reference comprise a discussion with his help. "Try a number eighty," or to a skinner, "Cut him up to the nose, but go easy on the borax." A grunt, a nod, or a wince answers most problems, but the tough ones he goes to work on himself.

"Actually, taxidermy is a very routine business here," Pflueger said. "A lobster, for instance, used to take hours of work; now we just soak 'em until the meat gets soft and then stick an airbrush in the joint of a leg, and *floom,* the lobster is clean as a whistle. I've been experimenting with plastics," he continued. "That's the future of taxidermy. If you could plasticize economically, you'd cut time and labor in half."

Pflueger demands and gets perfection from his staff. Although there are over seventy people working in the shops, about ten of them are key people, highly skilled airbrush artists, mold makers, and sculptors who elevate the fish from a bag of skin to a thing of beauty. The tricky job of getting the stripes on a bonefish in just the right pattern and intensity is done by an airbrush man who gets the fish after it has been sprayed with background colors of silver, pale green, and pearl, and with remarkable speed fires his needle-nose spray gun in horizontal and vertical sweeps, creating the grass-shadow markings worn by a living bonefish.

"We don't use paintbrushes for many operations," Pflueger observed, "except for the spots on dolphin, grouper, and hind. Hand painting is slow and unlifelike." For reasons of color, Pflueger rarely mounts freshwater fish. "They're too tricky. There's so much variation in their color that getting accurate results is almost impossible. A guy sends me a brown trout from Maine, and another one from California, and they're entirely different. We'd have to have good water-color drawings to copy from," Pflueger said. "My art man,

Deckert, has made over five hundred watercolors of different Florida fish just as quick as they were caught."

Part of Pflueger's daily routine is to check his refrigerators, which range from small apartment-size boxes that hold unique specimens—like sea snakes, a Pacific swimming relative of the cobra; a chimaera, which is a weird-looking link between the sharks and the bony fishes; a tail-chewing mot-mot bird from British Guiana, and a common garden-variety fried chicken belonging to one of the skinners—to a huge bolted-door locker that holds everything from yellowfin tuna to queen triggerfish. "We always have a thousand fish waiting for work," he said, "and it's a tough job keeping track of 'em. Somebody misplaces one and I have to turn the joint upside down. Not much chance of losing a customer's fish, though," he continued. "They're all recorded in the office and marked with the owner's name. When the skinners get through with a fish, they save the meat and divide it among the help. Beats me how they can eat so much of it."

Pflueger's most difficult reconstruction job was an 1,180-pound broadbill swordfish, which the press jumped on last year because the skin of the fish wasn't used. The cry of "Fake!" echoed from New York to Miami, but Pflueger was unmoved by this reportorial homily. "What I object to is that we always mount big-game fish intact, just like any other fish. But the guy who caught this particular broadbill didn't have the skin to send us. People get talked out of a marlin or swordfish by the dockhands or boatmen who want the meat. They can't sell the meat without the skin. So they send us the fish's head and some body measurements, and we have to work three times as hard making a body to fit between the snout and the tail. Work like this is so hard that one big marlin can hold up our production line for three months.

"Now, with a whole fish," Pflueger continued, "we make a plaster mold of both sides of his body before he's skinned. The fish is sent off to the skinners, then for degreasing, and with the two molds we make a complete plaster body. All we have to do is put two halves together, and we have an exact replica of the fish. This model will be rough in spots, because the body of a big-game fish will shrink or collapse in places

341

by the time it arrives here; so then a sculptor goes to work smoothing the cast out. When the model is absolutely perfect, we make a final shell. The shell is a plaster model reinforced with laminated paper, and it's only one-eighth inch thick, which makes the body easy to handle. All we have to do then is mount the fins, tail, and head, and pop the skin over the finished model. Nothing to it.

"The only big fish I don't like to do is a shark. The skin has to be tanned to leather before you can pull it over a mold. That takes too much time for commercial work. If the skin isn't fully shrunk, the mold explodes. Hell of a mess, with plaster all over the place. We make models of sharks that are better than the live beast. But for museum work you have to do it right."

There'll be no return to the native valley for Pflueger. "I never want to go any further north than the Saint Johns River," he says reflectively. "A man can live well in Florida. If I do move it will be some place down in the islands, or to Mexico. As long as I can get in some duck and goose shooting once in a while I'll be happy. After twenty-nine years in this business, I'm ready to bail out." Looking at the matchbox village moving in from the east, he continued: "All that over there happened in two years. It used to be one of the greatest bird fields in the state. Now the doves water in cement baths. Guess I'll have to move. I'm just a country boy at heart."

[1954]

43

Is Paradise
Lost?

Happily, and fifteen years after this article appeared in Field & Stream, *paradise may actually be improving. True, and as McClane points out, there aren't now nor were there ever 20-pound trout stacked in every riffle. What has happened is that the catch-and-release ethic that's become so prevalent here in recent years is catching on in Argentina, too. This has happened to a point now at which several professional guides in the Bariloche/San Martín/Esquel areas insist on a catch-and-release understanding before a client is even booked.*

Just as important for the long-term future of Patagonian trout fishing is something relayed to me recently by the owner of a large estancia, *or ranch, that happens to include one of the better rivers in the San Martín area. While operating expenses are going up, many of the larger ranches are depending on income from an increasingly depressed world market for cattle and sheep products. Many of the estancia owners, I'm told, are beginning to realize just how marketable their heretofore private fishing can be—*

especially to visiting Americans. It's entirely possible that a whole new world of angling access—managed for quality angling and (of course) for a fee—will be opening up in the next decade or so. Considering that some of these ranches amount to private national parks by American analogy, this is no small matter.

Unlike the average trout size here, travel costs have increased substantially. Round-trip air from Miami to Buenos Aires will now run you about $1,200 or more, with another $200 or so for a round-trip ticket down to Bariloche. Full-service guiding, including first-class lodging and meals, guide, transportation, boat (if you're floating), and so on, prices out at about $2,200 per angler per week based on double occupancy, which also includes transfers and hotel in Buenos Aires. If this sounds expensive, consider that it's much less than a full week at a deluxe Alaskan lodge and the scenery is equally spectacular.

When I first visited Argentina, which was more years ago than I care to remember, the quality of its angling was, at the least, superlative. It never did produce any number of 20-pound trout, but fish of this size always get press notices, and by repetition the exception becomes the rule. On an average day I could expect a modest number of trout over 5 pounds and many smaller fish, which is very satisfying indeed, when one wades a crystalline stream and casts a fly. By pounding the *bocas,* or river mouths, in the evening or by trolling lakes with a spoon, I could reasonably expect a fish in the 10- to 15-pound class—maybe bigger. After four trips I succeeded in taking an 18½-pound brown. Nevertheless, Argentina, like New Zealand, developed a double-figure reputation, and many tourists went home disappointed.

While staying in Bariloche last April, I met an angler from California who complained he had a "lousy" day, for his biggest fish was only 7 pounds. Unfortunately, the South American syndrome is self-perpetuating. The belief that paradise *is* lost has no basis in historical fact for the simple reason that it never existed on so grandiose a scale, except uniquely in Lake Titicaca, Bolivia—which was the world's greatest rainbow fishery in the early 1950s. But what was average for Titicaca is as typical of the Andean ridge as Raquel Welch is typical of North American womanhood.

On a recent trip to Argentina my total for twelve fishing days was sixty trout of over 5 pounds, mostly browns, for an average of five per day. The largest was about 7½ pounds. These are only estimated weights, since we killed very few trout. For stream fly fishing, this is as good as I've experienced anywhere and is comparable to the late 1940s. Fish of below 5 pounds were numerous, and I suppose twenty "small" trout per day would be a fair average. I also lost two heavy fish—a brown of perhaps 12 pounds and another that I didn't get to see—and Laddie Buchanan hooked an 8-pounder that tail-walked all over the Limay River.

In all, it was a very satisfying trip—but it was Laddie's knowledge of the various places we fished that made it successful. Gone are the days when you could drive to the nearest stream and expect to fill the frying pan. There are newly paved roads and considerably more angling pressure as endless balls of monofilament in the handiest streamside willow testify. Hydroelectric impoundments are already a threat to the rivers of southern Patagonia. Yet there is still solitude, miles of it, and more pretty streams than any man can fish in his lifetime.

One aspect of the local scene that has changed dramatically is the fishing in Lake Nahuel Huapí. This 330-square-mile body of water is probably the most productive spot in South America today. It drops to 1,600 feet in depth and is divided into many branches that vary in character biologically. Twenty years ago the lake was primarily a brown trout fishery (record 36 pounds) but, as is typical of brown trout in an ocean-size environment, it produced little for the fly fisherman. Rainbows were in the minority then and, like the brownie, were taken mainly by deep trolling. On previous visits I caught trout in the 15-pound class with deep-swimming spoons and plugs, but to me a stopover in Bariloche was merely a pause between flying and driving. Despite the creature comforts of a resort town, serious anglers either headed north or south another 200 dusty miles and stayed at a *hostería* or camped out. A man doesn't travel halfway around the world to sit in a boat and blindly hope for three or four strikes.

Today, rainbows not only dominate the lake, but you can wade knee-deep and cast to risers within sight of town. In fact, two of the hottest stretches of shore are directly in the village. Some idea of the angling quality is reflected in these facts: Last season 398 trout of over 7 pounds were registered at the Nahuel Huapí Fishing and Hunting Association. Bear in mind that this is a small local club and doesn't reflect the tourist catch. Of these, 123 weighed over 12 pounds and the 2 largest were a 24-pound brown trout and a 26-pound rainbow trout. Among the qualifying fish were 22 brook trout exceeding 7 pounds. The majority fell to spoons and spinning lures, but a good percentage were taken on flies. The 24-pound brownie was caught on a fly in the lake's outlet river, the Limay, in one of the big pools about six miles downstream, and Laddie and I saw a fish of almost that size actually *rising* to mayflies along the far bank in the same location. The presence of such large fish is not something I remember during the river's halycon days when gringo anglers first arrived.

We did comparatively little fishing in Lake Nahuel Huapí because I wanted to visit some of my favorite rivers to the north—the Chimehuin, Malleo, Collón Curá, and finally the beautiful Traful. Laddie and I ventured up to the Aluminé one morning, and this proved to be our poorest choice of the whole trip. The river is congenitally silty with a substrate of sharp ankle-turning rock. The best we could do here was a half-dozen rainbows from 1½ to 3 pounds after many hours of casting. Fishing in the Chimehuin, however, is about the way I remember it, with a pair of 2- to 5-pound browns and an occasional larger trout, particularly at its mouth where the river leaves Lake Huechulafquén.

By the time we returned to Bariloche the early winter winds made fly casting on Nahuel Huapí virtually impossible. We drove along the shore each morning and evening hoping for a break, but whitecaps pounded noisily against the gravel. This didn't discourage the spin fishermen who paraded their catches to the local smokehouse, which, incidentally, is precision-operated by the village watchmaker at the rear of his shop. But during a brief lull in the wind, I managed to take a 6-pound steelhead while wading at the mouth of the Ñirihuau and saw a 14-pounder beached by a fly fisherman after a spectacular half-hour fight.

The radical change in Nahuel Huapí's fishing is more accidental than a management coup. The pivotal point was the introduction of steelhead or *plateado.* When local anglers began taking these silvery fish, it was believed that a new species had evolved in the lake. Unlike the familiar Argentinian spotted trout with a prominent red band at maturity, which claims some seventy years residence in Nahuel Huapí—the deep-bodied, almost spotless plateado began raiding the shores and busting tackle. In paradise past an abundant shallow-water fishery didn't exist at all. The phenomenon of habitat segregation by two or more separate populations is not unknown among salmonids, with one form living mainly in the littoral or shoreline regions of a lake and the other living pelagically or in the open water. The Bariloche hatchery is a kind of international supply house, and it appears that steelhead were among some of its imports in the past decade, although nobody recognized the difference.

As every student knows, the rainbow trout is a widely variant species consisting of many integrating geographic races. Most of these have been given subspecific status at one time or another. California, for example, officially lists six forms of subspecies. In my opinion this is the only intelligent way to deal with salmonids from a management point of view, and while certain other states have been reluctant to accept trinomials, the fact remains that there are major differences between strains. This indecision is compounded in Argentina because since the early 1900s it has obtained trout from at least a half-dozen different countries and countless hatcheries. The original rainbow plants were Shasta and Kern River strains from California, but in recent times fish of unknown bloodlines from Denmark and Germany have

347

been stocked. This has changed the picture to the extent that Argentina now has both spring and fall spawning rainbows. Natural reproduction must be at optimum, as we observed vast quantities of trout fry in Nahuel Huapí's tributary streams.

The Danish trout are a mystery. Denmark, of course, obtained *its* original rainbows from the United States and for some years had a trout-farming program that became one of the country's leading industries. This highly domesticated stock is bred for the restaurant trade, and in Jutland streams I found it an otherwise dull but accommodating fish ready to play games. However, the trout that arrived in Argentina are flighty, ill-tempered creatures with all the instincts of a piranha. We spent an afternoon with the director of the Federal Hatchery in Bariloche, Dr. Miguel de Lourdes Baiz, a serious young man who told us that a Danish rainbow actually bit a visitor on the forefinger as he pointed at a large trout in one of the rearing pools. Even though we approached the water cautiously, they panicked like wild fish. Dr. Baiz installed a screen over the pool—not to keep predators out but the fish in. "Every time anybody walked by the pool some trout jumped out," he said. It's impossible to relate these fish to any I ever saw in Denmark. By contrast, the rainbows from Germany were a sorry-looking lot unable to thrive on the 100 percent liver diet that cattle-rich Argentina still quaintly dispenses. They were ulcerated and lethargic.

Despite a brood stock of brilliantly colored 6- to 7-pound wild brook trout that he proudly displayed, Dr. Baiz was gung-ho about the Canadian Assinica strain that he hoped would arrive from New York. "Their longer life span should produce fish of record size in our waters," he said. Argentina made its first brook trout plants with fish from Maine. These were widely scattered throughout Patagonia by airdrops, and some major fisheries developed, particularly in remote Lake General Paz and Lake Hui-Hui, where 5-pounders are quite ordinary. But squaretails also became established in pine-shrouded Brazo Bonito, a cold-water arm of Nahuel Huapí less than a two-hour drive from Bariloche. A 9½-pounder was caught here in 1970. Landlocked salmon, another Maine import, thrived in only a few watersheds (although the local record is 31 pounds), possibly because the piscivorous diet associated with good salmon growth is generally absent here. Argentinian waters contain only one smeltlike forage fish that has a scattered distribution, and it occupies the lakes where salmon are established.

The initial introduction of trout into Argentina was an ecologist's dream. No predator fish existed, and only two native fish species of any size occurred in freshwater—the *trucha criolla,* which translates to "native trout," is not a trout at all, nor is it a perch (as it is often described), but a member of the drum family; there are at least three of these serranids in Argentinian streams, and they are a valuable market fish. The pejerrey is one of the silversides, the same little baitfish so popular in U.S. Atlantic ports with the difference here of growing to a length of 18 inches or more; both landlocked and sea-run forms exist. Fortunately, the colorful Argentinian sea lamprey has never found access to Patagonian streams, and barring human error in future hydroelectric projects, it may never become a dangerous parasite. So trout were literally planted in a vacuum in 1903. Although there existed an equal scarcity of small forage species, the pound-per-acre production of trout was, and is, incredible.

The main item of trout diet in Argentinian streams is the *cangrejo,* a small freshwater crab that the fish literally gorge on. There are true crayfish present also, but the more abundant crab is consumed in such quantities that the belly of a big trout sometimes feels like a sack of gravel. As a result, the flesh of Argentinian trout is a brilliant red, the coloration deriving from dietary fat-soluble carotenoids found in crustaceans. A dark Woolly Worm is about as effective an imitation of the crab as any, particularly when the hackle is given a pumping action in short, quick jerks on the retrieve. Streamer flies in black, brown, tan, and dull green also score. The volume of insect life varies greatly from river to river, but large nymphs are generally productive, and at times during a hatch the dry fly excels. On my last trip we had only three real opportunities with the floater: a mayfly emergence on the Collón Curá, a tremendous swarm of flying ants on Lake Nahuel Huapí, and a caddis flight at the mouth of the Limay. This is about average. Except on small streams with eager trout, the chuck-and-chance-it method of dry-fly fishing seldom pays off in Argentina. A sinking-tip line and sunken fly is the first fundamental.

A trip to Argentina hasn't changed much as far as the economics are concerned. I flew down on Braniff Airways and the tourist-class fare is $533 round trip from Miami to Buenos Aires. By jet, of course, the journey is measured in hours; in the piston-engine era it required two days or more, and you had to have an iron butt to survive. From Buenos Aires to Bariloche add another $90 on Austral—the only airline whose stewardesses sell trout flies in-flight. The trip begins to amortize itself when you can stay in a first-class hotel like the El Casco at about $11 per day with meals included. The option then is to rent a car and drive to the local hot spots or, better still, hire a capable guide like Laddie Buchanan; his fees vary according to the number of people in your party at a low of $45 per day in a group of four to $80 per day for one person. Bear in mind these charges include accommodations, meals, and all ground transportation. An Argentinian fishing license costs $5—a mere pittance in paradise.

I had to leave for home on the last official day of the trout season, and as we drove to the airport it was obvious that April 15 was the break we had been waiting for. New-fallen snow sparkled on the Andes and the azure lake was as calm as a mill pond. Laddie told me that he was going to try the shore around the mouth of the Limay after he dropped me off. I wasn't surprised when he wrote some weeks later to say that he registered four trout at the club that day, two 9-pounders, one 12-, and a 17-pound steelhead. He broke off on four other fish. Mr. Buchanan is helping to perpetuate the double-figure syndrome, but the truth is that paradise is not lost—it's prospering in the age of the plateado.

[1972]

44

The Saturday of Marten Van Kleek

The early history of angling in America is much like a worn antique quilt—now seen as fragments of loosely bound and odd pieces of cloth with pieces missing here and there to add dimension to the puzzle. For the uninitiated, much of the following may seem as interpolation from history, and there is indeed some interpolation here—the legitimate guesswork found often in a historical essay. What surprises me, as the director of a museum devoted to angling history, is that there is so little in this essay that isn't accurate as a matter of historical fact as we know it. Edward Pole, for example, the Philadelphia tackle dealer mentioned in this chapter, is one of the earliest American tackle dealers of whom we have accurate record at the museum. I shouldn't be surprised, however. In this case, as in so many others, McClane offers the extraordinary attention to detail that brought him to the top of his craft. As an introduction to early American angling, his story here is without peer in popular print. Join us, then, for an angler's tour of Manhattan as it was in 1776.

When he awoke at dawn there was already a heat haze over the city, a luminous steam that smelled of wood smoke and souring salt herring left to dry on his neighbor's roof. Marten Van Kleek planned to go trout fishing, so he dressed quickly. It was a three-mile hike to the Great Kill, and he could be there before the humidity got any worse. It was his fifty-seventh birthday and despite living in the British Colony of New York, like his father before him, he still thought of the island as Nieu Amsterdam. A widower, whose young wife had died of the pox, Van Kleek was a tanner by profession, and his three sons had migrated from Manhattan: Johan to Germantown in Pennsylvania, Aaron to the valley of Merrimack in New Hampshire, and Basil, his youngest, to the *Katzberg*—the mountains of the wild cats. Basil was looking to the future, as Manhattan's forests were being burned over to pasture sheep and cattle. The vast hemlock stands of the Catskills promised an endless supply of bark, the source of acid for converting skins to leather. That his son Aaron would soon perish in a war was preordained on April 23, 1775, when another young man, a twenty-three-year-old post rider, galloped from Boston to New York, then on to Philadelphia shouting "To arms, to arms, the war has begun!" This young crotch-bruised patriot, Israel Bissel, spent horse after horse traveling at a rate of more than 100 miles per day. He was no more recognizable as history-in-the-making than the man that Tory New Yorkers considered a radical— George Washington. Bissel would die at the age of seventy-one, a Massachusetts sheep farmer without legacy, a faceless and otherwise voiceless clarion in mud-covered breeches "charged to alarm the Country."

But on this hot Saturday with the campaigns of Lexington, Concord, Boston, bloody Ticonderoga, and Quebec behind them, the British fleet led by General Sir William Howe was at anchor off Staten Island, its sails popping in a vagrant breeze. Washington's exposed flanks across the East River on Long Island and strung along the Hudson were of no interest to Howe at the moment. He awaited the arrival of more ships.

Many citizens were fleeing the city that day, going north over the King's Bridge into Westchester, but others went about their business as usual, confident that the Colony would not seek independence (indeed it twice abstained from voting until July Fourth) or that the reluctant Howe would destroy "Little London." Marten Van Kleek intended to abandon Manhattan—permanently. He had been thinking about it for a long time, but the muffled memories of fifty-seven years set up an echo in his heart. This was why he wanted to go trout fishing that day. Talk in the coffeehouses was confusing, as New York was a colony divided. As one sees disembodied things in the mirror of a dream, so he could see himself clearly in the flowing crystal of a stream. To a bilingual member of the Dutch Reformed Church, all the parading, speech making, and acts of rebellion in the year past were as foreign to his thinking as the dozen trout flies he had carefully placed in an envelope, which were tied on "the best silkworm gut newly come over." These were a gift from his son Johan, who had visited the tackle dealers Edward Pole and William Ransted at Arch Street in Philadelphia. Although there was one major supplier in Manhattan, The Sign-of-the-Sportsman on Broad Way, the city was only half the size of Philadelphia, with its population of 40,000, and exotic items such as silkworm gut, horsehair lines, and winches had been more readily obtained through the Delaware shipping from England.

While seines and traps were widely used in both fresh and salt water throughout the Colonies, the City of New York had passed an ordinance as early as 1734 restricting *Kalck Hoech*, or Collect Pond, to hook-and-line only, a legislative effort inspired by the complaints of citizens who took their "pleasure" seriously. Its legal success was evidenced by the fact that the cold depths of Collect (also the source of the city's water supply) continued to produce trout until 1816, when the pond was drained. Collect was eventually filled and sealed over to become the site of Tombs Prison. The only voice raised against the rod, and then allegorically, was that of Puritan cleric Cotton Mather, the hot-tempered witch-hunter of New England. Mather often cited fishing anecdotes to point up his sermons, and in one he noted that "ministers were like rod fisherman; they spent too much time on indi-

353

vidual cases. Nothing like the net," he advised, "whether you are fishing for souls or trout."

The tackle Van Kleek carried that morning consisted of a 16-foot hickory rod and brass "rings" that lay flat against its four sections when not in use. His tiny brass winch was single-action and fastened to the rod with a circular spring clip, a vast improvement over earlier reels that had to be mounted with a pin that fitted into a hole in the rod handle. Although William Brown, the tackle dealer at The Sign-of-the-Fish on Fleet Street, and the firm of Bowness at Bell Year (both in London) had advertised "multiplying winches" as early as 1750, these were so poorly made that it remained for a Kentucky watchmaker to perfect the idea fifty years later.

But Van Kleek's reel was spooled with ten yards of horsehair line, an extravagance as compared to cheap "Indian grass" plaited from dried milkweed. Horsehair, which had been in use since at least the first century (Plutarch recommended the hairs of a stallion for their strength as opposed to those of a mare, which were "weaker due to her urination"), would persist until 1840, when fly lines evolved through cotton, hemp, flax, and silk with a waterproofing of tar, varnish, rubber, and finally linseed oil on plaited silk. The makers did not think of casting weight (that was a technical accident), but merely tried to prevent the line from rotting—a terminal condition that did not occur in the tails of horses. Marten often discussed tackle and fishing with his friends at Queen's Head Tavern, and, in fact, they met so regularly that it was looked upon as a kind of club.

Fishing and hunting were formally recognized as sports in America in 1732 with the formation of the Schuylkill Fishing Company, the oldest club in the world in continuous existence. The rod-and-gun social concept had been instituted at an earlier date in England, but these organizations did not survive 243 years. Founded as the Colony in Schuylkill (pronounced *School-Kill,* which means "Hidden Stream" in Dutch), it has its own flag of state, emblazoned with a crown and three perch in white against a red background. Despite this flag, the company remained faithful to his Majesty George III. When the Revolution began, it was changed to red, white, and blue with thirteen stars and stripes. Symbolically the stars surrounded the silhouette of a perch. The gregarious and delicious white perch was so abundant in the lower Delaware and its tributaries that it became a standard-bearer at every meeting, which included meals of fish and game freshly killed for the occasion. Patriots all, fifty-nine members of the Schuylkill Fishing Company rallied to the Philadelphia Cavalry, and one Samuel Nicolas became the first commissioned officer of the Marine Corps in 1775. Generals Washington, Lafayette, Meade, McClellan, and Pershing would sit at the company's long table in the course of history; but far from being militaristic, the club was dedicated to "recreative amusement" in angling and shooting. To the average citizen throughout the Colonies, however, a rod and gun was the way of life.

Armed with a smoothbore musket, one could stalk the marshes and great oak, chestnut, and beech forest of Manhattan for black bear, deer, wild turkey, grouse, woodcock, geese, and ducks. The wild pigeons and heath hen were so numerous that they "shut out the sunlight." The trapping of mink, otter, muskrat, and beaver was an industry in itself. When Marten Van Kleek's father arrived from Vacht, Holland, in 1715, the abundance of game found on the island staggered his imagination. The fishing was incredible, and one could gather all the lobsters, oysters, mussels, clams, and crabs that a hungry man needed. The road along the original waterfront, Pearl Street, was an endless mound of "pearly" shells, where people had harvested the East River shore.

To a European accustomed to private ownership of hunting and fishing rights, the privileges guaranteed in the English charters of the Thirteen Original Colonies ("it shall be free for any man to fish and flow there, and he may pass and repass on foot through any man's property for that end, so that they trespass not upon any man's corn of meadow"), the long history of royal prerogative was an ancient abuse. In 1549, another tanner by the name of Robert Kett sent a petition to King Richard asking that "ryvers may be free and common to all men for fyshing and ffree passage," and the king delivered his answer in the person of the Earl of War-

355

wick at Mousehold Health near Norwich. Kett and his constituents were butchered—hanged, drawn, and quartered in the name of the Lord. But to what extent the charter designer had "freedom" in mind (for the right to bear arms was an essential but fatal agreement on the part of the British) is debatable.

Commercial fishing, so valuable to the Empire, began in the Colonies with the settlement at Gloucester, Massachusetts, in 1623, and ultimately this would be significant in yet another war with England in 1812. The early-day Gloucestermen first went to sea in little Chebacco boats, and as they ranged farther offshore and eastward, worthier craft, the ketches and pinkeyes with their ladylike sheers raised gracefully aft, went in search of the cod, haddock, and halibut. Thousands of English, French, and Portuguese fishermen with an older maritime tradition were already harvesting the Grand Banks, a series of shoals extending about 350 miles off the southeast coast of Newfoundland and ending at Georges Bank east of Massachusetts Colony. The cold Labrador Current and the warm Gulf Stream join in this area creating ideal thermal conditions for plankton growth, and this plankton growth affects vast quantities of fish. But this same union creates fog, and the shallow banks build huge seas that were then, as now, a sailor's nightmare, particularly in the winter months. To survive the rigors of Grand Banks fishing, where ships and men went down in a solid block of ice, the swiftest and most weatherly fore-and-aft rigged vessel came off the ways in 1713—the New England schooner. This was the prototype of future ships of war. Running for market at twelve knots in heavy swells without wetting a lee rail was a tactical exercise that Yankee fishermen learned well.

Despite the variety of seafood caught around Manhattan, the demand for salt cod was insatiable; a valuable export item of the Colonies, most of it was being shipped to Europe. In the darkest years of American history, the cod would support its slave trade in that infamous Golden Triangle: cod for Europe's gold, gold for Africa's slaves, and slaves for sugar of the Indies, which fermented into the golden rum of New England. But that was in the future, and Marten Van Kleek lived in the past, where he never did anything worse than become happily drunk on Old Madière two or three times.

Walking along the now-polluted, yet pretty, spring-fed brook on Maiden Lane, where seemingly every woman in Manhattan came to wash her laundry (although it still held a few trout), he was aware of the changing values in his lifetime, not in a political sense, for he was not a political person. Not like that *fericht* Gilbert Forbes, the owner of The Sign-of-the-Sportsman, who had been arrested for selling muskets to Tory sympathizers and using the money to recruit disenchanted Colonials for the British Army. Marten remembered a line from the favorite passage of his father, who read the Book aloud each night, "the fool shall be bound with the cord of his own sins."

He jumped over a foul-smelling open sewer, wondering who could be depended on for the truth. The war would be decided in far off Philadelphia in any case. Beaver's Path or Beaver Street, which had given the Van Kleek family well over 10,000 pelts in its halcyon years, was now a ditch, and at the end of it, at Broad Street, the swamp that attracted so many ducks and geese was reclaimed. But waterfowl still arrived in noisy legions all around the island. There were more rabbits now (the cottontailed *coney* had become such a menace east of Manhattan that the Dutch called the place Coney Island) and more deer as the land was cleared and more farms or *bouweries* were cultivated. The city was small in area, being limited to the south end of the island, having grown very little beyond the old wall. During the war between Holland and England a fortified wooden barricade had been built to protect the city's north flank, but like the fort in the south at the Battery, it was a token bulwark to the vastly outnumbered Dutch who didn't fire a shot. It had long ago been torn down and used for firewood.

Once beyond the city limits at Canal Street, Marten came into open country. The woods were quiet in the growing heat. The Great Kill was his favorite spot for trout. He had caught fish here up to a pound and a half in size. But there were other trout waters like the Minneta Kill, which flowed along what is now Fifth Avenue, from Twenty-first Street to Eighth

Street, then to the Hudson between Houston and Charleston streets. He also fished the Saw Kill at Seventy-fourth Street and the Montagne's Kill at 108th Street. There were streams of a different character, like Stuyvesant Creek and Mill Creek draining the lower salt meadows, which held white perch, pickerel, and striped bass. These marsh lands were peculiar. Although wolves still played havoc with the cattle, cows more often disappeared in Manhattan's bogs. One day "sidewalks" would curl and buckle as wetlands settled and underground streams changed their courses.

The place called *Manhatte,* or simply "the island," was a campsite for hunting and fishing before the coming of the white men. When Giovanni da Verrazano arrived in the spring of 1524, he encountered Indians ashore, but in the winter following, Estaven Gomez, a Portuguese explorer, found the island deserted. During the cold months when damp and bone-chilling winds roared over its hills and marshes, the Indians moved. It was only after Englishman Henry Hudson probed the river in the service of the Dutch that the first white settlers arrived in 1624 and set up their crude shelters, when the Indians made camp. They established themselves to trade in a village called Greenwich. The *Manhattans* were one of eight tribes in the Wappinger Confederation, related to the Mohicans of the north and the Delawares to the west. Like the members of the Montauk Confederation on Long Island, who were almost extinct through the ravages of smallpox but once numbered 6,000 under their great sachem Wyandanch, they were all Algonkians. Among the riverine tribes, the favorite food dish was striped bass. John Josselyn observed in 1672 that "the Indians have in the greatest request, the Bass, the Sturgeon, the Salmon, the Lamprey, the Eel, the Frostfish, the Lobster and the Clam."

There were no black bass in New England and none around Manhattan, although the smallmouth was well known among the French colonists of the Saint Lawrence River valley where the fish was called *achigan,* the Algonkian word for "ferocious." The largemouth had a wider range, from the Great Lakes south into Florida and along the Gulf

Coast. But the black bass didn't appear in the East until the opening of the Erie Canal in 1825. Despite the great river that flowed past Manhattan, no Atlantic salmon invaded its currents.

Beginning with Henry Hudson, early-day and some contemporary records refer to "salmon" in the Hudson River. Although attempts were made to establish the fish here and in the Delaware, these projects failed, and the natural range of the species never extended farther south than the Connecticut River. Atlantic salmon did thrive in northern New York in the Lake Ontario and Champlain drainages and were taken in tremendous quantities, particularly in the Chazy, Oswego, Saranac, Ausable, and Salmon rivers until the 1830s. But elsewhere when the Colonists weren't familiar with a fish, they merely attempted to describe the quality of its flesh rather than a species. Early settlers in the Ohio River valley referred to the muskellunge as a "white salmon." Even the walleye (apparently introduced by a Jesuit priest who stocked them in the Chemung River, a tributary to the Susquehanna's North Branch in 1812) was commonly known as "Susquehanna salmon." While the Atlantic salmon was of great food and trade value to the New England Colonies, it was no more important than the shad and eel. In fact, salmon was so plentiful that it was often written into the articles of indenture that servants must be fed salmon no more than three times a week. The fish were taken with spears and nets, and while some were probably caught with a rod, the first record of a salmon taken on the fly in North America was that of a British colonel, John Enys, on the Saranac in 1787.

When the _Mayflower_ left Delftshaven in Holland, it was headed for Captain John Smith's Virginia Colony, but the 102 souls aboard suffered from seasickness in the teeth of gale-force winds. Finally, as their food supply dwindled, "especially our beer," they were forced to seek a more northerly landfall in Massachusetts. During the century that followed, America's coastal towns spread from harbor communities up the lush riverine valleys as agriculture became increasingly important.

To these pioneers there were two important seasons:

shad time and eel time. Autumn was eel time, and during the month of October they were taken in such numbers on the Merrimack River that Derryfield (then the name for Manchester, New Hampshire) "beef" became synonymous with a winter diet. One historian observed "that enough eels were salted down in a single year to be equal to three hundred head of cattle."

The unrelated sea lamprey was considered just another kind of eel. Aside from being jawless, it is also, except for its head, boneless, a virtue "made safe food for children." Ironically, the parasitic lamprey, which is capable of boring a fatal hole in other fish with its rasplike tongue, was in such demand that as late 1887 attempts were made to "restore" it by stocking New Hampshire's rivers, and even a ten-dollar fine was levied for killing one out of season.

Although the shad was not sought by rod and reel (according to the Schuylkill Club records, the capture of one with any bait was novel), it was one of the most important food fish from the Virginia Colony to New Hampshire. Along with salt cod, trout, and oysters, the shad was held in high esteem by George Washington, whose secretary sent frequent missives to his Philadelphia fishmonger, advising him on the quality required at the general's table. Washington, soon to be called the Father of his Country, also became the Father of Partyboat Fishing by chartering a vessel in 1784 to take members of his staff out for a day of sea bass fishing at Sandy Hook, New York.

When the English first settled in the Connecticut River valley, the shad "was despised and rejected," yet it was wryly observed that in spring New Englanders couldn't get their shirts off without help because of the shad bones that stuck out of their skins like porcupine quills. Even the fierce Pawtucket Indians had their shad "cookouts" below the falls of the Merrimack River at Lowell, and the party-loving Winnipesaukees invited all the neighboring tribes of the Pennacook Confederacy to assemble for this joyous feast. Those shad not immediately consumed "were handed to the squaws, who stood ready, knife in hand to split the fish and hang them up to smoke for winter on the centre-pole of the wigwam or laid them out to dry in the sun." But before the

Revolution, the art of boning this tasty fish became common knowledge, and by the time Washington's army marched back to the Hudson River in 1778, "some thousands of barrels of shad were put up in Connecticut for the troops."

As Marten threw his rucksack on the bank, he recalled the letter his son Aaron had written in April the year before, which was over a month in reaching Manhattan by way of Boston from remote New Hampshire. News of the clash at Concord had caused him to "address himself to the militia" and that was the last word he heard. Aaron, still unwed, had farmed for a year, but he could "no longer stand idly by while seeing his freedom lost." Is this the Promethean fire that lifts man above animals? With a vague sense of detachment, Marten tried to shift focus to the maiden of his youth in her cheap cotton dress, as though trying to blow dust off a long-faded picture. Too many years had passed.

Decision, Marten thought, must be a privilege of the young. Even deciding which fly to use seemed too much that morning. He had some tied on horsehair snells, and of course the newer ones on silkworm gut; some were dressed without hackles and other were palmer-tied, looking much like a caterpillar. He selected a Shell-Fly pattern, and after tying it carefully to the single horsehair strand at the end of his line with a water knot, he stripped the single-tapered line from his winch until he reached the six-hair portion. This line was plaited or "twisted" on a simple device consisting of a horizontal wheel below which the hairs were suspended and attached to a weight. A bottle cork was inserted between the hairs to create a tight plait as the wheel was turned. Then the cork was removed. The line maker used a varying number of hairs in making each "link," knotting them off until a sufficient number of links was twisted to make a line. Double-tapered lines would evolve in the age of oiled silk, which sooner or later rotted, and thus the angler could use one end until it became worthless, then reverse the line and use the other end.

In these hot and bright hours, Marten felt he would have better luck fishing the more turbulent main stream, which splashed downhill toward the Hudson River. One day it would run under the asphalt and be called Forty-second

Street, but now it danced freely over boulder outcroppings. He was lost in thought when the first trout eagerly snatched the Shell-Fly, and despite its small size, the fish snapped the horsehair at his surprised reaction. Marten was prepared for the next trout, which he gently led out of the water by slowly walking back into the meadow until the fish was flopping on the bank. The winch, with a spool diameter of about 1½ inches and a spindle of no more than ¼ inch, made cranking a hopeless task. Many anglers simply tied the line to their rod tops and hoisted the fish out of the water or into a hand net; for this reason 16- and 18-foot rods were still popular. But ever since Bowleker's *Art of Angling* appeared in 1747, the trend in Europe had been toward shorter lengths of green-heart from British Guiana, and Cuban lancewood.

One builder in London, Simon Ustonson, was experimenting with glued strips of cane in making split-bamboo rod tips to provide more "spring" when joined to sections of other woods. However, it remained for an American gunsmith, Samuel Phillipi of Easton, Pennsylvania, to produce the first six-strip bamboo rod in 1872, the strips so finely matched that the joints couldn't be seen with a 10X magnifying glass.

Marten continued downstream, casting the same length of line, letting the fly float, then sink. Many little trout followed the fly and splashed behind it, then a half-pounder nailed it in midstream and was eased out flopping on the quick-stones to be added to his stringer. Before noon he reached the Van Coenis *bouwerie* where, amid cackling hens and the lowing of a calfless fresh cow demanding to be milked, he crossed their barnyard to reach the last pool. Below this point the stream spilled into a marsh, becoming tidal, but the sea trout never tasted as good as those brightly colored ones in fresh water. Marten tied on a Green Drake pattern, and within the next hour took a fine fish of about 1 pound and several smaller ones, which he also slipped on the stringer. He heard wild turkeys talking in some far-off copse. Like the deer and rabbit, they seemed to flourish around grainfields and orchards, and despite more and more hunting, some persisted from Central Park north into Harlem Village.

Marten sat in the shade of a tree and ate his coarse bread and cheese. He drank some water from the brook, then took his rod down and started for home. He intended to stop at the Queen's Head for a pipe and tankard of ale before curfew, but after he reached the old and rutted Indian trail, or Broad Way, he was soon caught in the flow of people who were going to the Battery. Howe's armada of 130 ships and over 9,000 men was an awesome sight across the bay. Everywhere he heard the sound of drums as the ragtag American militia held its daily roll call. They were bright-eyed and rheumy-eyed, skinny and fat, dressed in linens, buckskins, and remnants of uniforms from long-forgotten wars. Even some of his neighbors, Van Buren, Stuyvesant, and Van Cleef, stood on the cobbles before City Hall. It reminded him of the Book and a census taken in another age . . . *"the children of Shallum, the children of Ater, the children of Talmon, the children of Akkub, the children of Hatita, the children of Shobai, in all an hundred thirty and none."* Perhaps they will tell me I am too old, he thought, but that is a chronological, not a physical, truth, and tomorrow after church I will bring my musket to stand and be counted.

There is no record in the Van Kleek family Bible of when Marten left Manhattan, but it's quite probable that he migrated, in 1784, shortly after the Revolution. He went to the land of his son Basil in the Katzberg to what is now known as Drybrook, then a wild and turbulent tributary to the East Branch of the Delaware. The name, a mistranslation of *Drie-Brugen,* described a trout-filled river crossed by three bridges rather than a waterless hollow. Marten hauled by wagon enough seedlings of Astrachan apple trees to lay claim to ten morgans of land. And thus his grave is in a long-untended orchard, the eroded stone partly legible but completely overgrown by the gnarled roots of a tree, as though protecting its ancestral life source. He died at the age of seventy-nine, faceless and voiceless in the reckoning of his country.

[1976]

45

From Aawa to Zooplankton

I had the recent good fortune to share a Bahamian bonefish flat with Fred Cushing, a retired publishing executive who, in his days with what's now known as Henry Holt and Company in New York, had much to do with getting McClane's Standard Fishing Encyclopedia *into print in 1965. I have always regarded this book as remarkable, and that evening—after swapping flies and lies with Fred—I found out that sales of the* Encyclopedia *are now approaching 900,000 copies in English plus assorted other languages. It seems the word* standard *in the title turned out to be more prophetic than anyone might have guessed.*

Comparative sales figures on older angling titles are almost impossible to obtain, but it seems relatively certain that this book is the best-selling angling title of this century and is close to the top of the list of all-time contenders. In this chapter, written not long after the book's debut, McClane offers a rare, behind-the-scenes look at what may eventually be judged his most important work.

When my publishers asked for a fishing encyclopedia, I don't suppose they expected a volume that exceeds the *Decline and Fall of the Roman Empire* in size, but looking back on the years of systematic confusion in compiling the work, it's remarkable that we condensed it to something around a million words. I'll never forget the expression on the cab driver's face when I had a redcap truck the first 6,000 manuscript pages out of Newark airline terminal. It was cased in what resembled a wooden coffin weighing eighty pounds.

"Whatcha got there, Mac, a body?"

"No, a book."

"Ye're kiddin'. How do you read it, on a stepladder?"

"No, I spread it on the floor and crawl past it."

He inspected me in the rearview mirror and never said another word. I wondered what he would think if I told him it was only half a book and I really did hunker over the pages. Periodically my wife chased everybody out of the house and I'd start with *A* by the living-room fireplace and follow a sixty-foot trail into the adjoining bedroom, which never got me much beyond *C.* When the day finally came that I had a *Z* to cross-reference, the pages stretched all over nine rooms. I enjoyed the Marine Ecology because it was in the kitchen and I could stand up for a coffee break. Maybe Webster had a better system, but I doubt it. For one thing, you can't remember the pages as a book progresses among 141 authors who are all writing on different yet related subjects, and you also can't run the risk of stacking 6,000 sheets like the leaning tower of Pisa. So cross-referencing became a mild form of mental and physical gymnastics.

I had hired a secretary to keep the copy moving, and one day a new girl came to the house for an interview. There happened to be a cross-reference session going on, and four of us, including my wife and an off-duty police officer who stopped by to talk about fishing, were hopping around on the living-room floor on all fours, like squirrels for nuts. The sweet young thing punched the doorbell, then glanced through the screen door. Before she could unhinge her jaws, Bob said, "I'm Sargeant Chadwell, won't you come in?" It took me a half-hour to convince her that she hadn't stumbled into the funny farm.

One night I even had to crawl around a cocktail lounge. Our phone rang about 1:00 A.M. My wife answered it.

"Wake up. It's Don de Sylva. I think he said somebody swiped his tuna fish," she yawned. That didn't make any sense, but anything could happen on this project.

I stumbled to the night table. "Whatsamatta?"

"I'm at the club. Come over and help me find my bluefin larvae. I had them in a half-pint jar of alcohol. I was talking with the boys when this lady came over and said she wanted to show them to her husband and—"

"Tell the janitor to keep the door open. I'll be right there."

The microscopic bluefins were a rare catch that the eminent Dr. de Sylva had donated to our project. Crawling around on a barroom floor searching for half a dozen larval tuna no more than 50 millimeters in length is a demanding sport. We had to look under cigarette butts, hairpins, and discarded olives. I found a woman's shoe. Don discovered the jar standing upright in a chair with the screw lid off. It was empty.

"Gad, he drank them!"

Obtaining as many as a thousand different species of fish was a job. The obvious ones like a bog brook trout from Gods Lake, an Arctic char from the Tree River, or an Atlantic sailfish practically on my front doorstep were easy. However, after we exhausted the list of common gamefish and needed oddballs like the jolthead porgy, shortnose batfish, longfin bonefish, and the freshwater sleeper, things got complicated. I remember trying to get through the Bahamian customs one day with Don de Sylva and Dick Youngers. We had snorkels, scuba equipment, underwater lights, twenty gallons of rotenone, electric reels, slurp guns, spear guns, a long line with a thousand hooks, seine nets, cast nets, and even milk bottles. (I am a milk-bottle specialist. It's remarkable what you can catch by putting a slice of bread in a milk bottle and lowering it to the bottom with a piece of string tied around the neck.) We had specialized tools like metal coat hangers that could be shaped to fit the burrow of a mantis shrimp. The customs man was skeptical. When we returned to clear out a week later he was incredulous. All we had to show as our "catch" was one small frozen squid. Dick had committed everything else to his sketchbook.

Richard Evans Youngers is a born naturalist, the kind of lad who spears an eagle ray as readily as he sketches one. For the most part he did his paintings on location. He'd set up his work board on a beach or in a boat, and when possible we'd capture a subject and have it posed while still kicking. Many species, of course, were out of our range or so rare that obtaining one depended on other people. It took us a long time to learn how to ship specimens properly. The system we finally worked out was to pack small fish in plastic bags of water with oxygen added and airfreight them alive. The method for large fish was worked out by Keen Buss, Chief Fisheries Biologist of the Pennsylvania Fish Commission. Keen drugged the fish while still alive with MS 222, then quick-froze them and packed them in Styrofoam boxes filled with dry ice. Specimens treated in this fashion kept their coloration perfectly. In remote areas one method or the other wouldn't work for the lack of materials, and several rare specimens took mysterious routings.

Take the case of the longfin bonefish. The longfin is a rare species restricted to isolated parts of the Caribbean. It sometimes appears in the Florida Keys, but many old conchs have never seen one, so our search for a specimen centered on Jamaica. Longfins are most often seen around the fresh-water creek mouths of the island. While visiting Port Antonio I asked a local expert, Jim Paterson, to keep an eye open for a longfin and if possible to rush it air express in ice to the nearest stateside location.

For almost two years I didn't hear from Jim; then shortly before our deadline he wired that two longfins were on their way to Miami, but I had worked out a fast routing north to Palm Beach via Greyhound bus, then west to Dick at Fort Myers. The snafu began when the fish arrived at a Miami motel. How, we never learned.

"Meester, a peckage of feesh you vant?" It was a woman's voice.

"Yes, where are they?"

"Vair dey are? At Beekman's Cabanas. Vy you send dem to me who don't *like* feesh?"

"I didn't send them to you ma'am, I've been looking for them."

"Lookink for dem? Meester, confidantschully a—a *blind* man could find dem. Dey're smailing up *my* lobby!"

I urged the lady to put them on the next Greyhound bus. Dick drove over from Fort Myers so he could get to work on them fast. The bus arrived but no package.

"Pardon me," said Dick, "do you have a pair of bonefish aboard?" The bus driver examined us with the friendly grin of a cougar. "You wise guys or somethin'?"

The following day the bus company called. "This is the baggage department," announced a voice in authority. "Are you expecting a carton of cheese?"

"No! I'm expecting some fish."

"Well, you better get over, buddy; it smells like limburger to me."

Dumb luck also played a role in our project. Snake eels are fairly common in the southern waters at certain times of the year, but naturally, when Dick had to paint one it was their off-season. Fortunately he made it a practice to dissect his subjects on location to determine the sex of the specimen, and after opening a Nassau grouper he found not one but five freshly swallowed still-living snake eels. On another occasion I was taking a swim with my daughter, Susan, when she spotted a "red thing" rolling in the surf. It turned out to be a beautiful specimen of the hard-to-obtain glasseye snapper. The glasseye is a deep-water species that never ventures inshore.

It was inevitable, of course, that some of our valuable fish would be eaten. One was the juvenile stage of the African pompano, rare as a Ming vase, that weighed about 3 pounds. Our cleaning lady (who had learned to expect a Friday dividend in a fishing household) said it was delicious. Although we rushed her home in a bath of tears to look for the all-important fins, which are its key characteristics, the city garbage collector got there first. Dick's house was always so backlogged with specimens that his wife was often confused about which ones were book material and which ones were a legitimate dinner.

Editing the encyclopedia and working with its authors and artists was a great adventure, but there is a curious sense of relief in seeing the manuscript gone from the house. It was like a visit to the dentist. The moment of unendurable pain when he yanks the aching bicuspid is the moment that cures, and the after-twitches of extraction are easily borne.

[1965]

46

The Lure of
the Trout Stream

*A really successful fisherman, I've always thought, is
as much a poet as a scientist. Success in these terms
means learning a river well, and this means hearing
and feeling its music as much as understanding
where trout hold in a myriad of currents. It's certainly possible to fish in empathy with the flowing
water, and McClane's descriptions here of several rivers are ample evidence of just that sort of feeling.*

*McClane is best known as a technical angling
writer—meaning instructive—but this and several
other chapters in this book offer solidly constructed
prose with a great depth of feeling for the waters he's
known and fished. A great technical writer, yes; but
it's always a delight to find that his superb talents are
equally at home with a river's lyric.*

There is something deep in the human spirit that responds to
running water. The trout fisherman knows it well, for a living
river has many voices—from the infant gurgling of a headwa-
ter brook spilling over mossy stones to the sibilant sound of
its youthful course as it dances on graveled riffles or its pro-

370

testing roar as it rushes between towering rock walls that threaten to hold it captive. The thundering passage of Montana's Madison River echoing through Bear Trap Canyon is awesome; yet before it joins the Jefferson and Gallatin to form the Missouri, it has the gentle and reassuring voice of an old friend at journey's end.

For much of my life, I lived next to a river, and each night its familiar sound always soothed my mind before sleep. But it is when trout fishing, I have learned, that you come to know a river intimately. I sometimes feel like a trespasser, scolded by squirrels, screamed at by kingfishers, even growled at by bears, but the current tugs at my waders, urging me to find that idyllic pool around the next bend where a great fish will rise to my fly. Perhaps my only reward will be silvery troutling, ruby-spotted with the brilliant jewels of youth, but for a few seconds I can hold it gently in my hand, feeling the pulse of the river. In more than half a century of angling, I have known hundreds of trout streams, from Hot Creek in California to the Au Sable in Michigan to the Allagash River in Maine, and each offers its own rewards.

Yellowstone National Park

Yellowstone National Park is a mecca for trout anglers, and among its many rivers is one of the strangest on earth: the Firehole. This river's frigid source is in snow-fed Madison Lake, where it starts as little more than a brook rushing through dense forests of lodgepole pine. Then, gaining volume, it flows into a series of geyser fields near Old Faithful. In this area of the park, thermal springs vent from hot bowels of the earth, spouting in steamy clouds that can be noisily unnerving at times, particularly when you are concentrating on the rise of a difficult trout. You almost expect to see a dinosaur strolling down the river instead of the shaggy-maned buffalo that wander along the stream bank. But the hot springs have no detrimental influence on the cold waters of the Firehole and its tributaries. Indeed, at Biscuit Basin you can cast to some of the wariest brown trout to be found in the West.

The Firehole is easily accessible, and places such as the

turnout at Muleshoe Bend—with its beautiful view of the river—are often crowded with anglers from every state in the nation. I sometimes think it's the camaraderie, rather than the fishing itself, that is the real attraction. Yet solitude is also possible to find in the park; it simply requires a little more effort.

Slough Creek, on the north side of the park, is one of those places that remains, for the most part, isolated. Each September, my daughter, Susan, and I hike those few steep miles from the campground entrance to fish for its beautiful cutthroat trout. This crystalline river comes down from the Beartooth Mountains near Grasshopper Glacier, and in its coniferous subalpine reaches beginning at First Meadows, brightly colored trout rise to our flies in whispering currents. This is catch-and-release water, so the quality of the angling is exceptional. The cutthroat—named for the patch of orange or red on the throat membrane—is the only trout species that was native to the Rockies back in the early 1800s when Lewis and Clark made their famous journey. Susan and I have a favorite spot between First Meadows and Second Meadows where we stop for our noontime sandwich; here we share a magical moment among the blue of the wild gentian and the crimson Indian paintbrush, waiting for a family of moose to appear, as they usually do at that hour. Somehow, in a world seemingly gone mad, the appearance of an old bull and his retinue has become, I suppose, a reassuring footnote to our trip. By late afternoon, when it's time to leave, the general order of life is once again in perspective.

Beaver Kill

No river of greater fame flows through American angling history than New York's Beaver Kill, which flows west out of the 272,000-acre Catskill Forest Preserve. Beginning in the early 1870s, when anglers from New York City journeyed north on a pioneer railroad to the Catskills, the pastoral beauty of the Beaver Kill's hardwood and hemlock forests became the perfect setting for what is regarded as the birthplace of American fly fishing. Although the trout had been "invented" before the first ice age, as angler-artist Meade

Schaffer once observed, "this is where they painted spots on him and taught him how to swim."

Of the forty-five-mile length of the Beaver Kill, almost all of its upper reaches are posted and in private hands; but the lower fifteen miles, from the village of Roscoe to the river's junction with the East Branch of the Delaware, is public water. And it is the lower river, with its more than thirty legendary pools—Barnhardt's, Hendrickson's, Cairn's, Wagon Tracks, Painter's Bend, Cemetery, Baxter's, the Acid Factory—that has challenged generations of anglers. Despite intensive fishing pressure, the well-stocked Beaver Kill still produces quality sport, especially when hatches of mayflies or caddisflies are fluttering over the water and fish rise with abandon. The most productive locations are the catch-and-release stretches whose boundaries are defined with roadside signs. It is not unusual for a skilled caster to release two-dozen brown trout in the course of a day.

Tailwater Fisheries

An infant river has responsibility beyond mirroring the works of nature. It is not expected to produce hydroelectric power, irrigate farmlands, or act as a reservoir for great cities. However, with age it often does all these things. At its headwaters below Lake Tear of the Clouds, New York's Hudson River retains the character of its youth, forming a bubbling Adirondack trout stream with quiet pools, where deer come to drink and otters slide merrily into the currents.

The Hudson's lower reaches, however, have joined a long list of rivers whose energies have been harnessed by man. One happy by-product of these attempts is that in building dams, man has created a new generation of trout rivers formed by the discharge of cold benthic waters from vast impoundments. These tailwater fisheries are too recent historically to have a Beaver Kill mystique; however, their productivity in some locations is phenomenal. I remember fishing the White River in Arkansas many years ago when it was a fabled warm-water bass stream; but after being dammed to form Bull Shoals and Table Rock lakes, it became trout habitat, so cold that the river in that narrow Ozark valley is often blanketed in fog on a summer morning. Crawling out of my sleeping bag, I could find the stream only by the voice of a nearby rapid.

The "Big" Delaware, a Catskill bass river of my boyhood, now under the hydrothermal influence of Downsville Dam on its East Branch and Cannonsville Dam on its West Branch, produces splendid rainbow trout as far downstream as Long Eddy. The mighty Missouri in Montana hosts several tailwater fisheries, and some of the largest riverine trout in America feed in its powerful currents below Toston and Hauser dams. (The local record for the seldom caught browns is 29 pounds, 7 ounces.) The Bighorn in Montana, by origin a free-flowing but silted trout stream in its prairie headwaters, is made even colder and sediment-free by the bottom discharge of huge Yellowtail Dam in the lands of the Crow Indian Reservation. Perhaps the most popular of all contemporary western rivers is Henry's Fork of the Snake, in Idaho—a meandering twelve-mile run below Island Park Dam. Here the big draw is the Railroad Ranch stretch, where spectacular rainbows trigger a stampede of anglers during the June stone-fly hatches.

Au Sable River

In a historical sense, Michigan's Au Sable River is often compared to New York's Beaver Kill, as they both came to prominence shortly after the Civil War. But physically, the Au Sable is totally different from the boulder-strewn, swift-flowing Beaver Kill. The main Au Sable is created by three branch streams born in springs and cedar-stained swamps, coursing though a poplar, birch, and pine-forested alluvial plain of the Lower Peninsula. The river bottom is composed mainly of sand and gravel, and its flow runs strong and deep—so deep that wading is not everywhere possible. Although the lumber industry that thrived in the area in the nineteenth century has since disappeared, logjams still provide sanctuary for the occasional old brown trout with nutcracker jaws who rises to the surface like a ghost out of the past.

The most popular area for the fly fisherman is on the Au

Sable's North Branch around the town of Lovells, where it is easy of access and wadable; brook trout are dominant here, and because of its shallow depth this section of the river—unlike others—is not plagued by "aluminum hatch." That modern metal phenomenon, consisting of hundreds of summertime canoeists joyfully paddling downstream, panics the trout and makes casting utterly impossible.

On the South Branch the best fishing is from Roscommon to the main river, and on the Au Sable proper it's found between the town of Grayling and Mio Dam Pond. Here canoes are a real traffic problem by day, but fortunately it is the nocturnal brown trout that provides all the action. The Au Sable is famous for its after-dark mayfly hatches, and the big fish that hide in the depths during sunlit hours rise greedily at night. Dulled senses become razor-sharp when you fly-fish at night, as you listen for the *plop, plop* of rising trout against river sounds and blindly estimate casting distances by the feel of line tugging against the rod. Personally, I love the Au Sable best in autumn. Most paddles are put aside after Labor Day and by the time the Michigan countryside is splashed with color, one can find quiet runs and see the river in its fairest possible light.

Big Hole River

So many streams flow past the windows of my mind—the glassy, weed-rich glides of Pennsylvania's Le Tort Spring Creek, the turbulent pools of Box Canyon on the Rio Grande in New Mexico, Colorado's Gunnison thundering into Black Canyon, the trout-dimpled meanderings of Wyoming's New Fork, that big spread of the Snake River in sight of Mount Moran in Grand Teton National Park, and the always difficult slow runs of the Batten Kill in Vermont and New York.

Then, I see a herd of antelope watching me from the height of a mesa, bordering the Big Hole River in Montana, and my longing for wild water becomes overpowering. The journey from the town of Divide upstream to Wisdom is through country that probably hasn't changed much since Chief Joseph and his Nez Percé warriors fought the U.S. Cavalry in 1877 at the Battle of the Big Hole. But the river, with its sinuous curves and nimble rapids flowing past cotton-woods, is a fly fisherman's dream. The way to enjoy it is to hire a guide with a double-ender or McKenzie boat and float-fish for eight or ten miles, just drifting from pool to pool, while willows toss in the breeze and clouds chase each other across an endless blue sky. The Big Hole has never disappointed me, although if you asked how many fish I released on my last trip, I don't remember—there were some big ones, though, black-spotted and golden with bellies the color of buttercups. I do recall that when the hills turned purple at dusk and we reached our takeout point, a pair of mule deer came down to drink, and a rainbow trout leaped in midstream. I drew a long breath of twilight's sweet air and saluted the Big Hole with my fly-bedecked hat.

[1985]

47

Cobras
of the Sea

Here's McClane in yet another dimension—that of a natural-history essayist on a topic only peripherally related to fishing. The rationale for the story in the first place, I suppose, might have been twofold: First, some fishermen in remote tropical areas might encounter sea snakes, and information about them would be valuable on premise. Second, and for the millions of McClane readers who will never see a sea snake, the critters are just plain interesting with the same sort of morbid fascination as is attached to the piranhas covered in Chapter 15 of this book.

In either case, here's an absorbing look at one of the oceans' oddest—and deadliest—creatures by a man who took the trouble to inquire and to inquire well.

Last year a Colombian commercial fisherman was running his haul seine at the mouth of the Jaenen River. His fourteen-year-old son was helping him by pulling the free end of the net in a circle with the lead line scraping over the sand bottom. The boy had to work hard to drag yards of mesh through the murky water, and from time to time he stopped to clear some trash from its path. About halfway back to shore he grabbed a spinachlike mass of weed and started to toss it over the floating corks. Suddenly the boy flailed his arm at the air and screamed. A snake had buried its fangs in the base of his thumb. Although the father was familiar with the procedures of first aid, within twenty minutes his son was in convulsions. Within a half-hour he was dead.

One of nature's strangest creatures is the sea snake, a reptile belonging to the family Hydrophidae whose members are uniquely adapted to life in salt water and have a toxin that is often more lethal than that of a cobra. The nostrils of a sea snake are provided with valves that permit air breathing and close up underwater to prevent drowning. Apparently its small lungs are highly efficient, because the sea snake can spend long periods under water. Usually it swims in lateral, wavy eellike movements, but it can also float on the surface and swim backward and forward with no effort. Anglers frequently encounter sea snakes far out on the marlin grounds of South America's west coast, but at least one species, the yellow-bellied sea snake, has been found swimming hundreds of miles from land.

With the puzzling exception of one species inhabiting Lake Taal, Luzon, all sea snakes are found in salt water. And except for the yellow-bellied sea snake, they all occur in the tropical Pacific and Indian oceans from the Persian Gulf to the Yellow Sea and south to Tasmania and western Oceania. Some primarily coastal species live in shallow water and invade river mouths. The yellow-bellied sea snake is more widely distributed, possibly because it is a marathon swimmer. It ranges from East Africa through the Indo-Pacific to the Gulf of California and south at least as far as Ecuador. Like its terrestrial counterpart the aquatic reptile is most apt to be aggressive when disturbed. Optimistically, sea snakes are said to be docile—but so is a sleeping tiger. One big difference between a sea snake and a Texas sidewinder, for instance, is that about 25 percent of the people bitten by the aquatic kind die violently. There are no statistics on mortalities, largely because sea snakes are common only in the more remote and primitive places of the world where nobody keeps records. The majority of cases that have been authenticated indicates that native fishermen who work with nets and accidentally handle the reptile are its most frequent victims.

What little is known about sea snakes is as diverse as it is mysterious. To reproduce, some species come ashore to lay eggs, even though sea snakes are relatively helpless on land. Others bear living young. Some are active only by day, others at night. Their food consists of small fish, so it's impossible to understand why they forage so far out in the ocean.

I have seen sea snakes floating on blue water off the coast of Panama like dozing sunbathers. At times they would swim rapidly toward the boat, then dart away. Or they would appear abruptly in a school of baitfish being hammered by dolphin or bonito. When at rest, their flattened, almost stick-like posture is so innocent that an unwary anchovy or mullet may easily wander within range, oblivious to the danger. Periodically, sea snakes congregate in huge masses at the surface. The reason for this "schooling" is not known but is presumed to be for copulation. Although most sea snakes are less than four feet long, a few twice that size have been captured. No sea snakes are found in the Atlantic Ocean, but the reptile has a look-alike counterpart there that is often mistaken for the deadly traveler.

The other day one of the neighborhood kids brought me a snake in a Cracker Jack's box. This lacked the showmanship of the lad who walked into Bob Kleiser's Tackle Shop and pulled a coral snake out of his pocket to be identified. Oddly enough, coral snakes, although members of the cobra family, are not always aggressive and have been toted about by small-fry. This is like walking around with a pinless grenade. But the one in the box didn't fit the "red against yeller, dangerous feller" adage that most Floridians learn if they spend much time in the woods. Its yellowish orange blotches over a scaleless pale olive body looked vaguely familiar, and after thumbing through a number of books I remembered where I had seen the critter. Once when cleaning a big grouper

I found several of these pointy-tailed eels in its stomach.

The snake eel is a member of another family, Ophichthyidae, and is related to the moray. It differs from the moray in having a tail that ends in a horny point (the moray has a continuous rayed fin around its body). A sea snake, on the other hand, has a flattened tail. Besides differing in other anatomical details, the snake eel usually has a blotched color pattern, a series of round blobs of color along the length of its body. There are about forty species of snake eels in the Western Hemisphere, and though they inhabit coral reefs and grass beds they are most often observed or "collected" in shoreside trash or weeds. Although perfectly harmless to man, snake eels are often eaten by tuna, barracuda, and grouper and can bore through the stomachs of their hosts into the body cavity. These escapees shrivel inside the fish and resemble mummies.

The venom of some sea snakes is far more powerful than that of land snakes. The toxin of one species was found to be five times more potent than cobra venom when used experimentally on rats, ten times more potent on rabbits, and fifty times more potent in cats and fish. All are neurotoxins that kill a human fast or slowly, depending on the species of snake, the victim's general health, and the amount of venom injected. The fatal dose from one kind of sea snake is 3.5 milligrams, or about one-third the amount in an average bite. Dr. H. A. Reid of the General Hospital in Penang, Malaysia, reported several cases in some detail to the American Association for the Advancement of Science. Two of these attacks were apparently unprovoked and occurred while the victims were bathing.

In one case, a Chinese boy, aged eight, was paddling in the sea about ten feet from shore when he saw a snake fastened to his ankle. He felt no pain but naturally was frightened. His father merely saw a drop of blood oozing from a few pinholes and thought no more about it. The boy went to play. An hour later he felt drowsy, his limbs were flaccid, and his tendon reflexes ceased. Although a physician was called and the boy was taken to the hospital, he died thirteen hours after being bitten. That same day at the same beach an adult was attacked by a sea snake while wading in chest-deep water. He lingered through seventy-seven hours of pain and vomiting before death.

Recently an angler in western Australia was killed by a sea snake. He was one of a party fishing from a boat about a hundred yards from shore. When the boat sprang a leak, several of the men jumped into the shallow water to lighten the load. As the men waded toward shore, the victim was attacked by the reptile. This man passed out instantly and never revived.

There is no known antivenin for sea snake bites. About the only thing that can be done is to apply a tourniquet, incise the wound, and use standard first-aid procedures. Of course, getting the patient to a hospital is of prime importance. The real killer in most cases is ignorance; because there is no real pain in the bite, nine times out of ten the victim ignores the wound, believing he has been nipped by an eel. There are snakes in the sea, and they are among nature's deadliest mysteries.

[1965]

48

Song of the Angler

In a way, I think I've saved the best for last. Here are McClane's thoughts on why people fish in the first place. This is purely and simply a superb essay, and to my own mind one of the finest pieces Al has ever written.

His discussion here brings to mind another thought I encountered recently, which is the difference between fishing *and* angling. *Modern fishing writers often use the two interchangeably, simply to avoid the use of one word over and over again. But before 1900 or so, the difference between the two was that fishermen were those who fished commercially, whereas anglers fished for sport. And just what constitutes that sport is what Al McClane so thoughtfully examines in this particular chapter.*

People often ask me why I enjoy fishing, and I cannot explain it to them because there is no reason in the way they want meanings described. They are asking a man why he enjoys breathing, when he really has no choice but to wonder at its truth. Psychologists such as Dr. Ronald Ley ["Why Anglers

382

Really Angle," *Field & Stream,* February 1967] have tried to explain its mystique in terms of behavioral conditioning, but this is as oddly misleading as his comparison of angling to golf. There are also pundits who believe that the rod provides an outlet for our hostilities, our frustrated egos, or our competitive instincts, or that it symbolizes the primitive feelings of man in his search for food, *ergo* the need to kill. To a degree I believe all these qualities exist in every participant in any sport, and if so, healthfully so, as it is far more harmless to vent one's spleen on a trout stream or a golf course than on one's fellowman. However, if this assumption is logical, then the rationale of *angling* is still without explanation.

The chirping plague of analysts who have invaded every chamber of the mind from the bedroom to the tackle room has missed one thing—angling is a robe that a man wears proudly. It is tightly woven into a fabric of moral, social, and philosophical threads, which are not easily rent by the violent climate of our times. It is foolish to think, as it has been said, that all men who fish are good men, as evil exists on all of life's paths; but to join Walton's "company of honest men" requires first the ability to accept a natural tempo of misfortune not only in the allegory where failure is represented by the loss of a fish (or success by its capture) but in life itself. In the lockstep slogan of young radicals thumbing their noses at their world, reality is no longer realistic; but I would argue that life is a greater challenge than death, and that reality is as close as the nearest river. Perhaps an exceptional angler doesn't prove the rule, but then anglers are exceptional people.

Lord Fraser of Lonsdale is not only a peer, but he wears the robe of an angler, as well. He is a skilled fly fisherman, and when last we visited together, he caught a 35-pound salmon, which was the biggest in the camp for many weeks. What's more, he could charm the socks off Willie Sutton, and I have heard him spellbind a roomful of strangers with tales of his life in South Africa, while sipping rare wines, naming each château and its vintage. This introduction would be fatuous were it not for the fact that Lord Fraser is totally blind. Both of his eyes were shot out in World War I. A profoundly intellectual man, Fraser has developed his other senses to a point that most of the people who sat with him that night had no idea that he was unable to see them; yet later he could summarize the physical characteristics of each person as though he were describing a rare burgundy.

I don't know if you have ever tried wading (unaided) and fly-fishing a stream while blindfolded. I cannot do it, and I would probably lack the guts if I *had* to do it. Fraser's explanation for his ability to do this is that he can hear all things around him: the changing tempo of deep and shallow water, the curling smack of a rapid against a boulder, even the roll or rise of a fish. His ear for the music of angling is incredibly keen. Is this Dr. Ley's behavioral conditioning? In terms of a compensatory development of the senses, perhaps, but it does not explain *why* a man, even a blind man, enjoys angling.

The music of angling is more compelling to me than anything contrived in the greatest symphony hall. What could be more thrilling than the ghostly basso note of a channel buoy over a grumbling surf as the herring gulls screech at a school of stripers on a foggy summer morning? Or an organ chorus of red howler monkeys swinging over a jungle stream as the tarpon roll and splash in counterpoint? I have heard them all—the youthful voice of the little Beaver Kill, the growling of the Colorado as it leaps from its den, the kettledrum pounding of the Rogue, the hiss of the Yellowstone's riffles, the sad sound of the Orinoco, as mournful as a G chord on a guitar. These are more familiar to me than Bach, Beethoven, and Brahms, and for my part more beautiful. If there are three "Bs" in angling, they are probably the Beaver Kill, the Brodhead, and the Big Hole.

Big-game angling has quite another music. The hull creaks and the outriggers clap as the ship comes into the wind, while the sea increases the tempo as she turns from stern to bow. Then the frigate birds scream at a ball of bait and you know the marlin are below. As the ship lurches over the chop her screws bite air in a discordant whine, and the mullet trails *skitter flap skitter,* until the pitching hull sounds like the soft rolling of drums.

At last one note assails the ears, the *snap* of white linen pulled from the outrigger. Now the water explodes in a crescendo of hot engines roaring into life before you lean into a quarter ton of shoulder-rocking fury. And in that ageless walking leap that follows no path in the ocean, the angler hears the most exciting sound of all—the wailing of a reel as stark and as lonely as a Basin Street clarinet.

But my protracted maundering leads us away from Dr. Ley's hypothesis, which he reinforced with the learned E. L. Thorndike's thesis of punishments and rewards. What *are* rewards of angling? A dead fish? A trophy? At some point perhaps, but then it takes years to become an angler.

There are tidal marks in our development. In the beginning, when one is very young and inexperienced, fish are measured in quantity. Then, only quality becomes important. Eventually even record fish lose their significance unless they are of a particular species, and ultimately the size doesn't matter, provided they are difficult to catch.

The latter condition is fairly easy to find in these days of declining resources. Trout in the upper Beaver Kill, for instance, are generally ½ pound in weight, but they can be the most demanding kind. The water is diamond-clear and at the shadow of a passing bird or the glint of sun against rod they instantly vanish under the nearest boulder. You must work with a leader of cobweb diameter and have enough control to drop your fly in a teacup target through a maze of overhanging limbs. There are large trout in the stream, of course, wise old browns that you might catch a glimpse of once in a while, usually in a pool that everybody believes has been emptied.

Recalling the years when anglers gathered at the old Gould cottage on the Beaver Kill—a temple now fallen to death and taxes—which Arnold Gingrich described in his wonderful book, *The Well-Tempered Angler* (you can even smell the waders drying in the rafters)—one man comes to mind who knew perhaps a bit more about the rewards of angling than most of us.

Ellis Newman could cast fly line to 90 feet with his bare hands. I saw him make three measured casts with tournament tackle, each of which fell short of 200 feet by inches. I doubt if a more polished caster ever lived. He had neither the time nor the inclination to compete in games (except for the pigeon-shooting circuit, which he did for money). We often fished along opposite banks of the Beaver Kill, or alternated pools, just for the pleasure of each other's company.

One day, when the mayflies were on the water, Ellis caught and released several good browns below the dam, one going about 3 pounds. At the top of the next run we met a young boy who proudly displayed a 9-inch brook trout. Ellis admired it so much that I thought we were looking at the biggest squaretail captured since Cook hit the jackpot on the Nipigon in 1914. When the lad asked Ellis if he had any luck, he looked very serious: "Oh, I caught a few, but none were as pretty as yours."

Ellis worked with underprivileged children and handi-capped people at his own expense. And the expense was ap-preciable. He designed Rube Goldberg wheelchairs and trac-tor-driven bucket seats for fishing and for hunting as well, and he even developed a method of running steel cable through a string of boulders to build "necklace" dams on his eroding Beaver Kill. Ellis never waited for the fulmination of a new idea to die down before putting it into practice, and the people who loved him may be consoled with the reflection that angling would have suffered a greater blow had he re-garded each new venture carefully.

Arnold Gingrich became, as Charlie Ritz once called him, "that terrible fishing machine" in the sense that he was on a first-name basis with every trout in the stream. He would appear with smaller and smaller fly rods, considering any stick over 2 ounces as heavy tackle, and any leader above 7X suitable only for salmon. But the publisher of *Esquire* maga-zine is a tremendously energetic individual and the piston-like style of casting with flea rods was duck soup for him.

Arnold earned his robe in my eyes the first time we an-gled together; in releasing a tired trout he held the fish under-water gently, almost lovingly, stroking its belly and talking to it. He is a master of conversation and, so help me, at times the fish swim away with an impossible but perceptible grin on their faces. Arnold has that passionate blood fire, typical of anglers, which no psychologist (or wife who hears her husband stumbling out into an April blizzard at 4:00 A.M.) has satisfactorily explained.

One morning I was crossing the Swinging Bridge Pool and happened to look down; there stood Arnold in an icy torrent, banging away with a little dry fly. Something was protruding from his mouth. I didn't recall that Arnold smoked cigars.

"When did you start smoking cigars?" I called. He pulled the bulbous object from his mouth and examined it as though he didn't know it was there.

"Oh. That's my stream thermometer."

"Your *what?*"

"I'm sick. I have a fever."

"Then what are you doing in the *river?*"

"Oh hell, it's only 99.8. If I break 100, I'll go to bed."

Whenever somebody asks me why I enjoy fishing, another thing that comes to mind is what it means in terms of friendship. General Charles Lindemann was always impeccably dressed, cologne lashed, and wearing his stiff upper lip as Counsel to the British Ambassador in Washington. During the years we fished together he had a running verbal duel with Charles Ritz for reasons that only an Englishman would feel about a Frenchman and vice-versa. There was no evil lurking beneath this play of wit; it had the woolly camaraderie of barracks talk. When Lindemann stepped into the river, Ritz would ask him "Where is your gaff, old boy? All Englishmen carry gaffs." Although a stranger would think that the general meant to hang Ritz with his old school tie, they were really fond of each other.

This good-natured combativeness continued until we stopped to lunch on the bank of the Stamp River one noon. A sudden change came over the general. For a moment he became misty-eyed. He told that he had sat in this very spot with his young wife a half-century before and made his life's plans. Now she was buried in France, a geographical anomaly that he made no attempt to explain except to refer to a wartime plane crash. Later that day, while I was beaching a steelhead, I saw Ritz crawling along the bank picking wild flowers. Swearing me to silence, he carefully packed a bouquet in his duffle bag. "I know the cemetery outside of Paris. I will take these to her. She would like that."

Lindemann didn't know what he had done, and despite my old friend's deserved reputation as one of the world's greatest anglers, I would embarrass him now by saying that Charles Ritz wears his robe because he is a truly kind and loving man. The general is gone, and it wasn't until his death a few years ago that a certain irony became apparent in our secret when we learned that General Lindemann had been Chief of the British Secret Service.

The only psychologist I have ever met who knew anything about angling was Dr. J. H. Cooper of Kansas City, Missouri. He made sense because he invented the marabou bonefish jig, which reveals him as a practical man. We met, as anglers so often do, through his giving me a duplicate of his lure at a time when I was having lousy fishing at Andros Island.

Have you ever noticed how often anglers tend to share their good fortune? I have seen this happen many times among perfect strangers who simply meet on a stream. I remember a man who, after landing a beautiful rainbow trout below the Fair Ground Bridge on the East Branch of the Delaware, turned to a bug-eyed kid holding a 98-cent telescopic fly rod, and snipping the March Brown pattern off his leader gave it to the boy. "See what you can do with it, son." That's all he said. I was that boy and I can't tie a March Brown on my leader today without blessing my Good Samaritan.

Before you conclude that the author has broken loose from his moorings and is bobbing impotently on a sea of virtue, let me reassure you that the world is full of narrowly shrewd self-seeking people, blind to God and goodness, and for all I know, Dame Juliana Berners could have been some piscatorial Mary Poppins or a grosser wart on the face of society than Polly Adler. But I would be untrue to my craft if I did not add that although we live in a curiously touchy age when Mom's apple pie, the flag, and the Boy Scout's oath are losing currency, these still make a better frame of reference than Harvard's pellet-fed rats or Pavlov's dogs.

Psychologists tell us that one reason why we enjoy fishing is that it is an escape. This is meaningless. True, a man who works in the city wants to "escape" to the country, but the clinical implication is that (no matter where a man lives), he seeks to avoid reality. This is as obtuse as the philosophical doctrine which holds that no reality exists outside the mind.

Perhaps it's the farm boy in me, but I would apply Aristotelian logic—the chicken came before the egg because it is real and the egg is only potential. By the same reasoning the fluid content of a stream is nothing but water when it erupts from a city faucet, but given shores it becomes a river, and as a river it is perfectly capable of creating life, and therefore it is real. It is not a sewer, or a conveyor of barges and lumber, although it can be pressed to these burdens and, indeed, as living thing it can also become lost in its responsibilities.

So if escapism is a reason for angling—then the escape is to reality. The sense of freedom that we enjoy in the outdoors is, after all, a normal reaction to a more rational environment.

Who but an angler knows that magic hour when the red lamp of summer drops behind blackening hemlocks and the mayflies emerge from the dull folds of their nymphal robes to dance in ritual as old as the river itself? Trout appear one by one and the angler begins his game in movements as stylized as Japanese poetry. Perhaps he will hook that wonder-spotted rogue, or maybe he will remain in silent pantomime long into the night with no visible reward.

And that, Professor, is why anglers *really* angle.

[1967]

Index

391

401